Sasan Samiei completed his PhD in Intellectual and Ancient History at University College London and also holds an MSc in Economics from the London School of Economics (LSE). He lives in Lewes, East Sussex.

ANCIENT PERSIA IN WESTERN HISTORY

Hellenism and the Representation of the Achaemenid Empire

SASAN SAMIEI

BLOOMSBURY ACADEMIC
LONDON • NEW YORK • OXFORD • NEW DELHI • SYDNEY

BLOOMSBURY ACADEMIC
Bloomsbury Publishing Plc
50 Bedford Square, London, WC1B 3DP, UK
1385 Broadway, New York, NY 10018, USA
29 Earlsfort Terrace, Dublin 2, Ireland

BLOOMSBURY, BLOOMSBURY ACADEMIC and the Diana logo
are trademarks of Bloomsbury Publishing Plc

First published in Great Britain by I.B. Tauris 2014
Paperback edition published by Bloomsbury Academic 2021

Copyright © Sasan Samiei, 2014

Sasan Samiei has asserted his right under the Copyright,
Designs and Patents Act, 1988, to be identified as Author of this work.

All rights reserved. No part of this publication may be reproduced or
transmitted in any form or by any means, electronic or mechanical,
including photocopying, recording, or any information storage or retrieval
system, without prior permission in writing from the publishers.

Bloomsbury Publishing Plc does not have any control over, or responsibility for,
any third-party websites referred to or in this book. All internet addresses given
in this book were correct at the time of going to press. The author and publisher
regret any inconvenience caused if addresses have changed or sites have
ceased to exist, but can accept no responsibility for any such changes.

A catalogue record for this book is available from the British Library.

A catalog record for this book is available from the Library of Congress.

International Library of Iranian Studies 47

ISBN: HB: 978-1-7807-6480-1
PB: 978-1-3501-9776-3
ePDF: 978-0-8577-2414-4
eBook: 978-0-8577-3606-2

Typeset by Jones Ltd, London

To find out more about our authors and books visit
www.bloomsbury.com and sign up for our newsletters.

In memoriam of my great-great-grandfather Mirza Mohammed Ali Khan Rahmat Abadi. A constitutional revolutionary, a parliamentarian (1906/7–1909), and a democrat

CONTENTS

Acknowledgements	ix
Preface	xii
1. Introduction	1
2. Setting the Scene: Anthropology, Linguistics and Romantic Hellenism in Victorian Britain	14
3. The 'Race–Culture' Debate: 1900s–1930s	48
4. The 'Diffusionism vs. Evolutionism' Theoretical Debate, Gordon Childe and the Prehistory of Europe	79
5. Hellenisms Reassessed (1890s–1940s): Part I	105
6. Hellenisms Reassessed (1890s–1940s): Part II	147
7. Hellenisms and the Historiography of Ancient Persia	179
8. Concluding Remarks	235
Postscript	246
Glossary	249
Notes	257
Bibliography	296
Index	311

ACKNOWLEDGEMENTS

The planning of this book goes back to 2006. My under- and postgraduate tutors started the ball rolling by recommending me for an MPhil place at the University College London (UCL). My thanks must therefore go to Jacek Rostowski (Professor of Economics, and the current Economic Minister of Poland), and Peter Howlett (Professor of Economic History, London School of Economics and Political Science).

Throughout my time at the UCL, Amélie Kuhrt (my first supervisor) was always at hand to offer learned advice. She read my work with the greatest of care, and when she offered guidance for various improvements, her proposals were always exquisitely judged. Moreover, when she challenged some of my outlandish ideas and assumptions, she probed me gingerly, and was gentleness itself in her criticisms. I believe that Amélie has moulded a historian with much improved reflective and analytical faculties. And for that, as well as for many other acts of kindness, I am eternally indebted to her.

My meetings with Stephen Conway (my second supervisor) were usually over lunch; the financial burden of which, more often than not, was incurred by him. This was only part of his wonderful generosity. He read everything that was asked of him and provided very helpful suggestions in how to improve things. The value of his continuing and enthusiastic support is truly beyond measure. I am extremely grateful to Stephen for expanding both my waistline and my intellectual horizon.

Even though I only spent a very short and soggy October afternoon in their company, my splendid examiners, Edith Hall (King's College London) and Roger Matthews (UCL), made a number of invaluable comments and proposals for improving the thesis and turning it into a monograph. The fact that it is being published here and now is very much a testimony to their kind efforts. In all probability we shall not meet again, but during the viva voce, as far as I could sense, the earth *did* move – intellectually, I hasten to add. And for that fleeting moment of cerebral rush, I am exceedingly grateful to both of them.

I should also like to thank a number of individuals and institutions for their help and guidance. My thanks go to all the helpful librarians at the various libraries of the UCL, the Senate House Library, the library of the School of Oriental and African Studies, the library of the Institute of Classical Studies, the library of the University of Sussex and the British Library. In addition, the archivists at the Oxford University's Bodleian Library (Mr Colin Harris) and the Royal Anthropological Institute (Ms Sarah Walpole) have helped me enormously, for which I am indebted to them. A number of academics were also helpful beyond the call of duty. Special thanks must go to some of the members of the History Department, in particular Christopher Abel, Simon Hornblower, Axel Körner and Hans Van Wees. I also benefited greatly from attending the research training seminars and discussing a variety of subjects with my fellow students. I must also thank Mark Pagel, professor of evolutionary biology at the University of Reading, for enlightening me in a number of relevant areas.

And of course without the wonderful support of I.B.Tauris – and in particular my editor, Tomasz Hoskins – what had started as a doctorate thesis (entitled: *Classical Scholarship, Anthropology and the Historiography of the Achaemenid Persia 1900–1940* (2010)) would have scarcely moved beyond the academic world. I am extremely grateful to all involved.

Finally, without the love, support, and enthusiasm of my wife (Véronique) and daughter (Zia), I could not have carried on as happily as I have done. I owe them both a debt of gratitude.

Sasan Samiei
February 2013
Lewes

PREFACE

In and around the turn of the millennium, my knowledge of ancient history was so derisory that until reading in *Europe: A History* (1997) that in 472 BC Aeschylus had written a play called *Persians*, my awareness of all things Aeschylean was confined to the third line of a Cole Porter ditty, called 'Brush Up Your Shakespeare'. It begins:

> The girls today in society go for classical poetry
> So to win their hearts one must quote with ease
> Aeschylus and Euripides
> One must know Homer, and believe me, Beau Sophocles...

Although the play – *Persians* that is, and not *Kiss Me, Kate* – does create, in Norman Davis's words, 'a lasting stereotype whereby the civilized Persians are reduced to cringing, ostentatious, arrogant, cruel, effeminate, and lawless aliens',[1] it also does something different and out of character: by asserting that the Greeks and Persians are 'sisters of one race',[2] it situates them 'intra-racially' – or at least that was how it seemed to me when I read the play for the first time. Some months later, I caught a review of Tom Harrison's *Emptiness of Asia* (2000), where the reviewer had no qualms about the Saidian framework that was adopted by Harrison.[3] Still adhering to my original reading, I wrote to the reviewer and presented him with my dilettantish thoughts. The following was part of his short reply:

While I agree that the history of classical scholarship is deeply complicit with a history of unpleasant Orientalism, I cannot agree that this does not stem from Greek culture and Aeschylus. The best book on the subject remains Edith Hall's *Inventing the Barbarian* where you will find the evidence laid out.[4]

And Edith Hall had, admittedly, laid out all the evidence as ably and astutely as Simon Goldhill suggested; but it was carried out with an approving nod towards Edward Said's *Orientalism* (1977), and no telling reference was made to the racial sorority passage of the play. Although I remained unconvinced, her analysis had by then (and thereafter) become such a well-entrenched academic orthodoxy that contradicting it would have exposed me as an eccentric, if not as an out-and-out fool. As I was about to throw in the towel and plead academic naivety in my defence, I came across Anthony Podlecki's questioning commentary of this section of the play; it was a minor revelation:

> Is there deeper significance in the fact that they are sisters of the same race, and again that one holds the territory of Greece merely as the result of an allotment? Or may Aeschylus be suggesting that Greece and Persia were of common stock and should have not fought each other?[5]

Armed with this very qualified affirmation of my own interpretation, I began the next phase of my autodidactic study of the classics and ancient history with renewed gusto.

In 2003, an essay in the *London Review of Books* informed me not only of the existence of Pierre Briant and his magisterial *From Cyrus to Alexander: A History of the Persian Empire* (2002), but also of the existence of a more objective school of Achaemenid historiography that has been going strong for the best part of two decades. I read Briant, Wiesehöfer and Kuhrt with great interest, and was amazed that by examining the Achaemenid Empire within the methodological framework of *longue dureé*, these historians were able to give the reader a more thorough and nuanced understanding of the empire than the one on offer from the unashamedly Hellenist chapters of the *Cambridge History of Iran*. Moreover, some of these historians, it seemed, were also willing to perform, if needs be, tasks which are usually reserved for public intellectuals. In a combative piece of journalism for *Le Monde*,[6] Briant, for instance, takes Oliver Stone's 2004 film *Alexander* to task and lambastes it for its Orientalist traits and Western triumphalism. Although ably argued, this article, in my judgement, was inappropriate for the purpose of analysing a filmic product. The skills of a historically-informed cineaste would have been perhaps more useful than the erudition of a Collège de France professor. This is so because the historical underpinnings (in this case, based on Robin Lane Fox's *Alexander the Great* (1986)) of a film are secondary to the primacy of what can be *seen* and *heard* on the screen. So what do the sights and sounds of *Alexander* convey? First, the Persians and other nationalities of the empire are lumped together higgledy-piggledy, and are underdeveloped dramatically and rendered two-dimensional, as opposed to the fully-rounded 'European' Greeks. Second, the racial depiction of the protagonists leaves nothing to chance. While all the leading Greek and Macedonian characters are portrayed by very attractive actors of North European descent, Darius is presented as an oriental despot who, according to Peter Green, has more than just a passing resemblance to Osama bin Laden;[7] and Roxanne is played by an actor of African descent. Finally, by slotting in seasoned English stage actors in some of the important Greek and Macedonian roles, Stone endows his 'Europeans' with the kinds of gravitas and oratorical skills that the Israeli actor playing Darius could scarcely have matched in a 'foreign' language.

The tendency to exaggerate or falsify the 'racial' or other characteristics of the Persians is not a predilection that only affects the likes of Stone and Lane Fox; it has a much longer pedigree. In a 2006 *Times Literary Supplement* review, it was stated that in his *Histoire d'Outremer*, William, the twelfth-century Archbishop of Tyre, described the wars of the Persians and Greeks 'as a conflict of West and East, in which Persians have turbans and black faces'.[8] A 2007 cinematic treatment of the same wars depicted the same Persians, in the words of one reviewer, as 'exotic, often black, frequently masked, elaborately decorated, elephant-riding, [and] despot-serving' characters.[9]

These two instances, admittedly, are too far apart to be suggestive of a discernible trend. As a consequence, a more detailed and systematic gander at the relevant historical writings took me from the ancient sources towards, *inter alia*, Herder and Gibbon and thenceforth, via Grote, Rawlinson, Renan, Breasted, Toynbee and Murray, towards Olmstead, Momigliano, Burn and, eventually, Boardman, Cartledge and Lane Fox. From what was read, I made two broad inferences. First, although the 'racial' othering which appeared in most of these texts was not as explicit and crudely drawn as in *Alexander*, *300*, or the *Histoire d'Outremer*, they nonetheless, by opting to situate the Greeks and Persians so firmly in 'Europe' and 'Asia', respectively, continued to display an almost pathological need to propel the ancient Iranian peoples towards an implicit but unambiguous 'non-white' status vis-à-vis the ancient Greeks. But why? One obvious answer could be that the 'white' status for the ancient Greeks and the 'non-white' for the ancient Persians were matters of physiognomic facts. This, however, is contradicted by my second inference. Some texts, dating roughly from the 1850s to the 1930s, had dispensed with these types of categorizations. This was because the supposed Indo-European backgrounds of *both* Greeks and Persians could no longer accommodate such a racial polarity. This was a remarkable discovery for me; it appeared that I had gone back, serendipitously, to my earlier intuitive 'intra-racial' reading of *Persians*. I therefore decided to put some carefully-chosen aspects of my preliminary readings and reflections at the core of a doctorate programme (whence comes this monograph). But right through the period of my research, contemplation and writing, I was highly conscious of one very troubling and morally haphazard question: why deal with the thorny issue of the Indo-European studies, which would invariably touch upon the still thornier issues of 'race' and 'racism'?

Some, no doubt, may argue that the racial depiction of the Greeks and Persians is, or should be, largely irrelevant to the liberally-inclined thinkers of the early twenty-first century. What should detain our attention is the manner in which their actions, their lives and their multifaceted humanities are depicted by historians. To have 'hang-ups' on 'race', they may add, is morally debatable and, intellectually, a retrograde step. Perhaps; but let me offer a threefold counter-argument. First, why have the producers of *300* chosen to cast actors of African descent for the Persian characters, but a 'Scotch'[10] for Leonidas? There seems to be an emotional need to underline unequivocally the complete otherness of the Persians, vis-à-vis the Greeks – and what could be more visually compelling than a racially-inspired assortment of *dramatis personae*?[11] Even eminent classicists are not entirely immune from this strange malady. Paul Cartledge, with his apparent fixation for the noun 'wog', is a prime example of this pathology. In *The Greeks* (1993), Cartledge translates the compound word *'philobarbaros'* as 'wog-lover'.[12] Four years later, in an essay entitled 'Historiography and Ancient Greek Self-Definition', he enlarges upon this noun:

> So far from according parity to non-Greeks, the Greeks now primarily effected their self-identification through the polar opposition of themselves to the morally inferior barbarians – 'wog', as it were, to borrow the language of a more recent colonial discourse.[13]

Cartledge's analysis and use of vocabulary are problematic on a number of fronts. First, why mistranslate *'philobarbaros'* as 'wog-lover'? After all, 'wog', meaning 'a foreigner, especially a non-white person or one of Arab extraction', was used mostly by the British empire-builders of yesteryear. Moreover, the noun itself is an abbreviation of 'golliwog': 'A black-faced brightly coloured soft doll with fuzzy hair.'[14] Are these terms (when used by the ancient Greeks) truly applicable to the Persians and other ancient Indo-Iranian peoples? If they are not (and I am assuming they are not), then why does Cartledge bring 'wog', hence 'non-whiteness', into his discourse? Would it not have been more accurate if he had opted for derogatory terms devoid of overt and absolute racial connotations, such as 'wop', 'boche' or even *'les rosbifs'*? Second, his claim that he is borrowing 'wog' from 'a more recent colonial discourse' is conceptually confused. In this 'more recent colonial discourse', 'wog' had always been used by the colonizers against the colonized. And as Cartledge must surely be aware, it was always the Greeks who were either in the process of being colonized, or under the constant threat of colonization by the Achaemenid Persians. In other words, the utility of 'wog' only makes sense if it is used by the powerful against the powerless. And prior to 331 BC, the powerful were seldom the Greeks; and thereafter, only intermittently so. And finally, in the above quote, the author presents the Greeks' sense of moral superiority as a matter of historical datum, hence neutral and bereft of value judgements. Elsewhere, however, Cartledge is not so circumspect and asserts that the clash between the Greeks and Persians 'was a clash between freedom and slavery',[15] thus implicitly (after all, who could ever be in favour of slavery?) justifying and admiring the moral superiority of the Greeks.

All of which takes me to the second portion of my counter-argument. These forms of 'racial' profiling in isolation are, admittedly, of no consequence. But when practised by the likes of Cartledge, Stone and Zach Snyder (the director of *300*), an ideological agenda becomes discernible: its overriding purpose is, arguably, to drum into the reader or the viewer an easily graspable and retainable mental construction, upon which the much-cherished narrative of 'self' and 'other' can be hoisted. When confronted with dubious (indeed, erroneous) 'racial' depictions and definitions, it surely impinges on all of us to expose them for what they really are (sophistries), and not hide behind morally-convenient platitudes. Finally, as pointed out in another context by the editors of the *Achaemenid History V* (1995),[16] populist and/or accessible works, such as *300*, *Persian Fire* or almost anything by Lane Fox do matter, not because of their inherent worth, but because they tend to be better-known and therefore more influential in popular culture than a scholarly work such as *From Cyrus to Alexander*. And what they relate, straightforwardly or subliminally, and how they racially or ethnically depict the protagonists on either side of the Graeco-Persian imbroglios matters. It matters because it is predicated upon a fallacious *idée fixe*; the best definition of which was rendered by Rudyard Kipling: 'East is East, and West is West, and never the twain shall meet.'[17]

I consider the application of this dichotomized formula to the Graeco-Persian world of the fifth and fourth century BC to be, at best, a geographical tautology (the Iranian plateau happens to be to the east of the Greek archipelago) and, at worst, nothing but an anachronistic cliché. In other words, I categorically and absolutely challenge the contention, as expressed by, *inter alia*, Anthony Pagden, that the Persian Wars should be regarded as the first round of a '2500-year struggle between the East and West'.[18] I deem this mindset to be problematic because it pays scant attention to the historical, geographical, demographical, linguistic and genetic realities of the ancient world (see Postscript), and relies far too heavily on a set of unsuitable teleological approaches. In addition, the tendency to link the undoubted 'glory that was Greece' to the ascendancy of the North European civilizations of the past few centuries without sufficient reference either to the non-classical influences and innovations (see Chapter 7), or the murkier episodes in the annals of the 'West' (burning of witches, the gulags and the Holocaust, to name but three), seems to be a *prima facie* reason for proceeding with care and scepticism.

(A coda: throughout this book, I have been extremely careful in differentiating between the *ancient* and *modern* Persians (Iranians). With massive and frequent migrations of Turkic peoples from central Asia, and of Semitic-cum-Islamic ones from the Arabian Peninsula and North Africa taking place from the seventh to the twelfth century AD, the ethnic make-up of the modern Iranians (this author included) is not even remotely the same as their pre-seventh century (distant) ancestors. The reader should not conflate between these two very different sets of Indo-Iranian-speaking peoples.)

CHAPTER 1

INTRODUCTION

When dealing either directly or indirectly with the ancient Iranian civilizations, European classicism, both in its incipiency and contemporary manifestation, has displayed a remarkable constancy in ideological perspective, historiographical methodology and textual tonality. If you were to pick a classical text on (say) the Persian Wars or the conquest of Alexander from the eighteenth, nineteenth, most of the twentieth and early twenty-first centuries, you would confront a number of literary and methodological topoi, all situated well within the boundaries of Orientalism, Hellenocentrism and now Islamism.

Johann G. Herder pondered the following question in 1775: 'Did any Persian ravager of the world found such kingdoms, cities, and edifices, as he destroyed?'[1] In *The Five Great Monarchies of the Ancient Eastern World* (1862), George Rawlinson queries the mental prowess of the Persians, especially when compared to the Greeks, and asserts that 'we cannot ascribe to them any high degree of intellectual excellence',[2] thus implying that the threat they had posed to Greece, had it been realized, could have been catastrophic for the intellectual history of the world. Indeed, it is this theme that G. W. Cox took forward some 15 years later:

> [T]he conquest of Europe was no longer a vision which could cheat the fancy of the lord of Asia. The will and energy of

Athens, aided by the rugged discipline of Sparta, had foiled the great enterprise through which the barbarian despot sought to repress in the deadly bonds of Persian thraldom the intellect and freedom of the world.[3]

In more recent writings, the oriental credentials of the Persians are signposted with greater stylistic subtlety. For instance, in *Persian Fire: The First World Empire and the Battle for the West* (2006) – a title that brings to mind Henri Bergson's apt phrase, 'the illusion of retrospective determinism'[4] (in this case, the question must be: what was this 'West' that they were battling for?) – the author opines that:

> the political model established by the ancient monarchy of Persia was one that would persist in the Middle East until 1922, and the deposition of the last ruling caliph, the Turkish Sultan. It is the stated goal of Osama bin Laden, of course, to see the Caliphate resurrected to its prerogative of global rule.[5]

Implicit in Holland's words here is the belief, held by many contemporary thinkers, that there exists an unbroken arc of statecraft that inexorably links the kingship of Cyrus the Great to the Islamic 'Wahabbism' of Osama bin Laden.

With regard to Alexander, his historical portrayal was always a question of benevolent leadership and a mission to civilize. '[T]he Macedonian king, the commander-in-chief of the Greek confederates,' wrote J. B. Bury in 1909, 'had set forth as a champion of Greeks against mere barbarians, as a leader of Europeans against effeminate Asiatics, as the representative of a higher folk against beings lower in the human scale.'[6] Although in recent years the use of such terms has become obsolete, the overarching idea that the consequences of Alexander's conquest were mostly benign still holds. According to a 2005 article in the *FT Magazine*, entitled 'Alexander, the First Neo-Con', '[t]he Hellenistic civilisation that flourished for two centuries in Alexander's wake from Egypt to India is one of the glories of mankind. It truly did bring east and west together, putting Hellenic inquiry and individuality at the core of a vast oriental culture.'[7]

As far as the Persian Wars are concerned, counter-factual and teleological forms of conveying history are usually the preferred modes of exposition. 'Had things gone the other way', asserts Peter Green in *The Years of Salamis* (1970), 'mosques and minarets would dominate Europe.'[8] In 1999, Victor Davis-Hanson ponders 'what if the Persians had won the battle of Salamis?' He confidently opines that '[w]e would live under a much different tradition today – writers under death sentences, women secluded and veiled,[9] universities mere centres of religious zealotry, thought police in our living rooms and bedrooms – had Themistocles and his sailors failed'.[10] In *The Classical World* (2005), Robin Lane Fox makes a similar argument:

> If the Persians had won in Greece, Greek freedom would have been curbed and with it, the political, artistic, dramatic and philosophical progress which has been a beacon to Western civilization. Satraps would have ruled Greece and dispensed personal justice [...]. Persians might have dined on sofas and encouraged and watched the Greeks' athletic games, although their kings would never have risked competing in them for fear of losing.

Moreover, he is adamant that in '480 brave Greeks and their families died for freedom not slavery'.[11]

Despite this, there was a period, roughly from 1850s to 1930s, when the Persians were characterized quite differently. In some intellectual quarters, they were no longer 'othered' in such an uncompromising and binary fashion. These novel forms of depicting the ancients not only refrained from othering the Persians, but had gone out of their way to consider them, along with the Greeks, as the kith and kin of the peoples of Europe. For Gobineau, the Iranians were the 'cousins' of the 'Germans and Scandinavians'.[12] And for Ernest Renan, who believed that 'progress for Indo-European peoples will consist in distancing themselves more and more form the Semitic spirit',[13] the Persians were 'Exhibit A' in demonstrating that this 'distancing' is entirely within reach: 'Persia here is the only exception. It managed to retain its own genius, and it did so because it was successful in safeguarding its own legacy from Islam.'[14] In addition, the nineteenth-century anthropologist, R. W. Jackson, in a paper entitled 'Turan and Iran', defines 'Iran' (which literally means the 'land of the Aryans') as an entity that possesses 'the essential character and quality of the hereditarily gubernational classes, from Persia to Ireland'.[15] He also tabulates the rivalry between the 'Aryans' and 'Semites' by citing as examples Cyrus' triumph over the Babylonians, the conquest of Egypt by Cambyses and the victories of the Frankish knights during the Crusades. It is worth noting here that in this scheme, Cyrus' compadre in history was not Saladin, but Richard the Lionheart. In other words, when looked at from Jackson's perspective, the idea that Achaemenid kingship could have provided the blueprints for a governance which stretches from the first Islamic Caliphate right through to Osama bin Laden is rendered a fanciful proposition.

In 1911, the Oxford ancient historian, Sir John Linton Myres, described in *The Dawn of History* the arrival of the Iranians and the Greeks upon the historical scene:

> The newcomers of the North marshalled the whole eastern world, from the Adriatic to the Caspian and the Persian Gulf, into final camps, Eastern and Western in name, but held and directed on both sides by long-last brothers and true kinsman. In the west, they were the men who had 'come from the north,' and changed the Aegean from Minoan to Greek. And if the others came from the east, they were yet the same clear-eyed, chivalrous horse-tamers; the Persian 'companion' of the King of Kings.[16]

This was echoed some five years later by Henry Breasted in *Ancient Times*. 'The history of the ancient world', according to the author

> was largely made up of the struggle between [the] southern Semitic line, which issued from the southern grasslands, and the northern Indo-European line [...] two great races facing each other across the Mediterranean like two vast armies

stretching from Western Asia westward to the Atlantic. The later wars between Rome and Carthage represent some of the operations of the Semitic left wing, while the triumph of Persia over Chaldea is a similar outcome on the Semitic right wing.[17]

In dealing exclusively with the attributes of an Achaemenid monarch, one of Myres' former students, Gordon Childe, invites the readers of *The Aryans* (1926) 'to compare the dignified narrative carved by the Aryan Darius on the rock of Behistun with the bombastic and blatant self-glorification of the inscriptions of Ashurbanipal or Nebuchadnezzar'.[18]

But why did such a phenomenon manifest itself in this period, and cease to do so thereafter? The response to the first part of this question can easily be ascertained from the above examples: the growth of comparative philology – and therefore Indo-European philology and mythology – within the very broad and inclusive context of anthropology permitted the opening up of new academic horizons for those interested in new ways of analysing the ancient world. Why this kind of Persian-positive pan-Aryanism dominated the discourse only briefly and does so no longer is a harder question to answer. But, putting it as concisely as possible, the tragic consequences of World War II had rendered unpalatable the kind of framework that classifies the world into certain type of groups and/or cultures. It appears that when it came to the questions of 'race' or 'ethnicity' (which, in modern parlance, have become erroneously and unhelpfully synonymous), the contemporary intellectual or academic is determined to sidestep the moral complexities that had bedevilled many of his or her pre-war predecessors. One of the ironies of this new and universal mindset has been the swift jettisoning of the Indo-European framework that had depicted the Iranian world more benignly. Two crucial caveats should be appended here: first, this more 'benign' framework was constructed *mostly* within the contours of the highly dubious foundation of 'Aryanism' and the accompanying pseudoscientific discourse of the day. Second, and as a result of this, its benignity was an unintended by-product of classifying, as a matter of conceptual necessity, the ancient Persians along with most of the modern Europeans as belonging to one specific Ur-culture. Nevertheless, the analytical probing of this framework should not be considered, in my tentative judgement, as a morally repugnant act. After all, the reason for carrying it out is to discover and rehabilitate *only* those aspects which can be shown to be useful and enlightening. Furthermore, it should be borne in mind that it is not being suggested here that this intellectual sprucing-up should be carried out in a cavalier fashion and without due reference to strict ethical codes and intellectual guidelines. This, to be sure, is a treacherous area: I am perfectly aware that some, come what may, would consider many aspects of Indo-European studies (apart from pure linguistics) as nothing but a tawdry exercise in resurrecting the 'Aryan myth' and indulging in 'neo-racist' fantasies – and, some of the time, rightly so. As a consequence, I am determined – doggedly determined – to approach this subject with a great deal of sober deliberation.

The present-day Galton Institute at the University College London, which was known as the *Eugenic Society* until 1989, has committed itself to 'environmental and genetic studies' and is no longer interested in the 'out-dated views of the eugenic movement'.[19] In the 'Introduction' to *Twelve Galton Lectures: A Centenary Selection with Commentaries* (2007), one of the editors states that 'it is readily evident how great was the change and how alien some of the attitudes prevalent in the 1920s and 1930s appear in the twenty-first century – indeed, they had no place in the Society and Institute of the second half of the twentieth century'.[20] Moreover, the author finds the contrast between the pre-1945 lectures with the more recent ones striking: 'One can see how from the 1960s onwards the Society became focused on advances in the life sciences, particularly reproductive health and technology, and on contemporary concerns about population, the environment and genetic disease.'[21] This intellectual and institutional transformation is indeed a far cry from the kinds of research that had preoccupied the minds of Francis Galton and his contemporaries.[22] It is my contention that the way in which modern genetics has successfully negotiated its way out of its less than flattering eugenic past can provide this discourse with the necessary ethical framework in its dealing with the relevant aspects of Indo-European studies.

I – Methodology, Contexts and Terminology

In 1869, only a few short years after the publication of George Grote's *History of Greece* in 12 massive and comprehensive volumes, George Rawlinson could only gather together four 'modern' titles that had any direct relevance to the Iranian world, one of which, a 1590 publication, was a borderline incunabulum. It is precisely because of the existence of such a bibliographical dearth that a book such as this can justifiably be described as an intellectual corrective. But what are its main research aims? First, the primary theme of the entirety of this work is the analysis of the paradoxical and confused way in which the classicists of the period (1860s–1930s) discussed the Graeco-Persian world within the constraints of comparative philology. Second, since the resultant 'cognitive dissonance' or 'doublethink' (Persia being both 'Asiatic' and 'Aryan' simultaneously) was itself underpinned by a number of spatial (Europe v. Asia) and political (democracy v. despotism) dichotomies, detailed and systematic discussions of those dichotomies, within our stipulated parameters, can scarcely be avoided. And finally, with these interconnected aims being largely ensconced within a number of intellectual and academic settings – such as Hellenism/s, prehistory, questions relating to race and culture, anthropology, linguistics and Romanticism – it is essential to scrutinize these settings as thoroughly as possible.

My methodology, broadly speaking, consists of three interrelated components. First, the nature of this work demands close inspections of a large and varied body of documents. Consequently, detailed textual, and at times, semantic *deconstruction* defines much of the analytical aspects of this work. This approach, however, is complex and multi-layered – and it needs to be. There are, after all, many different types of texts or terms, each requiring their own bespoke exegesis. As far as the second component is concerned, it is necessary to *reconstruct* a number of specific historical, intellectual and institution-building trends of the period. The analytical reconstructions of how the fields of anthropology, philology, prehistoric archaeology, as well as Romanticism and Hellenism developed and evolved are needed, because it helps to contextualize the first component of my methodology, namely, the deconstruction of texts and terms. The final component is included as a contingency, but has come into play in a very substantial way. At the outset of this research, it was not clear that the tools of *philosophical enquiry* were a requirement for what I had in mind. As my thoughts matured, however, I realized that at certain points of this discourse, the application of philosophical analysis would become an unavoidable necessity. And as a consequence, I familiarized myself with a variety of relevant schools of philosophical thoughts, such as history, science, and aesthetics.

There are two contexts within which the overwhelming body of this work dwells. First and most importantly, there is the *narrow* or the explicit context. The manner in which comparative philology in general, and Indo-European philology in particular, had impacted and, arguably, manipulated questions relating to 'race', 'culture', ancient history, and prehistory during the 80 years from the 1850s to 1930s (concentrating on the last four decades of this period) defines this narrow context. This context is also where the core of this thesis lies. The *broad* or the implicit context, in contrast, exists in the margins of this discourse. It is to be found in the preface, endnotes and in the introductory passage of this chapter. Although this broad context deals with the same issues as the narrow one, it does so outside the boundaries of the narrowly defined period under investigation. In other words, it positions the detailed analysis of the first 40 or so years of the twentieth century within a context that includes, *inter alia*, contemporary classics, new Achaemenid historiography and populist works, such as journalism, fiction and cinema. It is my belief that in order to assess how this particular intellectual enquiry can best be furthered, it is necessary to acquaint oneself with the present state of the relevant debates in a critical manner – be they in the academic environment or beyond.

What do we mean when we speak of 'Iran' or of 'Persia'? The peculiar way in which these two terms and their cognates have been used requires clarification. In everyday discourse, these two terms are often used synonymously. Among the post-1979 émigrés, however, it has become customary to use 'Persia' and its cognates to denote a 'better' place, a grander, a less confrontational and a more sophisticated set of cultural co-ordinates than those being offered by the hierocratic diktat of the Islamic Republic. Until quite recently, I followed a very simple formula: 'Persia' for the pre-Islamic period; 'Iran' for the post-Islamic. Through the process of pondering the ways in which this book should be framed, I have come to the conclusion that such a simplistic labelling no longer suffices: the picture is much, much more complicated than I had anticipated at the outset.

'Persia', at the very least, has a threefold definition. First, it was the official name of a state until the 1930s.[23] Second, and following Josef Wiesehöfer's schema,[24] it describes a realm ruled by a number of monarchs, beginning with Cyrus in the sixth century BC, and ending with Yazdgird III in the seventh century AD. And finally, since the name refers to a specific area in the south-western extremity of the Iranian plateau, whence the Achaemenid clan came into prominence, it describes, in a narrow sense, the Achaemenid Empire. 'Iran', in contrast, is paradoxically both a harder and an easier term to define. It is easier because there is a state with such a name. It is harder because 'Iranians', or to be more accurate, 'Indo-Iranians' dwell and have always dwelled in many places outside the Iranian plateau.[25] In other words, from the perspectives of ethnicity, geography and history, there has been, since time immemorial, a 'Greater Iran'.[26] This entity extends from southern Russia, the Ukraine and the Danube Basin, right across the Caucasus Mountains, the Caspian and towards the vast plains of central Asia and the rugged region of north-west India. In this discourse, the Achaemenid Empire ('Persia' in the narrowest sense) is, to all intents and purposes, a proxy for this 'Greater Iran'. But how can the Achaemenid Empire, itself an amalgam of Indo-Iranian and non-Indo-Iranian (Elamite, Assyrian, Babylonian, etc.) cultural and ethnic variables represent this idea of 'Greater Iran'? The manner in which the Persian Wars and Alexander's adventures is discussed, as witnessed here and, in due course, in Chapter 7, often renders the Persians as the oriental 'other'.[27] By transcending the arbitrary line that divides the two continents of Europe and Asia, this notion of a 'Greater Iran' and a shared Indo-European cultural heritage makes it conceptually and intellectually more difficult to 'orientalize' the 'Persian' component of this Greater Iranian world so freely. Since there continue to be those who are unwilling or incapable of differentiating between ancient Persia and the modern Arabo-Islamic world, this situating of the Persians where they arguably belong – namely within the *Eurasian* family of Indo-Iranian peoples[28] – is, in my view, a much-needed analytical corrective. It is with this in mind that this work intends to explore how the Persian civilization was characterized during the 'high' Indo-Europeanism of the first 40 years of the twentieth century.

II – Structure

The central aim of the next chapter is to provide all the historical, intellectual and institutional backgrounds that are necessary for the unfolding of this narrative. The methodology adopted for this purpose is, broadly speaking, a chronology of events and ideas germane to the subject-matter. It is needless to say that the new sciences of anthropology and comparative philology did not emerge in isolation, but within a number of already existing contexts. Those relevant to this work are classicism and classical education in general, and Romantic Hellenism in particular. Consequently, after describing the evolution of these sciences, the rest of the chapter deals with the all-important contexts. In this section, the works of German Romantics, such as Winckelmann, Lessing, Goethe, Hegel and Nietzsche, are discussed in conjunction with those who were influenced by them in Victorian Britain, such as Walter Pater and Mathew Arnold. This chapter concludes by arguing that instead of speaking of Hellenism in the singular, it is more appropriate to consider it in the plural.

In the nineteenth century, a simplistic formula integrated comparative philology with physical anthropology, and as a consequence, fused the cultural-cum-linguistic characteristics of a population group with their arbitrarily drawn 'racial' attributes. One of the most pernicious consequences of this was the very popular idea of the 'Aryan race'. Chapter 3 sets out to investigate how and if this idea experienced any decipherable alteration during the first four decades of the twentieth century; and if so, how these modifications manifested themselves. The method used here is a detailed analysis of many of the anthropological or ethnological relevant writings of the period. The chapter begins with a background treatment of the state of anthropology in the United Kingdom, which is carried out by examining the archives of the Royal Anthropological Institute. This archival work, moreover, is extended to cover how 'race' and its relationship to 'culture' and 'language' were discussed by the relevant committees of this Institute, with particular attention paid to a document produced by its 'Race Committee' in 1935. The Hellenist context, however, that was touched upon in the preceding chapter cannot be forgotten. Thus, a closer look at the writings of Myres – who was an anthropologist and an ancient historian, as well as a member of this Committee – seemed at the beginning of my research to be a thoroughly sensible idea. Subsequently, however, I decided that the multifaceted quality of Myres' *oeuvre* enables it to be employed judiciously as the textual, intellectual, and chronological anchor for this monograph (see Glossary for an extended profile of Myres).

One area on which Myres had rather less to say was prehistory. In Chapter 4 the output of one of his former students, the eminent prehistorian Gordon Childe, is discussed. This chapter continues the themes of 'race' and 'culture' within the context of how the latter phenomenon emerged in prehistoric Europe. Did it evolve independently, or was it diffused centrifugally from the Near East? Childe's mindset proved to be of some interest. During the earlier part of his career, he produced *The Dawn of European Civilization* (1925) and *The Aryans: A Study of Indo-European Origins* (1926). These works suggest that the author was in favour of the 'evolutionist' stance. Much of this was predicated on his belief that by distinguishing unambiguously between 'ethnicity' and 'race', one was at liberty to comment about the various types of 'Aryan peoples' in a complimentary fashion. He seemed to be unaware that often, 'ethnicity' can and does act as a synonym or a proxy for 'race'. As a result of this unintentional approving nod towards 'Aryanism', he swung his intellectual pendulum towards the other extreme and adopted a fairly radical diffusionist stance by the 1930s. The overriding purpose of this chapter is to contrast Childe's treatment of the matrix of 'race', 'people', and 'culture' with the one pursued by Myres.

The debate concerning 'race' and 'culture' is only one of the two main themes of this book. The other, and more substantial theme, is Hellenism; or, to be precise, Hellenisms. Whereas in the nineteenth-century debate, an aesthetic form of Hellenism was the context within which the sciences of anthropology and philology functioned, during the first 40 years of the twentieth century, these roles were reversed. In Chapter 5 it is argued that as far as 'aesthetic' Hellenism was concerned, Gilbert Murray and his intellectual entourage carried on the Romantic traditions of Winckelmann, Goethe, Arnold and Pater with only minor modifications. However, it was Myres' more anthropological approach, together with its 'race-culture' foundation, which ushered in a new form of Hellenism. It is demonstrated in Chapter 5 that Myres' approach is distinguishable from that of Murray because of its 'scientific' underpinnings. The discussion which unfolds in Chapter 5 is only the first part of a longer discourse concerning Hellenisms. It merely examines the outer or the textual characteristics of the available published and unpublished evidence. It does not delve into the philosophical cores of these expressions. What makes Murray and Myres 'tick', philosophically speaking, cannot, of course, be ignored. In the second part of this analysis (Chapter 6), I try to pinpoint what kinds of thinking had gone into producing these two kinds of Hellenisms by pursuing a number of philosophical exegeses. As a result, it is ascertained that 'aesthetic' Hellenism resides within the compass of the philosophy of beauty, with ideas concerning 'truth', 'perfection' and 'wonder' (*thauma*) dominating. This mode of Hellenism engages far too uncritically with the literary legacies of the ancients. The anthropologically-minded approach, however, is shown to be a more complex phenomenon. This approach, as argued in Chapter 6, is underpinned by two distinctive philosophies – that of R. G. Collingwood's philosophy of history, and Thomas Kuhn's conceptualization of 'normal science'. In other words, the analysis in Part II augments the discussions in Part I by demonstrating that Myres' 'scientific' approach is also historically aware, hence the need for the new label of 'historico-scientific' Hellenism. This way of looking at the Greek civilization is, however, not an end in itself, but a means to another, albeit related, end: its overarching purpose is to investigate how within these contexts, ancient Iranian history (which almost always means the Achaemenid Empire with soupçons of the Parthian and Sasanian empires thrown in) is recounted in the historical writings of the period covered in this monograph.

This task of textual deconstruction is undertaken in Chapter 7. The bulk of this chapter deals with the manner in which Greek historiography and, to a lesser degree due to the unavailability of material, the Iranian historiography of the late nineteenth and the first four decades of the twentieth century dealt with the Persian Wars, the conquests of Alexander and the template that divides the ancient world between the 'Europeans' and the 'Asiatics'. The aim of this chapter is to acquire a better understanding of how comparative Indo-European philology and mythology, coupled with ideas concerning 'race', 'culture', and 'people', affected, narrowly speaking, the depiction of these important historical episodes, and more broadly the way in which the Iranian world vis-à-vis the Greek world was rethought. Once again, the 'aesthetically-informed' and uncritical history writing of the mainstream is contrasted with that of Myres. It is suggested that by relying on Collingwood's ideas along with the puzzle-solving tendency of a 'normal scientist', Myres sidesteps the 'presentism' that had pervaded much of the output of the period.

Finally, Chapter 8 brings all the discussions to a critical focus and denouement. It also reappraises Myres' multifaceted contributions to my discourse by referring directly to a 1953 paper which, at first glance at least, appears to go against many of his earlier core inferences.

CHAPTER 2

SETTING THE SCENE: ANTHROPOLOGY, LINGUISTICS AND ROMANTIC HELLENISM IN VICTORIAN BRITAIN

Introduction

By the beginning of the nineteenth century, the Renaissance humanism of early modern Europe gave way first to neo-classicism and then to 'Romantic Hellenism'. In parallel with these developments, major advances were taking place in other spheres, such as the natural sciences, anthropology and linguistics. This chapter is concerned with the manner in which these new fields had developed within the context of Hellenism.

There are two general aspects to this. First, by examining anthropology and linguistics, this chapter intends to demonstrate the growing tendency of the period to link 'race' to 'language', and which considered the notion of the 'Aryan race' as a matter of scientific fact (section I). Second, by an examination of both the Germanic and British (Victorian) brands of Hellenism, it tries to illustrate the intellectual pervasiveness and plurality of Hellenism (section II). Section III, in turn, discusses the phenomenon of Hellenism fusing with 'Aryanism'. This chapter concludes with a trio of brief résumés looking forward to the subsequent chapters (section IV).

I – The New Sciences of Anthropology and Language: A Historical Analysis

As a recognizable academic discipline, anthropology has only been with us since the second half of the nineteenth century. Due to its ambitious remit – nothing short of the science and study of 'Man' – it, by definition and design, could not do otherwise but capture and transform a number of academic disciplines and situate them within its intellectual and/or institutional structures. This is precisely what had happened in the nineteenth century. It is worth underscoring the point that the intellectual climate of this period was particularly propitious for an overarching supra-structure to assert itself. Many new and revolutionary ideas were aired in this period: Hegel's theories of state, Darwin's theory of evolution, Marx's dialectic materialism, Comte's sociology, Lyell's geology, Müller's linguistics and J. S. Mill's eclectic output were clamouring for some form of academic-cum-institutional order. Anthropology was at hand to provide some of that order.

In his *A Hundred Years of Anthropology* (1952), T. K. Penniman considers the first half of the century as a period of 'convergence' and the latter half, separated somewhat arbitrarily by the 1859 publication of the *Origin of Species*, as the 'constructive' period.[1] Questions concerning race and empire – not to mention the ending of slavery throughout the British Empire in 1834 – were partly responsible for the formation of anthropological institutions throughout Europe. The Ethnological Society of the United Kingdom, for instance, was founded with the aim of becoming a 'centre and depository for the collection and systematization of all observations made on human races'.[2] In addition, tentative inroads were made during the 'convergence period' in archaeology, sociology and relevant natural sciences. The prehistory of Europe had also become an area of avid archaeological interest, particularly in Britain, Germany, Denmark and Italy. No less important in this period was the study of 'Man' in his social environment and the manner in which he chose to negotiate rules governing social interactions. And finally, in natural sciences, Darwin, much influenced by Lamarck's precise classification of organic life, was already laying the groundwork for his groundbreaking theory. 'With the publication of the *Origin of Species* in 1859,' as Penniman avers, 'the Constructive Period of anthropology as a single, though many-sided science, begins.'[3]

The theory of evolution put the science of (human) biology right at the intellectual heart of anthropology. It facilitated and accelerated the formation of the physical, as opposed to cultural, aspect of anthropology, thereby rendering it, arguably, the most significant half of the anthropological whole. This process was augmented institutionally by the merging of the Ethnological and Anthropological (formed in 1863) Societies into the Anthropological Institute of Great Britain and Ireland in 1869. The work of this Institute was further supplemented by the peer-reviewed publication of *The Journal of the Institute of Anthropology* in 1871. Thus by the last quarter of the century, the science of anthropology had come of age. However, whereas it was fairly straightforward to classify, say, technology, archaeology, zoology, and palaeontology as belonging to either the cultural or physical branch of anthropology, the science of language or linguistics was proving harder and more controversial to define and classify.

The science of language or comparative philology had its earliest antecedence in (Late) Renaissance Europe. The Italian traveller F. Sassetti,[4] for instance, had remarked in 1587 on the lexical similarities between European and some non-European (Indic) languages. Moreover, over a century or so later, scholars such as G. W. Leibniz (1646–1716) and L. von Schlozer (1735–1808)[5] began to cast doubt on the consensus that Hebrew was the progenitor of all languages. Consequently, they divided the known languages into Semitic and Japhetic families, but their approach was speculative and lacked systematic rigour. It was not until the wholesale opening-up of India to scholars that lingual investigation moved into a new era.

The close study of Sanskrit by William Jones (1746–94) and his discovery of the Indo-European languages were the decisive factors in the formation of comparative philology as an academic discipline. Furthermore, he had also anticipated the eventual formation of comparative mythological studies by observing 'striking similitude between the chief objects of worship in ancient Greece and Italy' and India (see de Coulanges, below). In a celebrated extract from 1788, Jones puts it thus:

> The *Sanscrit* language, whatever its antiquity, is of a wonderful structure; more perfect than the *Greek*, more copious than the *Latin*, and more exquisitely refined than either, yet bearing to both of them a stronger affinity, both in the roots of verbs and in the forms of grammar, than could possibly have been produced by accident; so strong indeed that no philologer could examine all three, without believing them to have sprung from some common source, which perhaps no longer exists: there is a similar reason, though not quite so forcible, for supposing that both the *Gothick* and the *Celtick*, though blended with a very different idiom, had the same origin with the *Sanscrit*; and the old *Persian* might be added to the same family.[6]

It has to be remembered that Jones' inferences were the product of a gifted dilettante. They had to wait another 30 years for some semblance of scientific conceptualization. This proceeded in an ad hoc and piecemeal fashion. The central question which had exercised the minds of the nineteenth century's philologists and underpinned the (anthropological) debate was a straightforward one: should the 'science of language' be grouped with the 'physical sciences' or the 'historical/social sciences'? There were enthusiastic advocates on both sides. On the physical sciences side of things, the Schlegel brothers, Friedrich (1772–1829) and August Wilhelm (1767–1845), for instance, considered language 'to be a concrete organism, independent of human volition and with a growth analogous to that of the plant or the animal' and that 'the laws of language [can be] explained without reference to the facts of psychology'.[7] Franz Bopp (1791–1867), similarly, asserted that language is 'not so much a social product', but 'a subject of physical enquiry'.[8] This overarching postulation was underpinned by Bopp's position as the first serious systematizer of language. He had divided languages into three groups: those without grammar (Chinese), those which acquire grammar by compositing monosyllabic roots (Indo-European languages) and those which express relations of grammar by internal changes (Semitic languages). Consequently, languages could no longer be traced back to a single source (Hebrew, for our purposes). It should be stressed, however, that Bopp's conception of physical here is not racial but largely laryngeal (phonetics). The tendency towards a more race-based analysis was furthered significantly in 1851 by the publication of Jacob Grimm's (1785–1863) treatise, *Ueber den Ursprung der Sprache*, which begins by 'comparing the science of language with the investigation of natural history'.[9] August Schleicher (1821–68) took Grimm's analysis a step further and argued that 'like the phenomena of chemistry or physiology, the phenomena of language must be regarded as so many material facts which can only be the subject matter of physical science'. In turn, this goes on to render language, in Schleicher's view, 'the most important, it may be said the sole, test of race and lineage'.[10]

The historical or social sciences counter-argument commenced in earnest with August Friedrich Pott's (1802–87) criticism of his immediate contemporary and former teacher, Bopp. According to Pott, 'the roots of language have no existence apart from the mind'. In other words, language was considered to be no more than the 'expression of thought' and thus one of the 'historical or social sciences'.[11] Pott's approach to this subject owed a great deal to ideas advanced by Wilhelm von Humboldt (1767–1835). Humboldt had maintained that 'language is the expression of national thought, that it must be treated as an organic whole; that, in short, its science is historical and not a physical one'.[12] Like Pott, Heymann Steinthal (1823–99) was also a follower of Humboldt, and as a consequence he couched his analyses in the context of the social sciences. Steinthal argued that since the 'first condition for the "birth" of language [is] that men should be united together in a common society', then it is the 'psychological phenomena' of the society in question that need to be investigated.[13] Moreover, writing several years after the airing of these debates, Archibald Henry Sayce (1846–1933), in his *Introduction to the Science of Language* (1880), assessed these arguments carefully and inferred that '[L]anguage is the creation of society. An individual speaks a certain language because he belongs to a certain society.' As a consequence therefore, 'language is no test of race, only of social contact'.[14]

Even though Sayce was firmly against tabulating language with physical sciences, he nonetheless recognized that the propensity to link language and race was becoming philologically and ideologically inescapable. Philologically, the idea that language was entirely due to 'social contact' could no longer be maintained without appropriate modification after A. H. Keane's 1896 publication, entitled *Ethnology*. In this work, Keane demonstrated that in the Basque region of Spain, 'language shows the existence of ethnic elements which without its evidence would have been unsuspected'.[15] This, in turn, helped to reinforce the ideological trends of the day. And no one represented this trend better than the philologist, Max Müller (1823–1900). The title of the first lecture in Müller's 1861 series of lectures, published as *Lectures on the Science of Language*, was unambiguous. It read: 'The Science of Language, One of the Physical Sciences.'[16] Müller's analysis does not begin with a race-language synonymy; it only meanders towards that destination because of his adopted methodology of induction. He considers the approach that emphasizes 'empirical' observations, followed by the 'classificatory' and 'theoretical' stages, as sound for the purposes of comparative philology.[17] 'There are two great divisions of human knowledge,' according to Müller: 'Physical science deals with the works of God, historical science with the work of man.'[18] The historical science of philology uses language 'as a key to an understanding of the literary monuments which by-gone ages have bequeathed to us'. But in comparative philology, in contrast:

> language itself becomes the sole object of scientific inquiry [...]. We do not want to know languages, we want to know language; what language is, how it can form a vehicle or an organ of thought; we want to know its origin, its nature, its laws; and it is only to arrive at that knowledge that we collect,

arrange, and classify all the facts of language that are within our reach.[19]

It is precisely the detailed analyses of the 'origin', 'nature', and 'laws' of language from which, almost as inevitable by-products, the questions of race-language linkages emerge:

> The genealogical classification of languages [...] has a historical meaning. As sure as the six Romance dialects points to an original home of Italian shepherds on the seven hills at Rome, the Aryan languages together point to an earlier period of language, when the first ancestors of the Indians, the Persians, the Greeks, the Romans, the Slavs, the Celts and the Germans were living together within the same enclosures, nay under the same roof.[20]

In *The Imperial Dictionary of the English Language* (1882), Müller is more explicit:

> In continual struggle with each other, and with Semitic and Turanian races, these *Aryan* nations have become rulers of history, and it seems to be their mission to link all parts of the world together by the chains of civilisation, commerce, and religion.[21]

Although Poliakov exaggerates a little when he labels Müller the 'godfather' of the 'Aryan Myth',[22] he does, nevertheless, capture Müller and his particular milieu accurately. For instance, within the context of the ongoing Franco-Prussian War of 1870, Müller was aghast at the sorry spectacle of two 'Aryan' nations unnecessarily at war. This is how he puts it in a letter to a French colleague:

> I know you are as strongly French as I am German, but that does not prevent both of us, I think, from feeling deeply the shame and degradation which this war has brought on the race

to which we belong as men [...]. We must all hide our faces in shame and grief.[23]

The fact that this French colleague was none other than Ernest Renan (1823–92) is noteworthy. After all, Renan was probably the most vociferous advocate of the race–language synonymy and racial hierarchism of the period under discussion. In his *Etudes Religieuses* (1855), Renan penned one of his first articles concerning his distaste for the 'Semitic race', among which he had regarded the historical Israel, according to Charles Chauvin's *Renan* (2000), to be its 'highest and purest branch'. As far as Renan was concerned,

> peoples' characters are related to their language: the Semite has a language with a geometrical structure which cannot manipulate the roots of the words. However, it is different for those of the Aryan languages: all large political, social and intellectual movements in world history can be attributed to races that speak them.[24]

Renan therefore infers from his analysis that 'the Jewish culture will amount to nothing, the Greek culture (its culture of scientific enquiry for instance), on the other hand, will be able to renew and revive itself indefinitely'.[25] Some seven years later, Renan summed up his analysis more succinctly in a lecture entitled 'The Part Played by Semitic Peoples in the History of Civilization':

> The future, gentlemen, is for Europe alone. Europe will conquer the world and spread its religion which is law, freedom and respect for mankind, the belief that there is something divine at the heart of humanity. In all areas, progress for Indo-European peoples will consist in distancing themselves more and more form the Semitic spirit.[26]

One of the major influences on Renan — if their correspondence is anything to go by — was Count de Gobineau (1816–82).[27] His *l'Essai sur l'inégalité des races humaines* (1853) was the 'respectable' textbook on racial discourse of the day.[28] Here is a relevant and revealing extract:

> If the empire of Darius had, at the battle of Arbela, been able to fill its ranks with Persians, that is to say with real Aryans; if the Romans of the late Empire had had a Senate and an army of the same stock as that which existed at the time of the Fabii, their dominion would never have come to an end. So long as they kept the same purity of blood, the Persians and Romans would have lived and reigned.[29]

This inability, on the part of the 'Aryans', to sustain 'purity of blood' imbued Gobineau's work with undisguised pessimism. In a letter to de Tocqueville, he writes: 'I do not say to people, you are to be forgiven or condemned, I say to them: *you are dying*.'[30] The successful nature of the 'Aryan' conquest, in his view, paradoxically allowed the 'infusion of inferior blood',[31] thereby undermining the 'racial instinct' that exists in all human species.

The anglophone debate[32] predates that of Gobineau and his intellectual descendents[33] by some years. Thomas Arnold regarded the 'Teutonic race' as the 'designated instrument of Providence'.[34] Germany, in his opinion, was 'the land of our Saxon and Teutonic forefathers; the land uncorrupted by any Roman or other mixture; the birthplace of the most moral races of men that the world has yet seen — of the soundest laws — the least violent passions and the fairest domestic and other virtues'.[35] Arnold had also made a distinction between the Greeks and Jews, which, in due course, would become much more prevalent (nowhere more so than in the writings of Arnold *fils*; see section III). He argued that the Jews communicated to mankind 'all religious knowledge' and the Greeks, those of the 'intellectual civilization'.[36] Within the capacious framework of anthropology, these types of arguments were bolstered even further. The *Anthropological Review*, for instance, published two articles by J. W. Jackson, entitled 'Iran and Turan' (1868), and 'The Aryans and Semites' (1869). Both of these articles took the language–race synonymy as a conceptual given.

Interestingly, the 'Iran' of the title is not a reference to the country of that name, but to an 'entire area of Iran', throughout which 'the essential character and quality of the hereditarily gubernational classes, from Persia to Ireland' could be investigated.[37] According to Jackson, 'there can be no doubt' that the Turanian (a person of Turkic background) is 'higher than the Negro and lower than the Caucasian ["Semites and Aryans"] in structure and intellect'.[38] This inference, in Jackson's opinion, is significant because the 'conflict between Iran and Turan'[39] has been with us for a long time and will be with us (almost) in perpetuity. In this conflict, the Semites are going to be, according to the author, mere spectators: 'The world is now in the process of recovery from the racial collapse of its higher types, and in this resurgence it is the Aryan and not the Semite who is the more immediate heir of empire.'[40] In his 1869 article, Jackson's treatment of the 'Semites' is not as blatantly racist as his earlier treatment of the 'Turanians': after cataloguing many of the historical conflicts between the two 'peoples', in which the 'Aryans' were triumphant, Jackson declared that, essentially, the 'hot wars' of yesteryear have now been transformed into a long-term détente:

> In truth, if the Semite represents the man of the South, with his moral exaltation and his theological mission, and the Aryan, in contradistinction, represents the man of the North, with his intellectual expansion and his consequent aptitude for literature, science, and art; then, as the racial embodiments respectively of faith and reason, they present the bipolar aspect of man's superior nature, whose harmony is the effect and expression of well-balanced antagonism.[41]

II – The Context: Victorian (Germanic) Hellenism

Writing about Greece was in part a way for the Victorians to write about themselves.[42]

The preceding discussions have illustrated that by the last quarter of the nineteenth century, race–language synonymy became, in some quarters, an academic and intellectual constant. Of course, developments in anthropology and linguistics did not take place in a vacuum. There were a number of contexts. This monograph, however, is solely preoccupied with one context in particular, or at last with one ever-changing context; a context of long pedigree and deep roots. The shift from Renaissance humanism to neo-classicism and thence to Hellenism defines one of the main strands of modern European intellectual development. This process can best be appreciated by considering the following three areas: classical education, classical ideas of governance and, crucially, (Germanic) Hellenism.

Classical Education and Ideas of Governance

The eighteenth-century variety of classicism – the classicism that followed Renaissance humanism – was almost exclusively Romanocentric. This 'Augustan Age',[43] or the era of 'neo-classicism', was, according to J. W. Johnson, 'temporally and ideologically differentiated from the earlier "Humanism", and the later "Romantic classicism" (often identified with Romantic Hellenism)'.[44] It was precisely in this period that the intellectual climate was becoming increasingly hospitable towards the potential flourishing of 'Romantic Hellenism'. This was primarily due to an increasing demand for classical education as well as because a revolutionary Europe (and America) was eager to refer back to the ideas and ideals of classical forms of government. In the domain of education, there was continuity from the eighteenth to nineteenth century. William Pitt the Elder writing eulogistically to his nephew in 1751 is illustrative:

> I rejoice to hear that you have begun Homer's Iliad; and have made so great a progress in Virgil. I hope you taste and love those authors particularly. You cannot read them too much; they are not only the two greatest poets, but they contain the finest lessons for your age to imbibe: lessons of honour, courage,

disinterestedness, love of truth, command of temper, gentleness of behaviour, humanity, and in one word, virtue in all its signification. Go on, my dear nephew, and drink as deep as you can of these divine springs: the pleasure of the draught is equal at least to the prodigious advantages of it to the heart and morals.[45]

This note of appreciation encapsulates the perceived advantages of a classical education perfectly. It seems plausible to assume that the talented bookish pupils would have opted for Homer; the politicos, for Pericles; the potential warriors, for Alexander; and the aesthetes, for Phidias.[46] This sense of a timeless and seamless continuity from the classical world to their own, which the British public schoolboy has always been encouraged to take for granted, is one of the defining characteristics of classical education in the United Kingdom. During the Victorian era, the purpose of this form of education was not merely pedagogic and scholarly, but to mould – 'breed', to use the lexicon of the day – a type of individual who saw himself as an (almost) organic extension or an offshoot of the great men of the Graeco-Roman world. This was not undertaken, it should be stressed, purely in order to drink deep at 'these divine springs', but for a more mundane, albeit important, reason: to govern an empire – the British Empire. The admission examinations for the Home and Indian Civil Services as well as the Royal Military Academy were conceived and put into practice with an emphasis on classics. This was also the case with regard to various political and ecclesiastical appointments.[47] In other words, the Britain of the nineteenth century was awash with classically-educated functionaries. This, of course, had a perceptible impact on the question of constitutional arrangement and governance. From the preliminaries of the American Revolution until the demise of Bonapartism (1760s–1815), European political thinking was preoccupied with thoughts on constitutional (re)arrangements. The debate, broadly speaking, revolved around the merits and demerits of democracy. In such debates, repeated references to Periclean Athens could hardly have been avoided.

During the eighteenth century, there was a very limited interest in Greek political history and what interest there was, was focused on Sparta. Temple Stanyan's (1677–1752) and Oliver Goldsmith's (1730–74) *The Grecian Histories* (1739 and 1774, respectively) praised an autocratic but stable Sparta at the expense of a democratic but anarchic Athens.[48] Meanwhile, among the more radical thinkers, the first barely audible pro-Athenian whispers were being heard. In a 1768 publication, Joseph Priestley (1733–1804) claimed that 'the convulsions of Athens, where life was in some measure enjoyed, and the faculties of body and mind had their proper exercise and gratification, were, in my opinion, far preferable to the savage uniformity of Sparta'.[49] Nevertheless, Sparta remained the favourite until revolutions in America and France, as well as pressure for parliamentary reforms at home, had decisively refocused the intellectual perspectives of the day. The first major narrative of Greek history to appear in English was the ten-volume *History of Greece* (1784–1810) by William Mitford (1744–1827). Apart from its encyclopaedic treatment of the subject matter, Mitford's *oeuvre* performed another function: it indicted the Athenian democracy. Mitford's Greece was 'a story of balanced Homeric monarchies declining into various modes of unhappy republican life'.[50] This ideology was very much based on the sensibilities of a man immersed in the politics of the 'Country Party' with its notion of a 'balanced English constitution' and monarchical conservatism. In addition, this viewpoint was complemented with an undisguised hostility towards the democratization of the electioneering process for parliament (where Mitford sat as a Tory MP). Mitford argued that by handing 'every free Athenian [...] his equal right to vote and speak', Solon (638–558 BC) had put 'unlimited power in the hands of those least capable of properly exercising any power'. By doing away with the representative principle, Solon had bestowed on Greece 'A TYRANNY IN THE HANDS OF THE PEOPLE'.[51] The temptation for England to adopt this Athenian model, in Mitford's view, should be resisted forcefully.

By the 1830s, however, there were strong reactions against the anti-democratic and pro-Spartan stances of Mitford and others.

Although Macaulay[52] was the first notable critic of Mitford, a thorough response had to wait for the publication of George Grote's (1794–1871) *History of Greece* (1846–56). Grote was a political radical. His attraction to utilitarianism and liberalism inevitably implied that his take on the history of Greece would be very different – diametrically opposed, in fact – from that of Mitford. He celebrated the Athenian democracy; and by so doing, he had also implicitly approved of the post-Reform constitutional arrangements of the British polity. He shared with Mitford a belief in the necessity of 'balanced constitutions', namely to provide protection against 'internal turmoil, moral corruption, and civic decay'.[53] But he believed that democratic structures alone, *pace* Mitford, are the sole guarantors of auspicious outcomes and what he called 'constitutional morality' which would, in turn, 'enforc[e] obedience to the authorities acting under and within those forms, yet combined with the habit of open speech, of action subject only to definite legal control, and unrestrained censure of those very authorities as to all their public acts'.[54] In other words, the liberty of the individual, freedom of thought and due process under the law could only be achieved under the auspices of a government by consent. Moreover, Grote maintained that Mitford had misrepresented the Athenian government under Solon:

> In the age of Solon there was no political idea or system yet current which could be assumed as an unquestionable datum – no conspicuous standard to which the citizens could be pledged under all circumstances to attach themselves. The option lay only, between a mitigated oligarchy in possession, and a despot in possibility; a contest wherein the affections of the people could rarely be counted upon in favour of the established government.[55]

Ultimately, for Grote as well as for many of his immediate contemporaries, what had held true for Athens was also holding true for Victorian Britain: 'democratic freedom was the best guarantor of both stability and civic virtue.'[56]

The German Connection and the British Response

The importance of German intellectualism can hardly be overestimated.[57] This is particularly so when it comes to what concerns us here: Hellenism. There are three aspects to the centrality of German thought to Hellenism. The first is the aesthetic appreciation of the Hellene, as delineated by Johann Winckelmann (1717–68) and other German Romantics, such as Lessing, Herder, Goethe and Schiller. The second is the sizeable contribution of Friedrich Hegel (1770–1854), and in particular his idea that what matters in writing and relating history is the existence or otherwise of a historical *geist* (spirit). The third is Friedrich Nietzsche's (1844–1900) unique take on the tragedy of Prometheus. Since these quintessentially Germanic schools of thought have placed Hellenism on a pedestal for over 200 years, it is imperative to have some awareness of their geneses and evolution. It is immaterial to the work at hand as to why the Germans had imitated the Greeks 'more slavishly' and more 'intensely'[58] than many of their immediate contemporaries. What matters here is the manner in which this imitative absorption of 'a Greece that never was on sea or land'[59] had been carried out, and seeped, via a process of intellectual osmosis, into the cultural life of Victorian Britain.

'The major figures of the Enlightenment', according to De Laura, 'had appealed to *truth*, not *beauty*, as their standard, whereas the German Hellenists had more frankly sought a belief or myth, more beautiful [and] more in keeping with the dignity of man'[60] than what had preceded them. The first effective formulator of this 'myth' of Greece was none other than Winckelmann. There were two aspects to his Hellenism. First, he considered the physical and cultural environments of Greece to be particularly conducive to humanistic endeavours. A temperate climate combined with the tradition of gymnastic exercise in the nude, for instance, gave Greek artists ample opportunities to observe and study the human anatomy in an entirely new way.[61] In addition, the 'fairness' of the Greek bodies was also a matter of some importance: 'The fairest amongst us would perhaps not approach the fairest Greek body.'[62] This idyllic depiction with racial undertones, as Frank M. Turner argues in *The Greek Heritage in*

Victorian Britain (1980), 'portrayed the Greeks as an aesthetic people who resembled children of Western Civilization'.[63] This healthy youthfulness was supplemented by lauding the uniqueness of the Greek form of aestheticism. But 'it was not only the lost beauty of Greek art which Winckelmann rediscovered for the modern world', as Eliza Butler puts it in her preface to *The Tyranny of Greece over Germany*: 'It was also the ethical standard which he associated with it: greatness, nobility, simplicity and serenity of soul.'[64] Or, as Walter Pater put it in his essay on Winckelmann: 'the supreme characteristics of the Hellenic ideal are *Heiterkeit* – blitheness or repose, and *Allgemeinheit* – generality or breadth.'[65] Many of these qualities, in Winckelmann's view, are to be found in Greek sculptures. Here is his 'perfect law of art':

> The universal, dominant characteristic of Greek masterpieces [...] is noble simplicity and serene greatness in the pose as well as in the expression. The depths of the sea are always calm, however wild and stormy the surface; and in the same way the expression in Greek figure reveals greatness and composure of soul in the throes of whatever passion.[66]

And he had one supreme example in mind: the first century BC statue, *Laocoön and his Sons*.[67] 'The pain of the body and the greatness of the soul are equally balanced throughout the composition of the figure, and seem to cancel each other out.'[68] It is precisely this type of analytical approach that directed Winckelmann to infer that the Greeks did not merely copy nature, but added something to it; they added *ideal beauty*. It is not nature at its best that can be seen in the works of the Greeks, 'but something more than nature; that is certain ideal beauties formed from pictures created only in the mind of the artist'. This ascendancy of the 'mind of the artist' over nature was – and still is – a potent message. From this it follows, according to Winckelmann, that 'the beauty of Greek sculpture is more easily apprehended than the beauty of nature'. Therefore, the best course of action is to recognize that 'the study of nature must be [...] a longer and more toilsome road to the knowledge of perfect beauty than the study of the antique'.[69] Moreover, this approach is also taken into other domains, such as literature and philosophy:

> Perhaps the first Greek painters drew in much the same way as their first good author wrote [...]. The noble simplicity and serene greatness of Greek statues, is the true characteristic of Greek literature of the best period, the writing of the Socratic school.[70]

This analysis of the intellectual worth of the ancient Greeks was not undertaken by Winckelmann without due reference to an appropriate historical context. In order to establish aesthetic originality or otherwise, it was a conceptual necessity to enquire what had preceded the Greeks and what was contemporaneous with them. At the very outset of *The History of Ancient Art* (1759), Winckelmann distinguishes between 'the origin of art and the causes of its difference among different nations' in the following manner:

> The art of drawing among the Egyptians is to be compared to a tree which, though well cultivated, has been checked and arrested in its growth by worm, or other casualties; for it remained unchanged, precisely the same, yet without attaining its perfection until the period when Greek kings held sway over them; and the case appears to have been the same with Persian art. Etruscan art, when in its bloom, may be compared to a raging stream, rushing furiously along between crags and over rocks; for the characteristics of its drawing are hardness and exaggeration. But, among the Greeks, the art of drawing resembles a river whose clear waters flow in numerous windings through a fertile vale, and fill its channel, yet does not overflow.[71]

These epigrammatic literary tableaux are, of course, very much of their time. By rendering the contrasts between 'arrested development', 'furious and raging streams' and the 'well-balanced flow of clear water' so memorably vivid, Winckelmann not only succeeded in fuelling the imaginative faculties of the young Romantics of the late eighteenth century, but also managed to specify, clearly if allegorically, the differences in the artistic grammar of the ancient peoples.

The Laocoön sculpture continued to hold the attention of the German Romantics for some time. Gotthold Lessing (1729–81) revisited it in his *Laocoön, or the Boundaries between Painting and Poetry* (1865). This treatise on the 'laws of aesthetics' is a critical response to Winckelmann's analysis of the sculpture. In this work, Lessing takes issue with Winckelmann's assertion that the Laocoön of the sculpture, unlike that of Virgil's poem, 'is raising no dreadful cry',[72] but merely sighing anxiously. This restraint, in Lessing's view, has more to do with the 'peculiar nature of Art and her necessary boundaries and limitations',[73] and rather less to do with the deliberate balancing of 'pain' and the 'greatness of the soul'. In other words, such an interpretation has led to a misreading of Virgil. The words *'clamores horrendos ad sidera tollit'* ('His roaring fills the flitting air around'[74]) are merely a short segment of the whole poem. Its fleetingness hints at a momentary and understandable weakness, which cannot 'alienate our sympathies from a man who has already given proof of so many virtues'.[75] Thus, both the sculpture and the poet were perfectly justified in the manner in which they handled their respective materials and aesthetic media.

According to Humphrey Trevelyan in *Goethe and the Greeks* (1941), Johann Goethe (1749–1832)

> saw in them [the Greeks] a people that had understood better than any other how to give form to life on a great scale. They had had the urge to strike out recklessly and know life to the limit; but they had known also how to keep this urge within bounds so that it never lost itself in formlessness.[76]

Goethe's Greeks, unlike those of Winckelmann's, were close to and in harmony with nature.[77] In other words, the notion that the study of nature was in some way 'toilsome' would have mystified both Goethe and his Greeks. Goethe was not, it has to be said, averse to extolling the qualities of the Greeks. His fascination, however, was, in the main, with the beautiful complexity of the inner life of the (Greek) man:

> Greek tragedy [...] stirred whole, great emotions in their souls, for it was itself whole and great. And in what souls! Greek souls! I cannot make clear what that means, but I feel it and appeal, for brevity, to Homer, Sophocles and Theocritus, who have taught me to feel it.[78]

The supreme example of this fascination can best be seen in *Faust Part II*. Here, Helen – after whom Faust lusts unrequitedly – is represented, allegorically, as beautiful both in body and soul. This allows Goethe to convey, at a deeper level, his take on Hellenism. In Act 3, Helen tells Faust that her 'life seems past, and yet is somehow new; I know not, a stranger, but I live in you'.[79] A little later in the same act, Faust sits himself beside her and intimates: 'now that we have achieved oneness, let what is past, be past for ever!'[80] Here Helen of Troy, the symbol of Greek beauty, according to Goethe, belongs to 'the grey Hades, overflowing with unseizable shapes, and eternally empty'.[81] Helen, in this guise, has become in Butler's opinion 'the symbol for something which never had a real existence in this life, and never can. Winckelmann's Greece, for all its beauty, was an illusion.'[82] From my perspective, what is also significant is the fact that there is a symbiotic unity between Helen (a representative of the Greek world) and Faust (a representative of the Germanic world). Since one resides in the other, then, a spiritual 'oneness', in the form of a symbolic infant son, Euphorion, has been achieved – at least momentarily, until Helen vanishes into the infinite ether.[83]

The situating of Greece at the core of European thought, however, was far from illusory. The discourse was lively and multifaceted. As shown, those who followed Winckelmann (both temporally and intellectually) were not averse to engaging with him in a critical fashion. Their engagement, however, stopped short of interrogating the complex underpinnings that had allowed Winckelmann to position Hellenism at the very core of German, and – very swiftly — of British intellectual life. What better demonstration of this than Goethe's assessment of Winckelmann's worth: 'One learns nothing from him, but one becomes something?'[84] In Victorian Britain, there were those who had 'become something'; chief among them were Mathew Arnold (1822–88) and Walter Pater (1839–94). It was Arnold, who, as Turner contends, 'set the tone for humanistic discussion of Greek virtues'[85] for the second half of the nineteenth century. There were two noteworthy and relevant sources of influence on Arnold's intellectual formation. First, as Dale illustrates,[86] there was Aristotle's *Ethics*, dividing virtue into two kinds, 'intellectual and moral', which underpins much of the analytical thrust of his 1867 article on Hellenism (see below). Second, there was Arnold's father and his adherence to the Viconian idea that history is a cyclical phenomenon, where civilizations grow, mature and then decay, repeatedly and ad infinitum. In his *History of the Peloponnesian War by Thucydides* (1835), Thomas Arnold suggests that the different cyclical stages of a given civilization can have less in common with each other than the commensurable stages (say, 'decay') of two temporally and spatially separate civilizations. This paternal influence was most apparent in Mathew Arnold's assertions that Periclean Athens and nineteenth-century Europe have one thing in common: modernity. These two corresponding stages of cultural maturation, in Arnold's view, display 'the intellectual maturity of man himself; the tendency to observe facts with a critical spirit; to search for their law, not wander among them in random; to judge by the rule of reason; not by the impulse of prejudice or caprice'.[87] It is understandable why Arnold was upholding the maturity of the Europe of his day; but why opt for the Athens of Pericles? Fifth-century Greece (or 530 to 430 BC, to be precise), as far as Arnold was concerned, was an epoch 'of the highest possible beauty and value'. It was the period that went a long way to make 'Greece the Greece we mean when we speak of Greece'.[88]

Arnold's most telling contribution on the topic of Hellenism came with the publication of *Culture and Anarchy* (1867) — or more specifically Chapter IV of that book, entitled 'Hebraism and Hellenism'. He begins by stating that Hellenism and Hebraism share a final aim: 'man's perfection or salvation'.[89] Despite this, they 'very often' relate to each other in terms of confrontation rather than agreement. This is so because Hellenism strives to 'see things as they really are', whereas Hebraism is perfectly satisfied with 'conduct and obedience'.[90] In other words,

> The governing idea of Hellenism is *spontaneity of consciousness*; that of Hebraism, *strictness of conscience*.[91]

Christianity, in all forms, according to Arnold, 'changed nothing in this essential bent of Hebraism to set *doing* above *knowing*' (my emphasis).[92] Indeed, Christianity was much more effective and influential than Judaism in inculcating 'conscience' and 'self-conquest' in the manner in which Christian (read, European) 'man' conducts himself.[93] The reason why Christianity proved to be so successful was the 'unsoundness' of the 'Hellenic conception of human nature'.[94] This 'unsoundness', as Arnold is quick to clarify, had nothing to do with the shortcomings of the Greeks, but with the 'prematurity' and unreadiness of Christendom for the 'spontaneity of consciousness'. The Renaissance changed everything; it was 'an uprising and re-instatement of man's intellectual impulses and of Hellenism'.[95] Arnold contends, however, that the puritanical component of the Reformation ('a Hebraising revival'[96]) checked the progress of the Renaissance: 'Yet there is a very important difference between the defeat of Hellenism by Christianity eighteen hundred years ago',[97] and the more recent historical phenomenon of Renaissance. This was so because 'the subtle Hellenic leaven of the [Renaissance] found its way [...] in the Reformation'.[98] Arnold, therefore, infers:

> Primitive Christianity was legitimately and truly the ascending force in the world at that time, and the way of mankind's progress lay through its full development. Another hour in man's development began in the fifteenth century, and the main road of his progress then lay for a time through Hellenism.[99]

In *Hebrew and Hellene in Victorian Britain* (1969), David De Laura argues (and Turner[100] concurs) that Arnold had an 'idealised and simplified' notion of Hellenism which was, largely, untouched by recent classical scholarship. This was precisely the converse of Walter Pater. Pater, according to De Laura, was 'far more alive, both temperamentally and for dialectical reasons of his own, to the "other" tradition (the Dionysian) in Greek art and religion'.[101] Moreover, 'his Hellenism was a deliberate response to, and modification of, Arnold's view of the Greeks'.[102] With his essay *Winckelmann* (1867), Pater almost single-handedly introduced German Hellenism to Victorian Britain. Winckelmann, according to Pater, was destined to 'supplant [the] flimsier, more artificial, classical tradition' of Voltaire with 'the clear ring, the eternal outline, of the genuine antique'.[103] But, as Pater opines, Winckelmann's 'affinity was not merely intellectual'; the 'subtler threads of temperament were inwoven in it' in the form of 'his romantic, fervent friendships with young men'.[104] In other words, Winckelmann's Hellenism was predicated upon a not uncommon dualism – that of intellect and homoeroticism. As Pater reminds the reader, however, the Hellenic tradition, ultimately, existed in order to satisfy the 'vital requirement of the intellect':

> The spiritual forces of the past, which have prompted and informed the culture of a succeeding age, live, indeed, within that culture, but with an absorbed, underground life. The Hellenic element alone has not been so absorbed, or content with this underground life; from time to time it has started to the surface; culture has been drawn back to its sources to be clarified and corrected. Hellenism is not merely an absorbed element in our intellectual life; it is a conscious tradition in it.[105]

And the 'supreme characteristics of [the] Hellenic ideal', blitheness and breadth, were the very bases 'of conceiving humanity in a new and striking way, of putting a happy world [...] in place of [a] meaner world [...] generating around itself an atmosphere with a novel power of refraction, selecting, transforming, recombining the images it transmits, according to choice of the imaginative intellect'.[106] As a consequence 'the liberation of [...] human sensuousness',[107] as took place in ancient Greece, is one of the prerequisites of this 'happy world'. In *Greek Studies* (1895), Pater examines Greek sculptures and infers that along with sensuousness, they also display 'intellectualized' aspects. Thus, one important question for him is the necessary link that needs to be made between the abstract beauty of sculptures and the quotidian side of Greek life: 'Use and beauty'[108] cannot be divided. The great works of Greek art cannot be disconnected from 'the minor works of price, *intaglios*, coins, vases; with the whole system of material refinement and beauty in outer Greek life'.[109] After all, Greek poets describe clothes, shields, and jewelleries 'with the same vividness and freshness, the same kind of fondness, with which other poets speak of flowers'.[110] As indicated earlier, by adding the Dionysian (sensuousness) tradition to the Apollonian, Pater, as De Laura argues, managed 'to advance his "enriched" view of Greek religion as a conscious alternative to a played-out Christianity'.[111] A corollary to this, in Pater's opinion, was the 'relationship between the Ionian and Dorian impulses'; the first representing craftsmanship and 'mechanical skills'; the latter, 'intelligent and spiritual human presence'.[112] Even though Pater considered the latter as *the* driving force behind Hellenism, nonetheless, 'this was', as Turner points out:

> a Hellenism far more complex, rich and dynamic than that of Winckelmann [or] Arnold [...]. Pater's humanism and Hellenism were not a set of essential values or attitudes to be preserved in good society; they consisted, rather, of an appreciation for the role of material civilization in providing a necessary foundation for the life of reason. Pater understood Hellenism to be just that dialectical combination of material and spiritual forces making for reason and human adaptation and growth.[113]

Some of the British response to German Hellenism, therefore, was not in any way passive, but dynamic, thoughtful and 'improving'.

The biggest intellectual influence on Pater's work was Hegel. Pater even begins his essay on Winckelmann by approvingly quoting Hegel's assessment of Winckelmann:

> Winckelmann, by contemplation of the ideal works of the ancients, received a sort of inspiration, through which he opened a new sense for the study of art. He is to be regarded as one of those who, in the sphere of art, have known how to initiate a new organ for the human spirit.[114]

It is worth remembering that Pater's alma mater, the Oxford[115] of the second half of the century, was deeply influenced by many aspects of Hegel's copious and multifaceted output, particularly his writing on history (see below). In *Greek Studies*, for instance, Pater echoes Hegel's notion that, historically, 'spirit' appeared for the first time among the Greeks, asserting that prior to the Greeks there was nowhere in the East (Phoenicia in his example) where there was 'an insight into or power over human soul'.[116]

What were Hegel's ideas concerning art and, above all, history, and how are they relevant to the present discussion? In their fundamentals, Hegel's inferences concerning art were not qualitatively different from those of Winckelmann. In *The Philosophy of Fine Art* (1916), there is a discourse on 'idealness' in classical art which is largely absent from, *inter alia*, the Egyptian artistic traditions. Hegel asserts that the 'ideality or spiritual sense' of the Egyptians was so 'imbruted', that they had 'no imperative desire to possess the precision bound up in a true and vital representation carried through with detailed accuracy'. But art can only be satisfied with itself when it can claim that it is the careful product of 'reason, science, motion, expression, soul, and beauty'. 'We find this artistic self-consciousness,' according to Hegel, 'first wholly alive among the Greeks.'[117] Having kick-started the ideals of the classical tradition, the Greeks embodied '*spiritual* animation'[118] and possessed '*spiritual* substance'.[119] One theme that comes up, again and again, in Hegel's philosophy of art is the concept of 'spirit' or *geist*. In the short discussion above, this word and its cognates have appeared four times. This phenomenon is central to Hegelianism and, as we shall see, it is also at the very core of his philosophy of history. In his *Lectures on the Philosophy of World History*, Hegel discusses the nature of *geist* within the context of three varieties of historical writing. 'Original history' describes 'an immediate unity between the historian's consciousness or *geist* and the *geist* of what he is describing.'[120] It is history as witnessed or near-witnessed. 'Reflective history' deals with past events from considerable temporal distances. The historian's consciousness, in this instance, cannot directly relate to the *geist* of what is being described. Finally, the variety which had detained Hegel and defined his conceptualization of history was of a philosophical kind:

> The third kind of history, the *Philosophical History of the World*, is related to [...] reflective history in that it also adopts a general perspective, but without focussing on a single aspect abstracted from national life to the exclusion of the rest. The general perspective of philosophical world history is not abstractly general, but concrete and absolutely present; for it is the spirit which is eternally present to itself and for which there is no past.[121]

But how is this 'spirit' determined? Spirit is 'consciousness, but it is also the object of consciousness – for it is in the nature of the spirit to have itself as its object'.[122] In addition, the ability to feel, to think and to be able to control impulses by possessing an 'ideal knowledge of reality' do go a long way in determining the 'essence of spirit', which is 'self-consciousness'. The spirit

> is essentially individual, but in the field of world history, we are not concerned with particulars and need not confine ourselves to individual instances or attempt to trace everything back to them. The spirit of history is an individual which is both universal in nature and at the same time determinate: in short, it is the nation in general, and the spirit we are concerned with is the *spirit of the nation*.[123]

Hegel saw world history as unfolding in phases, beginning with the 'Oriental' world, passing through Persia,[124] Greece and Rome and progressing towards the spirit of a particular ethno-lingual nation, namely the Germanic Christian world. 'Hegel thinks', according to Stephen Houlgate, 'that all major developments in history' can be explained by a process which make explicit the implicitness of the 'self-determining consciousness'. 'This means that we must come to be self-consciously what we already are "unconsciously".'[125] Hegel puts it thus:

> What is implicit in man must become an object to him, come into his consciousness; then it becomes *for* him and he becomes aware of himself, explicit to himself. In this way he duplicates himself: first, he *is* reason and thinking, but only implicitly; then, secondly, he thinks, makes his implicit self into an object of his thought [...]. What was *potentia* comes into appearance *actu* [...]. The whole difference between Orientals and peoples amongst whom slavery does not prevail is that the latter know that they are free and are aware of it explicitly. The Orientals are free too — implicitly — but they are not free in fact.[126]

Freedom, moreover, as a political concept, increases numerically. In the 'oriental' state, one is free; in the classical world, a few are free; but in Christian Europe, all are free. It is, however, this decisive move from *one* to *more-than-one* that represents, to apply a later vocabulary retrospectively, a paradigm. In other words, when the mode of statecraft moves from the oriental and into the Hellenic (classical) world, fundamental alterations in the nature of the overarching historical process manifest themselves. As a result, spirit is engendered. 'Among the Greeks,' according to Hegel in *The Philosophy of History*, 'we feel ourselves immediately at home, for we are in the region of Spirit.' Furthermore:

> Greece presents to us the cheerful aspect of youthful freshness of Spiritual vitality. It is here first that advancing Spirit makes *itself* the content of its volition and its knowledge; but in such a

way that State, Family, Law, Religion, are at the same time objects aimed at individuality, while the latter *is* individuality only in virtue of those aims.[127]

Moreover, Hegel links this historically-obtained 'spirit' to sensuousness by averring that 'in Greek beauty the Sensuous is only a sign, an expression, an envelope, in which Spirit manifests itself'.[128] *Geist*, therefore, not only defines Hellenism aesthetically, but it also underpins it historically. We have gone full circle, back to the 'sensuousness' of Pater.

Hegel's treatment of history, however, should be put in its proper context. There were other – very different – forms of history writing in the German-speaking world. Although these, along with the salient aspects of Hegelianism, will be dealt with in Chapter 7, it is worthwhile at this juncture briefly exploring these other forms of history writing. Predating and following Hegel, there were the noteworthy contributions of academics belonging to the University of Göttingen (founded in 1734). Both philology and history, two of our three domains of interest here, were highly valued in this institution. Many of the philologists discussed in this section either studied or taught classes on at Göttingen. In the discipline of history, 'a more concrete treatment of politics' was encouraged. Moreover, 'it gave itself', as Herbert Butterfield argues, 'not to speculative adventures, but to the study of history'.[129] As a consequence, it was the right and proper setting for later, non-Hegelian historical scholarship. Indeed, one of the earliest chairs of history, Johann Gatterer (1729–99), championed 'Universal History' and 'foreshadow[ed] Ranke in his argument that the mere history of the Emperors was not enough [...] the Germans should [also] turn their attention to the proceedings of the Reichstag'.[130] A century later, Leopold van Ranke (1795–1886) took the study of history towards a more inductive, empiricist and textual plane. A synthesis of two related concepts defines Ranke's methodology. First, '[e]xact research, [and] step-by-step comprehension and penetration of documents' were considered to be the essential axioms of this new form of scholarship. But hoarding of facts and 'the sequence of causation of one fact by another', by themselves, were not deemed sufficient for meaningful scholarship. Thus the second concept: there has to be 'something of an idea' that rationalizes and embodies the facts. So Ranke infers that 'after having examined the details we must concentrate upon the idea'. After all, when dealing with a given people, 'we are not only concerned with the prominent individual facts in its history, but with the idea which we can see in the totality of its development, its deeds, institutions, and literature'.[131] This form of scholarship, as will be discussed in Chapters 6 and 7, had an indirect but crucial impact on Hellenism. There was, however, another equally important development in nineteenth-century studies of classical Greece, namely the impact of 'Aryanism'.

III – 'Helleno-Aryanism': A Late-Nineteenth-Century Phenomenon

By the 1870s, there was a European-wide consensus to attach the linguistically-derived adjectives 'Aryan' and 'Semitic' to the noun 'race'. Since the designated category of the first adjective included not only the modern Europeans, but also nearly all Europeans since ancient Greece, its attraction for Hellenism was quite understandable. Mathew Arnold is an interesting case in point. As discussed earlier, Arnold situated European civilization within a Hellenic–Hebraic framework. At the very beginning of Arnold's analysis, however, we are confronted by a conceptual anomaly. He argues that Hellenism and Hebraism share the same aim: 'perfection or salvation'. But it is not a given that these are synonymous goals; one can approximate towards one, without necessarily moving towards the other. It becomes clear soon enough that, first, Hellenism is the perfecting 'spiritual discipline'; and Hebraism, the salvational one. Second, the perfecting role of Hellenism is based on rationality and reason, whereas the salvational function of Hebraism is mostly confined within the fuzzy theology of Judaeo-Christianity. In other words, the Hellenic world, manned by 'the delicate and apprehensive genius of the Indo-European race',[132] will always have the upper hand in the weightier matters of human life. By anchoring it in the 'science' of race, Arnold puts the finishing touches to his amalgamation of Hellenism and 'Aryanism':

> Science has now made visible to everybody the great and pregnant elements of difference which lie in race, and in how single a manner they make the genius and history of an Indo-European people vary from those of a Semitic people. Hellenism is of Indo-European growth, Hebraism is of Semitic growth; and we English, a nation of Indo-European stock, seem to belong naturally to the movement of Hellenism.[133]

An interesting, albeit non-literary, advocate of this mode of thinking was the English painter and sculptor, Frederic Leighton (1830–96). Leighton had echoed Arnold by seeing, in G. L. Hersey's assessment, 'Aryanism and Semitism as two great contraposed disciples, the one of intellect and beauty, the other of conscience and will'.[134] He considered the effect of the Semites on art as irredeemably pernicious and that the more exposed a culture was to Semitic influences, the more it would suffer artistically. The Assyrians, for instance, had worse art than the Egyptians, because they were more Semitic than the Egyptians. 'The Jews, being the most Semitic of all,' Leighton concluded, 'were utterly "void of the artistic impulse."'[135] In his 1870 novel, *Lothair*, Benjamin Disraeli takes a satirical swipe at Aryanism in general and Leighton in particular:

> 'Aryan principles', said Mr Phoebus [the Leighton character]; 'are not merely the study of nature, but of beautiful nature; the art of design in a country inhabited by a first rate race, and where the laws, the manners, the custom, are calculated to maintain the health and beauty of a first rate race. In a greater or lesser degree, these conditions obtained from the age of Pericles to the age of Hadrian in pure Aryan communities, but Semitism began then to prevail and ultimately triumphed. Semitism has destroyed art; it taught man to despise his own body, and the essence of art is to honour the human frame.'[136]

Three years prior to the publication of Arnold's *Culture and Anarchy*, Fustel de Coulanges (1830–89) published *La cité antique* (*The Antique City*, 1864). By situating his work on an anthropological plane, de Coulanges tried 'to show upon what principles and by what rules Greek and Roman society was governed'. Moreover, the reason for choosing to treat these two peoples as one, interestingly, had nothing to do with the fact that they resided, culturally speaking, under the same rubric of 'classics'. It was all 'because these two peoples, who were two branches of a single race, and who spoke two idioms of a single language, also had the same institutions and the same principles of government, and passed through a series of similar revolutions'.[137] In other words, it was their perceived Indo-European heritages which made them ripe for an anthropological treatment. One of the main interests of de Coulanges, for instance, was the manner in which the Greeks and Romans responded to the ideas of death and afterlife: 'Go back far as we may in the history of the Indo-European race, of which the Greeks and Italians are branches, and we do not find that this race has ever thought that after this short life all was finished for man.'[138]

More recent scholarship on *La cité antique* is divided. Arnaldo Momigliano, for example, senses, not unreasonably, a whiff of anti-Semitism in this work. 'The main attraction of the Aryan idea for [de Coulanges],' according to Momigliano, 'was that it freed him from having to include the Semites – and therefore the Jews and dangerous Bible – in his discourse.'[139] S. C. Humphreys, in contrast, argues that 'there is no reason to reject a priori the idea that something may be learnt by comparing the kinship systems of the different Indo-European societies',[140] but warns against what had undone Coulanges' arguments, namely 'the vitality of his reactions to the beliefs and problems of his own society'.[141] In an essay published in *Cultural Responses to the Persian Wars* (2007), Clemence Schultze contextualizes the main work that she is discussing (Cormon's *Les Vainqueurs de Salamine*) within the writings of de Coulanges. She does so, however, without making any reference to the Indo-European framework in which *La cité antique* was so unmistakeably situated. All that she is willing to concede is that '[T]he work lucidly expressed a theory of the origins of the state and the nature of human society in the Graeco-Roman world'.[142]

The most intriguing advocate of the Hellenism-Aryanism synonymy of the period was Friedrich Nietzsche. In *The Birth of Tragedy* (1872) he takes issue with 'our contemporary cultured historiography', which tended 'to appropriate the ancient Greek world "historically", alongside other ancient worlds'.[143] This is quite interesting. Nietzsche seems to be implying that Hellenism –delicate, refined and idealistic – is not designed to cope with the realities of factual and historical accounts. As a consequence, it should not be exposed to them. This concession that Hellenism, as an overarching idea, has no history or autochthonous roots, although implicit in many writings of the period, was to all intents and purposes an original contribution to the debate. Nietzsche's assault on the accepted depiction of ancient Greece – Apollonian in his lexicon – was a deliberate moving away from the relentlessly upbeat and positive gloss of 'discipline and clarity' (represented by Winckelman and his followers) towards what he considered to be a more complete rendering of the Greeks. By allowing them pessimism and passion, and describing this condition as Dionysian (hence wine and intoxication), Nietzsche endowed the Greeks with complex psychological insights.[144] Of course there is a paradox here: his Greeks were of an unreal and ahistorical variety. In *The Birth of Tragedy*, where Nietzsche dichotomizes the 'Aryans' and the 'Semites' in the manner of Arnold, his chosen Greek[145] (Aryan) is, notably, from the mythical world. He is Prometheus:

> The story of Prometheus belongs from the beginning to the entire Aryan community of peoples and is evidence of their gift for the profound and the tragic, indeed it may not be beyond the bounds of probability that this myth contains precisely the same characteristic meaning for the Aryan character which the myth of the Fall possesses for the Semitic character, and that these two myths are related to one another like brother and sister [...]. The best and the highest blessing which humanity

can receive is achieved through sacrilege and its consequences must be accepted, namely the whole flood of suffering and troubles with which the insulted gods have no other choice but to afflict humanity as it strives nobly upwards: a severe thought which, through the *dignity* ascribed to the sacrilege, stands in strange contrast to the Semitic myth of the Fall, in which curiosity, dissimulation, the susceptibility to be led astray, lasciviousness, in short a series of eminently feminine feelings, are viewed as the origin of evil. What distinguishes the Aryan conception is the sublime view of the *active sin* as the real Promethean virtue: what at the same time reveals itself the ethical substratum of pessimistic tragedy as the *justification* of human evil, and even of human guilt as the suffering is caused by it.[146]

This analysis is quoted in full because the underlying current is crucial. By stealing fire from the gods and handing it over to mortals, thereby assisting 'humanity as it strives upwards', Prometheus' act of 'sacrilege' has become an 'Aryan' and masculine ('brother') virtue. The myth of the Fall, in contrast, with its decidedly feminine ('sister') shortcomings, is nothing less than sacrilege without 'dignity'. It is a sin. Hence, 'the contradiction at the heart of the world reveals itself to the contemplative Aryan', according to Nietzsche, 'as a collision of different worlds [...] each of which individually has right on its side, but must suffer for its individuation as an individual world alongside others'. Moreover, there is always a tendency 'to step outside the spell of individuation and to become the *single* essence of the world'. By doing so, Nietzsche avers, the individual 'commits sacrilege and suffers'. Such a sacrilege 'is understood by the Aryans as male, sin by the Semites as female'.[147] It has to be borne in mind that this type of gender-based analysis was extremely common and in all probability resonated with the widespread misogyny of the period. Still, by gendering the debate in this way, Nietzsche had effectively established a new and powerful distinguishing feature for his brand of Hellenism: the heroic masculinity of the 'Aryan' man/god.

IV – Conclusions

This chapter has depicted in broad sweeps a number of interrelated historical and conceptual phenomena. First, it has tried to situate the growing synonymity of race and language of the period within the institutional disciplines of linguistics and anthropology. It was inferred from the ensuing analysis that the hypothesis of the 'Aryan race' was becoming increasingly accepted in academia; it even managed, quite successfully, to reconfigure Hellenism – one of the main intellectual underpinnings of the century – in its own image. The second purpose of this exercise was the examination of the multifaceted concept of Hellenism. This was effectively the relevant and dynamic context within which the race–language debate unfolded. By dwelling on its ubiquitous plurality and alleged sublimeness, I have therefore tried to account for why the Victorians were so infatuated with Hellenism.

Hellenism, as discussed, comes in a variety of guises and as such it is more correct to speak of it in the plural. Hellenism*s*, although sharing a common core, diverge in a number of ways. It is precisely in these areas of divergences where I intend to situate the overarching thrust of my unfolding discussions. There are three strands to this. First, Winckelmann's and most of his followers' brand of Hellenism is predominately an aesthetic concept. It is the ideal beauty of Greek sculptures and other cultural products which informs their sensibilities. The fact that 'the beauty of Greek sculpture', as Winckelmann cited earlier would have it, 'is more easily apprehended than the beauty of nature' is the chief definer of this brand of Hellenism. Moreover, this is the form of Hellenism which, broadly speaking, is still with us. It is what Gilbert Murray described in 1921 as 'a style of scholarship which consist[s] essentially in the perception of beauty, and to some extent in the representation of it'.[148] The second form of Hellenism, which approached the subject from an anthropological perspective, had its roots in the kind of historical scholarship that was partially informed by Ranke. This approach (the subject of Chapters 5 and 6) was adopted, *inter alia*, by Sir John Linton Myres. In *Who were the Greeks?* (1930), he sets out to shine 'the light of modern advances in the study of race, language, [and] religious beliefs'[149] onto the topic of Hellenism. The third kind of Hellenism was 'Helleno-Aryanism', which, in its twentieth-century manifestation, went on to prop up the racist ideology of National Socialism.

The investigation of the first two of this trio of Hellenisms[150] also has an indirect purpose: to understand the changing nature of the modern European/British treatment of the Achaemenid history – particularly during the first 40 years of the twentieth century. These *scientific* and *aesthetic* Hellenisms can, I believe, reveal a great deal concerning the depiction of the ancient Persians, as well as how the Europeans, at the zenith of their intellectual and imperial powers, visualized themselves through their understanding of the ancient Greeks. The first portion of this is discussed in Chapters 5 and 6; the latter, in Chapter 7. Before all that, it is necessary to scrutinize the race–language debate further and see whether or not this debate changed significantly during the first four decades of the twentieth century.

CHAPTER 3

THE 'RACE–CULTURE' DEBATE: 1900s–1930s

Comparative philology, as discussed in the previous chapter, had a huge impact on the nineteenth century's obsession with 'race': it had effectively become one of the chief underwriters of the pseudoscientific notion of the 'Aryan race'. Thereafter, however, it appeared to have a more benign influence upon British academia; first by becoming a useful tool (with a number of other interrelated disciplines) of anthropology, and second, by beginning to play a more subtle and constructive role in the post-'Aryan race'[1] discourses of the period.

The aim of this chapter is to examine the debate concerning 'race' and 'culture' in the 1930s with extensive references to two specific documents: first, the interim report published in 1935 by the Royal Anthropological Institute (RAI, henceforth) and Institute of Sociology, called *Race and Culture*; and second, an unpublished paper by John Linton Myres, entitled 'Races and Cultures'.

After the institutional and historical résumé (I), this chapter concentrates on three decipherable modes of analysis that were current in the period. Section II discusses the move to *delineate* between race and culture in a mutually exclusive manner. Gordon Childe was one of the keenest advocates of this school of thought. The following section (III) concentrates on the interim report. It is argued that the contributors to this work had attempted – with mixed

THE 'RACE–CULTURE' DEBATE   49

results – to *rationalize* the ground rules of the racial discourse. And finally, section IV scrutinizes Myres' paper. It is suggested that this paper had *synthesized* race and culture without resorting to 'Aryanism'. Before drawing some conclusions (VI), section V brings the previous three sections into an analytical focus and poses a number of pertinent questions.

I – Historical Background

In the first decade of the twentieth century, the anthropological syllabus was coterminous with the embryonic and now infamous discipline of eugenics. The publication of the guideline (for lecturers) by the Board of Studies in Anthropology of the University of London[2] coincided, more or less, with the very first instalment of the *Eugenic Review* in 1906. 'Physical Anthropology' and 'Cultural Anthropology' were the two main divisions of this guideline (each with their own subdivisions). With some prescience, however, the comparative studies of the 'various races' and 'various peoples' were apportioned to the *physical* and *cultural* ethnologies respectively (see below). Moreover, and germane to the interest of this thesis, the 'comparative study of language' was one of the five subdivisions of 'Cultural Anthropology'. These clear markings of the academic and intellectual territories were further buttressed by the growing importance of psychology – both in holding its own as an independently robust discipline as well as its perceived usefulness as a putative link (the body to the mind) between the two primary anthropological divisions.[3]

This simultaneous process of convergence – with RAI becoming the main institutional locus – and specialization had engendered a climate, although uncertain and in flux, of opportunities and possibilities. There was a huge amount of intellectual fluidity in the system. Many were in a position to don a number of academic hats. Myres, for example, was a classically-trained ancient historian, geographer, anthropologist, geologist and Hellenist. As Sherratt points out in *Economy and Society in Prehistoric Europe* (1997), when it came to revise Myres' contributions to *The Cambridge Ancient History* some 50 years later, 'it required six specialists to cover the ground'.[4] Childe, moreover, a generation younger than Myres, had toyed with the idea of either accepting a tenure at Leeds as an ancient historian or opting for classics at Durham, before settling for prehistoric archaeology at the University of Edinburgh in 1925.[5] These far from unusual instances of 'anything goes' had one unique outcome. Whereas previously academics had tended to fill specialized vacancies for which they had been specifically trained, the new arrangements had given specialized disciplines themselves (many of which were fairly new and untested by the rigours of intellectual life) the novel opportunity to condition and mould the mindsets of those academics chosen to fill these new vacancies. This phenomenon in which subjects defined the attributes of their personnel and not vice versa brought about, as we shall see, an innovative way of framing hypotheses and encouraged the greater use of interdisciplinary methods of enquiry. Within the boundaries of anthropology, it was becoming increasingly acceptable – and common – for, say, ancient history to be 'cross-fertilized' with cultural ethnology and/or comparative philology.

The beginning of it all, however, was quite a mundane affair. In order to justify the funding and the *raison d'être* of the RAI, the needs of the British Empire were upheld in the first half of our period of interest. 'I feel that it is of utmost importance,' wrote Henry Balfour on 30 August 1914, 'that the Empire, in its own interest, should encourage and subsidise schools of Anthropology which aim at promoting Imperial interests & endeavouring to equip future administrators with some of the knowledge which is essential for a just, hard-minded and sympathetic treatment of the natives under our control.'[6] The (internal) memorandum of May 1922, which surmised that in the interests of the empire, the 'knowledge of Anthropology should be more widely disseminated',[7] was one of the last instances of such pronouncements. Thereafter, a vaguely detectable shift manifested itself, which put the purely intellectual merits of anthropology squarely in the foreground. 'I find that anthropology,' E. N. Falaize (the honorary secretary of the RAI in 1923) pronounced, 'comes into nearly every section – art and archaeology, history, linguistic[s], and theology.'[8] Unsurprisingly therefore, one of the subjects up for discussion at the newly-created Committee on Anthropological Teaching (meeting on 29 May 1923) was the '[a]nthropological point of view in the teaching of history, geography, etc'.[9] Moreover, for this to be taken further, Sir Grafton Elliot-Smith was given the task of 'prepar[ing] a memorandum on the relation of anthropology to [the] teaching of history'[10] for their next committee meeting. In other words, anthropology, as a multifaceted academic discipline, was – or, at least, appeared to be – on a progressive march onwards and upwards.

In his 1931 inaugural lecture as the new president of the RAI, however, Myres was saddened by the fact that 'old prejudices against a new subject like Anthropology die hard [...] and systematic provision for anthropological studies, like Anthropology itself, which is still a very young science, is in its infancy'.[11] It was within this tumultuous epoch of methodological flexibility, new academic fields and the trial-and-error nature of institutional structuring that there emerged the tentative and multi-vocal responses to 'the whole complex of race, culture and environment',[12] thus initiating the further downgrading of the pseudoscientific notion of the 'Aryan race' and much more besides.

II – Differentiating between 'Race' and 'Culture': A Critical Response to the Concept of the 'Aryan Race'

Some time in 1906, Myres jotted down the following in a notebook:

How are we to classify man?

Now, it would seem, at first sight, natural to classify varieties of Man according to the more specially *Human* characters: language, civilization, religion.

Notoriously, all these *can be acquired*, during the life time of a single individual [therefore] we must fall back upon purely *zoological* characteristics (esp. we must get behind the conception of an 'Aryan Race' evolved in XIX cent. from conception of Aryan 'family' of languages[)].[13]

The overall thinking of this aide-memoire was given a more robust turn-of-phrase by the author in the first volume of *The Cambridge Ancient History* (1924):

> By *races* of men, are meant groups and sequences of such selves linked by corporeal similarities propagated by natural process within each group: by *peoples* or *nations*, groups of selves exhibiting peculiarities of interpretation, invention, and effort sufficiently similar for their results to be cumulative and coherent; and by *cultures* or *civilizations* the accumulated and coherent results of such similarities in the activities of selves like you and me. [emphasis in the original][14]

It seems that the shift towards differentiating between races and peoples/cultures had begun not only prior to the root and branch restructuring of British academe, but also decades before the esoteric concept of the 'Aryan race' had been transformed into the emotional controversy that was the *Rassentheorie* (race theory) of the 1930s. Since many of the subjects of British India were Indo-European speakers, some had begun, most determinedly, to consider themselves as bona fide Aryans, and hence connected, at some deeper level, to their British rulers. The publication, for example, of *The Arya* journal in Madras in 1901 was very much an Indo-European calling-card. The need to consider 'modern north Indians as an equal', argues Ballantyne in *Orientalism and Race* (2002), was tidily dealt with by the British rulers in the following manner: 'As the Aryans pressed south and south-east, some intermarried with the weaker Turanian and Dravidian peoples. This intermarriage slowly introduced both inferior "blood" and superstition into the Aryans.'[15] According to this narrative, therefore, well before the nineteenth century, the subcontinent had had an amalgamation of races (with the Dravidian dominating) on which rested a largely Indo-European lingual, societal and religious culture.

The institutional and other developments, discussed in section I, also contributed towards a fundamentally new approach – best represented by the University of London guide for the study and teaching of anthropology – to racial and ethnic sensibilities. The 'ethnological' subdivision of the 'Physical Anthropology' section sought to undertake 'the comparative study of the physical characters which distinguish the various races and sub-races of man'. The same subdivision ('ethnological') of the 'Cultural Anthropology' division, however, aimed to embark on 'the comparative study and classification of peoples based upon cultural conditions and characteristics'.[16] This clear separation of 'race' and 'people/culture' effectively underpinned the study of Man via the multifaceted science of anthropology. In this intellectual atmosphere, therefore, the concept of the 'Aryan race' could no longer dominate the anthropological field in the way it had done for over half a century. It had found itself increasingly exposed, on the one hand, to the growing influence of the *narrow* and precise racial classifications, based on cranioskeletal and palaeontological evidence. Terms such as brachycranic (round-headed) and dolichocranic (long-headed) together with regional classifications such as 'Nordic' (long-headed), 'Alpine' (round-headed) and 'Mediterranean' (long-headed) began to influence a range of academic literature. On the other hand, *broader* and earlier accepted definitions such as Caucasian, Mongoloid and Negroid continued to hold academic currency. Accompanying these developments was the publication of a plethora of monographs and books. This new form of literature was predominantly concerned with the physical and physiognomical attributes of humankind, and deemed areas such as culture and language to be beyond its primary remits.

Joshua Whatmough, in his scathing review of the now infamous *The Aryans: A Study of Indo-European Origins* (1926), accused Childe of having no qualms in overusing the term 'Aryan' as well as employing it as a category of race.[17] This was indeed the case. It can, however, be argued on Childe's behalf first that he had made it clear in the preface of the book that the only reason he had used the term 'Aryan' was due to its 'brevity and familiarity' and not for its 'scientific' value.[18] Second, the usage of the term 'Aryan race' was justified on the ground that he had, unambiguously, defined his terminologies right at the outset of the book: '"[R]ace" has different connotations for the physical anthropologists and the philologists.'[19] It is this difference that transforms 'race', as understood by philologists, into 'people'. He augmented this by stating that 'we cannot argue from unity of language to unity of race'.[20] By the early 1930s, however, he had not only distanced himself from *The Aryans*, but had also endeavoured to establish his credentials as an academic wholly uninterested in the question of race and the classification of races. His 1933 paper titled 'Races, Peoples and Cultures in Prehistoric Europe' was, arguably, penned with this in mind. 'Swarthy Hindus, Greeks and Italians of small stature and generally narrow-headed; blonde round-headed Prussians; dark round-headed Swiss; and tall blonde Swedes,' he contended (not atypically for the 1930s), 'obviously do not belong individually or in mass to a single physical type or breed.' In his opinion therefore, '[L]anguage goes not with race but generally with the group we term people, and so it is generally linked with culture'.[21] Furthermore, and unlike much of today, Childe did not treat ethnicity and race interchangeably. 'If ethnic [is] the adjective for people, we may say that prehistoric archaeology has a good hope of establishing an ethnic history of Europe, while a racial one seems hopelessly remote.'[22] As far as Childe was concerned (see Chapter 4), the disentanglement of these two terms was sufficient for a serviceable framework for the purposes of prehistory and archaeology. In *The Danube in Prehistory* (1929), he explains thus:

> We find certain types of remains – pots, implements, ornaments, burial sites, house forms – constantly recurring together. Such a complex of regularly associated traits we shall term a 'cultural group' or just a 'culture'. We assume that such a complex is the material expression of what would today be called a 'people'. Only where the complex in question is regularly and exclusively associated with skeletal remains of a specific physical nature type would we venture to replace 'people' by the term 'race'.[23]

In a letter written some eight years later, Childe, still faithful to his earlier framework, reminds the addressee that 'I deal with cultures and peoples and not with races and breeds'.[24]

III – The Rationalization of 'Race' and 'Culture'[25]

The overall approach towards the question of 'race' and its immediate conceptual associates, such as 'culture', 'language' and 'people', progressed significantly in 1934. In the spring of that year, 'a committee was set up under the auspices of the RAI and the Institute of Sociology to consider the significance of the racial factors in cultural development'.[26] The members of this committee (12 in all) consisted of the leading experts of the day in a number of relevant fields. Among them were classicists, anthropologists, geographers, biologists, sociologists, anatomists, geneticists, philologists and statisticians. The committee published a report in 1935 called *Race and Culture* and set itself the not inconsiderable task of clarifying the term 'race'.[27] It began by defining race:

> Race is composed of one or more interbreeding groups of individuals and their descendants, possessing in common a number of innate characteristics which distinguish them from other groups. The innate characteristics mentioned are held to be such as usually apply to the generality of the individual studied, and not to be pathological characters, or features which characterise only a relatively small percentage in a population.

Alternatively:

> By Race is meant a biological group or stock possessing in common an undetermined number of associated genetic characteristics by which it can be distinguished from other groups, and by which its descendants will be distinguished under conditions of continuous isolation.

Culture was defined thus:

> Culture includes the activities involved in man's collection, cultivation and preparation of food, his implement making, his method of warfare, his magical and religious ideas and

practices, and his social and political relations. These activities and ideas are embodied in institutions, which work in essential interrelation in the society or group. It is through his culture that man in his group or social life adepts himself to his environment, and adapts his environments to his requirements.[28]

With the definitions out of the way, the rest of the report was given over to the views and personal analyses of seven of the committee members.

Sir Grafton Elliot-Smith (1871–1937) argued that the 'conception of race is analogous to the biologists' idea of species' and therefore should not be confused with nationality, which is 'a man-made assemblage of peoples, usually of various races'. With this as his guiding framework, Smith unequivocally dismissed the Aryan question by pointing out that 'the acquisition of culture is not due so much to innate qualities as to historical circumstances and quite arbitrary factors'. He concedes, however, that temperament may 'play some part in the acquisition of culture, but it is difficult to obtain any precise evidence in substantiation of this general impression'. He further downgrades his earlier assertion by pointing out that 'among a population even so mixed as that of England, it is not difficult to find among members of the same family individuals exhibiting different racial traits, who have been brought up under identical social and environmental conditions'. The problem with this, as Smith sees it, however, is the difficulty in defining the racial differences in temperament and character precisely or giving them 'numerical expression' – 'even if their social significance is definite and far-reaching'.[29] In addition to this published analysis, Elliot-Smith made two highly telling observations elsewhere.[30] First, he thought far too many anthropologists were making far too many 'loose statements': 'Only too often slovenliness of thinking in anthropology is reflected in slovenliness of language.' Far too frequently, maintained the author, race and nationality are conflated:

> When anthropologists are frequently guilty of such solecisms it is not surprising that laymen, politicians and publicists, in

their appeal to anthropology are too often not distinguished by either accuracy of information or cogency of argument.

And second, while admitting the validity of the hypothesis that the development of the original Indo-European language 'necessarily implied the existence of the people who spoke it', Smith is adamant that it 'affords no warrant for the use of the word "Aryan" in the twentieth century as a distinctive label for the uncircumcised gentile,[31] as part of the campaign for imposing disabilities on the Jews'.[32] All this, however, should be read with some care. Elliot-Smith was a firm believer in cultural diffusion (see Chapter 4). Furthermore, he argued very strongly that we should look to Egypt and Egypt alone for the source of this global diffusion.[33]

Herbert Fleure (1877–1969) begins at the beginning – with *Homo sapiens*. Some people, he argues, have, through isolation, kept their distinctive racial characters (the north-western quadrant of the Old World and large swathes, for instance, of Africa and China); and it is to these groups to which '*Race* is most often applied in general discussions'. The problem arises, therefore, from on the one hand the inapplicability of any suitable form of racial theories to those parts of the world where distinctive racial characters have scarcely been kept (i.e., everywhere else but China, Africa, and north-west Europe), and on the other hand, by the 'considerable [racial] divergences' that exist within these 'interbred' parts. Thus, treating these billions as broad categories of homogeneous races is, in Fleure's view, analytically flawed and conceptually unhelpful:

> [T]he averaging of whole populations regardless of these diversities of strain or breed obscures important biological facts and gives results which are sometimes too abstract to be of great value.[34]

Raymond Firth's (1901–2002) contribution to the report made a very useful distinction between the scientific and popular conceptions of race. The scientific conception concerns itself 'with observable physical characters as criteria of classification and the distribution of these characters is related to the geographical distribution of human groups'. The popular conception, on the other hand, deals with the way that 'physical differences [...] are used as a basis for cultural evaluation of an aesthetic, ethical and political order'. Firth concludes thus:

> It is essential then that the wide gap between the definition of race acceptable to a biologist or anthropologist and the current idea of 'race' in political discussion should be made clear, and the lack of validity shown in the common assumption that the cultural achievement of a people – their material equipment, social institutions and language – are necessarily a simple correlate of their physical character and the nature of their geographical environment.[35]

Although Firth does not directly object to the idea that there might be some form of relationship ('correlation') between 'cultural achievement', 'physical character' and the 'geographical environment' of a given people, he is nevertheless reluctant to give credibility to the notion that culture has an exclusive functional relationship with race and physical environment. In the report, Firth did not take his argument further, but in *Human Types* (1928), he was not entirely convinced that a recognizably veritable pure race had ever existed: 'Purity of race is a concept of political propaganda, not a scientific description of a human group today.'[36] Only 11 per cent of the Swedes, 'generally acknowledged to be one of the most Nordic of the European populations', Firth maintained, can be described as '"pure" Nordic types'.[37]

In his contribution, Geoffrey Morant (1899–1964) gave a mainly biometrician's view of race in humanity, which 'is derived primarily from the statistical study of samples' of certain kinds, such as '(a) head and body measurements; (b) skin, hair and eye colours; (c) physiological measurements'. 'By themselves,' Morant concedes, 'they clearly provide insufficient evidence to establish racial identity, but they may profitably be used in conjunction with anthropometric characters.' The general thrust of Morant's argument is, primarily, a statistical one. In other words, if large enough samples were, after careful examination, found to show

> differences which are no larger than the ones which can be attributed to chance selection in drawing up the samples – i.e., in statistical terms, when they show no 'significant' differences – and when the necessary conditions regarding the nature of the samples are fulfilled, then it will be safe to assume that as far as can be told from the available evidence, the two samples represent the same race.[38]

In other words, Morant nudges the overarching analysis forward by steadfastly adopting a methodology which is 'essentially descriptive and [it does] not presuppose any particular theory of individual or racial heredity'.[39] Nowhere was his approach better represented than in his 1939 inference, based on blood groups and anthropometry, that the Germans, *pace* the Nazi theories, were the most racially heterogeneous group in Europe.[40]

Although John Haldane (1892–1964) stated the obvious point that human diversity is a given and predicated upon innate and environmental causations, he nonetheless makes a number of salient observations in his piece. First, he argues that 'any definition of race must include a reference not only to human characters, but to geographical distribution'. Second, since most of humanity consists of mixed populations, special attention must be paid to them. 'It is only legitimate', expounded Haldane,

> to define a race by certain physical characteristics if those characteristics are, or were, confined to the inhabitants of a certain area. If they are found outside it in mixed populations it is not legitimate to assume either of two propositions. First, that the mixed population was derived from mixture of ancestral races one of which possessed the character in all its members. Secondly that, if this is believed on other ground to be the case, those members of the mixed race possessing the

character or groups of characters necessarily had more ancestors possessing it than the other member of the race.

There is an important caveat, however. This analysis breaks down 'not only when it is applied to such a population as that of Europe, but to population intermediate between the great racial types, such as those in Nubia or Northern India'.[41] Interestingly, in the preface to Morant's *The Races of Central Europe* (1939), Haldane, after congratulating Morant for his meticulous response to the German claim that 'linguistic divisions in Central Europe correspond to racial divisions', concedes that 'the answer is not so simple. Some linguistic divisions correspond in a rough way to those based on innate physical characters, others not at all. And nowhere are racial boundaries as sharp as the linguistic.'[42]

While Haldane was inching closer towards a matrix of race and culture without quite getting there, Ruggles Gates (1882–1962) had, tentatively and implicitly, reached the environs of that destination some years earlier. In *Heredity in Man* (1929), he stated that 'a knowledge of inheritance must form the basis of any enlightened attempt to influence the future development of the human race'. Moreover, he lambasted 'popular writers' for denying 'the importance of heredity in mankind'.[43] In his contribution to the report, Gates contends that any definition of the term race was only truly acceptable if biologists choose to utilize it. However, he qualified this substantially by contending that, since methods of transport have 'obscured the geographical lines of distinction between races', it would be sensible to make two types of racial classification:

1. A backward-looking or biological classification which attempts to classify races and other groups according to their evolutionary origin, history and former relationships, as far as they can be determined.
2. A forward-looking, political or modern classification, which recognises that the civilised man is unique in his power of

organisation, transportation and government, and that this has affected the development of races within historical times.

Thus, '[a]ny adequate biological classification of the Hominidae', argued Gates, 'should therefore begin by recognising the existence of larger and smaller categories – groups within groups – beginning with genera and species and ending with geographic "races" or smaller population groups'. Consequently what we are left with is that the 'biological classification of the species can be divided into smaller units'. In other words, say, 'the Caucasian "species" of man [...] may then for example be separated into Nordic, Alpine and Mediterranean'. Although Gates conceded that no present population 'belongs exclusively to any of these races', he nevertheless subscribed to the real 'value of these types of anthropological conceptions'. The value resided, according to Gates, 'in recognising the genetical differences between the various types of mankind and of gaining some conception of the paths and the factors by which racial evolution and differentiation have taken place'.[44]

What was strongly hinted at in Gates's piece was made explicit by the last of the seven contributors. George Pitt-Rivers (1890–1966) made a number of notable observations. He concurred with the others that 'Race must refer primarily to ethnic identity and distinction without necessarily involving the difficult and uncertain question of ethnic origin'. He furthermore averred that 'the use of the terms Aryan, Anglo-Saxon, Indo-European, [and] Celtic' as racial categories was unhelpful. 'These terms', in his view, 'describe languages or peoples but not races or race-types. On the other hand, Nordic, Alpine, Mediterranean, properly describe recognisable and measurable, although arbitrary, standardisations of the characteristics of existing race-types.' Pitt-Rivers, an increasingly bellicose anti-Semite in the inter-war years and a future war internee, dismissed the furore over the use of the 'Aryan race' theories in Germany as a purely political undertaking that focused, exclusively, 'on the Jewish problem'. In his view, the 'Aryan race no less than English race should not be interpreted in either country as the adoption of a scientific terminology. Such a term must apply to a race–culture complex, that is to say, an ethnogenic or environmentally-conditioned racial complex, not to a true racial group.' He therefore felt that there was 'an urgent need for a term to express race, population and culture, interacting and evolving. The term I have proposed is ETHNOGENICS. It means the study of human history in term of changing race, population and culture.'[45] In his 1934 essay, 'The Anthropological Approach to Ethnogenics', Pitt-Rivers asserted that this 'new synthesis will work for a correlation between somatic and psychical forms, and on the physiological side for a standardization of criteria similar to past groundwork on the side of physical forms'.[46] Armed with his race–culture complex, Pitt-River stressed that he

> cannot accept the claim made by Sir Grafton Elliot-Smith that his researches seem 'definitely to establish the fact that the acquisition of culture is not due so much to innate qualities as to historical circumstances and quite arbitrary factors' [...]. With equal confidence the ethnogenist, insisting on the value of function for survival, claims that the diffusion of cultural elements between races in contact by borrowing is a process which involves the selection of some elements only, their modification or adaptation to the need of the borrower and the complete rejection of incompatible elements.[47]

In other words, the innate quality of 'man', in the author's scheme, governs what elements should be selected, modified, adapted, or rejected: racial attributes beget cultural ones.

With what had gone before and what was going on in much of the Continent in the 1930s, the publication of this committee's report was, arguably, a step towards a more sophisticated discourse. It hailed, at least within the context of British intellectual life, the arrival of an analytical modus operandi, which would no longer brook dogmatic assertions of a pseudoscientific variety. Even the most 'racist' member of the committee, Pitt-Rivers, had to concede that 'Aryan', as an adjective, should not be attached too readily to the noun 'race'. All in all – and bearing in mind the importance of the racial discourse among the European intelligentsia of the time – this was not an unhealthy state of affairs to take forward.

Along with the downgrading of the notion of the 'Aryan race', the committee's report also managed to move the debate on in a number of interesting ways. First, it demonstrated that a debate on race and all its conceptual associates can be had soberly and rationally without resorting to the Aryan myth. Second, it had compelled a number of diverse specialists to work on a given subject, thereby equipping the subject itself with a number of academic perspectives. Finally, this interim report was more than an adequate preamble to what was supposed to follow. It helped to define the central terminologies of race and culture, as well as allowing the individual participants free rein to express their learned opinions on the alleged linkages between race and culture. And yet, these tentative steps were not free from some institutional and intellectual deficiencies. Institutionally, the committee met for the last time in the winter of 1935 and was not convened thereafter. Despite the interim nature of the report, no final report was ever published. It seems, therefore, with a quasi-racist war in the offing, the RAI had, understandably, very little appetite for discussing matters pertaining to race.[48] The possibility of establishing another committee did not arise until 1943, but that was also abandoned soon after.[49] Moreover, although the participants had, in one way or another, worked within the scope of the RAI for many years, there was, nevertheless, a reluctance to turn the report into a point of departure for further debate. Each, it seems, was content in presenting his views without demanding critical feedback (maybe that was pencilled in for the final report which never appeared), thus giving the impression that the report was not as interdisciplinary a product as it could, or should, have been (see section IV). This lack of cohesion had its intellectual counterpart in the fact that the report, broadly speaking, gave race more conceptual coverage and analytical weight than it was willing to offer culture – which, as we shall see, should have caught the imagination more keenly. This tendency was not suited for the most important, *ex ante*, objective of the report, namely the understanding of the 'racial factors in cultural development'. How to tease out the complex, multifaceted and at times paradoxical connections and relationships between these two phenomena was beyond the scope of this dissonant but nuanced interim report. For a more thorough and sophisticated discussion, we must look elsewhere.

IV – Synthesizing 'Race' and 'Culture': 'Neither Race Purely nor Culture Merely'

The committee had five other members who had refrained from presenting papers at the meeting or for publication, one of whom was Myres. It is not certain why he, along with the other four, had not presented a paper at the meeting. After all, various drafts of most of the above contributions can be found in his papers at the Bodleian Library. In addition, the same papers hold large files pertaining to race, culture and other relevant topics,[50] thus hinting at Myres' undoubted and lifelong intellectual interest in the subject. One explanation could be that his contributions were intended for future committee meetings which, as already indicated, failed to materialize. My reasoning for this straightforward explanation is based primarily on my discovery of an unpublished, 10,000-word, pencil-written, rough first draft (apparently) of a paper or possibly the synopsis of a planned book, called 'Races and Cultures'.

To understand Myres as a versatile thinker, although not incorrect, tells us precious little. His knowledge of ancient history, geography, anthropology, archaeology and prehistory had had a single purpose: it was required in order to tease out interpretative and analytical connections in his overarching inquiry, and thus render a complicated study comprehensible without sacrificing its complexity. So what was this study that had subsumed much of Myres' output? It was nothing less than the study of 'Man' in his historical setting. As an academic paper, 'Races and Cultures' is no more than a work in progress. It is an unedited compilation of the ideas of a formidable intellect, thinking aloud. The material is rewardingly paradoxical: it displays a number of profoundly worked-out analyses while remaining true to a number of well-established sensibilities: it alternates between tightly-focused passages on the main topics of the paper and 'free associative' writings, dealing with subjects as temporally and spatially remote as the quality of life in the Palaeolithic grassland of Asia and the effects of Italian immigration on the English-speaking mining communities of California, in between which Myres manages also to bring in, among others, the Greek *polis* and medieval London. In a nutshell, this work is not a document that demands unabridged and uncritical reading. Although those passages which focus tightly on race, culture and language are, perhaps, some of the most interesting ideas of our period of interest, one should, nonetheless, be continuously reminded that these passages – both textually as well as for the author in his given milieu – were merely the very first cerebral inklings of an overarching framework, and not the planned final product. The incompleteness of the framework however, can be rendered methodologically advantageous. First, the ambitious scope of the paper and the confident manner in which Myres presents his arguments are indicative of a subject in good health. Second, this literary sketch provides an insight into a fast-moving, often confused and politically-charged debate that marked much of the 1930s.

One constant in Myres' academic life was Herodotus. Herodotus was much more than just 'a mine of information'; his endeavours to ascertain 'the reason they [the Greeks and the Persians] fought one another', had rendered him, as Myres expounded in *Herodotus and Anthropology* (1908), the 'Father of Anthropology no less than the Father of History'.[51] But what made Herodotus invaluable to Myres' grand perspective was his ethnological description of Greekness in the often-quoted passage from Book VIII of the *Histories*. From the first decade of the century, via his seminal *Who Were the Greeks?* (1930), right through to his last work, *Herodotus: the Father of History* (1953), Myres remained resolute in his intellectual attachment to the idea of the commonality 'of descent, of language, of religion, of observances'[52] as the central definers of a given people. It is not surprising therefore that in the preamble to the paper, Myres had considered these definers as the 'bonds which make a people one, and make its welfare a higher, dearer thing than life'.[53]

In his 1910 inaugural lecture on becoming the Wykeham Professor of Ancient History at Oxford, Myres was sanguine that his main field of academic endeavour would benefit from the challenges and opportunities thrown up by the new sciences of archaeology, philology, and 'economic biology'.[54] He further buttressed this stance repeatedly throughout his career, nowhere more comprehensively than in his 1933 pamphlet, *Science and Humanities: The Uses and Abuses of Information*:

> This extension of the scientific outlook from 'natural sciences' to new 'sciences of man' has very greatly enhanced the philosophic interest and anthropological significance of these studies in themselves; they have severely acquired standards of scholarly technique which demand long and laborious apprenticeship; their output of research, in the sense of detailed 'information', is enormous.[55]

It is within the flexible boundaries of these 'sciences of man' that Myres situated his paper on 'Races and Cultures'. 'At first sight,' Myres admits, '*Race* and *Culture* might seem to have nothing to do with each other.' After all, '*Race* is, first and last, a matter of physical descent, of natural history, of biological science, like the races and breeds of any other animal. *Culture* – whether we include in it speech and cult or not – is specifically a human manifestation, an activity of the mind, an interaction between minds'; the study of which ought to be considered as 'a major branch [...] of the humanities; the interpretations of all arts and sciences, all practices and beliefs, as works of men, and of the Man'.[56] 'But historically the matter is not so simple,' asserts Myres. Hence:

> if we are not to take a quite superficial view of the variety of races and of cultures [...] we must regard them not only as an ephemeral pattern on the earth's surface, but as historical factors in one and the same process from the past, through the present, into the future of our world.

This historical outlook presents us, in Myres' view, with the unavoidable challenge of understanding and explaining 'the wide incongruity and discrepancy between the geographical distinction of Races and Cultures and of languages, because it was the unconformities between Language and Race that first called attention to unconformities between Language and Culture, and between Culture and Race'.[57]

Despite this, 'historical retrospect', Myres avers, 'has done little to reconcile the larger distributions' that have hitherto been examined. Our ability to account for discrepancies from more recent dates, such as 'the suppression of Celtic speech by Romance and Teutonic languages', can only get us so far; but 'when we make use of prehistoric evidence and analyse into fundamental elements the oldest types of culture that can be associated at all with the remains of modern breeds of Man', Myres argues, 'we begin to find [...] Cultures and Races beginning to cohere in their regional distributions and historical spread from period to period; and by this time we are beyond the point at which we can do no more than conjecture what sort of speech these populations had'.[58] The key phrases here, which are central to Myres' intellectual *Weltanschauung* and encompass both the overriding hypothesis of the paper ('Cultures and Races beginning to cohere') and the adopted methodology ('in their regional distributions, and historical spread'), are given a much more precise wording in the following passage:

> And the perspective of the past has become wonderfully deeper, while that of the present has become wonderfully wider: There has come into general experience a new kind of scientific knowledge and scientific method, distributional rather than systematic, historical and geographical, rather than physical or biological.[59]

The rationale for the methodological necessity of the geographical component of this dual approach (which Myres concedes has little direct relevance to the subject of race and culture) is highly illuminating. Putting it concisely, the 'geographer of the current-affairs' has to exist in order to differentiate between 'Historical Myths' and 'Geographical Facts'. Myres, writing and thinking in the 1930s, was in a unique position to recognize the potential dangers of the sort of solecism that states: 'it matters far less whether a thing happened than whether it was believed to have happened.' Furthermore, one is fully aware of the background to Myres' assertion that 'there is always a mythical element in history and occasionally that myth is allowed, or encouraged, to dominate historical teaching, or paralyse historical research'.[60] He was, of course, referring to the myth of the 'Aryan race' that was current in this period. Countering this tendency, according to Myres, there had emerged (under the auspices of the anthropological and ethnological sciences) in the distributional and the geographical studies of Man:

> significant advances during the last two or three generations, as the linked but distinct studies of race and culture – or better (because abstractions are nowhere more dangerous than in geography and history) of races and cultures – or (once again to be more concrete) of the racial and cultural resemblances among men on this earth.[61]

These advances were mostly due to the 'rapid increase of facilities for intercourse' between various peoples and their habits; the increasing availability and ubiquity of 'the produce and productions of other communities into our hands'; and finally, the growing uneasiness about the prospect of 'put[ting] ourselves back into mental isolation'.[62]

It is worth noting how doggedly determined Myres was to give as accurate a definition of 'the link between race and culture' as possible. This disposition supplemented what he considered to be the shortcomings of 'Physical Anthropology': because of its close affinity to the biological sciences, it was an unsatisfactory partner for the related subjects of prehistory and ethnology. Thus,

> Physical Anthropology [...] is felt to be unable to retain the dominant position it had been accorded formerly, at the cost of

ceasing to be merely a physical science. Both on its psychological and its historical frontiers, it has once more debateable ground with the humanities, if it claims to be other than one of the biological sciences.[63]

But since it is highly unlikely that it would make such a claim, what are we left with? According to Myres:

This leaves Prehistory a historical science, the past tense, so to speak, of Ethnology, and chiefly of the technological department of it; for it is only by inference from material remains that we can reach conclusions about the social or intellectual activities of primordial Man.[64]

In order to arrive at his synthetic framework, concerning the concepts of race and culture, Myres, hereafter, opted to proceed by examining a number of relevant historical instances. He begins with the 'Retrospect of Prehistory'. The simple material archaeological remains of prehistoric man had shown both 'diversities of technique, and widely distributed uniformities with those contrasted techniques'. This suggests '[the] long previous isolation of the Men who severally practised them'.[65] Moreover, these groups of 'isolated Men' had resided in a number of very different environments, such as grasslands, forests, prairies, parklands and so forth, thus equipping these various 'breeds' with fundamentally different abilities and attributes. When such populations were secluded for long enough periods, then, a 'genetic equilibrium' was reached and a 'racial type' created.[66] In order to substantiate this, Myres gives the 'old Greek type' as a salient example. By looking at the pictorial and figurative representations of the 'inhabitants of Greek lands [...] executed in the centuries from around 1600 to 1200 BC', Myres inferred that the 'classical Greek' type appeared only very rarely among the several distinct and available types from Crete and southern Greece.[67] With the arrival of the newcomers 'from the south and north-west',[68] sometime in the thirteenth century BC, however, a stable 'racial type' had gradually come to the fore:

Within the next five hundred years, then, from about 1100 BC to about 600 BC, the Greek people, as we know it in the Greek Age of Hellas, literally came into being, with a racial physiognomy which cannot be clearly recognised, there or anywhere else, before that period of racial and national gestation, but remained characteristic until it was merged in a fresh mixture of peoples freely circulating round the Mediterranean 'ring of lands' under Roman administrations.[69]

A similar phenomenon had also occurred in England; where, although not entirely secluded, the number of newcomers in the period between the Saxon conquest and 1700 AD was demographically insignificant, thus allowing the slow concoction of a unique 'racial type'. These 'fractional instances of the processes by which stable racial types are created'[70] are, according to Myres, highly revelatory:

> The process looks at first sight like a biological process; and in part no doubt it is biological, and must be examined biologically. But every one of those courtships and unions was also a social and a historical event; a struggle of human personalities with each other, and with economic, and even political incentives and obstacles, under the shifting, but also under the persistent controls of a community as well as a site. When we are told, sometimes vehemently that Culture is the product of Race, it is well to remind ourselves that in a very real sense Race is a product of Culture: *Manners makyth Man.*[71]

Although he begins his analysis by conceding that 'racial types' are invariably created by biological processes, nevertheless, the main thrust of his analysis concentrates on non-biological phenomena. In other words, it is a matrix of social, political and economic factors which tend to arrange future 'racial equilibria'. In addition, the controversial and intellectually messy subject of eugenics was ill-equipped to provide the methodology and context that Myers' analysis had called for. The manner in which he takes the natural sciences out of the equation and relies, almost exclusively, on what he calls 'the distributional and historical sciences' for both the foundation and the building blocks of his analysis should be noted. The above quote, for instance, reiterates the importance of 'historical and social events', as opposed to 'biological processes'. And, more importantly, the widely-accepted formula (stated by Pitt-Rivers above) that culture is a function of race, although not rejected by Myres, is depicted as only one aspect of a larger dualism; the other aspect being the converse of this case, namely, that race is a function of culture. It is precisely within the context of this symbiotic relationship that Myres situates his historical insights concerning interactions between 'race' and 'culture':

> Retrospect of Race and Culture as Coefficients – There have been illustrations, on a relatively minute scale, of processes both race-creating and culture-creating which we seem obliged to postulate as operative during the longer and more obscure period which connects the latest Palaeolithic Age with the beginnings of historic civilisation. So far as our analogies go, it is difficult to give either Race or Culture priority; coeternal together and coequal, the fruit of Man's body and the offspring of his mind are concurrent factors in the process from which emerge neither race purely nor culture merely, but a people.[72]

Why no other, more concrete and less compromising inference would have done for Myres was primarily due to the difficulties he envisaged as being inherent in 'classifying either Races or Languages or Cultures'.[73] For a chemist or a biologist the task of classification is essentially a pedantic one; hence, easily achieved. His classification of races and all its immediate associates, however, is not so straightforward. He writes:

> In what sense does it give any sort of priority to a physical, morphological unity, if members of such a class express their wants and thoughts by a particular sort of speech? Even supposing that there is any biological or philological connexion

between breed and speech, or between particular strains and
particular languages, on what principle of classification in any
language or groups of languages to be regarded as of higher
type than another?[74]

Unlike the biologist or the chemist, Myres is aware that a racialist is
compelled to make subjective judgments concerning *value*:[75] how
good or bad, how superior or inferior a particular entity such as a
language is compared to another. Languages, he argues, 'like varieties
of races, are not easily or cogently arranged in any hierarchy from
primitive to advanced';[76] unless, of course, one were to come into the
debate with an already chosen 'pre-eminent' language (and here
Myres' explicit example, revealingly, is the Indo-European group of
languages[77]). This, for Myres, could never do. The general propensity
to evaluate humanity in such fashion was a gross deviation from the
true task of the historically-literate distributional geographer. By
considering the complex relationship between 'race' and 'culture' as a
dynamically symbiotic phenomenon (the final result of which was
'people'), Myres was not merely inaugurating the 'sciences of man'
but, specifically, endeavouring to place the methodology of the
'distributional and historical sciences' within the easy reach of the
racial and cultural discourses of the period.[78]

V – 'Race' and 'Culture': An Analytical Overview

One of the main problems arising from the neat distinction between
physical and cultural anthropology was the tendency, on the one
hand, to think of 'people' as an entity devoid of racial attributes, and
on the other hand to consider race as a purely zoological phenomenon.
Even though Myres, in 1906 and 1924, had fallen back 'upon purely
zoological characteristics', he had nonetheless moved the debate on
significantly. Although cultural anthropology had many of the
necessary sub-disciplines for what Myres had in mind, it had a
singular deficiency: because it was largely unhindered by the question
of race, it had effectively rendered the disciplines of prehistory and
geography (or more accurately, geographical distribution) – which

are, by definition, programmed to factor in the racial aspects of human existence – largely superfluous. But since 'Prehistoric evidence', according to Myres, had demonstrated that 'Cultures and Races begin to cohere in their regional distributions and historical spread', the potential of this highly-relevant discipline could no longer be ignored.

It is a counter-factual argument, but if the committee had not been disbanded, then it is not altogether fanciful to think that, in the long term, academic robustness and diversity on matters pertaining to race and culture would have perceptibly progressed within the institutional framework of the RAI. This having been said, however, with Myres there is substantially more than just robustness and diversity in the analysis; there begins to be the shaky and tentative outline of a possible paradigmatic shift in the race–culture discourse of the period. One discernible difference between the report and the paper was the fact that Myres was quite successful in integrating a number of relevant disciplines, thereby endowing his narrative with the conceptual prerequisite of cohesion, which, in turn, should be regarded as a first imperative step towards grasping not only the 'racial factors in cultural development',[79] but also their converse: the cultural factors in racial development. This symbiotic relationship had evidently passed many of the committee members by; all that they wanted to do was to examine 'race' and 'culture' within the narrow confines of their respective specialized fields, while sensing no urgency for the bigger picture. Pitt-Rivers, admittedly, came close with his 'race–culture complex', but his underpinnings were governed by human ecology, hence non-historical and static. Myres' race–culture mix, however, was informed temporally and spatially – the proportions of the cultural and racial components varying (reverse convergence) through time and place – hence historically and distributionally.

But why should this insight be of any significance? After all, the inference 'neither race purely nor culture merely, but a people', had been reached – much more straightforwardly and without subsuming race within it – by Childe. Although Childe had not dealt with the concept of 'race' in much of his work, he had, nevertheless, understood the term within the agreed definitional boundaries of the day: there was, as stated earlier, on offer a broad (Caucasian, etc.) and a narrow (Alpine, Nordic, etc.) set of racial classification. The conceptual problem with this twofold racial classification was that one set was too broad and the other set too narrow. In other words, one set was too abstract to be meaningful, and the other was too (micro-)descriptive to be of any utility. From this conceptual predicament, there arose another: there were no intermediate racial categories available in order to fill the void between the broad and narrow classificatory sets. Thus the supposedly neutral category of 'people', unencumbered by 'race', was compelled, by default, to fill this void. In Childe's scheme of things, it had inadvertently become the *proxy* for racial classification. By making the term 'race' secondary, and hence methodologically largely redundant, he had left himself very little wriggle room. He was fenced in by the conceptual inadequacies of the clear-cut difference that separated 'race' from 'people/culture'. As a consequence, Childe could only pass highly questionable judgements within the confines of his not entirely apt concept of 'people'. In the 1920s and the early 1930s, Childe was fulsome in his praise[80] for the Indo-European peoples and even titled a book *The Aryans: A Study of Indo-European Origins*. In the late 1930s and beyond, however, he was less forthcoming and regarded the term 'Aryan' as meaning as 'little as the words "Bolshie" and "Red" in the mouths of crusted Tories'.[81] It is noteworthy that as early as the autumn of 1911, Myres, Childe's supervisor at Oxford, wrote the following words to an academic colleague:

> As to the term Aryan; it is habitually used as a comprehensive term for the whole Indo-European speaking group of peoples, but it has the disadvantage that originally, it meant the Indo-European speaking invaders of northern India, and is still commonly used in a specific sense to denote the Eastern group of Indo-European languages, in contrast with the European sections. It is for this reason that I have employed the word Indo-European, and not the word Aryan to describe the whole group. Nobody, except Germans and disciples of Germans, use

the word Indo-Germanic, which appears to me to have been invented to reinforce some political aspirations which are no better based than the name.[82]

Childe's simple conceptual definitions of 'race and 'culture', as far as they went, were a significant improvement from what had preceded it, i.e., the 'Aryan race' theory. This scheme, however, proved to be problematic. Its central weakness corresponds with what made Myres' unpublished rumination so analytically compelling: the latter, as opposed to the former, had accommodated 'race' *and* 'culture' within its compass. It was not an equation of mutual exclusivity, where 'race' and 'culture' did not interact; but an equation of *mutual inclusivity*, where race and culture did more than just interact: they, historically and geographically, co-varied. By transforming 'race' and 'culture' into *co-variances*, Myres managed to keep the discourse well within the racial schemata of the day. Moreover, unlike Childe's praise of the 'Aryan' peoples and languages,[83] by dealing head-on with the question of *value* in relation to the classification of races, cultures and languages, Myres placed the entire race–culture discourse on a very different and relatively neutral intellectual plane.

Some, however, may argue that even though, superficially, the race debates of the 1930s seemed to have moved on from the Gobineauism of the nineteenth century, they had not done so decisively enough to be considered as an altogether new phenomenon. In *The Retreat of Scientific Racism* (1992), Barkan, for instance, writes that in relation to the committee on race:

> Anthropologists and biologists were presumed objective in their scientific analysis of the question of race, and there was not even a hint that the reverse might be the case, namely that prejudice was the source of scientific justification and that scientists were trapped by the same blindness as the public at large.[84]

This assessment indicates that Barkan was not uncritical of the composition of the committee, its remit and the report that it eventually published. He divides the committee members into 'racists' (Pitt-Rivers and Gates) and 'anti-racists' (the rest), and contends that even this 'anti-racism' aspect of the committee should be understood within its peculiar 'historical context', in which Jews were excluded 'from the Committee because they were deemed too subjective to participate in a scientific elucidation'.[85] As far as the report was concerned, Barkan calls it 'unsatisfactory'[86] and relies heavily on critical quotes taken from *Nature*, which had argued in an editorial that the committee, after taking two years to come up with a user-friendly definition of race, had only managed to produce two 'inexceptionable' definitions, as well as a number of unintentional 'minority reports'.[87]

Barkan's criticism of Myres ('the British diplomat of anthropology'[88]) relies almost entirely on a single paper, entitled 'Correlation of Mental and Physical Characteristics in Man'. According to Barkan, Myres 'bas[ed] his argument on personal impressionistic observations', and 'concurred with the view that these characteristics "are sufficiently widespread over large areas as to claim provisional acceptance as racial qualities"'.[89] Although Barkan admits that Myres had 'suspended judgement on the ethical superiority of one race over another', nevertheless, he goes on to observe that 'Myres broke no new ground, yet as a commentator from within the discipline he underscored the contradiction and paradox in contemporary evolution theories of anthropology, according to which a constant racial type was set within a dynamically developing world'.[90]

While Barkan makes some pertinent points concerning the shortcomings of the committee, its published report and Myres, there are a number of issues with which one can quibble. First, Barkan's work is overall informed by what he calls the 'Boasian' 'egalitarian' approach to anthropology. In *The Mind of the Primitive Man* (1911), Franz Boas, according to Barkan, stated that 'race, culture, and language are independent variables, and should not be confused'.[91] It is, however, worth remembering that Boas was thinking and writing within a very challenging academic context. Contrary to much of Boas' outlook, the United States of the period was always too eager to measure 'racial mental differences' and to assess the neurological attributes of those belonging to the 'lower and higher races' of mankind.[92] In addition, Boas was working against the intellectual grain in another, albeit related, area: as a cultural diffusionist (who subscribed to the notion of culture diffusing gradually from the Near East), he was also at odds with the evolutionist (culture as an independent invention arising spontaneously in many places) consensus that was widespread in the US. Where one stood with regard to this debate mattered because many German nationalists of the period (Kossinna for instance) maintained that sophisticated cultures had evolved in north-central Europe largely due to the innate abilities of the German race (see Chapter 4). Although Boas was known in Britain, the discussions in this paper suggest that the notion that there are no tangible links between race, culture and language could not have been institutionally prevalent in the United Kingdom. Indeed, even the 'anti-racists' of the committee did not entertain *complete* independence regarding these three variables. Second, it is not helpful to label some members as "racists". A more neutral approach to assessing the views concerning the nature or the degree of linkages between race and culture would have been advisable.[93] Besides, things were not as clear-cut as Barkan would like to have them. For instance, Elliot-Smith ('anti-racist') edited three volumes of Pitt-Rivers' essays for posthumous publication, and according to Slobodin, 'distorted Rivers's [the 'racist'] level of support for diffusionism'. Third, Barkan, erroneously in my view, does not dwell on the significance of the interim nature of this report. Finally, although it is clear that Barkan has some familiarity with Myres' unpublished manuscripts, he seems to have had no knowledge of the 'Races and Cultures' paper. That paper, as has been argued here and contrary to Barkan's suggestion, *did* break 'new ground', and *did* move Myres away from his 'impressionistic observations' of the early 1920s.

VI – Conclusions

A complete delineation at the one end, and a thorough synthesis at the other, describe the two conceptual extremities of the race–culture debate in this chapter. The fact that such a framework manifested itself in so many different voices is, to say the least, noteworthy. In addition, the fact that there was a collective desire to wrestle with the morally difficult issues of race and culture suggests, if not progress, then at least, a welcome dose of intellectual dynamism. There is of course a disadvantage with so many viewpoints expressed so dynamically: a lack of coherence and analytical focus invariably presents itself. The aim of this chapter has been to try to ameliorate these problems. By framing the supposed interaction between race and culture in this way, it has been possible to provide a rendition of the debate that is qualitatively different from the one provided by Barkan and his division of the committee into 'racists' and 'anti-racists'. As far as Myres (the axis upon which this entire work hangs) is concerned, it is the contention of this chapter that his numerous historical analyses (see Chapters 5, 6 and 7) can best be appreciated and understood within the context of his contributions to the race–culture debates of the period.

It should also not be forgotten that this report was a partial response to the *Rassentheorie* emanating, with a varying degree of shrillness, from a number of European sources. In other words, it was a reactive phenomenon, caused primarily by the 'Aryan race' theories which were still current (and growing) in many of the European political and academic circles of the day. Consequently, in addition to a more thorough analysis of race and culture, there was an implicit recognition that the term 'Aryan' could not just be excised from academic discourse without a plausible and neutral replacement. The term 'Indo-European', applicable to language, culture and people (but, crucially, not to race) and much in use in the British academia, appeared to have been the favourite replacement until the consequences of World War II altered the intellectual map of Europe beyond recognition.

CHAPTER 4

THE 'DIFFUSIONISM VS. EVOLUTIONISM' THEORETICAL DEBATE, GORDON CHILDE AND THE PREHISTORY OF EUROPE

The debate on which this chapter concentrates is the one between the Orientalists (diffusionists) – who believed that Europe was a barren continent before the culture of the more advanced Near East had begun to diffuse gradually – and Occidentalists (evolutionists) – who contended that most important aspects of the early European civilization were *sui generis*, hence, largely, of (Indo-)European cultural origin.

In the period considered here, Gordon Childe was *the* prehistorian of Europe par excellence. His six editions of *The Dawn of the European Civilization* had spanned a period of 32 years (1925–57). With regard to the 'diffusionist v. evolutionist' debate, he claimed that he stood somewhere in between. This chapter aims to show (via close textual analysis) that he tended to tilt towards evolutionism in the 1920s and towards diffusionism in the 1930s and beyond. After a historical background of the debate (I), section II scrutinizes Childe's most relevant works comprehensively – in particular *The Dawn of European Civilization* of 1925 and 1939 (henceforth, *The Dawn*), and *The*

Aryans: a Study of Indo-European Origins (1926), (henceforth, *Aryans*). Section III will analyse these textual deconstructions with reference to relevant secondary literature. Section IV pulls the results together.

I – Configuration of Cultures: A Historical Background

The question of whether cultures diffuse from a single spatial source or evolve endogenously and in relative isolation was very much in vogue during the latter half of the nineteenth century. From James Fergusson's *Rude Stone Monuments in All Countries* (1872) to Oscar Montelius' *Der Orient und Europa* (1899), a gradual propensity towards a consensual diffusionist stance was becoming an academic reality. During the first four decades of the twentieth century, the desire to analyse these issues had not gone away. On the contrary, there was a growing tendency to re-examine these questions from new perspectives, such as from within the context of Indo-European philology. Within this context, however, how Europe had developed was no longer a purely academic question; it had become an increasingly political one as well. The debate revolved around two conflicting hypotheses. The diffusionists argued that Europe was a culturally barren continent with an underdeveloped and primitive cultural heritage, which did not improve until the arrival of sophisticated cultural forms from the East. At the other end of the spectrum, there was a growing belief that much of the cultural achievements of Europe were home-grown. The (Indo-)Eurocentric account went something like this: it was the Indo-European peoples of the Bronze Age who, *ab initio*, had sown the seeds of the eventual flowering of European cultural life. Grafton Elliot-Smith and Gustav Kossinna were, respectively, the central figures of these two schools of thought.

When asked by the cultural anthropologist, William Perry, 'what was taking place as regard the development of culture in the rest of the world, while Egypt was laying the foundation of our civilization?', Elliot-Smith made a one-word response: 'Nothing.'[1] The built-in assumption and the curt but unambiguous reply reveal a great deal concerning the status of this debate in 1915: diffusionism was a given. Elsewhere and somewhat later, Elliot-Smith elaborated on this with great confidence:

> Practices such as mummification and megalith building present so many peculiar and distinctive features that no hypothesis of independent evolution can seriously be entertained in explanation of their geographical distribution. They must be regarded as evidence of the diffusion of information, and migration of the bearers of it.[2]

Kossinna's stance was very different. This is how he describes the situation in the third and second millennia BC:

> The great folk movement [...] went out [...] from north-central Europe, from this side of the Baltic and beyond, and then further, from the middle and lower Danube, populating all Europe, and especially southern Europe and the Near East, with the people who speak our tongue, the language of the Indo-Germans. Everywhere people of central European blood became the ruling class.[3]

As in many similar cases, however, extreme positions seldom represent the accepted norm. Within set limits, they merely define the contours of what is broadly permissible. A watered-down diffusionism — which still chimed with Elliot-Smith's central tenets — formed the general consensus in the United Kingdom concerning European cultural attainments in the prehistoric period. This consensus remained largely in place until the discovery of radiocarbon dating in the late 1940s, and dendrochronology in the 1960s shifted the paradigm once and for all.[4] These new scientific techniques demonstrated that diffusionism, as a working hypothesis, was now redundant. In the wake of this shift, the early Europeans could no longer be dismissed, in Colin Renfrew's phrase, 'as uncouth yokels on the remote Atlantic fringe of Europe, far removed from the so-called "heartlands" of the civilized world'.[5] But does this imply that Kossinna, his chauvinism notwithstanding, was closer to a more convincing framework than most of his non-German contemporaries? Kossinna's position had certainly been significantly strengthened *post ipso facto* by the inferences from the new scientific methodologies of dating archaeological finds. Even Renfrew – who is at pains to assert that the paradigm shift has nullified diffusionism *and* evolutionism equally[6] – has substantially more to say regarding the shortcomings of the former.

Broadly speaking, the moderate diffusionist stance was countered, not by a Kossinna-type framework, but by a modified form of evolutionism. This form of evolutionism did not reject diffusionism in its totality. It accepted that a large number of cultural forms were transmitted via a number of obvious conduits, such as trade, migration and warfare. But there were two crucial caveats to this proposition. First, as Bronislaw Malinowski warns in *The Life of Culture* (1928), that 'in the case of every invention, we know that it is invariably made and remade time after time in different places, by different men along slightly different roads, independently of one another'. Consequently, 'every cultural achievement is due to a process or growth in which diffusion and invention have equal shares'.[7] Secondly, and related to this, there is also a possibility of convergence, even if independent invention is denied. Here is Wissler in *Man and Culture* (1923):

> Since in all matters of invention one step leads to another, we may suspect that trait complexes evolve from simple beginnings. So it is conceived that, in the course of time, two or more quite different traits, originating in widely different cultures, may come to be similar.[8]

It is noteworthy that most of the arguments in support of moderate evolutionism were emanating from the United States: a land where the probability of independent invention was hard to deny, and that of diffusion harder still to substantiate. As early as 1945, several years prior to the advent of radiocarbon dating, Leslie White, with some prescience,[9] took diffusionism within the American anthropological context to task:

The triumph of the 'diffusion negates evolution' argument and its success for so many years presents an interesting problem for the student of the behaviour of scientists and of the growth of scientific tradition. How could an error, which when exposed seems almost absurdly obvious, have had such a run?[10]

Within the context of European prehistory, however, things were quite different. There existed within the immediate vicinity, indeed on the very edge of the continent of Europe, a rich source of diffusible cultural ideas and materials. This, understandably, put the onus firmly on the evolutionists to substantiate their assertions. After all, European civilization took off in the region closest to Mesopotamia and Egypt. This gave the European diffusionists a comparative advantage vis-à-vis their American counterparts. But that does not necessarily imply that the theoretical analyses of the American evolutionists were not applicable to the Old World. As a matter of fact, Gordon Childe, had adopted, early in his career, an approach not too dissimilar to them.

II – A Bibliographical Survey

a) *The First Two Editions of* The Dawn of the European Prehistory: A Comparative Analysis

In a 1923 letter to his former tutor, Childe mentions the idea for 'a book about the European Neolithic and Bronze ages'. 'There must come a day,' he continues revealingly, 'when Aegean students will notice that the world is not bounded by the Alps and Balkan mountains and will become conscious (as you [Myres] & Evans & Petrie alone among Aegean archaeologists are – as yet) that axes, daggers [...] have a scientific if not aesthetic value.'[11] In reply, Myres is supportive: 'A short book on the early European cultures is much needed; I hardly realised how much until I discovered what elementary questions people are prepared to ask after a first reading of my sketch in CAH.'[12] And two short years later, *The Dawn* was published.

Childe was always steadfast in his belief that cultural diffusion from east to west was primarily responsible for kick-starting the European civilization. What makes Childe interesting, however, is how he evaluates the nature of this 'kick-start' throughout his career. In the preface of the 1925 edition of *The Dawn*, Childe takes as his overarching 'theme' 'the foundation of European Civilization as a peculiar and individual manifestation of the human spirit'. In order to tackle this, he, at the very outset, confidently asserts that he can subscribe neither to the school which maintains that 'Western Civilization only began in historic times after 1000 BC in a little corner of the Mediterranean and that its true prehistory is to be found not in Europe but in the Ancient East', nor to the notion that 'the origin of all the higher elements [lies] in human culture of Europe itself'. 'The truth,' according to Childe, '[lies] between them.'[13] The exact location of the truth that lies between these two schools of thoughts is left unspecified, but there are strong hints:

> The Occident was, I would submit, indebted to the Orient for the rudiment of the arts and crafts that initiated man's emancipation from bondage to his environment and for the foundation of those spiritual ties that co-ordinate human endeavours. But the peoples of the West were not slavish imitators; they adapted the gifts of the East and united the contributions made by Africa and Asia in a new and organic whole capable of developing on its own original lines. By the sixteenth century BC the new organism was already functioning and the point had arrived when the Westerners were ready to assume the role of masters. Among the early Bronze Age peoples of the Aegean, the Danube valley, Scandinavia, and Britain, we can recognize already the expression of those very qualities of energy, independence, and inventiveness which distinguish the Western world from Egypt, India, or China.[14]

This passage is instructive for a number of reasons. First, it is noteworthy that the Orient furnished no more than the rudiment – the 'imperfect beginning of something underdeveloped or yet to develop'[15] – of what were the prerequisites of emancipating the European man from 'bondage to his environment'. This had to be so, simply because the Occidentals were no 'slavish imitators', but organic adaptors par excellence. Second, the early Bronze Age of the sixteenth century BC – when the Westerners 'assumed the role of the masters' – is also significant for another reason: it was the broadly agreed-upon date for the arrival of the Indo-Europeans upon the European scene. Finally, with the European-wide (from the Aegean to Britain, via Scandinavia) expression of 'energy, independence, and inventiveness' being absent in much of the East, Childe is, clearly, signalling no more than a niggardly appreciation of the eastern portion of the world. Although Childe asserts that he believes the truth to lie between diffusionism and evolutionism, his failure to provide the exact co-ordinates of that position does not conceal his tangible belief that it lies closer to evolutionism than diffusionism. All of which, arguably, suggests that diffusionism was, at best, secondary; perhaps even ephemeral in his overall thinking in 1925. He seems to have opted for evolutionism; or to be more precise, he regarded diffusionism not as the main narrative of European prehistory, but its necessary, albeit modest, prologue. The story that mattered was not only what was taking place in the Aegean, but, more crucially, what was unfolding beyond the bounds of the 'Alps and Balkan mountains'.

Now, when we turn to the preface of the 1939 edition, the tendency to highlight the superior qualities of the Europeans has been drastically downgraded. Here he contends:

> Our deepened knowledge of the archaeology of Europe and of the Ancient East has enormously strengthened the Orientalists' position. Indeed we can now survey continuously interconnected [European] provinces throughout which cultures are seen to be zoned in regular descending grades round the centres of urban civilization in the Ancient East. Such zoning is the best possible proof of the Orientalists' postulate of diffusion.[16]

This explicit move towards the idea that the Europeans were beholden to the East for substantially more than the mere rudiments of culture was a decisive shift of his intellectual and conceptual perspectives. In order to tease out narrative discrepancies and methodological incongruities, it is best to undertake a comparative textual examination of these two editions of *The Dawn*.

The two Aegean chapters were entitled 'Minoan Crete and the First Civilization in Europe' and 'The Orient and Crete', respectively. This renaming is noteworthy. The former focuses, almost entirely, on the genesis of the first *European* civilization, which is unmistakably situated, spatially, in Europe. This European aspect, however, is erased from the 1939 edition, and is replaced by the centrality of the Orient in the scheme of things. This same refocusing continues throughout. The original text here (1925 edition) is very much preoccupied with the 'result of the diffusion and adaptation of the discoveries of the Orient'[17] by Europe. But a number of asides and unvoiced assumptions hint at another, very different perspective. The discoveries of the East were not merely adapted by the Europeans, but *improved* upon:

> The true originality of our ancestors was displayed not in inventing what early climatic conditions had reserved for others, but the manner in which they adapted and improved the invention of the Orient. In this sense the early inhabitants of our continent were truly and remarkably creative and before the end of the Second millennium [BC] had outstripped their masters and created an individual civilization of their own.[18]

It is also worth noting that even when Childe admits to the inventive contributions of the Orient, he qualifies them by introducing climatic factors into the discourse:

> While conditions in our Continent only permitted the sort of life still lived by Esquimaux [Eskimos], the contemporary inhabitants of North Africa and Western Asia enjoyed an environment eminently favourable to cultural progress.[19]

Now that he has contextualized a marginalized Orient, Childe goes on to argue that 'the Minoan civilization was European and that it acted as the intermediary in the transmutation and transmission of oriental discoveries to other parts of our continent'. Although he acknowledges that Crete was 'deeply indebted both to Mesopotamia and Egypt', however, he insists that 'it was no mere copy of either, but an original and creative force'.[20] Childe buttresses this further:

> The Minoan spirit was thoroughly European and in no sense oriental [...]. We find in Crete none of those stupendous palaces that betoken the autocratic power of the oriental despot [...]. The Cretan artist was not limited to perpetuating the cruel deeds of a selfish despot nor doomed to formalism by the innate conservatism of priestly superstition. Hence the modern naturalism, the truly occidental feeling for life and nature that distinguish Minoan vase paintings, frescoes, and intaglios. Beholding these charming scenes of games and processions, animals and fishes, flowers and trees we breathe already a European atmosphere. Likewise in industry the absence of unlimited labour-power at the disposal of a despot necessitated a concentration on the invention and elaboration of tools and weapons that foreshadows the most distinctive feature of European civilization.[21]

By insisting on the multiple superiorities (governance, art, economic efficiency, etc.) of the *European* Cretans, Childe is in no doubt – nor does he wish to leave his readers in any doubt – as to how he views the real contributions of diffusionism to the discernable assemblage of the first European civilization in Crete. In order to drive home his central point, the second half of the chapter is given over to a close analysis of tools and weapons. These archaeological finds, according to Childe, 'will serve to illustrate the originality of the Minoans and their wide influence in Europe'.[22] In the domain of tool-making, the Minoans had 'outstripped the dwellers on the Nile'[23] by improving the technologies of axe and dagger manufacture.[24] Discussing weaponry such as Minoan rapiers, Childe applauds the 'remarkable metallurgical achievements' and 'aesthetic genius' that was 'displayed in the inlaying of the hilts and the spiral decoration of the blades'. He also writes:

> At the same time these enormous swords vindicate conclusively the supremacy of the West over East, both in technical skill and originality, for nothing to compare with them was ever born in Mesopotamia or Egypt. European civilization is henceforth armed to defend its independence.[25]

It is my contention that the primary purpose of the 1925 edition of the book was also to 'vindicate conclusively the supremacy of the West over East'.

The aim of the 1939 edition, in contrast, was almost the reverse of this categorical assertion. In 'The Orient and Crete', Childe begins by giving a fuller description of the Orient: the climate, topography and urbanization of the East are discussed in more detail than in the 1925 edition. Furthermore, none of the above quotes, which foreground the contributions of the Europeans' 'genius', are repeated in the new edition. The only exception to this is a watered-down version of the assessment of the Cretan artists:

> So professional potters from Asia may have introduced the potters' wheel and trained native apprentices in its use. And other specialists such as fresco-painters may have arrived to minister to courtly desires for refinement. But if new arts were introduced by immigrants, the Minoan schools founded these were original and creative both in devising fresh techniques and in creating a new naturalistic style that owed little to Oriental models. In beholding the charming scenes of games and processions, animals and fishes, flowers and trees that adorned [...] the palaces and houses we breathe already a European atmosphere.[26]

All references here to 'oriental despotism' and the uniqueness of European civilization have been profoundly modified. It is worth commenting on the fact that whereas in the 1925 passage the contribution of the East was perfunctorily dealt with, in the 1939 revision the *direct* involvement of the 'oriental' artisans, both in producing 'courtly refinements' and training apprentices, is unequivocally stressed.

There are many other instances of extensive revision. For example, a whole chapter in the 1925 *Dawn* deals with the 'Peoples of the Steppes'. In this chapter, Childe reviews a number of competing hypotheses. One school of thought contended that these peoples had, in reality, 'advanced from Scandinavia and Germany to colonize South Russia. The other school, however, asserted that their cradle can be traced back to "Inner Asia".'[27] Childe averred that the matter could only be settled by ascertaining the nature of the growth of battleaxe culture in Northern and Central Europe. His analysis of the available archaeological finds led him to infer that since 'all the European battle-axes are [. . .] derived from South Russia; it is likely that their wielders came thence too'.[28] In concluding this chapter, Childe comes closest to proclaiming an explicit Indo-Europeanist stance, which was to become more pronounced in his 1926 book, *The Aryans*:

> An equestrian population, warlike and nomadic, ranging the steppes, came into contact with the Sumerian civilization in the Caucasus region. They adopted and adapted some elements of the higher culture and brought these with them to Northern and Central Europe [. . .]. We have found, if not the origin of the Neolithic civilization of Europe, at least a possible explanation of that element which [. . .] gave to the copper and early bronze age civilizations of the North their peculiar vigour and genius.[29]

This chapter, along with the above analysis, was deleted from the 1939 edition and was replaced by a subsection called the 'Pontic Cultures'. The emphasis on the peoples of Southern Russia was replaced entirely by a more diffusionist approach. This is signified by the introduction of phrases such as 'in connection with Oriental civilization', 'Oriental types' and 'Oriental imports'.[30] Henceforth, these peoples of the steppes were doing something, qualitatively, different. They were no longer adopting and adapting '*some* elements of the higher culture', which had equipped the European civilization with 'vigour and genius'. All they could now do was to absorb, rather inefficiently, the incoming 'cultural forms and accessories' from the East, with South Russia losing its importance. The 'battle-axe folks' were now considered as having no 'ethnic unity'; and furthermore, 'if it be desired to equate the archaeological facts with philological speculations, the Indo-European languages might be regarded as the consequence of adapting a series of *savage dialects* [italic added] to be the means of intercourse in pastoral, warlike, and patriarchal societies with new interests, material and social'.[31] This 1939 concluding paragraph is in complete contrast to that of 1925 (see above) and what had followed in 1926.

In a similar fashion, the first edition makes a great deal of the material advances made by Scandinavia and the British Isles. The 'history of Scandinavia', according to Childe, 'is one of continuous progress'[32] – with the southern parts developing with greater rapidity than the western and northern parts, in accordance with the 'hypothesis of an invasion from South Russia'.[33] Britain, although stifled by 'cults and superstitions inherited from the Atlantic culture', had still managed to achieve 'a truly original and independent civilization already in the Early Bronze Age by 1600 BC'.[34] He sums up unequivocally: 'Scandinavia and Britain were the only megalithic regions in the whole of Europe where the rise of a truly progressive civilization can be traced.'[35]

The 1939 edition contains none of this. Here, the north-western periphery of Europe has transmogrified into either 'self-sufficing Neolithic societies [South Scandinavia]', or 'groups barely emerging from savagery in the far northern forests [Scandinavia]'.[36] Much of this analysis was framed by what he called the 'principle of zoning': 'cultures [...] zoned in regular descending grades round the centres of urban civilization in the Ancient East.' This analytical structure is revisited in the last chapter of the work and categorical inferences are drawn. The descending grades, *c*.1400 BC, commence with the 'fully-literate, city dwellers' of Greece and ends with the 'savagery' that was rife in northern Europe. Consequently, 'Egypt and Mesopotamia',

Childe affirms, 'retain their capital status. The Aegean world, and with it Sicily, descend one grade in the scale. Central Europe [...] and Britain still rank as Bronze Age, Scandinavia [...] remain[s] Neolithic. But South Russia loses grade.'[37] It is highly significant that the 1939 narrative puts Egypt and Mesopotamia at its very core so very explicitly, with various European 'zones' being no more than mere satellites revolving around this powerful and all-encompassing gravitational field. This overwhelmingly centripetal schema was absent in 1925. In its stead, there was no more than an arbitrary, slow-moving and somewhat ad hoc diffusion of culture from the Near East to Europe.

b) *The Aryans: A Study of Indo-European Origins*

The first edition of *The Dawn* was in many ways the prelude to another publication. The texts analysed above have demonstrated what types of ideas or theories had underpinned the 1925 version. The Indo-Europeanist aspects of the book were lightly drawn. The reader was seldom burdened by them; and yet, one could scarcely escape their subtle and cumulative influences. In this respect, it served as the precursor to *The Aryans* in C. K. Ogden's *The History of Civilization* (a series of publications). His fascination with the Indo-European question went back, at least, to his Oxford days. There, he produced a now vanished BLitt thesis, called 'The Influence of Indo-Europeans in Prehistoric Greece' (1917). His interest in this topic clearly remained strong right throughout his early academic life. Years later, in order to justify his fascination with these matters, Childe argued that what had gripped his attention was the desire to discover the 'cradle of the Indo-Europeans'.[38] This may be so, but it was not the entire story: he was also fascinated by the historical role of the Indo-European peoples. A cursory glance at the contents page of *The Aryan* provides a good starting point. Only half of the book is devoted to investigating this 'cradle'. The rest consists of a description and analysis of the cultural influences of these peoples, ending with an examination of 'The Role of the Aryans in History'. Why should a search for the birthplace of a set of peoples require an examination of their eventual role in history? In what way are their contributions to human history germane to the geographical whereabouts of their 'cradle'? After all, one of the references that Childe cites is Harold Bender's *The Home of the Indo-Europeans* (1922). This work, unlike *The Aryans*, is *exclusively* preoccupied with a spatial investigation of the 'cradle' (he settles for Lithuania) of the Indo-Europeans, and has very little to say concerning the attributes of these peoples. Why did Childe not follow suit? Moreover, the ideological tone of the narrative and the tendency to pass judgement and generalize freely signalled a definite departure from Childe's usual inductive methodologies, based almost exclusively on the examination of concrete archaeological data. Here, he is *emotionally* involved, as represented by his liberal use of superlatives. While the discussion in the half of the book devoted to the 'cradle' is conducted soberly (he settled, as he had hinted in *The Dawn*, for South Russia as the cradle), his assessments of the worth of the Indo-European peoples, however, are marred by dubious assertions. Here is a typical example:

> The Indo-European languages and their assumed parent-speech have been throughout exceptionally delicate and flexible instruments of thought [...]. It is no accident that the first great advances towards abstract natural science were made by the Aryan Greeks and Hindus, not by the Babylonians or the Egyptians [...]. The first great world religions [...] Buddhism and Zoroastrianism were the works of Aryans, propagated in Aryan speech.[39]

And here he is drawing a direct and explicit contrast between the 'Aryan' and the 'Semitic' peoples, to the detriment of the latter:

> To whatever physical race or races they belonged, they must have possessed a certain spiritual unity reflected in and conditioned by their community of speech [...]. Anyone who doubts this would do well to compare the dignified narrative carved by the Aryan Darius on the rock of Behistun with the bombastic and blatant self-glorification of the inscriptions of Ashurbanipal or Nebuchadnezzar.[40]

The 'Diffusionism vs. Evolutionism' Debate 93

In the concluding chapter, Childe reviews the 'glorious' role of the Aryans in history, before deciding where their role was most decisive. It is, however in continental Europe that the work of the Aryans as the founders of Western Civilization is most readily apparent.'[41] Europe prior to the Bronze Age, according to Childe, was a superstitious, stagnant and barbaric place. 'Left to itself,' he avers, 'it might have remained on the level of a totemic society in Melanesia or North America.'

> The Aryans [however] imposed their authority and their culture on the whole region, welded the disparate racial groups and the scattered clans into a national unity in which western and eastern ideas were blended to an European whole and called forth a progressive society no less brilliant in trade than in war.

Thus, Childe infers, 'the Aryans do appear everywhere as promoters of true progress and in Europe their expansion marks the moment when the prehistory of our continent begins to diverge from that of Africa or the Pacific'.[42] Moreover, on the question of race,[43] he skates, perilously, on very thin ice. This is the concluding paragraph of the book:

> [T]he fact the first Aryans were Nordics was not without importance. The physical qualities of that stock did enable them by the bare fact of superior strength to conquer even more advanced peoples and so impose their language on areas from which their bodily type has almost completely vanished. This is the truth underlying the panegyrics of the Germanists: the Nordics' superiority in physique fitted them to be the vehicle of a superior language.[44]

III – Analysis

Two pertinent questions arise from this bibliographical survey. First, why was there such a dramatic change of views and emphases from one version of *The Dawn* to another? And second, why was a book such as *The Aryans* ever written and published?

The preface of the 1939 edition maintains that 'the essential outlines of the thesis, originally advanced [in 1925], still hold good';[45] thus indicating that Childe had not shifted his position. In the light of what has already been discussed, this assertion is difficult to maintain. Meanwhile, archaeological discoveries in Europe and the Near East, according to Childe, were proving to be so revolutionary[46] that it would have been unfeasible for them to continue to remain outside his prehistoric scheme of things. But is that really the case? Both editions of this work stay faithful to a simple approach. The raw data that provide the backbone of the narratives are, unsurprisingly, archaeological finds. Around 400–500 such items are sketched in these works. Cumulatively, they legitimize and underpin those inferences which the author wishes to draw. It would thus be right to assume that if certain core inferences were to be comprehensively reformulated, then this could only be done by employing a new set of archaeological finds. Alternatively, at the very least, a sufficient number of fresh finds would need to be adduced in order to support a changed framework.

This prerequisite was absent from Childe's revisions. The 1925 edition had 148 listed multiple-illustrations, many of which were, faithfully, reproduced in the 1939 edition. Moreover, the edition that claimed as its *raison d'être* the availability of revolutionary archaeological discoveries appears to have found their inclusion unnecessary. This obviously raises the following question: how can theories alter, if the available facts/data remain broadly the same? Some may counter that it is fatuous to claim that no new interpretations can ever be formed, if the body of facts remains unchanged. This is a fair point, but it does not apply to the case under review. The change in ideological tone of the narrative was not due to some groundbreaking archaeological finds: none were highlighted in the 1939 edition. The reason for the shift in Childe's works lay elsewhere (see below). All he did was to rearrange and re-title chapters, move the same illustrations from the first edition around and refer to a number of relevant but far from 'revolutionary' recent publications.[47] The analysed archaeological data and the additional footnotes and references of the 1939 edition do not truly signal fundamental changes. For instance, the archaeological items described and analysed in the chapters on Crete and the steppes were almost[48] identical, but inferences drawn from them differed enormously from the first to the second edition of *The Dawn*.

The manner in which Childe had approached his subject-matter in 1925 proclaimed itself to be a straightforward matter of induction: all available and relevant finds were assembled in order for them to yield a number of working hypotheses. In other words, in 1925 Childe gave the impression that facts recovered from the ground were mostly responsible for his particular take on European prehistory. But then how could, broadly speaking, the same facts furnish him in 1939 with a totally different prehistory? 'Childe became convinced,' according to Grahame Clark, 'that it was possible to extract from raw archaeological data the kind of information needed to understand the genesis of "European civilization as a peculiar and individual manifestation of the human spirit."'[49] Indeed, if one were to examine many of his archived sketch-cum-notebooks,[50] one would detect that his overarching approach is not too dissimilar from that of a master mosaicist: assembling disparate archaeological pieces to form a preconceived historical picture. With this in mind, it is therefore surprising to note that his 1939 'principle of zoning', while exposed to almost the same evidence as 1925, managed to draw very different types of conclusions.

It can, however, be argued that an alteration in a given epistemological approach should not, in itself, be a point of dispute. Childe, admittedly, had every right to introduce the 'principle of zoning' into his debate. There are, however, two reasons why its introduction should be handled critically. First, it is not made at all clear how regions such as Scandinavia had been relegated from the 1925 status of 'a truly progressive civilization' to a region that was 'barely emerging from savagery'. Such complete inferential reverses require, in my view, the clearest of expositions regarding the reasons for such reversals. In the 1939 edition of *The Dawn*, none are given. Second, it is unclear whether the 'principle of zoning' is an inductive framework or a deductive one. On the one hand, the structure of the book, as well as the nature of the evidence, is more or less the same for both editions: the framework appears at the end of the (1939) book, and not as an a priori hypothesis at the beginning of it. On the other hand, however, since the reasons for Europe (Russia and Scandinavia in particular) losing grade are not adequately explained, then it is not altogether out of the ordinary to surmise that some form of a priori methodology or perspective must also be at work.

As discussed in the previous chapter, by cancelling out the 'race' variable from his equation, Childe brought to the fore the activities or the supposed achievements of peoples or their cultures. Peoples' actions, both past and present, could now be judged with candour and without the fear of incurring the opprobrium of racism. Childe felt secure in the knowledge that when he discussed the Indo-Europeans, he was discussing peoples and not races. This meant that there were no limits, either conceptually or morally, to the levels of permissible subjectivity and value judgement. By opting to feature the word 'Aryans' so prominently in the title of his book, Childe had made an unfortunate decision; and by not handling the race–culture matrix dexterously, he had constructed an inflexible foundation upon which nothing durable could ever be erected. In addition, his failure to anticipate that the term 'people' (even if defined *sans* race) can be and inevitably is taken as a proxy for race demonstrates fuzzy thinking. Bruce Trigger, however, attributes these tendencies to the influence of Childe's tutor, Myres:

> It is clear [...] that the fundamental formulation of *The Dawn*, which has the idea of material culture coming from the Near East being transformed within the European context by the genius of the Indo-Europeans, is derived from J. L. Myres. Indeed, the title of Childe's book echoes the title of Myres's *The Dawn of History*, published in 1911.[51]

It is worth recalling the letter quoted at the beginning of the last section: Childe seems to have had no need to be prompted by Myres to look beyond the 'Alps and Balkan mountains' for evidence.

Furthermore, on all of the main points Childe and Myres are at variance (see Chapter 3). By arguing for a synthetic culture–race arrangement ('neither race purely nor culture merely, but a people'[52]), as well as by reasoning that as we go back in time, these entities tend to converge – Myers had recognized, contra Childe – the difficulties inherent in a strict separation of race and culture. In addition, Myres had also counselled against evaluating peoples. Moreover, as early as 1911, a decade and a half before the publication of *The Aryans*, Myres had shunned the term 'Aryan', and was well aware of the political trends in Germany.[53] It is also worth remembering that Childe had a great and continuing fascination with Indo-European ideas. The following archival materials are of some significance in relation to this. Childe wrote to Myres in 1935:

> I've just done a slashing review of Eyres's hotchpotch [*European Civilization: Its Origin and Development* (1935)]; your section was the welcome relief [...]. If there is an archaeological solution to the Indo-European problem it must be based on the relations between Europe and Iran. After all, Aryan languages were spoken over an area as large as that of all the European Indo-European languages together![54]

This letter is interesting on three counts. First, it shows that even at the height of his diffusionist rewrites, Childe was still gripped by the 'Indo-European problem'. Second, the Myres chapter that came as a 'welcome relief' was entitled 'The Ethnology, Habitat, Linguistic, and Common Culture of Indo-Europeans up to the Time of the Migration'. In 1957, the year of his death, Childe had made the following final (?) comment in an unpublished first draft of his posthumously published essay, entitled 'Retrospect' (1958):

> I doubt whether the Indo-Europeans had a 'culture' in the sense of an assemblage of distinctive ceramic types [...]. Still I do believe that the Indo-Europeans had a 'culture', as well as a linguistic tradition & that it is quite legitimate object of arch. Research.[55]

Furthermore, in the published 'Retrospect', Childe wrote:

> In rewriting [*The Dawn* in 1956] I began to realise how right Hawkes had been in 1940 when in his *The Prehistoric Foundations of Europe* he had insisted that by the Bronze Age Europe had achieved a kind of culture distinctively its own.[56]

What was the core of Hawkes' argument?

> From Greece to the British Isles, and from Italy to the Baltic, the tongues that dominated Bronze Age Europe were the languages of the Indo-European or Aryan family, the diffusion of which has on every account to be equated with the spread of our warrior-culture peoples. That spread was largely accomplished before and in the beginning of the Bronze Age; but the ethnic and cultural disharmony created by those centuries of migration, conflict, and change was not resolved until the Middle Bronze Age, and the even balance of culture that it brought, whether Germanic or Illyrian, Celtic, Italic, or Mycenaean Greek, into a coherent unity of European civilisation.[57]
>
> Its [Europe's] foundations were formed of a balance of cultures, in which Mediterranean and Western, Alpine and Danubian, Nordic and East European elements of Stone Age inheritance were poised against the civilizing influence of the Orient, in an equilibrium dominated by the peoples of Aryan speech and warrior tradition, who from the years before and after 2000 B.C. onwards have given so much to the moving pattern of European achievement.[58]

All of which brings us to the third point of interest regarding the letter, namely the analytical position of 'Iran'. There is a paradox at the heart of Hawkes's analysis: if the 'foundations' of Europe were predicated largely upon the 'domination' and 'achievement' of 'peoples of Aryan speech', then why not also include the 'Indo-Iranian' world – many of the population of which happen to have resided in Europe – into this definition of 'Europe'? Surely, when situating the 'peoples of Aryan speech' within the narrow context of the Bronze Age, it seems to be a matter of elementary logic to refrain from creating a Europe with arbitrary boundaries. The letter suggests that Childe had understood this analytical anomaly. By envisaging that the 'Indo-European problem' can only be solved by investigating 'the relations between Europe and Iran', Childe appears to be thinking of the Iranian world, in a manner of speaking, as Europe's antechamber.

By implying that changes in views over time and without the presence of new evidence is unsustainable, I am not merely dabbling in naive empiricism, but I have also forgone the opportunity to examine the workings of a fertile, creative and changing mind. It can further be argued that my failure to situate Childe's writings within the context of his 1939 warning – 'over a large part of our Continent prehistory has been harnessed to the service of a political dogma [Nazism]'[59] – is nothing but moral laxity. And as far as *The Aryans* is concerned, it is more accurate to see it as a late and misguided publication of his 1917 thesis, and not as a direct and mature follow-up to the first edition of *The Dawn*.

The formal definition of 'archaeology' is, according to the *Oxford English Dictionary*, 'the study of human history and prehistory through the excavation of sites and analysis of physical remains'. And what could be more empiricist than the 'analysis of physical remains'? The more specific quandary that confronts us here, however, is essentially delineated within the contours of the following questions. What is better, the safeguarding of the prehistory of Europe from the influences of 'political dogma' by relying on the most accurate and truthful renditions of what are generally believed to have been the events and processes of the second and first millennia BC? Or the forgoing of good and evidence-based analyses and responding to the perils of such dogmas by producing a prehistorical narrative specifically and primarily designed to deal directly with the unpalatable consequences of these ideologies and precious little else? As I shall argue, much of the recent writing on Childe has failed to address the relevant issues within this paradoxical framework. Colin Renfrew, for instance, follows the example of Glyn Daniel in defining Childe's approach as 'modified' diffusionism, which 'did more than any other to maintain a balance and further the international approach on the foundations laid down by Montelius'.[60] Not entirely satisfied with 'modifying' Childe's diffusionism, some other writers go even further and explain its championing by Childe on 'ethical' grounds. Trigger, for example, asserts:

> For him [Childe], the concept of diffusion had strong ethical implications. It expressed the mutual interdependence of all mankind and was a powerful weapon for opposing doctrines which asserted the superiority of one racial or ethnic group over another. He believed that demonstrating that Europe owed its early technological development to the diffusion of knowledge from the Near East served to counteract the myths of European, and specifically Teutonic, superiority [...]. Childe's insistence on the uncreativity of prehistoric Europe and the debt its peoples owed to the Near East markedly increased during the 1930s in response to the threat of National Socialism; while a more balanced view reasserted itself as racism and ethnocentrism receded following World War II.[61]

And here is Michael Rowlands putting a similar point more forcefully:

> It is well known that Childe's particular brand of diffusionism was motivated by a wish to counteract the rise of racism and nationalism in archaeology and to absolve his own guilt over his previous adherence to the Aryan hypothesis.[62]

If diffusionism is a theoretical framework, then it has only one paramount function: to explain the nature and origins of Europe's prehistoric cultural developments and nothing else. The notion – as presented by Childe and endorsed by others – that it is academically admissible to use diffusionism as an ethical response to Hitler and

The 'Diffusionism vs. Evolutionism' Debate   101

Nazism, and without due reference to what had actually taken place millennia ago, is peculiar. Many, however, do not share my sense of unease. Renfrew argues that Childe opting for 'modified' diffusionism 'was largely a very natural revulsion from the extreme racism of Kossinna'.[63] But cultural diffusionism was not, in origin, a politically motivated hypothesis, designed to cater for what was taking place in the Europe of the 1930s. It was designed to be a value-free structure and an analytical framework, constructed for the purpose of ascertaining a number of verifiable postulates. It was therefore not meant to provide absolution for Childe and his 'guilt over his previous adherence to the Aryan hypothesis', but to furnish us with some semblance of historical verisimilitude concerning European prehistory.

This barely hidden tendency to relativize Childe's legacy, in my judgement, is a disturbing intellectual development. In *Fear of Knowledge: Against Relativism and Constructivism* (2007), Paul Boghossian observes that '[t]he core constructivist conviction [...] is that knowledge is constructed by societies in ways that reflect their contingent social needs'.[64] He goes on to say:

> One source of their [constructivist ideas] appeal is clear: they are hugely empowering. If we can be said to know up front any item of knowledge only has that status because it gets a nod from our contingent social values, then any claim to knowledge can be dispatched if we happen to share the values on which it allegedly depends.[65]

When situated within the context of this constructivist insight, Childe's adherence to diffusionism does appear to be intellectually and conceptually unsound. This is so because its existence is largely due to the 'nod' it gets from the social, political and ethical (anti-Nazi) values of the 1930s (indeed, this 'nod' represents what I had called earlier, with reference to the 'principle of zoning', 'some form of an a priori perspective'). Trigger's concession that after the use of diffusionism as a response to Nazism, 'a more *balanced* [my emphasis] view reasserted itself as racism and ethnocentrism receded following

World War II'[66] is a good example of constructivism at work. The notion that actual and evidence-based historical interpretations can be sidelined from elevated discourse —for however long necessary — until the influence of a number of morally dubious values (racism, ethnocentricity, etc.) begins to recede is precisely what is conveyed by the term 'fear of knowledge'. Moreover, a less philosophical and more methodological deficiency of this approach lies in an over-reliance on teleological thinking. To 'respond' against the threat of Nazism is indeed a worthy thing to do; but to respond to it by rewriting what was, hitherto, sincerely believed to have been a verisimilar interpretation of the past, smacks of historical 'presentism' — which, by definition, cares less for what *had* probably happened in the past, and more for what is happening in the present.[67]

In his 'If Childe Were Alive Today' paper, Trigger has a list of 21 works from Childe, the earliest from 1931.[68] This quietism concerning Childe's 1920s output sits uneasily with Grahame Clark's judgement that he 'had achieved what he was going to achieve in this genre [prehistoric archaeology] by 1930'.[69] Who is right? There are three reasons why one would tilt towards Clark. First, and as discussed at length, it is the first and not the second edition of *The Dawn*, that is not only faithful to the archaeological evidence but also does not dwell, inordinately, upon the European political climate of the inter-war years. Second, there is no question whatsoever that *The Aryans*, within the context of Ogden's book series, was the planned follow-up to *The Dawn* – and not a published version of his 1917 thesis[70] – thus hinting at the centrality of an Indo-European mindset dominating Childe's early thinking. Finally, and as a consequence of this, by asserting as late as 1956 that Hawkes was right to suggest that 'by the Bronze Age Europe had achieved a kind of culture distinctively its own' (bearing in mind that Hawkes situated this within 'an equilibrium dominated by the peoples of Aryan speech'), Childe appears to have been inching back towards his Indo-European framework of the 1920s.[71]

IV – Conclusions

If Isaiah Berlin[72] was to classify Gordon Childe, he would put him down as a hedgehog: an intellectual who knew one big thing, or, to be precise, an intellectual who had a lifelong passion for one big thing.

'Indo-Europeanism' was, truly, the single defining characteristic of Childe's tumultuous academic career. It defined Childe's formative years of the 1920s. It defined the reaction and the *mea culpa* of the 1930s. It defined the partial return to the earlier formative template in the 1950s. Even at the height of 1930s revisionism (as his letter to Myres demonstrates), Childe had more than just a nominal interest in matters Indo-European. It was, therefore, quite natural for him to infer that the main problem with his framework was precisely his single-minded passion: his adherence to the Indo-European methodology. As a result, he found it hard to see the wood for the trees, and diagnosed the shortcomings of his framework incorrectly. The problem lay with the foundation upon which this methodology was predicated (namely the race–culture dichotomy), and not the methodology itself. This situation was aggravated further by his unique way in dealing with the hard evidence. His archived notebooks, with hundreds of archaeological sketches, demonstrate that Childe was a systematic compiler of artefacts, which, in turn, allowed him to form narrow and tightly-focused hypotheses without paying due attention to the bigger picture. In his final published work, Childe recalls the beginning of his 'thrilling' Indo-European journey:

> Like Gustav Kossinna I came to prehistory from comparative philology; I began the study of European Archaeology in the hope of finding the cradle of the Indo-Europeans and of identifying their primitive culture. Reading my Homer and my Veda with the guidance of Schrader and Jevons, Zimmer and Wilamowitz-Mollendorf I was thrilled by the discoveries of Evans in Prehellenic Crete and of Wace and Thompson in Prehistoric Thessaly.[73]

Of course, as discussed, the finding of 'the cradle of the Indo-Europeans' and the identification of 'their primitive culture' was not *all* that Childe had undertaken in the 1920s. Indeed, very much like Kossinna, he had also drifted into the treacherous ideological and political terrains of the day. Unlike Kossinna, however, it was done inadvertently and was largely due to faulty assumptions that he had adopted early in his career. In the following chapter, this particular shortcoming will be compared and contrasted with Myres' works pertaining to race, culture and Hellenism.

CHAPTER 5

HELLENISMS REASSESSED (1890s–1940s): PART I

At the turn of the last century, as discussed towards the end of Chapter 2, the sketchy outlines of three decipherable types of Hellenisms became apparent: 'aesthetic', 'scientific' and 'Nietzschean'. This chapter is only concerned with the first two of these. *Aesthetic* Hellenism can be described as a set of ideas which emphasizes the supreme beauty of the classical Greek culture. *Scientific* Hellenism is harder to define. This approach, although stemming from the traditions of aesthetic Hellenism, does not begin with an a priori assumption that the Hellenic is uniquely beautiful, but proceeds in utilizing all the available scientific and historiographical tools to ascertain the nature and the context of classical Greek culture and people. Between 1900 and 1940, scientific Hellenism was asserting its youthful yet vigorous credentials at the expense of the established aesthetic Hellenism. This chapter, broadly speaking, is an account of how this episode unfolded in the intellectual history of British classicism.

Most eminent classical scholars of the period were enthusiastic adherents of the aesthetic variety of Hellenism; Gilbert Murray (1866–1957) being, arguably, its most fervent and noted advocate. Conversely, very few intellectuals had noticed the emergence of a science-based Hellenism as a viable alternative for examining the classical Greek world. The adoption of scientific methodologies in Hellenic studies was, largely, the work of one man: John Linton Myres.

Section I begins with a discussion of mainstream Hellenism that defined the sensibilities of Murray and his like-minded colleagues. Myres' work is analysed in section II. In this section, most of his relevant published and unpublished writings are scrutinized in order to piece together his intellectual makeup. Section III brings these two discussions into analytical focus. With the first part of my overarching reassessment of Hellenisms complete, a number of questions are posed in section IV in order to set the scene for Part II.

I – Mainstream Hellenism: 1890s–1940s

The generation of classicists that succeeded Mathew Arnold and Walter Pater (see Chapter 2) were confronted with new and unforeseen challenges. The trend that had begun with Winckelmann's notion of Hellenism in the latter half of the eighteenth century continued with some élan into the early twentieth century. This new generation, however, found itself in an era of exciting archaeological discoveries while at the same time its terms of reference had to take on board the new scientific disciplines of the day. The discovery of the Bronze Age treasures of Troy by Heinrich Schliemann (1822–90), and the unearthing of the palace of Knossos in Crete by Arthur Evans (1851–1941) fuelled the imagination of many up-and-coming classicists of the period. But they found themselves to be no longer the sole custodians of these discoveries. Anthropologists, prehistorians and comparative philologists began to move, albeit tentatively, into their intellectual terrain. These new specialists were becoming stakeholders in this multifaceted and fast-moving academic enterprise. In a sense, Hellene ceased to be the exclusive domain of those belonging to the classical nobility and began to be a subject for study across a number of disciplines. Two interrelated questions arise from this new academic constellation. First, how did the Hellenists of the period manage to pursue their subject-matter while compelled to accommodate these new sciences? And second, were they able to shift Hellenism away from its predominantly German Romantic axis?

Writing to a colleague in 1921, Gilbert Murray, the doyen of mainstream Hellenism, expounded his idea of how classics should be framed in modern education:

> If I felt more confidence about the future of education in general and classical edn in particular, I should say that a group of us – you [J. A. K. Thomson] and I and Livingstone and Zimmern and Cornford and J E H [Jane Harrison] and Robinson of Eton and some others in England – had a very good chance of establishing a style of scholarship which consisted essentially in the perception of beauty, and to some extent in the representation of it. As it is I do not feel able to prophesy but we still have a chance.[1]

Richard Livingstone's (1880–1960) *The Greek Genius and its Meaning to Us* (1915) is perhaps the clearest demonstration of the rationale for Murray's assertion of this new 'style of scholarship'. Livingstone gives this 'genius' a glossary of notes: the note of beauty, of freedom, of directness, of humanism and of sanity and many-sidedness. 'The study of these men and their writings can give us', according to the author, a set of rules 'by which we can live'. In addition, those 'prizing the Greek spirit in its graver and more serious aspects, turn to Greek literature as other men turn to the Bible'. Here, Livingstone is thinking of 'certain expressions used by Professor von Wilamowitz-Moellendorff' and 'passages in Professor Murray's book on Homer'.[2] Livingstone, however, is also aware of the historiography of Hellenism. In congruence with two essentially nineteenth-century mindsets, he follows, first, Mathew Arnold's example and argues that for a Greek, unlike a Jew, who 'was deeply interested in morality, his attitude to it was one of reason rather than of passion'.[3] Second, the German Romantic connection is not forgotten: 'The modern interest in Hellenism really dates from Winckelmann, and Winckelmann drew his ideas of the Greek mainly from their art.'[4] He does, however, take issue with the 'Mid-Victorian' idea of Greek beauty, which consists of 'beautiful statuary' and 'a population almost entirely consisting of beautiful young men, who spent their lives in admiring the beauty around them'.[5]

Beauty, in this strict sense, was not the main definer of the Greeks. 'The Greeks,' in Livingstone's view, 'were not aesthetes, and they had many qualities besides a love of beauty. Yet they are the authors of the most beautiful statues, the most beautiful buildings, and the most beautiful poems in the world. In mere beauty their art and literature has never been equalled.'[6] But, according to Livingstone, Hellenism in its most 'truthful' has a core of 'aesthetic morality'. In this context, '[v]ictory, temperance, eloquence, the punishment of vice, frankness, wisdom, and readiness to listen to wisdom, were not merely good, they were "beautiful"'. Furthermore, '[a]n Englishman would admire these qualities and praise them. A Greek spoke of them as if they gave him the same emotions as the sight of a beautiful human being.'[7] It therefore seems that the tangible difference between the Victorian Hellenists and Livingstone and his contemporaries is the latter's insistence that there is much more to Hellenism than a narrow definition of beauty.

In order to get a better purchase on what Murray means by 'a style of scholarship which consists essentially in the perception of beauty, and to some extent in the representation of it', it would be best to examine Murray's relevant published and unpublished works directly. In addition, the works of James Alexander Kerr Thomson (1879–1957), one of his main interlocutors (the addressee of the letter quoted above), and Arnold Toynbee (1889–1975), his like-minded son-in-law, are revealing and significant.[8]

Approaching this field from a non-specialist perspective, Toynbee goes further than Arnold and Mahaffey (see Chapter 2) and draws more than just a parallel between the ancient Greece and modern West. He considers that there is a robust intellectual 'relationship between Ancient Greek and the Modern Western Civilization'. In a chapter for *The Legacy of Greece* (1921), Toynbee asserts: 'That portion of contemporary humanity which inhabits Western Europe and America constitutes a specific society, for which the most convenient name is "Western Civilization", and this society has a relationship with Ancient Greek society which other contemporary societies – for instance, those of Islam, India, and China – have not. It is its child.'[9] Moreover, the answer to the question 'why study Hellenism rather than our own history'[10] is, first, in 'Greek history the plot of civilization has been worked out to its conclusion'.[11] This provides us, to all intents and purposes, with an almanac of events and eventualities. The second reason is largely aesthetic: 'the historical experience of the Greeks has been more finely expressed than ours.'[12] Third, 'tragedy' – and here Toynbee is inspired by Aristotle – is a concept that imitates 'an action that is serious, complete, and of a certain magnitude', which through 'pity and fear' results in purgation or purification.[13] It is 'the emotional value which is peculiar to the study of a different civilization, and which one cannot get [...] by the study of his own'.[14] Fourth, the study of 'Ancient Greek is generally admitted to have more educative value for an Englishman than the study of modern French or German, because Greek and English embody the fundamental principles of human language in entirely independent forms of expression'.[15]

Whether or not Toynbee's advocacy of Hellenic education convinces is not relevant here. What is of interest, however, is twofold. First, every single meme, in a manner of speaking, appears to have been present in the historical experiences of the Greeks. This sense of 'everything-ness', as will be seen, was an ever-present phenomenon among the leading Hellenists of the period. Second, the desire to couple the Greeks not only with modern Europeans but, specifically, with the Englishmen of Toynbee's education and worldview is noteworthy because it implies a tendency to appropriate the Greeks for a specific type of people.

Informing Murray of his forthcoming book, *Greeks and Barbarians* (1921), Thomson concedes that as far as the main chapter of the book is concerned ('Classical and Romantic'), 'I feel somehow that I have not made a proper acknowledgement of the debt it owes to your writings'.[16] So what ideas underpinned this chapter? The book itself is largely a historical account of the Greeks and their unhappy dealings with the non-Greek 'barbarians', with the Persian Empire taking a characteristically starring role (see Chapter 7). The chapter in question, however, situates the Greeks and an unusual assortment of 'barbarians' not historically, but thematically. Thomson begins by suggesting that 'classical art is an expression of Hellenism and

Romantic art of Barbarism, so far as Barbarism is capable of expression'.[17] He also sees one glaring difference between Romanticism and Classicism: the aesthetic grammar of the former is based on magic[18] and the latter on reason.[19] Thereafter the work justifies this by demonstrating that Greek literature 'deals sparingly' with 'the magic of fairies and witches'.[20] The only reason that in the later Hellenistic period 'there existed a great body of magical writings', was, according to the author, due to 'the contact between Greek civilization and Oriental superstition'.[21] In other words, 'Hellenism, the flower of the Greek spirit' had no choice but to grow 'in a soil impregnated with superstition [and] with a religion containing many elements of magic'. What no one can deny, however, is that 'Hellenism tends to reject magic, and tries to expel it from human life. Magic was barbaric, and Hellenism was in reaction against Barbarism.'[22] Moreover, 'the great vice of the Barbarian', according to Thomson, 'is that he has no self-restraint, and the Barbarian *pur sang* [...] must be incapable of art'.[23] With his innate inability to refrain from crude exaggerations, the 'barbarian' is set — unlike the Greek, whose literature is 'marked by a unique sincerity, or veracity, or candour'[24] — on a path towards artistic mediocrity and, eventually, oblivion.

Ultimately, '*Beauty is Truth, Truth Beauty* is very Greek.' But Thomson takes issue with Keats' *Ode to a Grecian Urn* and asserts that 'it is not Greek to forget the second half of this aphorism. So the Greek poets aimed less directly at beauty than at the truth of things, which they believed to be beautiful.'[25] This second aphorism seems to have been central to Thomson's overall thinking. He concludes the chapter and the book with the following remarks:

> To see that essential beauty is truth and truth is beauty — that is the secret of Greek art, as it is the maxim of true realism. To keep measure in all things, that no drop of life may spill over — that is the secret of Greek happiness. To be a Greek and not a Barbarian.[26]

To connect the entire European Romantic movement[27] with barbarism is perhaps a little overdone, but what is novel in

Thomson's approach is his wide definition of barbarians; they no longer solely dwell in the East. In other words, he would not have written, as Toynbee had done in *Greek Historical Thought* (1924), that the use of the word 'barbarian' is 'wholly misleading when it can be *bettered* [my emphasis] by "Oriental"'.[28] Thomson's barbarians can also reside in Europe and produce entirely bona fide Occidental art and literature. One only has to compare, according to the author, 'the greatest poem in the world', the *Iliad*, with the 'comparatively rude and primitive'[29] *Táin Bó Cúalnge*[30] of early Celtic literature to fully grasp the tangible differences between the Celts and the Greeks. This tendency to categorize post-classical Europeans as Romantics, hence largely barbaric, was a peculiar approach and very much at odds with Toynbee's assertion that 'Western Civilization' is the talented and sole offspring of the Greeks. Murray's response to this book was complimentary[31] but without explicitly agreeing with Thomson on the question of equating Romanticism with barbarism. Does this imply that on the fundamental definitions of Hellenism, Murray was in disagreement with Thomson? Was Thomson merely ingratiating himself with Murray by stating that he owes a debt of gratitude to his writings?

In order to make headway with such questions, it is imperative to look closely at Murray's relevant works. In the preface to *A History of Ancient Greek Literature* (1897), Murray looks at the past and the present of Greek studies:

> The 'serene and classical' Greek of Winckelmann and Goethe did good service to the world in his day, though we now feel him to be mainly a phantom. He has been succeeded [...] by an aesthetic and fleshy Greek in fine raiment [...]. He is a phantom too, as unreal as those marble palaces in which he habitually takes his ease [...]. There is more flesh and blood in the Greek of the anthropologists, the foster-brother of Kaffirs and Hairy Ainos. He is at least human and simple and emotional and free from irrelevant trappings. His fault, of course, is that he is not the man we want, but only the raw material out of which that man was formed; a Hellene without beauty, without the spiritual life, without the Hellenism.[32]

Three years later, Murray, in a letter to his mother-in-law (31 January 1900), expresses the following forthright views:

> For the future, I have been more and more inclined towards the plan of devoting myself to a large and full history of Greek Literature [...]. But I think that a large Hist. of Gk. Literature would not only exercise all my powers in a very full way, but also might be of value to 'Humanity' – which is on the whole my great object. Greece has a profound and permanent message to mankind, a message quite untouched by 'supernaturalism' and revealed religions; it is human and rational and progressive, and affects not Art only but the whole of life. I think [...] that I may be the most suitable person to interpret Greek Poetry.
>
> The work as I conceive it might be something really great, if carried out by a person with the great powers. I think it unlikely in the extreme that I could achieve any result of the sort – anything comparable to what Ruskin or Renan might have made of the subject. But I think it also very unlikely that I shd completely fail [...]. I *have* got a faith and a message: thy way be mistaken or vulgar or valueless, but thy are there, and I want to speak them out. And I think that the subject which I happen to know best is also a vehicle very well fitted for expressing them. Greek Lit. contains the genus of almost everything; so you can treat of almost all tendencies in treating of it.[33]

The contrast between these two texts is noteworthy and well worth an extensive commentary. The prefatory extract is generously laced with irony (one phantom replacing another) and sarcasm meshed with racism[34] ('the foster-brother of Kaffirs and Hairy Ainos'). A candid Murray, however, does not disguise his sense of frustration and unease: this 'simple and emotional' person is not the 'man that we want'. To be more precise, he is not the man whom Murray wants. After all, if he was willing to accommodate such a man, then Hellenism would be deprived of its beauty. This said, Murray seems to be resigned to the fact that anthropology has rendered the Greek not only human, but human with warts and all (there is an echo of Nietzsche here, see Chapter 2). The sentiment expressed in his letter of 1900, in contrast, is of a different order. He is in no mood to reach any pragmatic compromise with the anthropologist. Greece has regained its beauty; its message continues to be a 'rational and progressive' force. The permanency of its message to humanity is qualitatively different from the successive and regressive redefinitions that the Hellenism of the preface had to endure. Murray's letter has also substituted the unenthusiastic concession to the inevitability of progress in the form of anthropology with an urgent need for a timely dose of intellectual pugilism. His clarion call ('Thy way be mistaken or vulgar or values [. . .] and I want to speak them out') defines how Murray chose to frame his extremely influential brand of Hellenism during the first four decades of the twentieth century.

The purpose of *The Rise of the Greek Epic* (1907) is a case in point. 'It is an attempt,' according to the author, 'to puzzle out a little more of the meaning of a certain remote age of the world, whose beauty and whose power of inspiration seem to shine the more wonderful the more resolutely we set ourselves to understand it.'[35] Moreover, the fact that Murray believed that 'Greek Lit[erature] contains the genus of almost everything' should be noted. This 'everything-ness' (which Toynbee had also taken on board) is absolutely central to Murray's Hellenic scheme of things. More importantly, it is, to all intents and purposes, a catalogue raisonné of the better or the best qualities that reside in 'Man'. It is their enviable self-restraint,[36] their stoicism,[37] their ingrained attachment to the noble ideas of freedom and justice, their singular aptitude for moving beyond the 'beauty of ornament' and towards the 'beauty of structure [and] the beauty of rightness and simplicity'[38] and, above all, it is their innate ability to construct for themselves a 'humane civilization' which aggregate harmoniously towards rendering the Greeks so valuable 'to the future of the world'. This civilization, Murray is in no doubt, has 'produced on a vast scale what Aristotle calls "a good life for man"; it produced security, law, art, science, philosophy, and religion, expressed in a very extensive and magnificent literature [. . .] we are its children and pupils'.[39] This legacy should not be neglected by the contemporary world: 'When the reasonableness of population control, the necessity of honesty among the judges, the fair treatment of prisoners'[40] have been accepted and implemented by a given society, then, according to Murray, that society has been Hellenized. Moreover, he is unshakeable in his belief that as far as the fruits of the intellectual enquiry are concerned, the Greek cultural outputs are the 'models of a finished and more or less unapproachable perfection'.[41] And what would become of the world, if it were to reject Hellenism and all that it has to offer? Murray in a 'stream-of-consciousness' frame of mind, juxtaposes a miscellany of Hellenism with its unattractive and ultimately futile alternatives:

> These ideas, the pursuit of Truth, Freedom, Beauty, Excellence are not everything. They have been a leaven of unrest in the world; they have held up a light which was not always comforting to the eyes to see. There is another ideal which is generally stronger and may [...] in the end stamp them out as evil things. There is Submission instead of Freedom, the deadening or brutalizing of the senses instead of Beauty, the acceptance of tradition instead of the pursuit of Truth, the belief in hallucination or passion instead of Reason and Temperate Thoughts, the obscuring of distinctions between good and bad and the acceptance of all human beings and all states of mind as equal in value. If something of this kind should prove in the end to be right for man, then Greece will have played the part of the great wrecker in human history.[42]

Another aspect of Murray's appreciation of the Greeks is the tendency to liken the sensibilities and proclivities of the ancient Greeks to those of contemporary Englishmen – often at the expense of other major European nationalities. In a 1941 paper entitled 'Greece and England', Murray asserts that there seems to be a unique love for Hellene that is largely absent on the Continent. When confronted with the mendacity of the everyday political life, the likes of Burke, Peel, Gladstone, Asquith and Baldwin preoccupied themselves with 'considerations more permanent, considerations of *wisdom* or *honour* or magnanimity or maybe of eternal right or wrong'.[43] He also contrasts the gentlemanly and amateurish behaviour of the Englishmen with that of the Germans. Murray recalls an amusing anecdote concerning the words of an anonymous German diplomat, who had allegedly said to his English counterpart, 'you will always be fools and we shall never be gentlemen'.[44] Murray asks: 'Is this British quality or weakness at all particularly Greek?' And he promptly replies: 'I think it is.' In order to substantiate this claim, he cites the occasion when a distinguished Austrian classicist[45] had come to Oxford to give a number of lectures. This visitor, according to an eyewitness Murray, was 'staggered' by the liveliness and the enthusiasm of the students. 'Our men,' Murray concedes, 'were not at all erudite.' They were something much more. 'They were only φιλόσοφοι ["lovers of wisdom"] they liked scholarship. They were φιλόκαλοι ["lovers of beauty"] they cared for beauty [...]. To a German professional scholar they would be mere amateurs, *unmethodisch*, almost *unwissenschaftlich*.'[46] In the quintessential spiritual sense, however, Murray's men had become Greeks.

Broadly speaking, the ingredients constituting Hellenism for Thomson were not qualitatively different from those which were upheld by Murray. Murray had merely added to the superlative qualities of the Greeks. Thomson's notion that Hellenism was predominantly defined by *truth, freedom, reason* and above all *beauty* was only enlarged upon by Murray, who added *humanity, progressiveness, stoicism,* and *perfection.* In other words, Hellenism, as a cultural ideology, became the sole depository of every good and beautiful thing that the human mind can ever possibly fathom (these acquired aesthetic qualities are of some significance and will be discussed in the next chapter). Moreover, Murray, as Toynbee astutely commented some three years after his death, 'identified both the Hellenic genius and modern Western genius with the liberal spirit, and so identified them with each other. This was the master idea that gave unity to all his pursuit.'[47] It was not, however, any old kind of Western liberalism, but its English mutation. It was a school of liberalism that had permitted John Stuart Mill to pronounce without even a hint of irony that 'the battle of Marathon, even as an event in English history, is more important than the battle of Hastings'.[48] It was also that very school of liberalism that had sustained an environment for the lively pronouncements of Murray's young Oxonian lovers of words, wisdom, and beauty.

Although a fuller response to the questions posed at the beginning of this section will be offered in the next chapter, it is useful at this point to make some interim observations. First, the overall response to the position of scientific methods in general and anthropology in particular vis-à-vis Hellenism was, at best, lukewarm. Murray's resignation to the paramountcy of anthropology in 1897 and his subsequent *volte face* are a case in point. Second, while the classical fraternity of the early twentieth century had truly moved on from the Victorian ideas of equating Hellenism with an easily graspable concept of beauty, they had not moved on far enough. Their idea of beauty as directly equatable to a Hellenism that embodied the notions of truth, humaneness, moderation and stoicism was, admittedly, a more complex and sophisticated phenomenon than what had preceded it. It was, however, still a cultural ideology predicated upon a philosophy of beauty; a philosophy of beauty more ornate and nuanced, to be sure, than that which Winckelmann had bestowed to posterity, but a philosophy of beauty all the same.

II – The Works of John Linton Myres: Going Against the Grain?

a) The Early Years: 1900s–1910s

John Linton Myres began his professional life as a historian, anthropologist, geographer, geologist and Hellenist with mainstream Hellenism as his intellectual backdrop. How did he fare? Two years before becoming the Wykeham Professor of Ancient History at New College, Oxford, Myres made his first of many forays into the field of anthropology. In 'Herodotus and Anthropology' (1908), Myres argues that in the period 'between Homer and Herodotus, Greek Reason has come into the world'.[49] In Herodotus, according to him

> we cannot but see a man who meant to be in the best sense 'a mine of information'. But it is the same Herodotus who put it

before him in his title-page 'to discover, besides, the reason they [i.e., Persians and Greeks] fought one another'; and that is why we hail him Father of Anthropology no less than Father of History.[50]

This Herodotean duality of history and anthropology was important to Myres and it went to the very core of his *Weltanschauung*. In his inaugural book, *Greek Lands and the Greek People* (1910), he argues that

> [t]he great problems of history are problems of determining precisely 'what it was that happened', when men, at a parting of the ways, chose deliberately this or that 'apparent good', and so, as we say, 'made history'. These problems are most strictly historical when the element of human choice is preponderant. In proportion as other factors predominate in our estimate of what happened, the problem becomes less one of history, and approximates to the problems of sociology or of human geography.[51]

After all, '[i]n what sense are there *Greek lands*, and in what relation of cause or effect do Greek lands stand to the Greek people? Or, to put it the other way round: Geographically considered, *who were the Greeks?* How did this unique flower of humanity spring into bloom just when it did?' Myres responds that 'this is not, in itself, a historical question; strictly speaking, indeed, it is a question of economic biology'.[52] We are already witnessing here the earliest manifestation of a scientific frame of mind that went on to define much of Myres' future output.

He takes this manifestation a step further in an essay published in the same year entitled 'The Value of Ancient History'. In this work, Myres avers that 'as an investigation of what really happened, [history] is as thoroughly a science as geology or botany'. It is, however, a science of a particular kind; 'it selects those things which happen [to be] of "human interest"'. Moreover, history 'regards only those things as being of interest which are seen to have been instrumental in bringing about "the present".[53] As a direct consequence of this manner of thinking, Myres concludes that history 'is only conceivable on an anthropocentric basis'.[54] Thereafter, Myres establishes the real differences between modern and ancient histories and the particular way in which they should each be approached methodologically. Whereas in modern history it is possible to go 'behind the work of previous historians', in ancient history, such an option does not present itself so readily. In the case of the latter, a great deal of time needs to be allocated to 'rediscover from the historians themselves what were the materials upon which they were working [...] first, how far these materials of theirs represented [...] the real state of the case; and then, how far the periods or topics about which these authors write were the only periods or topics worth studying'.[55] With methods available to 'the historians of modern times' being largely 'insufficient for any reconstruction of antiquity',[56] Myres contends that ancient history, having become a part of 'a wide group of "historical sciences"', is now largely 'concerned with the collection and arrangement of new classes of materials for history'.[57]

In *The Dawn of History* (1911), Myres' first major publication, he reasserts this point more unequivocally by stating that 'the general history of the human race is commonly resigned to another science, Anthropology'.[58] It is within this subordinate status that history holds in relation to anthropology that 'the question, how, when, and where, each of the peoples whose doings have most affected the course of human history made its first historical appearance'[59] can properly be answered. This approach is particularly relevant to an exercise, such as the one covered in this publication, where prehistoric times move towards historic ones 'not suddenly, but by degrees'.[60] Frequently, according to Myres, 'we know a good deal about the art, the trade, and the manufactures of a people, before we know much about their language or their institutions'.[61] There are two chapter titles in this book which are revealing: 'Coming of the Semites' and 'The Coming of the North'. The first, as it clearly suggests, deals with the Semitic peoples and civilizations. The second title, which is much more ambiguous and vague, accounts for emergence onto the scene of peoples of Indo-European descent. In Greece, for instance, 'first was the "Coming of the Achaeans", blonde, fair-skinned giants, "tamers of horses", "shepherds of the people"'.[62] This was followed a century or so later, circa 1100 BC, by another wave of Indo-European migration, namely the 'Dorian invasion'.[63] 'Like Semitic intruders in Babylonia and Syria,' according to Myres, 'these folks of northern nomad origin and "Indo-European" ways of thought, brought with them qualities, traditions, and institutions which offered a new standpoint for looking at Aegean nature, just because in origin they were independent of it. The result was Greece.'[64] This assertion represented a work in progress; some 20 years later, it was given a thorough and more 'scientific' treatment in *Who Were the Greeks?* (see below).

Before all that, however, Myres establishes his anthropological credentials much more fully by producing an overview of the subject-matter. Myres begins his *Influence of Anthropology on the Course of Political Science* (1916) in the following manner:

> Anthropology is the science of Man. Its full task is nothing less than this, to observe and record, to classify and interpret all the activities of all the varieties of this species of living being.

Thereafter, he takes the reader through the various historical and intellectual epochs of anthropology, beginning with ancient Greece, travelling via the Renaissance and right through to the modern academic treatment of the subject in his day. This exercise allowed Myres to conclude that '[e]ach fresh start on the never-ending quest of *Man as he ought to be* has been the response of theory to fresh facts about *Man as he is*'.[65] According to the author, this is science at work. When the 'perspective of anthropology shift[s] and the standpoint of observation advance[s]', then what was seen 'as problems' simply melt away: 'This is no new experience; nor is it peculiar either to anthropology among natural sciences, or to political science among the aspects of the study of man. It is the common law of the mind's growth, which all science manifests, and all philosophy.'[66]

b) The Formative Years: 1920–1930

By the 1920s, Myres' dual perspective of ancient history/Hellenism and science/anthropology became thoroughly entrenched. To the first volume of *The Cambridge Ancient History: Egypt and Babylonia to 1580 BC* (1924), Myres contributed two chapters ('Primitive Man, in Geological Time' and 'Neolithic and Bronze Age Culture'). These entirely pre- and non-Indo-European discussions of prehistory had very little to do, in the strictest sense, with the discipline of ancient history; they were used solely to set the scene for the impending chapters. Within the context of Myres' published *oeuvre*, however, this work takes what had preceded it since *The Dawn of History* to a new analytical level, thus demonstrating the author's serious intent and credentials beyond the disciplines of classicism or Hellenism; it essentially foretold what was to come in 1930. In addition, after being the RAI's honorary secretary for some years, Myres became its president in 1928. In other words, Myres' ability to bestride two very (seemingly) different academic disciplines could no longer be doubted. As we shall see, it had a number of unpredictable and interesting consequences.

The more straightforward or orthodox form of Hellenism in Myres' work is best represented by his 1927 publication, *The Political Ideas of the Greeks*. He begins by way of a contrast. The Greek political legacy and folk-memory is discussed alongside those of the 'Hebrews'. 'Hebrew philosophy,' according to Myres, is a subtly compounded essence of the Wisdom of the Ancient East.' Greek philosophy 'is in the same way the Wisdom of the Mediterranean region'.[67] There is, however, a fundamental difference between these two wisdoms:

> [W]hile it is on its political side that Greek thought has been most obviously operative, and Hebrew thought in its moral aspect, it is essential that we should realize that the political thought of Greece stands as intimately related to a characteristic conception of individual morality as Hebrew morals are to the political philosophy of the Theocratic State.[68]

This tendency to counterpoint the Greeks with the Jews, as discussed in Chapter 2, was very much in vogue during this period. Although much more circumspect in making unsubstantiated assertions than either Mathew Arnold or Nietzsche, Myres is not averse to situating the Jews well within the geography of the Ancient East, 'with its great river-valley cultures, its Semitic nomad-pastoral motive-power, and its "theocratic" organization'.[69] Furthermore, in order to understand this uniquely Greek and non-Semitic 'conception of individual morality', Myres, after accounting for the 'main phases of Greek history',[70] analyses, in some detail, a number of salient political 'notions' of the Greeks.

Polis (society) was an ever-changing phenomenon. It 'originated in tribal society, and represents a rearrangement of tribal units in a new political relation to each other.'[71] The Homeric conurbations of the Heroic Age, for instance, were entirely different from those of the more sophisticated *polis* of the fourth century. *Themis* (ordinance), according to Myres, was *the* prerequisite for citizenship. It 'formulates a normal mode of behaviour, and supplies guidance in repairing a breach in normal behaviour'.[72] This in turn is supplemented by *arkhé* (initiative), an ability to 'push', to 'drive', to have 'vim', to be able to 'get things done'.[73] *Diké* (justice) defines the nature of the 'way a thing happens'. It is, among other things, 'the clearest ruling on the point of custom which governs the matter in question'. It is 'a ruling of a judge or other wise men on a dispute between parties'.[74] And in order to have justice, one must also have the regulative function of the law. *Physis* and *nomos* are, respectively, the customary and natural laws, which an efficient *polis* would invariably require. All the above notions go on to fortify the final two notions: *eleutheria* (liberty) and its flip side, *isonomia* ('equity of allotment'). By allowing 'equality in public meeting' and 'in public speech', liberty, in Myres' scheme of things, becomes the midwife of what truly defines Hellenism: 'Grown-up-ness', in Myres' lexicon.[75] These concisely presented 'notions', in a manner of speaking, can arguably be seen as the more specific and precise categorizations of what he had alluded to so forcefully in 1911, namely the 'Indo-European ways of thoughts' that had resulted in Greece.[76]

The type of analysis which Myres had adopted in 1927, although still well within the orthodox boundaries of Hellenism, differed in two ways from the general trend discussed in section I. First, it had nothing of substance to say concerning the aesthetic qualities of the Greeks. Myres' 'notions' were neither reliant, as in the case of Livingstone, on beauty nor were they a function of 'a style of scholarship which consist[s] essentially in the perception of beauty, and to some extent in the representation of it'.[77] Second, and more importantly, Myres, the anthropologist, was always present. The very first sentence of this book reads: 'Man is always trying to live well.'[78] Again, what underpins Myres' work was his preoccupation with 'Man'. This fixation with what 'Man', or to be precise, what the Greek man (not person) was and wanted to do or become took centre stage in arguably his most important work, *Who Were the Greeks?* (1930). It begins unambiguously:

> The purpose of these lectures is to examine the Greeks' own beliefs about their origin, in the light of modern advances in the study of race, language, religious beliefs, arts and crafts, observances and institutions: to supplement and revise their notions from sources of information and method of enquiry not available in antiquity; to take note of our own ignorance in many of these matters; and to submit a program of research.[79]

The desire to understand Greece or the Greeks' sense of themselves by examining new 'sources of information' is not particularly noteworthy. After all, Murray and his like-minded contemporaries were not averse to infusing their works with recently revealed sources of information. What makes Myres almost unique is his propensity to give serious considerations to a 'method of enquiry' which gave due attention to 'the study of race, language, [and] religious beliefs'. Moreover, he was not altogether unreceptive to the accepted view of Hellenism. 'In the representative art,' Myres opines, 'we are confronted [...] with the Greek conception of human beauty, physical perfection of anatomical type, based on intimate observation of what we shall find to have been living types among the artists' contemporaries'.[80] There are faint echoes of Winckelmann here, but he qualifies this by stating that 'by looking rather deeper, below the surface of literary and artistic achievement, we learn to know the Greeks as exponents of a Greek "view of life", based on the mode of life austerely imposed on them by the rigid conditions of their geographical surroundings'.[81] This keen interest in space and time – 'regional distribution and historical spread', as discussed in Chapter 3 – is indicative of the importance that Myres had always attached to a scientific 'method of enquiry'.

As is often the case with Myres, it all begins with Herodotus. Taking his cue directly from the historian, Myres devotes the bulk of his lectures on what had defined Greekness for Herodotus: Common Descent, Common Language, Common Beliefs and Common Culture (Myres also introduces Common Abode into his framework). He does, however, subject these categories of Greekness to the most relevant scientific approaches that were available in the 1920s. 'Physical Anthropology' is brought in to deal with 'descent'; 'Comparative Philology' with 'language'; 'Comparative Religion' with 'beliefs'; and 'Prehistoric Archaeology' with material 'culture'.[82]

What were the inferences that were drawn from this multi-layered and multifaceted exercise? The overarching inference was a straightforward one: racially, linguistically and culturally, the Greeks had a mixed and not a very pure 'Greek' (Indo-European) heritage. First, no particular racial type, according to Myres, was the definition of Greekness. Within the Greek racial profile, the Mediterranean, the Alpine, the Armenoid and the Nordic types were all represented throughout the ages, with many coming in a variety of skull shapes. Second, although an Indo-European language, at least 40 per cent of the Greek vocabulary contains 'words which are not recognised as belonging to any Indo-European root or stem'.[83] Myres, therefore, opts to examine the non-Greek elements of the language and as a consequence looks closely at a number of relevant languages, both Indo-European and non-Indo-European. In his view, it was the movement of the 'Indo-European speaking peoples' from the north into Asia Minor and the Greek archipelago that was the beginning of the Homeric or Dorian Greek. Third, the belief system was an amalgam of the pre- and non-Indo-European elements (mostly Minoan and Egyptian) together with those of Greek Indo-European ones, such as the 'Olympian and Heroic' entities. Finally, the analysis of 'the material cultures of the Aegean shows a confluence of elements derived respectively from other shores of the Mediterranean, from the continental interior of Asia Minor, from the Danubian cultures [...] and from the "painted-ware" culture of the steppe region'.[84] In other words, and in every relevant area of human endeavour, Greece was a composite of both Greek and non-Greek elements.

Some of the inferences drawn by Myres, such as those based on cranioskeletal and dermatoglyphic evidence, are no longer academically tenable. But these retrospective shortcomings do not explain the reason why this work, despite its positive reception at the time of its publication,[85] fell into historiographical neglect. It cannot be underlined sufficiently that the real importance of Myres' work in general and this 1930 publication in particular, lies elsewhere. It is not the 'enquiry' itself or the results of that 'enquiry' that is of any durable value or interest to this narrative and beyond, but the 'methods' adopted to pursue this 'enquiry' which are of immense relevance. This chapter is primarily concerned with the manner in which Myres approached the study of Ancient Greece. It is his multifaceted scientific methodology that renders him historiographically an interesting subject for scrutiny and investigation. Myres marshalled the sciences of geography, anthropology, comparative philology, comparative religion and myth and archaeology in order to ascertain what had gone into forming the peoples of Ancient Greece. As a consequence, a number of approaches, many of which were beginning to be accepted as decidedly scientific, were extensively used for this overarching purpose.

Geography was brought in to discuss the 'Common Abode' of the Greeks. Where the Greeks dwelled is of some significance to Myres because it is

> a region of peculiar structure and configuration, climate, and resources; minutely subdivided and presenting so many different types of environment locally that it is itself a *microcosmus*, a

miniature universe; almost competent to maintain human communities self-sufficiently, and consequently fertile in solutions of the supreme question 'how to live well'; but never immune against intrusion.[86]

It is precisely this likelihood of 'intrusion' that makes Myres' comparative analyses (language, religion, and myth) compelling and crucial to his broader Hellenism.

The anticipated link between physical anthropology and comparative philology is asserted categorically in the first few pages of the book:

> We shall find that one outstanding contrast in physical type between the classical Greeks and both their predecessors and their successors demands special consideration, and points to the Greek language as likely to furnish the clue to an explanation, through its structure and the geographical distribution of its dialects.[87]

The physical anthropological approach produced, unsurprisingly, very few clear-cut inferences; hence the need to introduce comparative philology into the scheme of things. All the available data on the physical aspects of the human types were used by Myres. Although he followed the academic orthodoxy of the day, nonetheless what he was able to infer was, at best, sketchy and inconclusive. The matrix of analysing the available skull types (quantified and compared by 'cephalic indices'), the broad racial categorization and their geographical distributions, the evidence concerning complexion,[88] hair and beard, as well as the historical veracity or otherwise of the existence of the classical ideal of beauty ('broad oval face, high upright forehead, full jaw and chin, recurved and sometimes almost sensuous lips, and its narrow straight nose descending in the same line with the forehead'[89]), yielded precious little. In consequence, Myres concluded: 'we have to look for some fresh source of evidence, as to early relations between Aegean and the regions north and south of it, the Mediterranean shores and the home of "northern" man beyond the Danube.' The examination of the former, according to Myres, is an archaeological undertaking (see below), but that of the latter — since 'we are confronted at once with the fact that Greek is an Indo-European language'[90] — requires a philological approach. It is worthwhile noting here that when a particular 'scientific' methodology (physical anthropology) proved less than entirely satisfactory, Myres did not hesitate to use other 'scientific' methodologies in order to augment or bolster the main tenets of his arguments.[91]

After giving the required background concerning the pre-Hellenic languages, Myres discusses, at some length, the 'first appearance of Indo-European speech in the Near East'.[92] The arrival of Indo-European speech in an environment already replete with other well-formed, pre-Indo-European languages shaped only the beginning of his analysis. Other, more distant, Indo-European languages were brought in for the comparative purposes of locating and understanding the mechanisms through which the relevant Greek languages or dialects were 'conserved and propagated'.[93] Myres, as a consequence, was able to account for the way in which these various Greek dialects were distributed geographically.[94]

In the domain of comparative religion, Myres is keen to distinguish between the 'principal elements in Greek religious beliefs, and ask which, if any of them are connected with the people who introduced the Greek language'.[95] Again we have gone full circle, back to the centrality of language and its conceptual inseparability from that of belief systems. After detailing the existence of the Near Eastern influences in Greece, Myres contrasts the 'Olympian deities in their mature form'[96] with other Indo-European gods and concludes that the Olympian gods have their immediate counterparts 'in Norse, and (above all) in Iranian belief, wherein it is only if all good things, and good men, do their utmost in support of the source and champion of all good, that the good cause can ultimately win'.[97] In addition, a number of deific traits are examined anthropologically, such as heroic behaviours, religious rituals and 'the personal appearance of Olympian gods'.

One of the key components in Myres' framework was the archaeological analysis of the material civilization of the Greek lands. It is the close scrutiny of what caused the 'important breaks' in the course of a number of cultural developments that can provide interested parties, according to Myres, with an explanation concerning 'the movements of all bodies of people competent to occasion changes of physical breed, of language, or of religious belief, of the kind already detected'.[98] In other words, archaeology for Myres was an indispensable tool for verifying this hypothetical construct. Here Myres dons his prehistorian hat and analyses all the relevant archaeological finds of Asia Minor, the Greek archipelago, the Danubean basin and much of the Near East within the temporal contexts of the Stone, Bronze and Iron Ages. The systematic approach is undertaken primarily to ascertain the way in which the indigenous populations of the Greek lands handled the repeated arrival of various peoples and their corresponding material cultures. Or putting it differently, what interests Myres is how they had managed to amalgamate and harmonize all the new inputs into what became recognizable as unmistakably Greek.

Having conducted this 'reconstruction of the historical origins of the Greek people', Myres aimed to test it 'by comparing it with the principal outlines of Greek traditional folk-memory';[99] or rather to estimate the degree to which folk memory and Myres' scientific conclusions corresponded. The desire on the part of the author to verify his scientific findings by cross-referring them with the available historical and other data is noteworthy. Myres carries this out by going back to Homer, by analysing the genealogies of Helen and other deities and, most importantly, by setting up a methodology to enquire whether or not and to what extent philological results concerning Greek dialects corresponded to folk-memory. Myres found that they correlated to a significant degree, but what makes this relevant for the purposes of this monograph is not that correlation in itself, but that the investigations were carried out within the methodological boundaries of anthropology, archaeology and, in particular, comparative philology.

Of course, this methodological endeavour, in its imposing totality, has an overriding purpose: it is to ascertain *who the Greeks were*. The final two chapters, entitled 'The Crucible and the Mould' and 'The Making of a Nation', attempt exactly that. As discussed extensively in Chapter 3, Myres regarded a given 'people' (say the Greeks) as a complex and dynamic amalgam of 'race' and 'culture'. His various methodological analyses in this work led Myres to conclude that Ancient Greece was the product of a number of disparate and varied racial and cultural components, hence 'the crucible and the mould'. Moreover, in the process of making this nation, the Indo-European ingredient was only one among many. Culturally and intellectually, however, it was its most important and consequential ingredient: it provided the Greeks with a new 'way of thought'. Thus, the Herodotean quartet of what constituted Greekness, namely blood, language, belief and customs, could only be adequately explained, in Myres' framework, within the compass of a comparative approach that took full account of this phenomenon.

c) *The Mature Years: 1930s*

Two further publications – *The Man of Science and the Science of Man* (1933) and the chapter in Edward Eyre's *European Civilization* (1935) entitled 'The Ethnology, Habitat, Linguistic, and Common Culture of Indo-Europeans up to the Time of the Migration' – go on to buttress the analyses which were pursued in *Who Were the Greeks?*

As late as 1933, Myres seems to have been exasperated by the reluctance on the part of the old universities to accommodate the newer scientific disciplines. Whereas physics and zoology, for instance, were absorbed by mathematics and medicine respectively, neither anthropology nor geography could be added to the 'old classical courses'. Philology and archaeology, according to Myres, had similar institutional problems:

> Philology, in the sense of scientific study of languages, was for a long while not very scientific, and borrowed more from classical 'scholarship' than it had to give in return. Archaeology was as slow to distinguish itself from art-criticism, as art-criticism was from the use of works of art to grangerize[100] classical literature. As an instrument of education, therefore, much of

the teaching of science was allegorical [...] people said one thing but meant another.[101]

It is worth noting that the disciplines for which Myres is arguing are precisely those disciplines which were indispensable to the overarching methodology of his intellectual life's work. What is of primary interest here is the level of confidence that Myres possessed in tackling the broad subject of 'science' by dealing directly with the issues of science in the fields of business, leisure, education, and modern life.[102] This was not, even remotely, the type of intellectual interest that one would have expected from a professional Hellenist of the day.

Much that is discussed in his 1935 chapter had been touched upon by Myres some 20 years earlier in *Influence of Anthropology in the Course of Political Science*. In this work, Myres expounds at some length upon the various theories of the geographical co-ordinates of the 'Aryan Home'[103] and, for instance, quotes approvingly from Henry Maine's *Ancient Law* (1861) that although patriarchy was prevalent in Semitic cultures, 'the legal evidence comes nearly exclusively from the institutions of societies belonging to the Indo-European stock'.[104] What the 1935 chapter does, as the title implies, is to go through the various aspects of the Indo-European peoples and cultures with greater deliberation. There are two interesting observations to be made here. First, in a work that deals with the 'European civilization', Myres sees nothing wrong with analysing those Indo-Europeans residing outside geographical Europe, namely some of the Indo-Iranians.[105] Europe, in the context of this publication at least, was much less of a tightly-defined geographical concept and more of a cultural and linguistic one than it is today. Second, even for a discussion on the Indo-Europeans, he follows the Herodotean classificatory system (genealogy, language, culture, etc.), and as a consequence, his analysis concerning the 'origin of the Greek people'[106] is contextualized within the larger question of the nature, origin and cradle of the Indo-Europeans. In other words, his depiction of the Hellenic world is, yet again, represented in such a way that it would have surprised and baffled those of more conventional leanings.

It is fairly safe to surmise at this point that the scientific approach was the intellectual and methodological driving force behind Myres' assessment of what had given form to Hellenism. To all intents and purposes, Hellenism, in his scheme, became a function of science; or to be more precise, it became a function of the 'science of man'. And anthropology, as discussed, was seldom far from the core of Myres' thinking. Indeed, his division of the areas of analysis in *Who Were the Greeks?* mirrored the division of the discipline of anthropology quite closely (see Chapter 3). But what had happened to the discipline of history? Was this professor of ancient history truly willing to conclude that all that was required was anthropology? Myres does offer an explanation of a sort in his 1911 work: 'the general history of the human race is commonly resigned to another science, Anthropology.'[107] This remark is significant for two reasons: first, it makes history subordinate to anthropology and not its substitute, and second it implies that history should also be considered as a science. But what this work is primarily interested in is Hellenism. So how does Hellenism fit into all of this? Or, putting it differently: where and how does Hellenism sit on this anthropology–history continuum? There is a fairly lengthy unpublished paper in Myres' archives, written in 1935,[108] that may shed some light on these questions.

'Hellenism in the Treatment of History' is a curious title. On its own it suggests not only a Hellenism that stands outside the discipline of history, but a particular variety of history that can only operate within a Hellenic context. In other words, Hellenism in this context has become a tool for organizing some of the philosophical and intellectual constituents of the discipline of history. To what extent can a close reading of this unpublished text substantiate these initial intuitive assumptions? Myres begins his paper by taking one of his immediate contemporaries, William Inge (1860–1954), to task. Myres is puzzled by Inge's insistence that 'the Greeks showed an intelligent curiosity about the past, but [...] they did not take time seriously'.[109] Furthermore, Myres disputes Inge's belief that 'a philosopher may be classified by his attitudes towards events in time, and by his estimate of the status of time in reality'.[110] Myres has a twofold response to this. First, 'Greek History, like all else that is Greek, has its value for posterity, by reason of its Greek-ness. It is one of the many aspects, of Greek genius, the Greek view of life.'[111] Second, and connected to this, 'Hellenism in history, then, is an aspect of whatever Hellenism was in science, in art, in morals and polities'.[112] Following from these premises, it becomes possible to characterize Hellenism in a particular way. First, according to Myres, it can be best put colloquially thus: 'wide-eyed comprehension of all that matters'.[113] It is the ideal nature of the city state, 'the increased pleasure in common things' and the consideration that time is 'the momentary between coming into being and passing away' that make this 'wide-eyed comprehensiveness' of Hellenism so readily attainable. 'A second characteristic of Hellenism,' in Myres' opinion, 'is literally grown-up-ness, adult-ness, like the libertas of a Roman citizen's liberi, his grown-up self-possessing sons.'[114]

With the definitions of Hellenism out of the way, Myres embarks upon examining the Greeks' understanding of chronology. 'The specific opinion that "the Greeks did not take time seriously",' in his view

> appears to overlook the fundamental constitutions of the Greek astronomical science of chronology, and of Greek genealogical research to supply their astronomical time piece with a minute-hand, so to speak, for the measurement of shorter intervals, and of Greek improvement in the calendar, which added a second-hand for intervals shorter even than Thucydides' war-time reckoning by summers and winters.[115]

Consequently, bearing in mind that the Greeks were more than adequate timekeepers, Myres finds 'Dr Inge's Definition of History' hugely problematic. He sets up Inge's position in the following manner:

> Dr Inge comes to the conclusion that the 'Great Tradition' in philosophy, which he appears to expound and commend, 'leaves to history the limited but surely quite adequate task of tracing the life, habits, beliefs, and aspirations of the species to which we happen to belong [. . .]'. In this 'limited task', he thinks that

'there can be no exact science of history, because we cannot deduce, from what we know of the past, causal laws of general application', that 'there can be no presentations of facts without valuation', and science itself 'concentrates upon truth, which is one of the absolute or intrinsic values'; that therefore 'a historian cannot promise to be impartial', but 'he can promise to be candid', and he 'has the right to interpret and appraise events, to the best of his ability, that is his business'. In this 'surely quite adequate task' for history, did the Greeks contribute anything either of method or content?[116]

Having presented Inge's arguments in this way, Myres proceeds to analyse them critically and, more crucially, with reference to his methodological approach to the subjects of history and Hellenism:

It is not quite clear from all this, in what category, other than 'exact science' Dr Inge places all those branches of knowledge which lie between the most nearly biological outskirts of organic or physiological chemistry, where experimental verification and prognostication becomes complicated by the differences between living and dead cells and the most nearly psychological outskirts of moral and political studies, where experimental treatment of mental reactions begins to be complicated by interactions between two or more minds.[117]

Myres concurs with Inge that it is unlikely that 'with our present method and equipment' we are able 'to deduce from what we know [...] causal laws of general application'.[118] He does, however, warn that even the biological science, with its focus on organism and environment, cannot do without enquiring 'how the organism, and also the environment came to be as they are'. This in turn compels the observer to examine not only the ability of an organism to survive in a given environment, but also the manner of its survival – in what 'particular grade in a scale of organisations'. Thus, the question of 'valuation' and 'subjective judgement' (areas which Inge regards as not belonging to natural science) all of a sudden are no longer out-of-bounds to the 'exact science'. Myres, therefore, is categorical: 'The distinction between history and other forms of knowledge is not an absolute line, but a graduated flatland.'[119]

'One reason why it may be difficult for a philosopher to detect a historical aspect among the multifarious expressions of Hellenism in extent literature,' in Myres' view,

> is that philosophers sometimes speak of science, or the sciences as if their aims and methods were uniformly the same; whereas a historian is necessarily aware of a broad contrast between two main kinds of approach to scientific problems, or rather between two main kinds of approach to scientific problems, or rather between two main kinds of scientific problems, to which the method of approach is necessarily different.[120]

Here again (see Chapter 3) Myres is extra careful about how he presents the nuances between these two kinds of scientific approach. From Chapter 3, as well as from the above analysis of his 1933 publication, Myres divides his sciences into two groups: *systematic* and *distributional*. Mathematics, physics, chemistry and biology are typical examples of this category. Myres quotes Aristotle's *Ethics*: 'Fire burns here and in Persia; has burned at Troy and Persepolis; and will burn as long as the natural world remains what it is.'[121] The distributional sciences

> are concerned with the distribution and especially the co-distribution of the objects and processes with the qualities and changes of which the *systematic* sciences deal. They are not concerned at all with *what* happens, but solely with *when* it happens or *where*; and further with the questions *when* does it happen *here* or *there*, and *where* does it happen *now* or *then*.[122]

These distributional sciences can further be divided into historical and geographical sciences. This would allow them to deal 'with temporal sequences and spatial extension'.[123] He also advises that in these forms of sciences, experiments are not the norm; in fact, they are generally precluded. This is so because 'any human interference with natural co-distributions damages the order of nature on the course of events; bringing the observer or experimenter himself into the distribution which he is trying to investigate; and introducing a factor [that] is usually almost unknown'. In order to underpin his argument, Myres quotes Heraclitus: '"you cannot cross the same river twice."'[124] Myres' analysis does not end here. In order to bolster it, he incorporates the work of one of his contemporaries, the philosopher of history R. G. Collingwood:

> Whatever its place among the sciences may be, History is not very easy to define, nor even to describe, and a mere historian's definition of it might not be accepted as a basis of discussion. But fortunately, within the last few months, Professor Collingwood, historian and philosopher in one, has formulated afresh the philosophical basis of history, and defined the historian's aims and procedure. And I propose to take his description point by point, and illustrate it by familiar extracts from Greek historians.[125]

Myres believes that Collingwood's understanding of history chimes with his own assessment of it:

> [it] differs from experimental science, in that the historian is never concerned, as is the laboratory-worker, with something that exists here and now. The first twenty chapters of Thucydides [...] illustrate, even better than Herodotus's account of Athenian & Spartan origins the depth of historical perspective which a Greek historian might presume in his readers, as well as assume for himself.[126]

In order to substantiate these assertions, Myres quotes Collingwood:

> whereas science lives in a world of abstract universals [...] the things about which the historian reasons are not abstract but concrete, not universal but individual, not indifferent to space

and time, but having a where and a when of their own; though the where need not be here, and the when cannot be now.

History then is 'wholly a reasoned knowledge of what is transient and concrete'. Of this concreteness in Greek history writing, Myres gives the reader a familiar instance: 'Herodotus, after reviewing what have been described as the *cherchez la femme* theory and the *East is East and West is West* theory of the clash between Greeks and Persians, sets both alike aside.'[127]

At this point in the discussion, Myres poses an interesting question: 'But how are the historian's fixed points themselves fixed?'[128] He considers the Greek historiographical tradition or 'historical thinking', and in particular that of Herodotus, as resembling the way in which a prey can be 'spoored'. In other words, it would not be sufficient merely 'to interpolate the continuous process of animals' wanderings from the discontinuous footprints of the trail; but to prognosticate whether the game has now gone, either straight ahead [...] or alternating to right or to left'.[129] The manner in which an experienced hunter can determine the approximate co-ordinates of his prey in time and space without interfering with it is analogous, in Myres' view and in Collingwood's phrase, to a historian's inherent need for 'the web of imaginative construction':

> 'The web of imaginative construction' in Collingwood's words, 'is something far more solid and powerful than we have hitherto realized': for 'just as there are properly speaking no authorities, so there are properly speaking no data.' So far as anything is given, 'historical thought gives it to itself' as a result or achievement of historical thinking.[130]

This being said, Myres introduces an important proviso at this juncture of his analysis:

> But unlike the constructions of the novelist or the dramatist [...] 'history' must be consistent with all these autonomous gifts of historical thinking to itself: for 'there is only [a]

historical world', located in space and time, most obviously so in the sky-clear retrospect of astronomy; less obviously to historians perhaps, but still appreciable by physicist, chemist, in geology; and needing at times to be explained by one philosopher to another, in geography, in history.

Historical structures, then, either must agree with the evidence, or must be so constructed that this or that which is offered in evidence so fails to cohere or construe with it, that the historian can reject and ignore it as an anachronism or a fake. Every geological prospector has had to deal with puzzles of this kind – and most excavators.[131]

Myres is keen at this point not to leave the reader in any doubt concerning the following two conceptual underpinnings. First, he contends that the place of history among the sciences can no longer be disputed with any vigour. 'If anyone now doubts whether history as Collingwood sees it in its place among the sciences, and its relation to the philosophy of history, and (what is no less important) to the history of history, was or was not practised, as a science alike and as an art,' Myres invites them to review 'the aims and methods' of the Greek writers for themselves.[132] If they carry out this task judiciously, then the 'wide-eyed comprehensiveness' of Hellenism becomes all too apparent and fathomable. He is adamant that it is necessary 'to collate [the] words and phrases from the [Greek] physicists and physicians, as well as from historians contemporary with them, because it is not proper, nor indeed possible, to put Greek studies of history into perspective without reference to other kinds of scientific methods'.[133] The second point which Myres wants to underscore is that empiricism is the most important defining characteristic of bona fide history:

The preliminary distinction too must be made, as in all departments of knowledge, and of life, between a) ideal aims and logical methods, on the one side, and b) attempts, more or less successful, to realise and apply them. The fact that many of Francis Bacon's speculations seem to us frivolous, and his experiments futile, does not seriously detract from his eminence as a pioneer in inductive method. The cumulative structure of knowledge scientific and historical alike, with which Herodotus set out in his [Histories] was fragmentary, incoherent, and for the most part ill-attested, by modern critical standards.[134]

But – and this is a pivotal point for Myres – this should not detract from the correctness and innovativeness of the adopted methodologies.

The overriding purpose of this paper, as the title suggests, is Hellenism. Or to be more precise, it is the 'history as science' which Hellenism proper usually gives rise to:

> Whatever Hellenism has done for History has indeed been only one phase of what Hellenism has done for Humanity, in its supreme activity of Humanism; itself the corollary of Greek acuity and clarity of observation; appreciation of forms and what they called 'rhythm', in nature and in the works of Man; freedom of thought and speech, and tolerant recognition of the same right in other men; right judgement, and especially right opinion about the judgements of others. Precision, directness and restraint of expression, in speech and by every other means; and a general interest in life, universal and profound, responsive to the smallest opportunity in the Greek world and among Greek people for the qualities and achievements proper to human beings, regarded as being innate in themselves fundamentally good, and competent, if endowed with their fair share of this world's external goods, to realise their goodness by their good will.[135]

III – Analysis

A number of questions come to mind at this point in the discussion. First, to what extent can a linear progression towards greater scientific methodology be ascertained from Myres' main body of work? Second, if such a trend can be verified, then how did history,

Myres' main preoccupation, react to it and interact with it? And finally, what was Hellenism's role in all these?

At the beginning of his academic career, Myres seems to have been trying on for size the various scientific terminologies that were available to him. By moving from 'economic biology' to 'human geography' and anthropocentrism before settling for the all-embracing anthropology, Myres was effectively situating his analysis of the ancient world, both institutionally and methodologically, within an unmistakable scientific context. Looking at Myres' works chronologically, one can decipher a tightening of methodological focus beginning with the ascendancy of anthropology over and above history in 1911, through the anthropological overview of 1916 and the prehistoric rendition of 1924, the multifaceted and complex scientific treatment of 1930, and culminating in the confident pronouncements of an increasingly self-assured scientist of 1933 and 1935. So how was this focus tightening? Myres managed to move from a vague assertion concerning the importance of scientific thinking – such as the paternity of history and anthropology belonging to Herodotus – towards a more detailed and complex application of that scientific thinking in the analyses carried out in his 1930 *magnum opus*. It is worth emphasizing at this point that at the apex of this approach resided an all-encompassing 'scientific method of enquiry'. This method, admittedly, did not filter out what were shown later to have been faulty and dubious inferences. Despite this, its central role was not to guarantee the quality of the inferences drawn, but to equip the whole undertaking with scientific rigour; and in my view, it succeeded in doing exactly that. After all, as Thomas Kuhn argues in *The Structure of Scientific Revolutions* (1962), 'out-of-date theories', such as Aristotelian dynamics for instance, 'are not in principle unscientific because they have been discarded'.[136] In other words, what can be profitably gleaned from Myres' works are not his many and varied and often incorrect conclusions, but the manner in which he had set up his framework for the purposes of reaching those conclusions. Moreover, Myres, as his comments above concerning Bacon and Herodotus show, was entirely cognizant of the inevitable pitfalls which one would invariably encounter when the consequences of the growth in the aggregate body of knowledge and methods begin to manifest themselves.

Why this fixation with science matters and how it relates to history and, more peculiarly, to Hellenism are conundrums to which Myres' unpublished paper may provide some possible answers. Myres begins 'Hellenism in the Treatment of History' by introducing the concept of time. This almost modern fascination with time[137] fulfils a twofold function. First, it is a concept which lends itself to both science and history rather well, thus binding them together philosophically. Second, since this takes the form of what he calls the 'distributional sciences' (which 'are not concerned with *what* happens, but solely with *when* it happens or *where*'), Myres is also highlighting Inge's reluctance to differentiate between different modes of scientific exercises ('It is not quite clear [...] in what category Dr Inge places all those branches of knowledge which lie between the most nearly biological outskirts of organic and physiological chemistry [...] and the most nearly psychological outskirts of moral and political studies').

Proceeding from entrenching this distinction between distributional and systematic sciences, Myres goes on to tackle three interrelated ideas. First, he fortifies and legitimizes the centrality and importance of scientific thinking for a better understanding of the historical world by subdividing the distributional sciences into historical and geographical sciences, as well as warning against any 'human interference with the natural co-distributions' of things. Second, and in direct relation to this, history, if not rethought anew, is, at the very least, reconsidered from a fresher perspective – that of Robin G. Collingwood. After giving numerous examples from Herodotus and Thucydides, Myres considers Collingwood's concept of the 'web of imaginative construction' as a very helpful way of thinking about a 'historical world' located within space and time. This is so because the engendered 'historical structures' need to cohere with the available historical evidence (this is precisely how *Who Were the Greeks?* was structured). Finally, the Hellenistic historical approach itself, according to Myres, was not too dissimilar from what he and Collingwood were advocating. Greek historical thinking in Myres' assessment can be, metaphorically, likened to a hunter spooring a prey: it would not be sufficient merely 'to interpolate the continuous process of the animal's wanderings from the discontinuous footprints of the trail; but to prognosticate whether the game has now gone, either straight ahead [...] or alternating to right or to left'.[138] This analysis implies that the Greek tradition had, already and more than adequately, factored in not only historical re-enactments, but also − because of what is involved in the practice of spooring − an appreciation of time and space. In other words, the 'distributional sciences' were well understood by the Greeks.

How, then, should Myres' methodologies be judged? His published works, in my opinion, have demonstrated the growing influence of a scientific mode of enquiry in ascertaining matters and phenomena pertaining to ancient Greece. Looked at in this way, science seems to be underpinning Hellenism. The analysed archival paper, in contrast, gives a somewhat contradictory perspective. It argues that when Hellenism is examined within the contours of Greek historical writing, one can only infer that this form of historical writing was, to all intents and purposes, implicitly scientific. Here, Hellenism seems to be underpinning history. So what is the overarching inference from these deductions? It is an inescapable inference that science, history and Hellenism (in Myres' vocabulary: 'distributional sciences', 'web of imaginative construction' and the metaphor of 'spooring', respectively) are inexorably and tightly linked in Myres' framework. As a result, these three concepts can best be comprehended as a *triangular relationship*, transcending the simple binary linkages between them. Indeed, by constantly utilizing Herodotus' classifications, but examining them 'in the light of modern advances in the study of race, language, religious beliefs, arts and crafts, observances and institutions', Myres situates his analyses well within this conceptual triangle. Moreover, by classifying history as a branch of science and equipping Hellenism with the attributes of the 'distributional sciences', Myres, in my judgement, seems to also be offering a fundamentally novel way by which to examine the ancient world and asking the kinds of questions that – entirely due to the manner in which he chose to conceptualize Hellenism – were not available to Murray.

It can be countered that the distinction made between Myres' 'scientific' approach and Murray's and Thomson's 'aesthetic' Hellenism is not entirely tenable. After all, does Myres not use similar superlative definitions for Hellenism as Murray and those affiliated to him? Surely, Myres' celebration of Greek humanism and its 'corollary of Greek acuity and clarity of observation', along with their 'freedom of thought and speech, and tolerant recognition of the same right in other men'[139] are aspects of Hellenism with which Murray can only concur wholeheartedly in recognizing and lauding. In addition, is it not also true that many of the writings of the more orthodox Hellenists are very much informed by the 'scientific' methodologies, discoveries and analyses as carried out by anthropologists, ethnologists, archaeologists and linguists? Is it not, therefore, invalid to depict their works as residing primarily in the domain of aestheticism and thus dismiss them as insufficiently scientific?

It is entirely correct to state that Myres, as a trained classicist, celebrated the contributions of the Greeks in as carefree a manner as many other classicists throughout the ages. It is equally true that Murray's work had indeed benefited from other, more scientific, academic disciplines. Thomson, in a 1936 essay honouring Gilbert Murray, entitled 'The Present and Future of Classical Scholarship', argues that the 'controversy about the relative importance in education of Science and the Classics' is now over. This is so because 'classical scholarship, which used to be an art, is becoming a science'.[140] Thomson asserts that the 'comparative study of language, palaeontology, epigraphy, archaeology, the study of art in bronze and clay and marble, numismatology [...] are now pursued by methods at least as scientific as those achieved in certain branches of psychology, sociology or political economy'.[141] This said, Thomson concurs with Myres that Hellenism – or, to be precise, 'classical scholarship' – is 'both an art and a science', but warns against divorcing one from the other and argues against further specialization:

No doubt there are people who would welcome such a result. But no scholar could be expected to welcome it [...]. It is [the scholars'] business [...] to reinterpret the classics to their own generation in the light of living thought and with the skill of the literary artist.[142]

If these discussions were to terminate here, then it must be conceded that the distinctions which have been drawn between the two Hellenisms, while tangible, are not substantial enough to merit this lengthy treatment. But these discussions do not end here. On the contrary, I would like to broaden the debate by making the following observations. First, it is important to remember that Myres had opted for Hellenic superlatives within a very tightly delineated and well-defined context. He had also rationed them both in frequency and manner of use. For instance, from what has been gathered of Myres in this work, it is hard to imagine that he could have penned any article remotely comparable to, say, Murray's 'The Value of Greece to the Future of the World', or 'Greece and England' or Thomson's *Greeks and Barbarians*. Second, Thomson seems to have been eager to acquire scientific credibility for his and Murray's brand of Hellenism without stipulating any credible reasons for its acquisition. Besides, he undermines this stance by insisting that classical scholarship should be carried out primarily 'with the skill of the literary artist'.

A close textual scrutiny of Murray's writings, for instance, reveals that he was extremely careful to differentiate his Hellenist self from the scientific disciplines auxiliary to classical scholarship. For example, Murray states somewhat airily that quite often 'anthropologists and measurers of skulls' 'tell' him things relevant to his field.[143] Or anthropologists have rendered the Greeks as 'the foster-brother of Kaffirs and Hairy Ainos'[144] without due reference or deference to the Hellenists in their midst. Or a certain 'great authority' (see the quote below) on comparative philology has pointed out certain things to Murray. In other words, the scientific contributions made towards Murray's variety of Hellenism are usually from external, non-classical, agencies. Despite this, even when other non-classical academic disciplines are in a position to further the aggregate understanding of ancient history, it is not a given that their offerings will necessarily be taken on board. Thomson, for instance, makes the following comment at the end of his *Greeks and Barbarians*:

> There is perhaps a growing tendency to find 'Mediterranean' elements in the Ionian stock, and this would explain much, if the Ionians of history did not seem so very 'Aryan' in speech and habits of thought. On the other hand the 'Aryan' himself is daily coming to look more cloudy and ambiguous, and so is his exact contribution to western culture.[145]

At the very beginning of the main text of the same work, he makes the following observation:

> There probably never was a time when she [Greece] had not something to learn from the Barbarians about her – from Persia, from Palestine, from distant China. But when all is said, we owe it to Greece that we think as we do, and not as Semites or Mongols. I believe that on the whole our modes of thought are preferable.[146]

Thomson accepts that the Greeks might possess 'speech and habits of thought' that could be defined as 'Aryan'. Indeed, in the second quote, he seems to underline this by stating that 'we owe it to Greece that we think as we do, and not as Semites or Mongols'. If you look closely at the second quote, however, the terms 'Semites' and 'Mongols' are there specifically to correspond with the actual 'Semitic' state of Palestine and the 'Mongol' state of China. But where is the corresponding term for the state of Persia? Herein lies the contradiction and the lack of analytical rigour at the heart of Thomson's brand of Hellenic conceptualization: if the term 'Aryan' is to be invoked, even implicitly, then the Greeks have no option but to share it with the Persians – or to be precise, with the Indo-Iranians. This, of course, would have been problematic within the contextual demarcation of *Greeks and Barbarians*. It was therefore entirely necessary to question the 'exact contribution [of the "Aryan"] to western culture', while leaving the role of the Greeks in the configuration of the West largely intact and paramount. Moreover, for a work produced in 1921, this was a peculiar position to hold. First, having largely abandoned the pseudoscientific notion of the 'Aryan race', the relevant sections of the European academia, as analysed in this and the last two chapters, were discussing matters concerning the Indo-European languages, cultures and peoples with a fair degree of intellectual originality and sobriety. It is therefore puzzling to read Thomson's assertion that the picture was becoming 'more cloudy and ambiguous'. Second, and more importantly, as outlined in Chapter 3, the general and overwhelming consensus in the 1920s concerning the configuration of Western civilization was the diffusionist ideas of Grafton Elliot-Smith. In other words, if the 'Aryan hypothesis' was to be discarded, as Thomson implies that it must be, then surely, it could not have been Greece that had primarily mattered to the civilization of the West, but Egypt and Mesopotamia.

In *The Rise of the Greek Epic* (1907), Murray, in a passage entitled 'The Northmen as Rulers', argues that despite there having been no racial or linguistic differences between the Trojans and Greeks, the 'later Greek imagination' nevertheless 'liked to think of Troy as an Asiatic city, and to make the Trojan War as a type of the age-long struggle of West and East, Aryan and Semite'.[147] The fact that these terms (West/Aryan, East/Semite) are used synonymously should be noted. In a 1931 paper ('The Beginning of Grammar'), however, Murray refines his framework considerably by asserting: '[A] great authority has pointed out that the various nations which spoke Indo-European languages differed widely in race, in build in climatic conditions and in most other things.'[148] This is a curious statement. Of course, on one level, it is correct. By comparing, say, the present inhabitants of Scandinavia to those dwelling on the European shores of the Mediterranean, the differences in 'race', 'build and 'climatic conditions' of these 'various nations' are very much apparent. But, in my judgement, this is not what underpins

Murray's assertion. In order to overcome the kind of problem that had dogged Thomson, Murray is attempting to attribute narrowly-defined racial and other particulars to a *specific* nation speaking a *specific* Indo-European language. One of the main consequences of this would be the underplaying of the connections and similarities (assuming that there are any) between the various Indo-European peoples and languages. If, for example, the Greeks and the various Indo-Iranian peoples are classified differently, then belonging to the same family of languages, *reductio ad absurdum*, becomes a matter of little or no importance.[149]

Now, contrast all this with how Myres had approached this subject-matter. First, as discussed in section II, his analyses have inferred that the Greeks were a mixture of races and not a single racial type. Second, his use of scientific methodologies and frameworks do not give the impression that Myres, unlike Murray, is somehow detached from them. He is an anthropologist and a geographer and a linguist as well as a classicist; and not a classicist who merely dabbles in other disciplines. Indeed, as the close analysis of his works in section II has demonstrated, Myres had managed, at the very least, to equip his work with more than just a veneer of scientific enquiry. Indeed, right at the outset of *Who Were the Greeks?* (1930), he contends that he is embarking on a 'scientific discourse'.[150]

IV – How to Proceed in Part II

The discussions in this chapter should have given a fairly adequate rendition of the state of Hellenisms during the first 40 years of the twentieth century. They have, however, also given rise to a number of important questions. First, do any of these differences between Myres and his immediate contemporaries render him a bona fide scientist? Putting it differently, would a Thomas Kuhn or a Karl Popper or a Rudolf Carnap be willing to categorize or recognize Myres as a 'proper' scientist? Second, is it reasonable to accept the contention that Myres' historiographical approach is in broad harmony with Collingwood's 'Philosophy of History'? Is 'history as re-enactment',[151] to borrow a phrase from William Dray, a good description of how historical narratives tend to pan out in Myres' works? Third, if Murray's brand of Hellenism cannot be defined within a scientific conceptual framework, then how should it be defined? Is it at all helpful to analyse this Hellenism within the philosophical compass of 'beauty' and/or 'aestheticism'?

CHAPTER 6

HELLENISMS REASSESSED (1890s–1940s): PART II

In the last chapter, extensive literary surveys and historiographical analyses of Hellenisms during the first half of the twentieth century were produced. The ideas or philosophies, however, that might have underpinned these Hellenisms were barely discussed. In many of the cited works, the authors, more often than not, did not explicitly rationalize the philosophies upon which they had situated their works. The philosophical moorings were usually implicit, suggesting that even the writers themselves may not have been conscious of them.

The purpose of this chapter is to utilize the tools of philosophical analysis in order to glimpse some of the inner workings of these innate philosophical underpinnings. Of course, this cannot be done in a vacuum; the works themselves must give some clues as to where to begin and how to proceed. John Linton Myres, for instance, writes appreciatively of Robin G. Collingwood and his philosophy of history, but as far his scientific outputs are concerned, he does not furnish us with any hint as to what had underwritten his scientific framework. It is therefore necessary to examine which philosophy of science can best describe Myres' methodological assumptions. Moreover, Gilbert Murray and others – by couching their conception of the Greeks within the notions of beauty, truth and perfection – have given clear indications that the philosophical core of their mainstream Hellenism resides in ideas gleaned from aestheticism.

Section I begins with a detailed analysis of Collingwood's philosophy of history, and then proceeds by asking whether or not Myres the historian can be regarded as a 'Collingwoodian'. Myres' scientific credentials come under scrutiny in section II. In this section, it is suggested that the best philosophical description of Myres the scientist is Thomas Kuhn's conception of 'normal science'. The relationship between 'truth', 'perfection' and 'beauty' defines the main points of analysis in section III. Myres, the linchpin of this discourse, takes centre stage in section IV, where his overarching framework is closely examined. Section V brings the debates in this and the previous chapter to a conclusion.

I – Myres and History

Myres' dealings with history appear to be seldom direct and nearly always subordinated to a scientific framework. His championing of Collingwood's philosophy of history in 'Hellenism in the Treatment of History' (1935), therefore, seems to be very much at odds with the intellectual makeup of the man. Did this truly signal the jettisoning of a lifetime dedication to the scientific approach and its application to the subject of ancient history? By explicitly adopting Collingwood's idea of a 'web of imaginative construction' as a methodological framework, Myres admittedly gives that very impression. This sudden interest in Collingwood's ideas could, however, equally be accounted for in another way. These ideas could have legitimized and entrenched the manner in which Myres had always carried out his responsibilities as a historian, as a scientist and as a Hellenist. But what was Collingwood's philosophy of history?

a) *Collingwood's Philosophy of History*[1]

The document that Myres described as having 'formulated afresh the philosophical basis of history, and defined the historian's aims and procedure'[2] was Collingwood's 1935 inaugural paper, entitled 'The Historical Imagination'. In this paper, along with the notion of the 'web of imaginative construction', Collingwood considers two other areas to be central to his overall analytical discourse: 'critical and constructive interpretations of evidence'[3] and 'the past and its relation to the present'.[4] Since it is within the boundaries of these three closely-related sub-headings that the main components of Collingwood's philosophy of history broadly reside, it seems prudent to acquire a firmer grasp of their underlying characteristics.

Collingwood begins his paper by stating quite clearly what types of knowledge are *not* historical. First, historical thoughts can never be 'a here and now': 'Only when they are no longer perceptible do they become objects for historical thought.'[5] Second, although, due to its 'inferential and reasoned' methodology, scientific knowledge resembles historical knowledge, they nonetheless differ in a fundamental way. Whereas 'science lives in a world of abstract universals',[6] history deals with the concrete and not the abstract, with the individual and not the universal; there is always a where and a when to preoccupy the historian. Having dealt with what is not historical knowledge, Collingwood, before setting out his own understanding of what history is, considers what 'most people believe, or imagine themselves to believe, when they first reflect on [this] matter', namely the 'common-sense theory' of history:

> According to this theory, the essential things in history are memory and authority [...]. History is thus the believing some one else when he says that he remembers something. The believer is the historian; the person believed is called his authority.[7]

There is of course a glaring defect with this theory: why believe in those who proclaim themselves to be authorities? After all, 'the authority may be garrulous, discursive, a gossip and a scandal-monger; he may have overlooked or forgotten or omitted facts; he may have ignorantly or wilfully mis-stated them'.[8] Since the 'common-sense' historian, by definition, is not in a position to query his authority's memorial integrity and put his own critical imprimatur upon the topic under examination, then all that his diminished role allows him to do is act (at best) as a neutral conduit. This state of affairs is hugely problematic for Collingwood.

Historians, even those explicitly subscribing to the 'common-sense theory', invariably partake, at the very least, in selecting from their authorities. Much like a landscape artist, who despite his best intentions always 'selects', 'simplifies' and 'schematizes'; a historian, so argues Collingwood, cannot 'merely copy his authorities',[9] but must always leave out things which he considers to be superfluous. 'It is he, therefore, and not his authority, that is responsible for what goes in.' Furthermore, a historian who is explicitly aware of these limitations begins to ponder matters concerning 'historical construction and criticism' with greater care and purpose; he now challenges the supposed omniscience of his authorities. As a historian learns his craft, he does not, according to Collingwood, neglect his authorities, but manages to weave the reliable and useful nuggets of information provided by them into statements which are reached 'inferentially from those according to his own criteria, his own rule of method, and his canons of relevance'.[10] As a consequence, the historian begins to rely 'on his own powers and [selects for] himself his own authority; whilst his so-called authorities are now not authorities at all but only evidence'.[11] A corollary to this new-found autonomy is the necessary development of critical faculties. By 'putting his authorities in the witness-box', a historian can extort from them 'information which in their original statements they have withheld'.[12] In other words, when criticism (which must be part and parcel of any durable methodology) is applied to a well-audited set of evidence, it is then that we can safely declare that the criterion for historical truth has finally been met. At this point in the epistemological evolution of the historian, '[e]ven if he accepts what his authorities tell him [...] he accepts it not on their authority but on his own; not because they say it, but because it satisfies his criterion of historical truth'.[13]

The inferences of his 1935 paper can be traced back to some of Collingwood's earliest writing on the philosophy of history. In 'The Nature and Aim of Philosophy of History' (1924), he defines history in its 'fundamental and elementary form' straightforwardly as 'perception'. Four years later, in 'The Limits of Historical Knowledge', Collingwood moves up a gear and deals directly with the criticism that history is nothing but 'the doubtful story of successive events'. He, on the one hand, argues for sharpening up the interpretative faculties of historians, which would invariably be required for the purposes of examining evidence; and on the other, that historians should consider themselves duty-bound to reflect rationally when dealing with evidence. The idea of reflection is indeed central to Collingwood's schemes of things. In *The Idea of History* (published posthumously in 1946), he remarks that 'a man should not only have experience of historical thinking but he should also have reflected upon that experience; be a philosopher as well as a historian'.[14] And this is how he sums it all up in his *Autobiography* (1939):

> History and pseudo-history alike consisted of narratives: but in history these were narratives of purposive activity, and the evidence for them consisted of relics they had left behind which became evidence precisely to the extent to which the historian conceived them in terms of purpose, that is, understood what they were for; in pseudo-history there is no conception of purpose, there are only relics of various kinds, differing among themselves in such ways that they have to be interpreted as relics of different pasts which can be arranged on a time scale.[15]

Clearly, therefore, 'purposefulness' is the analytical antidote to the notion that history is always 'the doubtful story of successive events'. But how does imagination fit in to all this? Collingwood begins by insisting that when he ponders on how to define imagination, he thinks of it not ornamentally but structurally. This is so because 'between the statements borrowed from our authorities', we require interpolation. Thus, 'what is in this way inferred is essentially something imagined' in an a priori fashion.[16] For Collingwood this 'historical imagination' has a specific task: to render the imagining of the past as 'an object of our thought'. He writes:

> The historian's picture of his subject, whether that subject be a sequence of events or a past state of things, thus appears as a web of imaginative construction stretched between certain

fixed points provided by the statements of his authorities; and if these points are frequent enough and the threads spun from each to the next are constructed with due care, always by the a priori imagination and never by merely arbitrary fancy, the whole picture is constantly verified by appeals to these data, and runs little risk of losing touch with the reality which it represents.[17]

These fixed points, Collingwood warns, are not unalterable *faits accomplis*, but intellectual underpinnings which can only be cultivated by 'critical thinking':

His [the historian's] web of imaginative construction cannot derive its validity from being pegged down to certain given facts. That description represented an attempt to relieve him of responsibility for the nodal points of his fabric, while admitting his responsibility for what he constructs between them. In point of fact, he is just as responsible for the one as for the other.[18]

The idea of re-enactment or reconstruction appears rather late in Collingwood's writings.[19] He only tackles this topic (its first brief appearance in his 1935 inaugural paper notwithstanding) in 'History as Re-enactment of Past Experience' (1946). The problem that he encounters when contemplating 'performing an act of rethought' is twofold. First, if the aim is to resemble the original thought, then this act of rethinking is what he calls the 'discredited copy-theory of knowledge'.[20] The second option is a conceptually impossible one: opting for a rethought that is 'literally identical' with the original. To get out of this quandary, Collingwood proposes that 'the object (in this case the past) would simply be incorporated in the subject (in this case the present, the historian own thought); and instead of asking the question how the past is known we should be maintaining that the past is not known, but only the present'.[21] Moreover, in 'Human Nature and Human History' (1937), Collingwood provides a concise definition of his idea of re-enactment:

> The historian not only re-enacts past thought, he re-enacts it in the context of his own knowledge and therefore, in re-enacting it, criticizes it, forms his own judgment of its value, corrects whatever errors he can discern in it [...]. All thinking is critical thinking; the thought which re-enacts past thoughts, therefore, criticizes them in re-enacting them.[22]

Or as he puts in his *Autobiography*, 'all history is the history of thought'; which implies that 'historical knowledge is the re-enactment in the historian's mind of the thought whose history he is studying'.[23] With this approving nod towards Benedetto Croce, Collingwood takes us towards the final component (if it is the final component and not just the continuation of the idea of re-enactment) of his philosophical trinity, namely the question of the past and its connection to the present. Elsewhere in his writings, Collingwood has a great deal to say regarding this point, but as far as his 1935 paper is concerned, he only tersely asserts that '[e]very present has a past of its own, and any imaginative reconstruction of the past aims at reconstructing the past of this present'.[24]

In 'The Limits of Historical Knowledge' (1928), he puts on record, possibly for the first time, his unique insight into the complex relationship between the past and the present: 'The past as past is wholly unknowable; it is the past as residually preserved in the present that is alone knowable.' Moreover, 'what the historian wants is a real present [...]. He wants to reconstruct [...] the process by which *his* world [...] has come to be what it is.'[25] Two years later in the 'Philosophy of History', he buttresses this stance by arguing that 'all history is an interim report'.[26] Collingwood's 1934 paper entitled 'History as the Understanding of the Present' deals almost exclusively with this aspect of his *oeuvre*, and declares unambiguously that 'the ultimate aim of history is not to know the past but to understand the present'.[27] He qualifies this by stating that there are limits to this process: 'The past doesn't *actually* ever explain the present in its entirety. It only gives part of the present – not a complete determination of it.'[28] In 'History as Re-enactment of Past Experiences', he delves a little deeper into this question and asks whether it is correct to state that 'an act of thought by being subjective ceases to be objective, and thus, by being present, ceases to be past'. He answers in the negative and argues that 'because a person who states this has understood by subjectivity not the act of thinking, but simply consciousness as a flow of immediate state.[29] Subjectivity for him means not the subjectivity of thought but only the subjectivity of immediate experience.'[30] This mistaken perspective, in Collingwood's opinion, has no relevance to the genesis of bona fide 'historical knowledge'; which, he asserts in his *Autobiography*, 'is the re-enactment of a past thought incapsulated in a context of present thought which, by contradicting it, confines it to a plane different from theirs'.[31]

These main components of Collingwood's philosophical synthesis are part of a broader intellectual canvas. In 'The Nature and Aim of Philosophy of History', he discusses two inappropriate ways of 'doing' history. He dismisses the tendency that searches for 'general laws' that aims to erect 'superstructures of generalisation based upon historical facts'.[32] He also has precious little time for those who see 'history as the unfolding of cosmic drama', in which 'a single concrete plan' is progressively worked out.[33] With regard to the first, he considers it to be 'entirely illusory', because not only can one never have the 'last word' on any given fact, but also and more importantly, conclusions 'are not abstract universal laws, because they are statements about a contingent and transitory subject-matter'.[34] As far as history being a cosmic drama is concerned, Collingwood admits that history can be seen as a drama, but a drama with an important caveat: 'an extemporised drama, co-operatively extemporised by its own performers.'[35] By using the unknowable complexity and mêlée of war (the Battle of Hastings in his vivid example), he avers that 'no historical statement can ever express the complete truth about any single fact'.[36] In addition to this, 'no historian imagines that he knows any single fact in its entirety, or that any historian ever will'.[37] In a 1930 paper, entitled 'The Philosophy of History', he contends that since the past has stopped happening, knowledge of it cannot be derived from observation or experimentation.[38] Thus, in order to know the past, evidence (data) must be interpreted. On the question of interpretation, however, Collingwood is alive to the dangers of a historian being accused of partiality. In 'Can a Historian be Impartial?' (1936), he opines that competent historians cannot be expected to be entirely without prejudice (his example is Rostovtzeff[39]). What a good historian should do is, first, discipline his prejudices; and second, come clean about them. After all, 'without judgement of value, there is no history.' Collingwood maintained that a historian should not only try to discover 'what actually happened, but judge it in the light of our own moral ideals'.[40] In other words, if a dutiful historian can manage to subscribe to and follow what Collingwood had already envisaged in 1924, then he is on the 'right' methodological path:

> [It] is the study of historical thinking: not only the psychological analysis of its actual procedure, but the analysis of the ideal which it sets before itself. Historical thought is one among a number of attitudes taken up by the mind towards the objective world; it is an attitude which assumes that there exists a world of facts – not general laws, but individual facts – independent of being known, and that it is possible, if not wholly to discover these facts, at any rate to discover them in part and approximately. The philosophy of history must be a critical discussion of this attitude, its presuppositions and its implications.[41]

b) Was Myres a Collingwoodian?

In his last major publication, *Herodotus: The Father of History* (1953), Myres begins with what can only be described as a textbook example of Collingwood's philosophy of history. He pictures an inquisitive five-year-old Herodotus watching the arrival of the Persian fleet following its defeat at the Battle of Salamis and asking his mother, 'what did they fight each other for?'[42] This contrived historiette, on the one hand, imagines what Herodotus the precocious child-historian thinks, and on the other, it imaginatively foretells what Herodotus, the fully-formed historian, will in due time think with respects to the events that he had witnessed in 480 BC. But to what extent had these Collingwoodian sensibilities defined the inner workings of Myres' intellect as a historian? The answer to this question can only be gleaned from analysing two conceptually separate but intellectually related areas. First, a simple trawl through the sizeable body of his work should provide clues to the degree to which his thinking had chimed, consciously or otherwise, with that of Collingwood's philosophy of history. Second, it is interesting to examine whether or not the manner in which Collingwood's philosophy of history was constructed was inherently amenable and accommodating to Myres' approach, not only towards history, but more generally towards Hellenism.

Whether it is the notion of the 'Indo-European thought', or the 'political ideas of the Greeks', or 'the common culture of the Indo-Europeans', or, indeed, who the Greeks were, Myres is groping for one overarching idea: what had constituted the thinking of the ancient Greeks. In order to give substance to this idea, he endeavours to rethink thoughts belonging to the Greeks and more narrowly (if not more problematically) to the Indo-Europeans. Moreover, it is worth recalling that the purpose of *Who Were the Greeks?* (1930) was 'to examine the Greeks' *own beliefs* about their origin, *in the light of modern advances*' (my emphasis).[43] This is also precisely what Collingwood argues in his discussions concerning the past and the present. Here the past (the beliefs of the Greeks) is examined in the present (the light of modern advances) very much along the line of Collingwood's assertion that '[h]istorical knowledge is the re-enactment of a past thought incapsulated in a context of present thought'.

It is in the area of evidence that Myres felt the need to revise aspects of the historiographical approach that was current at the turn of the century. In his 1910 paper, entitled 'The Value of Ancient History' (see Chapter 5), he draws a very clear distinction between the methodologies that are available to modern historians and those available to ancient historians. The scope of the former, in his view, is 'insufficient for any reconstruction of antiquity'. What is required, therefore, is an entirely new way of 'collect[ing] and 'arrang[ing] new classes of materials for history', thereby facilitating ancient history to become part of 'a wide group of "historical sciences"'.[44] Even this aspect of his methodology, which appears at first to deviate from Collingwood, is still within the remits of Collingwood's views on ancient history and historians. There is a passage in *The Idea of History* that deals critically with the historiographical legacy of the Greeks. Collingwood argues that there is a tendency in Greek thought to be 'anti-historical'.[45] Since history for the Greeks was transitory, then, according to him, 'it can only be a matter of perception'. This was so because the Greek metaphysics dictated that only 'what is unchanging can be known'. Consequently, all that history can ever be is 'an aggregate of perceptions' (that brings to mind the 'doubtful story of successive events')[46] that solely require eyewitness accounts. It was within these limits, in Collingwood's opinion, that Herodotus and Thucydides had to operate. In fact if one were to examine Myres' 'Races and Cultures' (see Chapter 3), and 'Hellenism in the Treatment of History' (see Chapter 5) with sufficient care, one would notice that although the ancient sources (Herodotus in particular) are present and are referred to liberally, they are no longer the only providers of evidence (albeit still important in framing the subject-matter). Although Myres at no point in his published works on Greek historiography questions the veracity of Herodotus' claims, he nonetheless concedes in his 1935 unpublished paper that many things which were in *The Histories* were 'fragmentary, incoherent, and for the most part ill-attested by modern standards'.[47] This is precisely the reason why a 'light of the modern advances' in a number of scientific disciplines was deemed necessary for ushering in a totally new way of studying Hellenism. By taking his inspiration partly from Collingwood, Myres sets out to overcome a double obstacle: the paucity of evidence and the manner in which it was gathered. It was his awareness of these deficiencies that had arguably persuaded him to use other methods in his understanding of the ancient Greeks.

II – Myres and Science[48]

As discussed in the last section, the concept of historical imagination was introduced by Collingwood in order to link together a certain number of 'fixed points provided by the statements of [an historian's] authorities'. Bearing in mind that the historian's *raison d'être* is to provide connections between these points, then a propensity to increase the number of these fixed points should be, more often than not, in the forefront of a historian's mind. By bringing in what he calls 'distributional and historical sciences' into the proceedings, Myres, while remaining within Collingwood's philosophical compass, posits his brand of Hellenism upon the foundation of the relevant historical sciences of geography, anthropology, comparative philology and archaeology.[49] These sciences, as discussed in the previous chapter, had enveloped much of Myres' thinking and many of his historical undertakings during our period of interest, resulting in his confident assertion that *Who Were the Greeks?* was first and foremost a 'scientific discourse'.

This, however, raises a question: in what way was Myres' Hellenism scientific? At first glance, Myres seems to have subscribed to what was the norm in late-nineteenth century scientific thinking, namely the method of induction, which tended to generalize a hypothesis 'from the results of observations and experiments'.[50] Francis Bacon and his idea that 'slow and faithful toil gathers information from things and brings it into understanding'[51] had shown great resilience and had indeed been picked up and expanded upon by, *inter alia*, John Stuart Mill in his *System of Logic* (1865). But Myres was also exposed to an alternative approach championed by, among many others, William Jevons, one of Mill's contemporaries, who argued against Mill's position and stated that a hypothesis can only be justified by it being 'consistent with other well-confirmed laws', while at the same time, its 'consequences inferred [should] agree with facts of observation'.[52] What Jevons is alluding to is of course the now ubiquitous method of deduction, designed to fit 'results and observation' into a priori hypotheses.

In *Who Were the Greeks?* Myres follows a straightforward inductive method in sections covering geography and physical anthropology (examining skull types and forming inconclusive and sketchy hypotheses from them), but, significantly, in the rest of the work, particularly those parts covering linguistics and myth, as well as the two analytical chapters, 'The Crucible and the Mould' and 'The Making of a Nation', he frames his arguments with a number of a priori hypotheses (see Chapter 5). For instance, the analyses of both language and myth are carried out predominantly within the theoretical contexts of Indo-European philology and mythology (expecting the Greek deities to resemble their Norse counterparts, for instance). In a manner of speaking and as far as Myres is concerned, whether or not his thinking was primarily based on hypothesizing either inductively or deductively is a matter of secondary importance. This is not because these methods are somehow deemed insufficient for the purposes of a scientific discourse. They should be considered as secondary because what ultimately makes Myres an intriguing subject of enquiry is the fact that he textures his thoughts with science *and* history – as his careful phrasing in the form of 'distributional and historical sciences' testifies. What is required therefore is a philosophy of science that is historically informed. 'The special features we associate with science,' according to Newton-Smith

> arise from the combination and interaction of two different kinds of activity – the orderly, organized, disciplined process of normal science, and the periodic breakdowns of order found in revolutions. These two processes happen in sequence, within each scientific field. Science as a whole is a result of their interaction and of nothing less.[53]

This, of course, is a brief description of science according to Thomas S. Kuhn. The first chapter of *The Structure of Scientific Revolutions* (1962) goes directly to the heart of the matter; its title is 'A Role for History'. Here, the history of science, in Kuhn's assessment, is no longer purely about tracing 'cumulative [and] developmental lines for the sciences', but to 'seek the permanent contributions of an older science to our present vantage'. For example, Kuhn regards it as more sensible not to ask 'about the relation of Galileo's views to those of modern science, but rather about the relationship between his views and those of his groups, i.e., his teachers, contemporaries, and immediate successors in the sciences'.[54] By placing a revolutionary scientist, such as Galileo, within *in situ* groups, Kuhn is trying to comprehend not only the scientific context of this revolution, but also its historical context. What he is definitely not trying to do at this point is to assess the quality of the final revolutionary product, but to inventorize all the historical and scientific variables that were responsible for its eventual production. What interests him above all else is what he calls 'paradigm' or 'normal science':[55] 'the activity in which most scientists inevitably spend almost all their time'.[56] In order to qualify as normal sciences, they must fulfil two criteria. First, their achievements must be 'sufficiently unprecedented to attract an enduring group of adherents away from competing modes of scientific activity'; and second, they must be 'sufficiently open-ended to leave all sorts of problems for the redefined group of practitioners to resolve'.[57] In *A Historical Introduction to the Philosophy of Science* (2001), John Losee provides the reader with a useful checklist of what normal science intends to do. The following aims are relevant for our discussion: science, according to Losee, aims to 'increase the precision of agreement between observations and calculations based on the paradigm'; to 'extend the scope of the paradigm to cover additional phenomena'; and to 'decide which alternative way of applying the paradigm to a new area of interest is most satisfactory'.[58] These are precisely the characteristics that define normal science as a puzzle-solving phenomenon:

> Bringing a normal research problem to a conclusion is achieving the anticipated in a new way, and it requires the solution of all sorts of complex instrumental, conceptual, and mathematical puzzles. The man who succeeds proves himself an expert puzzle-solver, and the challenge of the puzzle is an important part of what usually drives him on.[59]

Even though the puzzle-solving activity tends to extend 'the scope and precision of scientific knowledge', it does not lead automatically to the emergence of scientific discoveries. By the logic of its conceptual construction, normal science, according to Kuhn, does not (indeed cannot) 'aim at novelties of fact or theory'.[60] This does not, however, imply that 'new and unsuspected phenomena' are not 'repeatedly uncovered by scientific research'.[61] All that it does suggest is that uncovering theory changes the rules of the game and leads to a 'paradigm change', as well as resulting in 'scientific revolution'. He puts it thus:

> Produced inadvertently by a game played under one set of rules, their assimilation requires the elaboration of another set. After they have become parts of science, the enterprise [...] is never quite the same again.[62]

As far as Myres' works are concerned, there is very little reason to go on and discuss Kuhn's fascinating theories pertaining to the 'emergence of scientific theories', and the 'nature of scientific revolution'.[63] This is so because Myres, having only operated within the contours of 'normal science', is the quintessential puzzle-solver. In many of his writings, Myres assigns aspects of ancient history to other disciplines, which seems to have the effect, intended or otherwise, of increasing the number of the Collingwoodian fixed points as well as strengthening the interpolative links between them. But how is it done? His 'program of enquiry' in *Who Were the Greeks?* suggests that Myres, by isolating a number of areas for scrutiny and asking narrowly-defined questions (what languages were there before 'the spread of Greek speech', what can archaeology tell us with regard to 'the principle phases and local varieties of material civilization' and so on[64]), is doing no more than extending 'the scope and precision of scientific knowledge'. Thus, by ensconcing Myres' approach in the idea of 'normal science' (which itself is historically aware), a plausibly historicized narrative of his 'scientific discourse' can be attained. Myres' scientific Hellenism, quite clearly, does not represent any kind of 'scientific revolution'. What it does, however, represent is a steady progress *within* 'normal science' and towards a distantly possible (but by no means inevitable or probable) shift in historiographical paradigm.

The concept of 'normal science' itself, it should be stressed, came under a barrage of fierce criticisms in the late 1960s. In 'Against "Normal Science"', J. Watkins contends that normal science is 'boring and unheroic'[65] and the idea that 'science progresses by accretion'[66] and then gives rise to 'revolutionary science' is a misguided assertion. In 'Normal Science and its Dangers', Karl Popper depicts the 'normal' scientist as being 'the not-too-critical professional [...] who does not wish to challenge ["the ruling dogma"]; and who accepts a new revolutionary theory only if almost everybody else is ready to accept it'.[67] Such an individual, moreover, is an 'applied' and not a 'pure' scientist, implying that he or she is formed and informed by a 'dogmatic spirit';[68] which, moreover, he or she is incapable of transcending. In addition, Popper dismisses the claim that each and every 'scientific domain' is served with one 'dominant theory' or paradigm.[69] In science, according to Popper, 'a critical comparison of the competing theories, [and] of the competing frameworks, is always possible. And the denial of this possibility is a mistake.'[70] In his reply, Kuhn argues that Popper's reasoning is confused. Popper has already conceded, according to Kuhn, that 'scientists *necessarily* develop their ideas within a definite theoretical framework'.[71] And since 'the science which I call normal is precisely research within a framework, it can only be the opposite side of a coin the face of which is revolutions'.[72] What follows from this, according to Kuhn, is the necessity of breaking *from* one framework (via revolution) and *into* another. All of which suggest that a scientist's perseverance with a framework is not always the result of the 'dogmatic spirit'.

Whether normal science is or is not methodologically 'dangerous' is a complicated philosophical debate that is beyond the scope of this analysis. So why situate Myres within the framework of 'normal science'? There are two reasons why this framework is useful for the purposes of this discourse. First, the main alternative to Kuhn, Popper's idea of 'falsification' and a science which is 'constantly and potentially on the verge of revolution'[73] (as opposed to the problem-solving aspect of normal science) does not (in fact, it cannot) satisfactorily explain Myres' use of science in ancient history. Second, and more importantly, it is Kuhn's awareness that in order to placate his critics he needs 'to retrieve from history'[74] examples of normal science, which can only be done by looking with the attentive eye of a historian (or a sociologist) at what he calls the 'community structure of science'.[75] 'Groups like these should,' he suggests, 'be regarded as the units which produces scientific knowledge.'[76] Since this work is an attempt to retrieve Myres' science from the history of academic Hellenism, then the path shown by Kuhn appears to be the most promising one.

III – Aesthetic Hellenism: A Philosophical Treatment

As discussed in Chapter 2, the intellectual and historical links between Hellenism and aestheticism go back a very long time. Renaissance humanism was followed by an Enlightenment that was largely concerned with the manner in which the Greeks had organized themselves politically; and of course there was that unabashed attachment to the Hellene of the European Romantic movement. The legacies of Winckelmann, Goethe, Arnold and Pater were modified and taken further by the likes of Murray and Thomson in the first half of the twentieth century (Chapter 5). For Winckelmann and his Romantic descendents, the beauty of Greek civilization was awe-inspiring and absolute; it was the *fons et origo* of high culture. Murray and others, however, mediated beauty through surrogate categories, mainly borrowed from methodologies belonging to the philosophy of beauty. The analyses of the previous chapter strongly suggest that for those of Murray's persuasion, *truth* and *perfection* were the main definers of the beauty that was embodied in Hellenism.

Questions such as 'is there artistic truth?' and 'must art tell the truth?', as well as phrases such as 'meaning and truth in art' have been in use regularly in the titles of books, chapters, and essays. One of the more mundane reasons for wishing to endow beauty with the discernments of truth was due to the fear that if the core essence of beauty was left without a considerable intellectual gravitas, then all that beauty would be able to engender would be the sometimes insalubrious sensation of pleasure.[77] Along with this puritanical censoriousness, there were more philosophical reasons for why the relationship between truth and beauty has generated so much interest among students of aesthetics.[78]

To begin with, there is – in the case of mainstream Hellenism – an element of internal logic to all this. Greek philosophy has always been hugely influential in the study of aesthetics. Although both Socrates and Plato were immersed in this topic,[79] it was Aristotle and specifically his *Poetics* that had, probably for the first time, linked truth with the aesthetic qualities of works of art. His example was that of poetry. He believed that since a poet only relates 'what may happen' in accordance with 'the law of probability or necessity', it means that poetry expresses 'universal' truths, whereas history, because it is preoccupied with 'what has happened', can only express 'particular' truths. As a consequence of this fundamental difference, poetry, according to Aristotle, 'is a more philosophical and a higher thing than history'.[80] The modern version of this debate does not stray too far from this general precept. It revolves around the question of how truth is embedded or embodied[81] in what is generally accepted as beautiful. E. F. Carritt in *What is Beauty?* (1932) begins by arguing that if Keats' assertion ('beauty is truth, and truth beauty') was to be taken seriously, then 'we should not need two words'.[82] A thing of beauty, according to Carritt, 'gives us some deeper insight than we naturally have into the nature of things of that kind'.[83] Moreover, when we acquire this insight, 'we are not thinking about its relations or about the law that governs its existence, as we should be in science'; but 'we feel it to be a little self-contained world by itself with laws of its own'.[84] But what has happened to history? Carritt is categorical: 'If beauty is in any sense truth it certainly is not historical or scientific or philosophical truth.'[85] In *Meaning and Truth in the Arts* (1946), John Hospers is in broad agreement with Carritt, contending that truth in arts provides us with an 'insight into reality'.[86] Arts in general and literature in particular[87] do not 'present us with propositions which are empirically verifiable like those of science and history [...]. And yet they are true-*to* human nature as we know it.[88] Thus in a way we can verify what the artist has presented; we can verify his insights in our own future observations of people and actions.'[89]

Hospers' views are reiterated by M. Weitz in his 1955 paper, 'Truth in Literature'. By examining Proust's *Remembrance of Things Past*, he avers that there are 'implicit truths' that can only exist in art – or specifically in literature – 'which were never thought of by anyone'.[90] While not disputing the fact that truth does indeed exist in art, D. N. Morgan in 'Must Art Tell the Truth?' (1967) maintains that there is nothing distinctively better about art furnishing us with truths; science and the 'vast majority of statements made in daily life' also give us truths. In addition, although some truths are only 'uniquely affirmable' in the arts and no other medium, truths, as claimed in science and everyday life, according to Morgan, can be disputed and proven false. This particular mode of conduct, he states, is absent when analysing truths in art: 'The truths supposed to be uniquely affirmable in a work of art are not relevantly contradicted by the truths affirmed in some other work of art.'[91] In other words, the insights that such truths can provide can scarcely be called 'universal', hence they are inapplicable to 'human nature'. All the same, the notion of truth in art as being an indispensable repository of insights has thus far been very much the consensus in this field.

Colloquially, perfection and beauty are very often used synonymously. For our purposes and the way in which it is used when referring to Hellenism, perfection is an 'aesthetic value'. It is a value judgement, which maintains the belief that there are *objective* aesthetic qualities in works of art that can be teased out in order to define entire artistic and intellectual traditions, such as those belonging to the ancient Greeks. It is precisely in this way that the whole notion of the 'unapproachable perfection' of the Greeks has been academically underpinned. It is the belief, current since the eighteenth century, that the 'works of classical antiquity [should be] considered by themselves [to be] a guarantee of the objectivity of beauty'. This is so because these works 'represent the major and the most probable occurrences of life and the fundamental aspects of human nature'.[92] In his introduction to *Introductory Readings in Aesthetics* (1969), John Hospers opines that T. E. Jessop, the über-objectivist, held to the belief that works of art possess 'objective properties' in the same way that a circle possesses circularity.[93] In the 'Objectivity of Aesthetic Value' (1932), Jessop presents his core theory thus: first, he makes the uncontroversial assertion that 'aesthetics is primarily concerned with aesthetic judgment'; second, and more arguably, he avers that in the exercise of this ability to judge, 'it is not about me [the judge] but about the object', or more accurately, the potency that the object wields over 'my power of judgment' is the determining factor; and finally, because of the object-centricity of this approach, Jessop deduces that 'aesthetic experience needs to be studied normatively (leaving room for a right and a wrong), and that the only feature of it that allows an aesthetic norm is the aesthetic judgement interpreted objectively'.[94] There is, however, a philosophical alternative to this, namely the fact that judgements concerned with the quality and value of art can be considered as a matter of *subjective* evaluation.[95] In his 1929 essay, entitled 'The Subjectivity of Aesthetic Value', C. J. Ducasse argues that 'there is no such a thing as authoritative opinion concerning the beauty of a given object. There is only the opinion of this person or that.'[96] This is the case because 'judgements of beauty have to do with the relation of the object judged to the individual's own pleasure experience of which he himself is the sole possible observer and judge'.[97] In addition, according to Ducasse, searching for objectivity is futile because unlike a scientific undertaking, no document of proof can ever accompany an aesthetic value judgment. In other words, the potency that Jessop had spoken of has, in this subjective context, moved away from the object and towards the now omnipotent (in an ontological sense) observer.[98]

Having followed the above discussions concerning the relationship between the grammar of beauty and truth, as well as the ins and outs of the 'aesthetic value', the reader may very well wonder that if the likes of Murray are determined to equip their Hellenism with the paraphernalia of aestheticism, then why should their actions be needlessly problematized? Indeed, it may seem to many that 'the extensive and magnificent literature'[99] which defines the core characteristics (law, art, science, philosophy, poetry, etc.) of

Hellenism can only be truly appreciated by a thorough aesthetic evaluation. But how viable is this assertion? There are two closely related problems with this viewpoint. First, by illustrating that historical truth is not the prerogative of beauty, as well as arguing that aesthetic judgement cannot, unlike science, be proven or disproved, Morgan and Ducasse *inter alia* have directed our attention towards the idea that what concerned many of the mainstream Hellenists may possibly touch on other philosophical domains, such as science and history. Second, by relying on the assumption that truth is first and foremost a 'universal' phenomenon with the solitary task of seeking insights into human nature, the role that historical truths were allowed to play in the Hellenist's scheme of things turned out to be meagre. This lack of historicity, in turn, permitted the formation of an imaginary commonwealth where Arcadia was no longer a rugged mountain district in the Peloponnese, but Hellas itself. In order to create a world with pleasing images, the Hellenophile aesthetes, in Theodor Adorno's paraphrased words, have relentlessly pursued 'a wilful cognitive distortion'[100] of the real world, thereby sacrificing even the pretence of loyalty to Clio. It can be countered that those writing history within the limits of aesthetic Hellenism can in no way be labelled as historically naive. On the contrary, their works suggest that they have read, usually in Greek, their Herodotus, Thucydides, Xenophon and Plutarch with care and diligence. Admittedly this is true; and herein lies the problem: they have followed what Collingwood termed as the 'common-sense theory of history' and believed nearly every assertion made by their ancient authorities without a great deal of critical demurring. Toynbee, for instance, contends, not disapprovingly, that Herodotus 'took his observations with the eyes of Odysseus and not through the lenses of Ranke'.[101]

But then again, why should this tendency undermine Murray's brand of Hellenism? After all, is it not the function of Hellenism to furnish us with the wherewithal of 'producing, on a vast scale, what Aristotle calls "a good life for man"'?[102] It is indeed commendable that there are those determined to utilize the sublime achievements of the ancient Greeks as an encyclopaedic guide for life, but, when inspected closely, all we find is essentially a set of abstract precepts ('Truth, Good, Beauty, Perfection, Unity, Harmony, Proportion'[103]), synthesized and presented as a cultural ideology and labelled 'Hellenism'. The problem here stems from the fact that Ancient Greece and the ancient Greeks did *really* exist. Or as Myres or Collingwood might put it: there was a *where* and there was a *when* and there certainly were many illustrious *whos*. The tendency to distil the delectable and beautiful from the historical and anthropological realities (often harsh and unappealing) of the ancient world should no longer be regarded as an exercise without externalities or moral hazard (see below). Those calling this ideology 'Hellenism' have effectively situated it within the well-regulated framework of history, but they have done so without supplying it with the accoutrements necessary for going beyond the 'common-sense theory of history'. As a consequence, the ideologues of this school of thought went on to write a copious amount of ancient history, but since their underlying philosophy was bereft of appropriate historical and historiographical 'aims and procedures', they produced precious little in the way of accurate canons (see Chapter 7). Interestingly, Murray was painfully aware of this fundamental shortcoming and in 'The Value of Greece to the Future of the World', after cataloguing all the glorious legacies of the 'Greek spirit', he allows himself to imagine what must be 'lurking in the mind of many readers':

> 'All this', they may say, 'professes to be a simple analysis of known facts, but in reality is sheer idealization. These Greeks whom you call so "noble" have been long exposed. Anthropology has turned its searchlight upon them. It is not only their ploughs, their weapons, their musical instruments, and their painted idols that resemble those of the savages; it is everything else about them. Many of them were sunk in the most degrading superstition: many practised unnatural vices: in times of great fear some were apt to think that the best "medicine" was a human sacrifice. After that, it is hardly worth mentioning that their social structure was largely based on slavery; that they lived in petty little towns, like so many

wasps' nests, each at war with its next-door neighbour, and half of them at war with themselves!'[104]

Murray concedes that '[t]hese charges are on the whole true', adding with some frankness that 'if we are to understand what Greece means, we must realize and digest them'. This can be done, in his opinion, by keeping 'hold of two facts'. First, 'the Greeks of the fifth century produced some of the noblest poetry and art, the finest political thinking, the most vital philosophy, known to the world'; second, those seeing, hearing and producing these wonders 'were separated by a thin and precarious interval from the savage'.[105] What Hellenism has allowed us to witness, therefore, is a unique form of cultural alchemy: transforming the basest materials provided by an unvarnished humanity into *the* finest man-made cultural and intellectual products. It is precisely because of such cultural metamorphoses – and not the 'remnants of savagery and superstition'[106] – that, in Murray's judgement, Greece should grab our attention and secure our permanent appreciation:

> It is not anything fixed and stationary that constitutes Greece: what constitutes Greece is the movement which leads from all these to the Stoic [...] who condemns and denies slavery, who has abolished all cruel superstitions and preaches some religion based on philosophy and humanity, who claims for women the same spiritual rights[107] as for man [...]. It is that movement which you will not find elsewhere, any more than the statues of Pheidias or the dialogues of Plato or the poems of Aeschylus and Euripides.[108]

Much of this thinking is predicated upon what is known as *Cambridge Ritualism*. According to Robert Ackerman, this idiosyncratic form of anthropological approach is largely based on the confluence of five distinct 'movements and tendencies': keen interest in the working of the 'unconscious mind'; the availibilty of numerous ethnographical examples of the belief systems of 'primitive peoples', thus allowing for comparative analysis; the two-centuries-old process of 'demythologization of the classics'; the nineteenth-century passion for seeking out origins; and finally, the triumph of the evolutionary process as an analytical framework.[109] Consequently, in Ackerman's view, 'it [became] possible to talk about the Greeks and the primitives in the same breath, but also to advance a general theory of the origins and evolutions of religions in term of social psychology based on collective emotion'.[110] Where the Greeks were concerned, however, this approach was extended well beyond just the 'evolutions of religions'. Other cultural activities, such as art, literature and philosophy, as witnessed in our discussions of Murray, were also situated within this decidedly ritualistic framework.

Murray's adherence to this school of thought is defective for one overarching reason: by attempting to define 'what constitutes Greece' in a way that only (or at least, largely) permits the comprehensive tabulation of all the stupendous wonders of the Greek art, philosophy and literature, without contextualizing them sufficiently within the grubbier side of the Hellenic life (he merely mentions them in passing, as the above quote demonstrates), Murray gives a very partial and censored rendition of the Greek civilization. Imagine if one were allowed to do exactly the same for, say, the contemporary German civilization. Would it be at all possible for a historian of Germany to be taken seriously, if he were to concentrate primarily on all the great and undoubted achievements of the German peoples, without analysing Prussian militarism, hyperinflationary pressures of the 1920s, Nazism, *Kristallnacht*, two world wars and the Holocaust? Can it ever be asserted that 'what constitutes Germany is the movement which leads from all these to Goethe, Beethoven's late string quartets, Lotte Lenya, the Bauhaus, and the slick design of a Porsche automobile'? Such an eccentric interpretation, surely, would not begin to be tolerated or even formulated. *Pari passu*, the Greek civilization should also be subject to similar methodological, intellectual and moral constraints.

Finally, and in relation to this notion of the sublime Hellas: it can be countered that the 'aesthetic' labelling of Murray's conceptualization of Hellenism is both inaccurate and philosophically meaningless. According to this perspective, words such as 'beauty', 'perfection', 'nobility', or 'truth' – in themselves and in isolation – do not signify the existence of a well-considered aesthetic framework.[111]

In *The Oxford Handbook of Aesthetics* (2005), Jerrold Levinson contends that 'one may usefully think of the field of philosophical aesthetics as having three foci, through each of which it might be adequately conceived':

> One focus involves a certain kind of *practice* or *activity* or *object* – the practice of art, or the activities of making and appreciating art, or those manifold objects that are works of art. A second focus involves certain kind of *property*, *feature*, or *aspect* of things – namely, one that is *aesthetic*, such as beauty or grace or dynamism. And a third focus involves a certain kind of *attitude*, *perception*, or *experience* – one that, once again, could be labelled *aesthetic*.[112]

From what has thus far been discussed in this section – and taking these classifications onboard – it is quite clear that the first two foci ('appreciating art' and 'property of things', such as 'beauty') have been well represented by many of those authors discussed here and in Chapters 2 and 5. It is, however, the shadowy presence of the third focus which is highly relevant to our discussions. Murray and others, in my judgement, bring to their conceptualization of Hellenism, in Levinson's words, 'certain distinctive experiences or states of mind';[113] and as a consequence, they can do no other but to frame it aesthetically. They do so not only because they employ (indeed over-employ) a certain number of words, but because their 'attitudes', 'perceptions' and 'emotion'[114] are very much conditioned by – as Richard Neer has recently discussed in another context (*The Emergence of the Classical Style in Greek Sculpture*, 2011) – the aesthetics of wonder (*thauma*). Since it is this ceaseless experiencing of wonder (the third focus) that has energized and enlivened the writings of these authors, it is not altogether inappropriate or incorrect to label and define Murray and others as 'aesthetic Hellenists'.

IV – Myres' Overarching Intellectual Template: An Analytical Audit

The discourse has now reached a juncture that requires a summing-up of Myres' works. To begin with, his methodology had seldom wavered from combining science and history. As the analyses of the previous chapter have demonstrated, this tendency was a permanent feature in many (if not most) of his published and unpublished writings; it can be detected as early as 1908 (*Herodotus and Anthropology*) and as late as 1935 ('Hellenism in the Treatment of History'). Collingwood's ideas of re-enactment and imagination were quoted approvingly in 1935, primarily because it chimed with Myres' own lifelong thinking, as laid bare in, among others, *Greek Lands and the Greek People* (1910), *The Dawn of History* (1911), *The Political Ideas of the Greeks* (1927), and, of course, in *Who Were the Greeks?* (1930). Collingwood's philosophy of history should be seen as lending philosophical legitimacy to what Myres had been pursuing for nearly three decades. In other words, since Collingwood came a generation later than Myres and therefore was not in a position to inform him philosophically until the 1930s, a better understanding of Collingwood is primarily required from the perspective of the intellectual history of the period. This is so because Myres left no indication of his own philosophy of history; we cannot speak of 'Myresian' philosophical ideas the way we can do so with regard to the Collingwoodian varieties. As a result, Collingwood's philosophy of history is the best proxy for Myres' implicit philosophical sensibilities. With respect to science, however, things have arranged themselves somewhat differently. Being a competent geologist, geographer, linguist and, above all, anthropologist, his immersion in 'distributional and historical sciences' was neither half-hearted nor dilettantish (see Chapters 3 and 5). It was not difficult to demonstrate his outputs' scientific traits; but, admittedly, it was a trickier affair to determine in which category of philosophy of science his undertakings belonged. In the final analysis, Kuhn's concept of 'normal science' appears to be the most appropriate for two chief reasons. First, being informed historically, it fits well with Myres' proto-Collingwoodian historical model. Second, its puzzle-solving element described Myres' scientific methods more than adequately.

But is it correct to differentiate so fully between history and science? Joynt and Rescher argue that the real difference between these two phenomena resides predominantly 'in the objectives of the research, and the consequent perspective that is taken in looking at the past. History does not collect facts to establish laws; rather, it seeks to exploit laws to explain facts.'[115] They expand on this by stating that '[h]istory must ever be rewritten if only because the progress of science leads inescapably to a deepening in our understanding of historical events'.[116] In other words, while science and history can and often do act in unison, they are nevertheless independent strands of philosophical thought. Here, with regard to Myres' approach, these two strands of thoughts have come together and produced a synthesis of a sort: a historico-scientific template. Why should this be of any significance? Within the confines of this narrative, this template suggests that the triangular relationship between history, science and Hellenism that was proposed in Chapter 5 does not entirely describe how Myres had conceptualized his ideas at a more fundamental level. This does not imply, however, that the inference drawn was an erroneous one. Within the evidential context of that chapter's analysis, the relationships between the three entities were accurately recounted. The identifiable alteration that has taken place is largely due to the extension of the overarching framework in the present narrative (see sections II and III). What we have now is a binary relationship, but a binary relationship of a special kind; between that of an interwoven and enmeshed history and science (foundation) and that of a Hellenism (superstructure) which is informed by it. Apart from the obvious significance of moving the debate on from Chapter 5, this new framework has also engendered two specific outcomes that are of some importance. For the sake of analytical clarity, I shall call these outcomes *primary* and *secondary*.

Putting it concisely, the *primary* outcome defines two central aspects of Myres' output: first, his thoughts on race and culture as well as the way in which they contrasted with other contemporary schools of thoughts; and second, depiction of Hellenism and the manner in which it deviated from the mainstream.

As discussed at length in Chapter 3, the debate concerning race and culture was one of the main areas of dispute in the pre-war years. Myres' unpublished writing on this matter was situated only adjacently to the accepted spectrum of views that were expressed by the Royal Anthropological Committee that produced the 'Race and Culture' document in 1935. At one ideological end of this it was asserted that any connection between culture and race is nothing but a racist fallacy (Elliot-Smith), and on the other end, it was firmly believed that race and culture are strongly connected to one another (Pitt-Rivers). Whereas the committee's central aim was to rationalize the alleged relationship between race and culture, Myres attempted to synthesize them. By insisting in 'Races and Cultures' that when we use pre- and ancient historical evidence, a cohering of cultures (which crucially includes language) and races 'in their regional distributions and historical spread'[117] manifests itself, Myres is underlining his continuing reliance on the utility of 'distributional and historical sciences'. With 'the perspective of the past becoming wonderfully deeper, while that of the present wonderfully widens', he avows that 'a new kind of scientific knowledge and scientific method, distributional rather than systematic, historical and geographical, rather than physical or biological'[118] is becoming a major part of the intellectual activities of the day. It is within the contours of this 'deeper' and 'wider' perspective that Myres posited his attempt to understand who the Greeks were.

The ideas concerning race and culture were representative of the more abstract aspect of Myres' grand template. The more concrete aspect of it was the historical narratives that were discussed in Chapter 5. The main reason why 'distributional and historical sciences' (anthropology, comparative philology, comparative mythology, archaeology and so on) were deemed necessary had to do with the recognition that the authority, evidence and analysis of the ancient sources were in need of qualitative improvement. They, as Collingwood had indicated, were to be the interpolative threads that connected one historical fixed point with another. Of course,

Myres adjusts Collingwood's prognosis considerably. He accepts that ancient history differs from modern history in many ways; hence similar approaches could not be countenanced. The introduction of scientific thinking enables him to deal not only with the shortcomings of his Hellenic authorities (Herodotus, etc.), but also to make headway with a number of other specific issues, such as the thorny question of 'race' and its relation to the multi-layered concept of 'culture'. This double-perspective suggests a symbiotic relationship, thus implying that his approach towards the question of 'who the Greeks were' was partly predicated upon how he viewed the relationship between 'race' and 'culture'. 'Neither race purely nor culture merely, but a people'[119] was how Myres saw the relationship between them. Moreover, he explicitly refused to attach 'value' to a given 'people'.[120] He had also considered the concepts of 'race' and 'culture' to be time-dependent variables, meaning that as you go back in time, they cohere; and as you go forward, they diverge. These three inferences (see Chapter 3 for extensive discussions) are central to Myres' thinking and his brand of Hellenism for a number of reasons. By giving the primary role to 'people', he endows ethnicity with greater weight than he allows for 'race'.[121] Furthermore, by resisting the temptation to compute a set of values for a given people, he avoids Gordon Childe's faux pas (see Chapters 3 and 4). In addition, by regarding the relationship between race and culture as a dynamic one, he implicitly rejects the idea that 'race' is a static phenomenon, which, in turn, undermines the notion that there could be this or that specific ('superior' or 'inferior') race. Finally, by describing 'race' and 'culture' as the 'coefficients' of 'people', Myres renders them secondary when compared to the primacy of 'people'. His overarching analysis can best be compared to that of a painting: what is visible as a pictorial narrative is the 'people'; what is invisible – namely, literary allusions, artistic influences, preliminary sketches, abandoned motifs, pencil-marks on the canvas, etc. – represent the concepts of 'race' and 'culture'. They are there, but they are there in a particular way, and they matter in a particular way: their contributions are palimpsestic; they represent the thoughts that the artist must have had before and during the execution of the final pictorial narrative.

The secondary outcome is what can specifically be inferred from the application of this twofold primary outcome. The discussion in the previous chapter suggests that Myres has rendered the Indo-European component of the ancient Greek composite as the most consequential defining characteristic of Greekness. This rendering does not take place in a void; unlike Childe's treatment of this subject in *The Aryans* (see Chapter 4), it has theoretical causalities. The way in which he perceives the relationship between race and culture, and the manner in which he augments his historical framework with science are precisely what differentiate Myres' Hellenism from that of Murray. The fact that aesthetic Hellenism is largely devoid of scientific thinking is neither surprising nor is it a reason for criticism. The fact that it takes very little account of the full discipline of history, however, is worrying. This is further compounded by a tendency to elevate the Greeks into some kind of deified figures and depict their doings in a reverential manner. The combination of creating figures detached from the human world and replacing critical historical thinking with a 'common-sense theory of history' and aesthetic sensibilities, the advocates of this school of thought have been producing, at best, lopsided history, and at worst, no history at all. Why should this matter? It matters because they have continued to write what is generally classified as history. Now if these writings were to concern themselves exclusively with purely Greek matters, then their writerly qualities are no concern of this work. What does concern it, however, is when these authors deal with the Persian Wars, the defeat of the Achaemenids by Alexander and, above all, the generic idea of 'East v. West'. The question that comes to mind when one is leafing through one of these documents is as follows: how can an important historical episode, such as the Persian Wars, be judiciously told, when the teller does not merely prefer one set of the protagonists over the other, but is positively bowled-over and smitten by it? Although such partiality in itself is disconcerting, it is only ephemeral to what the 'uncritical acceptance of the ancient sources' and the 'love of beauty' have been responsible for. The debate needs to move on, and the question needs to be rethought. But how should it be rethought?

V – Conclusions

At first glance, the scientific and aesthetic classifications of Hellenism seemed to have been a case of straightforward correspondences – the first, an offshoot of the Enlightenment; the second, an offspring of Romanticism. Although there is more than an element of truth in these categorizations, whence they came is ultimately of little significance. This is so because the process of categorizing in itself cannot reveal all there is to know regarding the characteristics and the inner dynamics of these two varieties of Hellenisms. A rereading of C. P. Snow's *The Two Cultures and the Scientific Revolution* (1959) impressed upon me that what must be looked at is, first, how the protagonists of these Hellenisms have gone about their academic and intellectual business (Part I); and second, what the philosophical precepts were that drove their works forward (Part II).[122]

In Part I, it was ascertained that for mainstream Hellenism, the beauty and perfection of ancient Greece were sufficient criteria for comprehending classical Greek civilization.[123] It was also established that the practitioners of this form of Hellenism were not entirely friendly towards a number of sciences, saving their most venomous antipathy for mainstream (physical) anthropology. Conversely, anthropology was very much part and parcel of another way of doing Hellenism. According to its main advocate, Myres, a 'triangular relationship' between science, history and Hellenism was the most accurate definer of how one should go about acquiring a comprehensive understanding of the Greek world. Having stipulated and contrasted the main characteristics of each Hellenism, Part I ended by enquiring what had philosophically underpinned these contrasting characteristics.

Within the analytical framework of this chapter, it has been inferred that not only were there a number of sturdy philosophical foundations upon which these Hellenisms were perched, but also, and as a consequence of examining these foundations, it has been possible to detect further contrasting characteristics that were not identified in the previous chapter. Moreover, by looking closely at the relevant aspects of the philosophies of history, of science and of aesthetics, the earlier-drawn inferences were reappraised and modified accordingly. Hence, it was inferred that, first, aesthetic Hellenism in its dealing with historical matters was bereft of adequate critical rigour; and second, the renamed 'historico-scientific' Hellenism was now something quite different from the one represented by the 'triangular relationship' that was distilled from Myres' texts rather than (crucially) deciphered from his philosophical subtexts.

Parts I and II should neither be seen as one instalment following the other analogously, nor should the second part be viewed as an improvement on the first. In their stead, Chapters 5 and 6 should be seen as representing the *inner* and the *outer* manifestations of the same phenomenon, namely the study of ancient Greece. When this complementary dualism is taken in parallel with the antinomy that resides within the body of Hellenism ('aesthetic' v. 'historico-scientific'), then we have the required contexts within which to think afresh the question that ended section IV: what can Myres' Hellenism (including its Indo-Europeanizing of the Greeks), his writing on race and culture, as well as his largely unpublished writing on the Achaemenids, tell us about the *historical framing* of the ancient Iranian peoples and their cultures?

CHAPTER 7

HELLENISMS AND THE HISTORIOGRAPHY OF ANCIENT PERSIA

Modern Europe's direct interest in Persian history is a relatively new phenomenon. Prior to the turn of the last century, it was not an easy task to compile a bibliography of more than a half a dozen publications which, in any significant way, could have related to the history of the ancient Iranian world or its peoples. The interested parties therefore found it necessary to refer to other genres of contemporary writings, such as travel writings, biblical studies and, of course, classics for a better understanding of the Persian world. This chapter concentrates on the classics.

While the state of literature concerning the ancient Persians can be described as barren, their Greek counterparts were supplied with what can only be described as an assembly-line of book production that churned out seemingly endless quantities of literature concerning their history and civilization. It is within the pages of these works that Achaemenid Persia was discussed at some length, and what was discussed remained broadly faithful to certain core assumptions, such as the idea that the Persian Wars should be seen as a clash between Europeans and Asiatics, between occidental freedom and oriental despotism; and that Alexander's conquest of the Achaemenid Empire was a much-needed *mission civilisatrice*.

Section I is a historiographical survey of these, mostly, Hellenocentric texts. The last portion analyses some of Myres' published and unpublished papers and tries to elucidate the very different nature of his contributions (he is interesting because his tendency, as discussed in the previous four chapters, was to approach these matters from anthropological and geographical perspectives). This analysis is extended further in the subsequent section (II), where questions relating to historical teleology and the appropriateness or otherwise of using certain terms and vocabularies are examined. Section III concludes the chapter.

I – Achaemenid Persia: A Historiographical Survey[1]

Towards the end of the eighteenth century, as discussed in Chapter 2, the introduction of comparative philology had altered the way in which ancient history as an academic discipline was framed. The dividing line between an Asiatic East and a European West ceased to be clear-cut. Within the limits set by the new Indo-European outlook, the old certainties concerning the 'orientalness' of the Iranians began to look increasingly outmoded and ripe for reassessment. The consequences of such a move for the way in which Graeco-Persian history was to be written appeared to be substantial. As a result, different attitudes were engendered; or to be precise, a single attitude with a wide conceptual range manifested itself: namely, cognitive dissonance or *doublethink* ('the mental capacity to accept contrary opinions or beliefs at the same time').[2] This attitude, for analytical clarity, can be divided into three broad segments. The first segment downplays the supposed Indo-European commonalities between the Greeks and the Persians almost to the point of ignoring them completely (I.a). Although the second segment accepts the Indo-European framework explicitly, it does so without foregoing the Orientalism embedded in mainstream Hellenism. The doublethink remains, in other words, in a state of perpetual irresolution (I.b). The third segment moves towards some form of resolution, but without quite getting there. In this segment, and largely due to the conceptual discipline of the Indo-European framework, the tendency to orientalize the Persians vis-à-vis the Greeks is substantially reduced, albeit not eradicated entirely (I.c). In parallel with these segments, there is a smaller mindset, which, largely due to a number of disparate analytical and/or ideological reasonings, did not display any form of doublethink at all (I.d).

a) Doublethink Downplayed

Those following this form of historical writing had either chosen not to mention the Indo-European aspect or had merely drawn attention to it sparingly and in passing. In his *Reflection on the Philosophy of History of Mankind* (1775), Herder was one of the first writers to acknowledge, in a roundabout way, the Indo-European background of the Persians by opining that if 'Xenophon [had] truly described the manner of the Persians', then, 'the German may be proud, that he is probably of a race allied to theirs, and may the Cyropedia be read by every prince in Germany'.[3] This passage notwithstanding, the general tenor of the writing is staunchly Hellenocentric. Herder distinguishes the Persians and the Medes by their love of luxury and 'Asiatic manners'.[4] In addition, Xerxes shed 'feminine tears'[5] and displayed what is described as the quintessentially Persian aptitude for destruction and damage. 'Did any Persian ravager of the world,' Herder asks rhetorically, 'found such kingdoms, cities, and edifices, as he destroyed, or endeavoured to destroy; Babylon, Thebes, Sidon, Greece, and Athens? Was any one of them capable of founding such?'[6] In dealing with the Greeks, Herder is full of poetic praise: 'With Greece the morning breaks, and we joyfully sail to meet it.'[7] After cataloguing the achievements of the Greeks, he deals with the Persian Wars, in which 'the Persians under Xerxes attacked as barbarians: in one hand they brought chain to enslave; in the other, fire to lay desolate'. But having 'conducted the war with a great force, and much fury; but without skill',[8] the Persians were not able to carry the day.

In a similar vein, G. W. Cox argues in *The Greeks and the Persians* (1887) that 'Eastern empires' have a tendency towards 'aggressive' conquest followed by 'satiety [...] luxurious inaction', and then 'speedy decay'. After all, with 'no national life, no growth of intellect, no spirit of personal independence in the individual citizen', such imperial structures can only remain in indefinite turpitude;[9] 'The struggle thus brought about between Europe and Asia was, in fact, between orderly government and uncontrolled despotism, between law which insures freedom of thought, speech, and action, and the licence of a tyrant whose iniquities can be cut short only by the dagger of an assassin.'[10] Cox, of course, acknowledges the 'Aryan' background of the Greeks and opines that 'we cannot shut our eyes to the evidence which traces back the polity of all the Aryan tribes or nations to the form of village communities';[11] *poleis* in their infancy, in other words. Furthermore, he asserts that the 'fabric of all ancient Aryan society was intensely religious',[12] implying that 'village communities' derived their political legitimacy, partly at least, from 'Aryan' forms of religious practices. Now with all these 'Aryan' sociological and theological underpinnings, Cox asserts that for the:

> Assyrian or the Persian [sic] the human body was a thing to be insulted and mutilated at his will, to be disgraced by servile prostrations, or to be offered in sacrifice to wrathful and bloodthirsty deities. For him woman was a mere chattel, while his children were possessions of which he might make profit by selling them into slavery.[13]

Conversely, the intellectual education and independence of the Greeks implied that of 'these abominable usages the Greek practically knew nothing'.[14] Furthermore, a Greek would rather return to 'primitive cannibalism' than adopt the slavish behaviours of the Persians. The coupling of the Persian with the Assyrian and the fact that the analysis takes place within an 'Aryan' context hints at some conceptual confusion. He further asserts 'that the natural tendency of the earliest Greek, as of other Aryan societies, would be towards an oligarchy of chiefs'.[15] Again, he refrains from acknowledging that the Persians, as a matter of definitional necessity, must have also the same social relationships. Instead, Cox argues that in the East there existed a 'servile awe of kings who, as representatives of the deity, show themselves only on rare occasions in all the paraphernalia of barbaric royalty, and otherwise remained in the seclusion of the seraglio, objects of mysterious veneration and dread'.[16] The result of the Persian Wars, according to Cox, was that:

> the conquest of Europe was no longer a vision which could cheat the fancy of the lord of Asia. The will and energy of Athens, aided by the rugged discipline of Sparta, had foiled the great enterprise through which the barbarian despot sought to repress in the deadly bonds of Persian thraldom the intellect and freedom of the world.[17]

Strictly speaking, Lord Curzon's *Persia and the Persian Question* (1892) was not a history of ancient Persia. It was more of a guidebook for the intended traveller or amateur archaeologist. Being a member of the ruling elite and a future foreign secretary, Curzon's considerations on Persia were part of the Great (imperialist) Game in keeping India, that 'inalienable badge of sovereignty in the eastern hemisphere',[18] from the clutches of a bellicose Tsarist Russia. He begins his lengthy work by asserting – only once and in passing – that 'it ought not to be difficult to interest Englishmen in the Persian people. They have the same lineage as ourselves. Three thousand years ago their forefathers left the uplands of that mysterious Aryan home from which our ancestral stock had already gone forth.'[19] Curzon has little to say with regard to the wars between the Persians and Greeks. His ancient Persia, the 'Persia of Herodotus and Xenophon',[20] is only discussed aesthetically. Persian art and architecture – 'the last expression of a strictly Asiatic genius, the heir of Chaldaea, and Assyria, and Egypt'[21] – were considered by him to be mimetic, largely inorganic and tediously repetitive:

> No one can wander over the Persepolitan platform, from storied stairway to stairway, from sculptured doorway to graven pier, or one can contemplate the 1,200 human figures that still move in solemn reduplication upon the stone, without being struck with a sense of monotony, and fatigue. It is all the same, and the same again, and yet again.[22]

Although J. B. Bury in *A History of Greece* (1909) concedes that 'the Persians and Medes spoke a language of the same stock as that of the Greeks', he, nonetheless, goes on to assert:

> [I]f the Persians had come under Greek influence, Iranian history would have taken a different course. For the Persians were a people marked out to fall under the influence of others and not to hew an independent path for themselves. [But] it was their inevitable doom to be led captive by their captives and to adopt the manner and ideals of more intellectual and original peoples. If Cyrus had transported the centre of his empire to the west, the Greeks might have been the teachers of their Persian speech-fellows; but such an idea would have occurred to no Mede or Persian. Consequently the new Iranian kingdom fell under the relaxing influences of the corrupt Semitic civilisations of Babylonia and Assyria; it had soon become a despotism so typically oriental that is hard to remember that the ruling peoples spoke a tongue akin to the Greek. Hence the struggle of two hundred years [...] between Greece and Persia, though strictly and literally it was a struggle between Aryan peoples [...] assumes the larger character of strife between east and west, between Aryan and non-Aryan, and takes its place as the first encounter in that still unclosed debate which has arrayed Europe successively against Babylonian, Phoenician, Saracen, and Turk.[23]

It is remarkable that Bury can simultaneously acknowledge that the Persians were Aryan and successfully 'other' them in a convoluted fashion that presents itself as perfectly reasonable – by invoking culture over ethnicity and rendering them 'Semitic', 'oriental' and 'non-Aryan'. A similar ideological flourish marks E. M. Walker's *Greek History* (1921). He states that in 'Persia we find the antithesis of all that is characteristic of Greece – autocracy as opposed to liberty; a military society organized on an aristocratic basis to an industrial society animated by a democratic spirit'.[24]

One of the major publications of the period was *The Cambridge Ancient History*, and in particular its fourth volume, entitled *The Persian Empire and the West* (1926). The 'main theme of the present volume', according to the preface, was 'the supreme struggle between the Persian Empire and the West'.[25] The preface also states that the 'Greeks and Greek states have been leading actors in the events recorded in the present volume'.[26] Since 'in the perennial debate between East and West this clash is the first of which the story is known in detail',[27] the editors are firm in their contention that its account should be told as comprehensively as possible. As in Curzon, the 'Aryan' background of the Persians/Medes is acknowledged only in passing, but curiously, especially when one recalls the title of the volume, a whole chapter is given over to the study of the Indo-European communities in Italy. As far as the Persian Wars were concerned, what was asserted in the introductory pages and the fact that the title of the relevant chapter was 'The Deliverance of Greece', as well as only devoting two chapters out of 16 to the Achaemenid Empire, the ideological aims of the editors could scarcely have been a better understanding of the Persians, but the manner in which 'the West' survived the struggle against them.

Although M. Laistner is silent on matters Indo-European, in *A Survey of Ancient History* (1929), he gives a fair summary of the relevant events: '[T]he preliminary round in the struggle between East and West began in 499 with a revolt of the Greek subjects of the Great King in Asia Minor.'[28] The author, however, acknowledges that under Persian tutelage '[t]yrannies were finally abolished and democratic governments were set up in the Greek poleis by Darius' orders. It was a remarkable example of broad-mindedness on the part of an oriental despot who would be least in sympathy with any form of popular government.'[29] Such benign views of the Persians (despite calling it a struggle between East and West) were not forthcoming in the publication, the same year, of R. W. Rogers's *The History of Ancient Persia* (1929). Although the author concedes, as it was the case with nearly all of the publications under examination, the 'Aryan'[30] background of the Persians, the title should not disguise the author's overriding aim, namely the recounting of the superior qualities of the Greeks:

> They [the Greeks] had won the contest not merely by fighting, not merely by skill in battle on sea and shore, but because in the deepest of all fundamental things they were a superior people, in civilisation indeed, as all later centuries have securely judged and determined, and also in the number of higher moral qualities.[31]

The other side of this 'superior people' argument has always been the deficiencies which characterize the Persian civilization. E. Herzfeld argues in *Archaeological History of Iran* (1935) that 'when the Persians attempted to accept everything that was Greek [...] they did not grasp the reason and proportion, but were satisfied with the semblance. The result is a hybrid art, if art it can be called, worthy to be studied only out of scientific and historical, not of aesthetic, interest.'[32] He also argues that 'while preparing the Western world for a great future, [Hellenism] had the most destructive effect on Iran'.[33] As far as the Sasanian era was concerned, he infers that a reversal from crude Hellenism ('European'[34]) was marked with 'weak activity'. This type of analysis was given a more general twist by J. M. Todd in *The Ancient World* (1938). It begins with what he considers to be self-evident:

> The European way of thought is far different from the Indian. If indeed we tried to define precisely the distinctions between East and West we should find some difficulties; but the broad contrasts remain, and they are thrown into high relief when some conflict brings the representative of one way of life face to face with his opposite.

One prime example of this was the 'clashes in the history of civilization [...] between the East and the West which took place [...] in the thousand years or so which began about 600 BC. It was a conflict as much of ideas as of armies.'[35]

When it was the Persians threatening to take over the Greek-speaking world, the Greeks, according to a large number of Hellenists of the period (and later), were safeguarding their freedom from the Asiatic Persians. Alexander's takeover of the Achaemenids, in contrast, has been depicted as a civilizing mission. 'No body,' according to J. Mahaffy in *Alexander's Empire* (1887),

> ever thought of going back beyond Alexander and his conquests to make a historic claim, or to demand the restoration of ancient sovranties [sic]. His conquests were regarded as perfectly lawful, the world his natural heritage, his will as a lawful testament. So, then, we may begin with him without much retrospect and see what he founded, and what he did for the advance of the world.[36]

In fact, Alexander was seen by many, in the author's judgement, to be 'the father and protector' of the orientals.[37] In a similar fashion, Bury, while discussing the 'spirit of Alexander's policy as lord of Asia', argues that 'the Macedonian king, the commander-in-chief of the Greek confederates, had set forth as a champion of Greeks against mere barbarians, as a leader of Europeans against effeminate Asiatics, as the representative of a higher folk against beings lower in the human scale'.[38] The fact that the '[m]ultitudes', which were recruited by the Persian army, 'were useless without a leader', and since 'money could not create brain',[39] the martial aptitude of the Achaemenid forces could not have been formidable enough to overcome the genius of Alexander or the competence of his armies.

Hutton Webster in *A History of the Ancient World* (1915) asserts that with the conquests of Alexander, '[E]verywhere into that huge, inert, unprogressive Oriental world came the active and enterprising men of Hellas. They brought their arts and culture, and became the teachers of those whom they had called "barbarians".'[40] Moreover, '[t]he ultimate result of Alexander's conquests was the fusion of East and West'. It was indeed Alexander's intention that 'the European and the Asiatic should gradually pass away'.[41] This belief was also shared by Bury. In *The Hellenistic Age* (1923) he writes that 'the change so suddenly wrought by Alexander in his ten miraculous years, substituting European for Asiatic rule all over the Near East, set problems which no European statesman had ever had to face before'.[42] The same type of argument was part of U. Wilcken's biography of Alexander. His *Alexander the Great* (1932) has nothing on the Indo-European front. The Persian/Iranians, although not Semites, are unquestionably orientals in the author's analysis. 'From the very first,' in his view, 'it was apparent to Alexander, the pupil of Aristotle, that this Asiatic campaign was to be not merely a military expedition but a great civilising event.'[43] Alexander had also managed to rule Asia and Europe according to what was customarily acceptable in each. 'As King of Asia,' Wilken contends, 'he was to the Asiatics an absolute ruler in the sense of the Achaemenids and sealed letters intended for Asia with the seal of Darius.' His less absolutist letters destined for 'Europe', in contrast, were sealed 'with his old Macedonian seal'.[44] Wilcken, moreover, echoes Webster by stating that 'the previous barriers between East and West were removed, and in [the] next generation thousands of Greeks traders and artisans entered the new world'.[45] This was so because 'Alexander reached these Oriental peoples, [when] the zenith of their development was past by centuries, or even millennia; their creative power seemed to have died out, and their condition was generally one of stagnation'.[46] Bearing in mind that Achaemenid rule lasted only two or so centuries, this assertion seems to be somewhat implausible; or at least, not entirely applicable to the Indo-Iranians.[47]

b) *Doublethink in a State of Irresolution*

In *The Five Great Monarchies of the Ancient Eastern World* (1862), G. Rawlinson has no qualms about the Indo-European background of the Persians and the Medes. He even buttresses this by taking Herodotus' contention concerning the remarkable thinness of Persian skulls as a matter of fact, and argues that this thinness implied 'a large brain-cavity and so an unusual volume of brain, which is generally a concomitant of high intellectual power'. He writes: 'The Persians seem, certainly, to have been quick and lively, keen-witted, capable of repartee, ingenious, and, for Orientals, far sighted.' Despite this, however, the author warns that 'we cannot ascribe to them a high degree of intellectual excellence'.[48] And one of the examples of their shortcomings was the lack of 'artistic genius'[49] displayed by their architecture. In *Parthia* (1893), he incorrectly infers that the Parthians were of Turkic background: 'their sculptures give them the large ill-formed limbs, the heavy paunches, and the general appearance which characterised Turanian races.'[50] Now that Rawlinson is contrasting the 'Turkic' Parthians against 'Aryan' Persians, the architecture of the latter suddenly no longer seems to be without merit: 'in the arts they [the Parthians] were particularly backward, devoid of taste, and wanting in originality. Considering the patterns that they had before their eyes [Pasargadae, Persepolis, etc.], it is simply astonishing that they could rise no higher than the mean palace at Hatra.'[51]

In relation to the Persian domination of the Ionian cities, Mahaffy, in *A Survey of Greek Civilization* (1897), contends that 'the loss of independence and of political liberty seems to have marred the bloom and blighted the growth of Greek genius. The whole greatness of these cities is before the Persian domination.'[52] He does, however, acknowledge that the artistic and lifestyle influences of the Persians had some benefits for the Greeks.[53] This was so because the 'eastern (Aryan) nobles were not barbarians in any reasonable sense, but civilized and probably cultivated men', many of whom must have resembled 'the old French *noblesse*'.[54] The author, interestingly, regards the Battle of Marathon as 'only a very unimportant skirmish'[55] and awards the role of decisive battle of the wars to Salamis, while at the same time conceding that 'the defeat was probably not so crushing to the Persians as the Greeks pretended'.[56] This type of New Achaemenid History, *avant les lettres*, was not, however, pursued by Edurad Meyer. In his contribution to the eleventh edition of the *Encyclopaedia Britannica* (1911), Meyer, admittedly, gives a sober and enlightened summary of the Achaemenid Empire, but he largely bases it on Herodotus and the Old Testament and thus succumbs to the pitfalls of the 'commonsense theory of history'. By not engaging with the *Histories* and the Old Testament in an appropriately critical manner, Meyer's account of the history of the Achaemenids – despite Momigliano's not incorrect contention that he was unfashionably fond of the Persians – is no more than a re-editing of the classical texts. This tendency is surprising, because it is at odds with the interest that he had shown some years earlier concerning matters Indo-European. As Momigliano established in his 'Introduction to a Discussion of Eduard Meyer', Meyer treated this subject matter in the first volume of his *Geschichte des Altertums* (1902) anthropologically;[57] and in the second, by indulging 'in arguments about their [Indo-European peoples] superiority of feeling',[58] historically. Although in the article he does not disguise the Indo-European background of the Iranian peoples, their alleged oriental tendencies are seldom forgotten:

> As early as 465 BC, Xerxes was assassinated by his powerful vizier (*chiliarch*) [...]. A similar instance may be found in Bagoas, after the murder of Artaxerxes III (338 BC). To these factors must be added the degeneration of the royal line – a degeneration inevitable in Oriental states. Kings like Xerxes [...] so far from being gloomy despots, were good natured potentates, but weak, capricious and readily accessible to personal influences.[59]

In *A History of the Ancient World* (1915), Webster begins with a 'racial' discussion and provides a map of how the Indo-European and other peoples were distributed geographically.[60] This Indo-European oneness is superseded some 140 pages later by the following topic under discussion: 'East and West in conflict: The Persian Wars.'[61] 'Orient and Occident,' in his view, 'for so many centuries sharply sundered, began now to draw together. Their contact produced the Persian Wars.'[62] He does not however situate these wars within the context of his earlier 'racial' discussion. In other words, he does not see that these wars can also be perceived, particularly within the confines of his own conceptualization, as an Indo-European 'civil war'. Moreover, for Webster the story of Greece's 'victory forms an imperishable record in the annals of human freedom'.[63] The reason why the Greeks were victorious is described as the superiority of their equipment, discipline and leadership:

The Persian wars were more than a contest for supremacy between two rival powers. They were a contest between East and West; between Oriental despotism and Occidental democracy. Had Persia won, the fresh, vigorous Western civilization then being developed by Athens and other Greek states would have submerged, perhaps for ages, under the influx of eastern ideas and customs. The Greek victory saved Europe for better things. It was a victory for human freedom.[64]

In D. G. Hogarth's view in *The Ancient East* (1914), 'the West did not assimilate the East except in very small measure'. For a variety of reasons, 'among which geographical facts – the large proportion of steppe-desert and of the human type which such country breeds – are perhaps the most powerful, the East is obstinately unreceptive of western influences, and more than once it has taken its captors captive'.[65] By asserting that the incoming Iranian peoples brought with them to the East 'the germs of higher development',[66] Hogarth seems to be situating the Iranian peoples outside what he means by the 'Ancient East'. This is stated at the very beginning of the work. Towards the end of it, however, the fall of Lydia to Cyrus is described as having effectively removed crucial 'buffers between the Orient and Greece', placing 'East and West [...] in direct contact and the omen boded ill for the West'.[67] Hogarth inserts a racial proviso at this point:

> It should be remarked that the new universal power {was} not only non-Semitic for the first time in well-certified history, but controlled by a very pure Aryan stock, much nearer kin to the people of the West than any Oriental folk with which they have had intimate relation hitherto. The Persians appeared from the Back of Beyond, uncontaminated by Alarodian savagery and unhampered by the theocratic prepossessions and nomadic traditions of the Semites. They were highlanders of unimpaired vigour, frugal habit, settled agricultural life, long established social cohesion and spiritual religious conceptions.[68]

In addition, 'free from the Semitic tradition of annual raiding, the Persians reduced the obligation of military service to a bearable burden and avoided continual provocation of frontier neighbours. Free likewise from Semitic supermonotheistic ideas, they did not seek to impose their creed.'[69]

When the subject of 'Persia and the Greeks' is discussed, these types of arguments, which are based on an Indo-European template, disappear speedily. In this new context, Persia imposes 'herself on cities which possessed a civilization superior, not only potentially but actually, to her own; on cities where individual and communal passion for freedom constituted the one religion incompatible with her tolerant sway'.[70] Hogarth, in addition, makes a great deal of Persia's reliance on 'Hellenic statesmen and men of science': 'Such an attitude towards Greeks was suicidal. It exalted the spirit of Europe while it depraved the courage and sapped the self-reliance of Asia.'[71] Stories such as 'how little ten Orientals availed in attack or defence against one Greek [which] one day would encourage a stronger Western power than hers [Sparta] to march to the conquest of the East'[72] are ubiquitous in this work. In the chapter entitled 'The Victory of the West', Hogarth argues that with the victory of Alexander, the Persian Empire and indeed 'the East' 'was subject to the European race which a century and a half before it had tried to subdue in Europe itself'.[73] 'The victory of the West over the Ancient East,' concludes the author, 'may be regarded as achieved on the day of Arbela.'[74] How and when these Iranian peoples – who were 'unhampered by the theocratic prepossessions and nomadic traditions of the Semites' – had metamorphosed from Aryans into bona fide orientals is not made at all clear by the author.

Henry Breasted's *Ancient Times* (1916) unambiguously divides the ancient world into Semitic and Indo-European portions (see Figure 1):

> The history of the ancient world [...] was largely made up of the struggle between [the] southern Semitic line, which issued from the southern grasslands, and the northern Indo-European

line, which came forth from the northern grasslands to confront the older civilizations represented in the southern line. Thus as we look at the diagram we see two great races facing each other across the Mediterranean like two vast armies stretching from Western Asia westward to the Atlantic. The later wars between Rome and Carthage represent some of the operations of the Semitic left wing, while the triumph of Persia over Chaldea is a similar outcome on the Semitic right wing.[75]

Moreover, Breasted expounds that we should:

bear in mind that we are watching a great racial change, and remember that these new Iranian masters of the East were our kindred; for both we and they have descended from the same wandering shepherd ancestors, the Indo-European parent people, who once dwelt in the far-off pastures of inner Asia, probably five thousand years ago.[76]

When it comes to the Persians as the enemies of the Greeks, however, the framework reverts back to the oriental/occidental and European/Asiatic

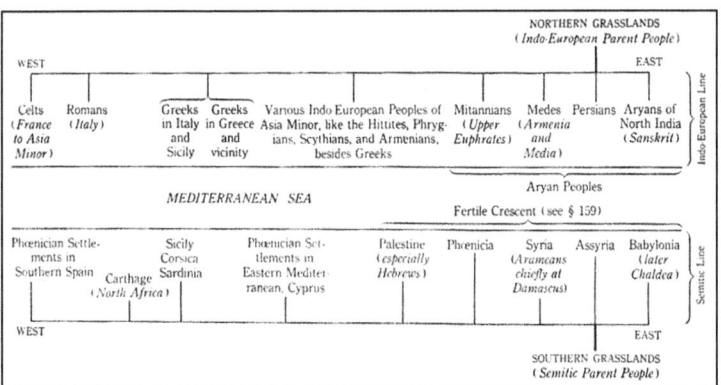

Figure 1 *Diagram suggesting the two lines of Semitic and Indo-European dispersion. Taken from Brested (1916), p. 239*

dichotomies. Persia, all of a sudden becomes 'the last of the great Oriental powers'.[77] Forgetting his own diagram (Figure 1), the author seems entirely unaware of the contradictions within his framework, and in a chapter entitled 'The Repulse of Persia', Breasted describes Persia as a 'despotic Oriental power',[78] and then goes on to discuss the various Persian 'invasions of Europe'.

One of the few books of the period on Persia exclusively was Percy Sykes' *History of Persia* (1917). This work deals extensively with the Persian Wars extensively. Before all that, however, Sykes praises Cyrus by asserting that 'we, too, may feel proud that the first great Aryan whose character is known in history should have displayed such splendid qualities'.[79] It also discusses in length the concept of the 'Aryan religious practices, vis-à-vis those belonging to the Semites and other non-Indo-Europeans'. 'With the Aryans there was not, as in the case of Sumerians,' writes Sykes,

> the propitiation of the evil spirit. Rather they had to be faced and overcome by the good spirits, who, in their turn, depended largely for success on the prayers and sacrifices of man. It is thus evident that, from the beginning, the position of man was one of assured dignity, with a manly attitude towards his deities.[80]

The tenor of the 'titanic campaigns' of the wars, 'in which the leading Aryan nation of Asia attacked its distant kinsmen in Europe', moves decisively away from these types of assertions and towards the more familiar terrain of Orientalism. The victory of the Greeks was attributed by Sykes to their 'wonderful moral[s]', advantage of fighting on rugged ground, armaments and the 'remoteness of Hellas'. From the viewpoint of the world, 'Marathon, Salamis, and Plataea were victories not only for Greece but for mankind. It was the triumph of the higher ideals.'[81] As a consequence, and for over two centuries, 'from Hellas to India, Semitic and Turanian states were alike ruled by Greek dynasties permeated with the Hellenic spirit'. The author, moreover, draws a close parallel between Hellenism and the British Empire:[82] 'Given then the Greek character, it is reasonable to suppose that in ordinary conditions the position of the subject races would be better than under the rule of Persia, just as the Englishman shows incomparably greater consideration to the Indian than the Indians do to their fellow countrymen.'[83]

In H. R. James's *Our Hellenic Heritage* (1921) there is a chapter on Persia, 'The Peril from the East',[84] which asserts that the term 'barbarian' was used by the Greeks against 'wild tribes of Thrace, Sicily, or Epirus, and savage Scythians, but also of Eastern peoples'. It is interesting to note that, unlike those dwelling to the north and west of Greece, Eastern peoples form an abstract monolith in the mind of the author. In a long footnote, he accepts that the Persians were largely of an Indo-European background, but they somehow do not behave accordingly: 'the Persian subjects of the Great King reckoned their lives as nothing, compared with the safety and comfort of their king.'[85] Moreover, the qualities which saved Hellas were the usual ones: equipment, discipline, etc., but also patriotism: with 'personal devotion to their king', the Persians lacked this patriotism.[86] Moreover, the Persians' love of luxury, 'which did not conduce to military efficiency',[87] was also blamed. By basing his argument entirely on an uncritical reading of Herodotus, James singles out the conceit and vanity of the Persians.[88] In a chapter entitled 'The Great Deliverance' (foreshadowing *The Cambridge Ancient History* by five years), James argues that 'the Persian failed against Hellas, because his cause was a worse cause, because the principles his power stood for were lower principles than the principles in which Hellenic life was rooted'.[89] The author, however, does approve of the 'high qualities of the Persian race as warriors and administrators'.[90] But the Greek victory 'meant in the long run for us the preservation of a distinctive European civilization and the emancipation of the human spirit'.[91]

G. W. Botsford's *Hellenic History* (1922) is an excellent example of 'doublethink' at its most extreme. On the ethnology of the Greeks, he states that the

> immigrants from the North were evidently a minority of the population; but superior virility gave their leaders a dominant place in their respective districts. It was not simply the

mainland that began in this way to fall under Indo-European control. Evidently individual adventurers [...] crossed to the islands, where by cleverness and personal superiority they attained to a place in the ruling classes and mingled their speech with that of the natives.[92]

The first military successes of this group, according to Botsford, were in Nineveh, when in 612 BC it 'was taken by a combination of highly civilized Babylonians with the Medes, a fresh virile Indo-European people'.[93] The 'revolution' that made the Median empire Persian 'placed in control a still more vigorously aggressive Indo-European race of mountaineers under a leader [Cyrus] of extraordinary genius and ambition'.[94] Yet again the mood music changes dramatically when the author concerns himself with the Persian War. 'The fundamental cause of the great war between Greece and the Asiatic empire,' argues Botsford, 'lay in the Persian policy of conquest. The chief interest in Oriental empire-building had always been predatory – the acquisition of slaves and other booty attending the subjugation thereafter imposed.'[95] The main outcome of Marathon was the demonstration that 'the Greek warrior was superior to the Persian', as well as the halting of the 'westward advance of the Asiatic empire'. In addition, 'the Greeks were inspired with a fair hope of maintaining their freedom'.[96] He also writes:

> [T]he permanent occupation of Greece [by the Persians] would doubtless have been a calamity for civilization. Although Greeks and Persians were alike of Indo-European speech, there could have been no considerable racial element common to the two peoples. Through the influence of environment the Persians were becoming essentially Oriental. Originally a fresh virile race of mountaineers, they rapidly submitted to the culture of the Tigris-Euphrates valley. It was a question [of] whether the Hellenes should be brought more or less directly under Babylonian influence. The half-century of Oriental domination over Ionia has been offered as evidence that Hellenism prospered under such conditions. In answer it may

be said that fifty years are but a brief season in the life of a people, and that in truth the cultural glory of the Asiatic Hellas had largely past [sic] away before the battle of Plataea.[97]

There is an obvious defect with this argument; Botsford does not make it clear how the Persians had succumbed, within a few decades, to the irresistible forces of environmental determinism, while the Greeks had managed to evade such a scenario.

C. Oman's *A History of Greece* (1924) defines Greeks as belonging to the family of 'Aryan nations'.[98] Meanwhile and as a consequence of the Persian Wars, 'Greece was saved, and with Greece the future of European civilization. The West repelled the invading East so thoroughly that for eleven hundred years no Oriental conqueror again approached the Hellespont to threaten the Balkan Peninsulas with annexation to an Asiatic realm.'[99] Oman of course sees no contradiction in these two statements; he nonetheless states that the Persians were a different (Aryan) race vis-à-vis the Semitic tribes of the East.[100] But belonging to the 'family of Aryan nations' did very little good for the character of Xerxes: 'The fair and stately face and form which seemed to mark him as a king of men, were belied by his intellectual feebleness and moral instability. His whole character was that of a mere harem-bred Eastern despot, and no spark of his father's genius inspired his actions.'[101] This kingly turpitude carried on, according to the author, for another 150 years, until a

> half-Hellenic race was developed all through his [Alexander's] wide dominion, and for a century it looked as if Hellenistic civilization was destined to dominate the whole of the East. But this was not to be; the Greeks were not numerous enough to raise the permanent level of oriental civilization, or to incorporate the Asiatics with themselves.[102]

In *The Ancient World and its Legacy to Us* (1932), Anthony Blunt states that the Chaldaean Empire was the 'last great Semitic Empire of the early East': 'In the struggle between Mountain and Desert [...] the mountain had at last won. The Indo-European had conquered the Semite.'[103] The Persians are described by Blunt as 'a very fine people': 'The various nations living in these provinces were justly treated, and, so long as they paid their tributes regularly and supplied their appointed number of soldiers for the Persian army, the Persian governors allowed them a good deal of freedom.'[104] Bearing in mind what he had said concerning desert and mountains, Blunt moves away from this analysis decidedly by stating that 'when Cyrus attacked the Greek cities of Asia Minor, he came in touch with a European people. For the first time a European and an Asiatic power met face to face.'[105] As a consequence of the wars, however, 'Persia was the last great Asiatic Empire of this early world. From henceforth the future lay in the hand of European peoples.'[106] Indeed, 'it was our battle that the Greeks were fighting, the battle of European freedom and civilization against eastern despotism'.[107] M. Rostovtzeff in his 1928 work, *A History of the Ancient World*, also notes in a similar fashion and not disapprovingly that 'it is still a commonplace to contrast West with East – Greece, as the bearer of a true and unique civilization, with the East, as the possessor of a different civilization, lower than the first and not measurable by the same standards'.[108]

Fleming Howell opines in *Our Aryan Ancestors: The World's Historical People* (1935) that the Aryans 'established under all climates, ranged along every degree of civilization, influenced by 30 centuries of revolution, show, nevertheless in its literature, and in its philosophies, the community of blood and of intellect which until today binds together all it offshoots'.[109] Furthermore, they 'have been more or less disposed to honesty, faithfulness, fairness, friendship and the better feeling of humanity, accordingly as their blood has remained more or less pure'.[110] 'Everywhere in the East as well as in the West these Aryans demonstrated their superiority over the earlier peoples.'[111] On Persians, whom Howell calls 'Asiatic Aryans', he is complimentary ('noble specimens of the great Aryan race'[112]):

> The general physical character of the ancient Aryan race is best gathered from the representations we have of the sculptures of the Achaemenian kings, which exhibit to us a very noble variety of the human species – a form tall, graceful and stately,

a physiognomy handsome and pleasing, often somewhat resembling the Greek.[113]

The reigns of Cyrus and his immediate successors, was the golden age of the Persian Empire. The people of Asia had always paid tribute to conquerors, and given Allegiance to despots. The Persians rendered them a service in subjecting them all to one master [...] it was a period of peace instead of ceaseless burning of cities, devastations of country, massacre and wholesale enslavement.[114]

'Had it not been for the Asiatic Aryans the hope of Israel, and of the world, would have been quenched in the darkness of perpetual Babylonian bondage.'[115] Despite all of the dubious praise (see full analysis, below), however, Howell was incapable of resolving his doublethink. A few lines after claiming that Achaemenid Persia saved the hope of the world, he writes the following:

Marathon, Thermopylae, Salamis, Platea, and Mycale, these five glorious conflicts decided forever the contest between Asiatic despotism and Greek freedom, the East and the West; the old civilization and the new; between darkness and light; between self indulgence and self culture; between effete orientalism and the magnificent possibilities of a future reserved for Athens, for Europe, and for the world.[116]

D. M. Robinson in *History of Greece* (1936) opines that the quality of Persian leadership and courage was so derisory compared to what was at Alexander's disposal, that 'it is little wonder that the forces of the illimitable East went down before a few thousand Europeans'.[117] The author also argues that Alexander's character underwent a marked 'psychological change' in the form of heavy-handed punishment of wrongdoers, but he promptly enjoins: '[I]t must of course be remembered in Alexander's favour that Orientals are most easily impressed by methods of punishment Oriental in character.'[118]

Despite this proviso, the author rues the real changes in the character of Alexander:

> He was no longer one of them [Greeks and Macedonians]. The aloofness of the despot replaced the easy courtesy of earlier years. He adopted [...] the robes and insignia of the Persian royalty. Native courtiers became his favourites; and, to cap all, since European troops alone could not suffice to hold so large an Empire, native soldiers were being trained in Macedonian tactics.[119]

When all is said and done, however, Robinson considers Alexander's genius to be 'beyond question' in giving to the East an entirely new intellectual and moral outlook upon life: 'There stands Alexander's true claim to greatness.'[120] Robinson also draws a parallel between Alexander and modern empire-builders: 'The fact is that Alexander was faced by the same problem which modern European nations have encountered in their occupation of backward countries.' It is not surprising, in Robinson's view, that Alexander only managed to make modest progress. After all, '[E]ast is East and West is West; and how to bring them together is a problem that still defies the power of human statesmanship'.[121]

c) Doublethink Moving Towards Resolution

G. B. Grundy's *The Great Persian War and its Preliminaries* (1901) has a number of modern sensibilities. 'Early in the course of my inquires,' Grundy writes, 'the results of investigation suggested to me that Herodotus' evidence as an historian differs greatly in value, according as he is relating facts, or seeking to give the motives or causes lying behind them.'[122] This seems to be one of the few instances of a Hellenist avoiding the pitfalls of the 'common-sense theory of history' (see Chapter 6). In the last chapter of the book, entitled 'Herodotus the Historian', Grundy directly questions the veracity of Herodotus' Persian 'tales' in the *Histories*,[123] and concludes that although Herodotus is usually accurate with statements of fact, he lacks information concerning the motives of those in command, as well as being bereft of the methodological know-how in deducing accurate hypotheses from them.[124] Having got his scepticism of *the* primary source in this field out of the way, he begins by considering the 'social question of the preservation of Hellenic civilization' vis-à-vis the Persian threat. He contends that many cities

> seem to have enjoyed a large measure of local independence under Persian suzerainty. Whatever the extent or nature of the tie which bound them to the sovereign government, it certainly does not seem to have been such as to crush social and intellectual development on Hellenic lines; in fact, with regard to intellectual development, these very cities seem to have been first in the field and to have been infinitely more prominent under Persian than under Athenian rule [...] it is plain, on the evidence of the Greeks themselves, that the Persian Government was extraordinarily lenient and liberal in its treatment of subject Greeks [...]. The Hellenism of the fifth century, social and intellectual, was, moreover, no tender plant requiring careful political nurture. It had struck its roots deep into the very being of the race; and it may be doubted whether Persia could, even if she would, have eradicated so strong a growth.[125]

By making a distinction between the political and intellectual/social development of the period, Grundy gives a very different rendition of the Graeco-Persian history. Although he states that 'from this time forward the Iranian took the place of the Semite as the suzerain of the East',[126] as well as making a number of explicit distinctions between the Iranian and Semitic 'races', he does not use the words 'Aryan' or 'Indo-European'; nor does he draw attention to kinship between the Persians and the Greeks.[127]

In his *A History of the Greek and Roman World* (1926), Grundy goes on to recognize the qualities of the Achaemenid kingship. 'If he [Cyrus] made one error, it was perhaps in liberality, in that he left the conquered peoples too much of their native institutions.'[128] In addition he warns against the temptation to cast 'the Persian as the villain of the plot' for seeking 'to rob the Greek of his political liberty' – if a villain, then a 'very civilized villain'. Indeed,

> if the proposed action of the Athenian democracy towards the revolted Mytilenians during the Peloponnesian War be compared with the policy which the Persian adopted to the cities of Ionia after the revolt, the brutality of the Athenian comes into strong contrast with the extraordinary humane treatment of the revolted subjects of Persia [...]. Even the most prejudiced Greek author was unable to rake up a grave charge of cruelty or even of severity against the Persian on this occasion. There was not even a restoration of tyrants to act as Persian agents. Popular governments were set up in the cities, and financial survey of their resources was made with a view to equitable taxation. They were moreover compelled to set up machinery for the peaceful settlement of inter-state disputes.[129]

In A. Jardé's *The Formation of the Greek People* (1926), the 'Forward' by Berr quotes the following from H. Ouvré:[130]

> Among the peoples whose ancient civilizations have been studied in the earlier volumes of the series,[131] the mind of men, 'essentially utilitarian', continued, in the same direction, the mental progress which we have seen taking place in the course of animal evolution and attaining remarkable results in the Anthropoid. 'All these hard working men [...] accomplish material work [...]. As against these mechanicals, the Aryan races think, or at least they think more; they have a singular aptitude for combining representations.'[132]

In the main body of the text, Jardé does not speak of the Greek racial type and regards the 'population of classical Greece as a mixture'.[133] He does, however, discuss the Indo-European migration and origin of speech with some degree of balance and sobriety. 'The "people of the sea" must be the ancestors of the classical peoples of Greece and Asia Minor. They are related, if not by race, at least by speech, for all their languages belong to the linguistic family which is called Indo-European.'[134] As far as the 'Persians of Darius and Xerxes' were concerned, they were

> by no means barbarians; their civilization, different though it was, was not inferior to that of Greece in brilliance or in moral worth. In material things the Persians had borrowed from their neighbours, but they had brought their own religion and lofty beliefs, on which the purest morality was based, and their whole conduct was inspired by this morality, which made them quite unlike the other peoples of the East [...]. While the kings of Egypt and Assyria left only ruin and devastation in their wake, the kings of Persia tried to conduct war with moderation and treat conquered with mildness and benevolence, allowing them to keep their religion, their laws, and even their national chiefs [...]. Thus Persian rule was mild and beneficent for the subject peoples, to whom it brought peace and prosperity.[135]

Jardé, moreover, argues that the Greek could not accept Persian domination not because of Persian barbarity, but because of the 'absolute incompatibility between the two forms of government, Oriental monarchy and Greek commonwealth'.[136]

Berr also provides the forward to Huart's *Ancient Persia and Iranian Civilisation* (1928) and states that 'the vast empire created by Cyrus, Cambyses, and Darius, that other "administrator of genius", astonished and frightened the free Hellenes; and yet, as a first attempt at an Aryan empire, it served as a model to Alexander'.[137] Despite the blatant Aryanism of the 'Forward', Huart's text substitutes this questionable framework with that of the equally questionable one of Orientalism. He opines, for instance, that Xerxes 'was violent, sensual, weak and indolent',[138] and concludes that 'the history of ancient Persia well illustrates the intellectual energy which was latent in the Greek, [which] gradually revealed itself'.[139]

H. G. Wells' *A Short History of the World* (1929) was aimed at a general readership. He, unequivocally, puts the 'Aryan' concept at the heart of this work: 'These Nordic people were destined to play a very important part indeed in the world's history.'[140] 'The Aryan peoples,' according to Wells,

> were learning the methods of civilisation and making it over for their own purposes in Italy and Greece and north Persia. The theme of history from the ninth century BC onward for six centuries is the story of how these Aryan peoples grew to power and enterprise and how at last they subjugated the whole Ancient World, Semitic, Aegean and Egyptian alike. In form the Aryan peoples were altogether victorious; but the struggle of Aryan, Semitic and Egyptian ideas and methods was continued long after the sceptre was in Aryan hands. It is indeed a struggle that goes on through all the rest of history and still in a manner continues to this day.[141]

It is interesting to note that this dichotomy is in contrast with the prevailing view which puts Persia and Greece in an epochal struggle.

Another publication which was intended for non-specialists was T. R. Glover's *The Ancient World* (1935). In it, he wonders 'what would have befallen Greek literature and art' if Persia had ended Greek freedom,[142] and asserts that the Persians were a very highly gifted people, 'more closely, indeed, related by blood to European races than to other Orientals, such as their neighbours the Syrians, the Jews, and the Arabs'.[143] But with 'the Persians getting a foothold in Europe as far as Macedonia',[144] Glover concentrates his analysis on the reaction of the Greeks. It was their belated unity 'that saved one and all from being the slaves of the barbarian'.[145] In other words, 'it was *Demos*, men said, who had won the war, who safeguarded peace [...]. They were the people; and one by one the old traditions were changed, and Athens became the standard democracy of the world, and of all time.'[146] Out of these two distinct narratives came a synthesis of a sort:

> A great race in conflict with another, both full of high intellectual qualities and high courage – it is a great spectacle. In the last big land battle of the Persian war Herodotus says the

Persians fought with strength and a spirit to match the Spartans, but the Spartans were in armour and the Persians in linen shirts. They were bowmen rather than swordsmen.[147]

When it came to the collapse of the Achaemenids, Glover asks the following question: 'Could he [Alexander] bring East and West to understand one another better, to share their gifts – the Greek to introduce the Oriental to intellectual life, and to learn from him something of the dignity and the princeliness and the royal outlook that Greeks so terribly lacked?'[148] Even within an explicitly Indo-European framework, the notion that Alexander was the harbinger of a civilization based on intellect was too attractive to be discarded unceremoniously.

d) No Doublethink

In *Lectures in the Philosophy of History* (1884), Fredrich Hegel asserts that the 'European, who goes from Persia to India, observes a prodigious contrast. Whereas in the former country he finds himself still somewhat at home, and meets with European dispositions, human virtues and human passions – as soon as he crosses the Indus, he encounters the most repellent characteristics, pervading every single feature of society.' It is with Persia, in Hegel's view, 'that we for the first time enter "continuous history": Persians are the first Historical People; Persia was the first Empire that passed away.' 'While China and India remain stationary, and perpetuate a natural vegetative existence even to present time, this land has been subject to those developments and revolutions, which alone manifest historical condition.'[149] This point is more clearly underscored in his *Lectures in the Philosophy of World History*:

> The Persians have ruled over many nations, but all of these have been allowed to retain their own peculiar character; their kingdom can therefore be likened to an empire. While China and India remained fixed in their principles, the Persians form the true transition from the Orient to the west.[150]

The operative word here, 'transition', suggests that Persia was, uniquely, in a dynamic and indeterminate state. Was it Oriental or Western; or did it cease to be one (Oriental), but had yet to become another (Western)? This placing of the Persians in his grand narrative of 'continuous history' was done with such subtlety that even some of Hegel's more careful interpreters seem to have failed to detect it. Karl Löwith in *From Hegel to Nietzsche* (1941), for instance, seems to have noticed neither this 'transition' passage, nor Hegel's view concerning the Persians, vis-à-vis the Chinese and the Indians. He writes:

> In his philosophy of history, the most important stages in the self-liberation of the spirit are the beginning in the East and the conclusion in the West. The world process begins with the great oriental kingdoms of China, India, and Persia. After the decisive victory of the Greeks over the Persians, it continues in the Greek and Roman political edifices on the Mediterranean.[151]

This assertion is completely at odds with what Hegel had in mind. This aspect of his work, however, was not lost on one of his modern interpreters. In his *An Introduction to Hegel: Freedom, Truth and History* (2005), Simon Houlgate argues that

> Hegel's claim [...] is not that there is one simple, conscious condition which constitutes 'history', but rather that within history we see a series of nations – the main ones being Persian Empire, Greece, Rome and Western Christian nation – each with its distinctive roots, but each able to appropriate the achievements of its predecessor and accommodate a level of self-consciousness, which its predecessor could not accommodate.[152]

Listed first in this quartet of nations, the Persian Empire's position as something more than just an 'Oriental kingdom' in Hegel's scheme of things is strongly suggested.[153]

Gobineau does not dwell at all on the cultural similarities of Greece and Persia. Indeed in *Essay Concerning the Inequalities of Races*

(1915), he states that 'their political ideas, their private habits, the inner meaning of their public rites, the scope of their art, and the forms of their government, remained quite distinct'.[154] But Gobineau situates these cultural and social differences within an Indo-European context. In *The World of the Persians* (1971),[155] he writes:

> Like their Scandinavian and German cousins, the Iranians have never been gifted artistically. Neither under the Achaemenids, the Arsacid dynasty, or later the Sasanians, or even in Muslim times, did Persia possess its indigenous style; but it did transform borrowed style [...]. Even the Greeks did not invent their own style; their basic conception came from Assyrians, and they only developed it gradually into a form which the original authors had not been able to achieve.[156]

This type of classification, along with a reluctance to give the Greeks more credit in artistic originality than they supposedly deserved, suggest that doublethink was absent from his framing mechanism. Gobineau was a representative of the school of the 'Aryan race' theories that was current in much of Northern Europe of the period. This school's most celebrated member, Ernest Renan, in an 1856 letter to Gobineau, described the *Essay* as ahead of its time and called it 'a remarkable book, full of vitality, and originality of spirit'.[157] In his own copious writing, Renan contrasts the Greek civilization not with that of the Persians, but with those belonging to the Semites. It is significant that it is in the *Histoire de Peuple d'Israël* (1889) where Renan declares that *'le plus grand des miracles de l'histoire, c'est la Grèce'*, and contends that 'the Jewish history, which always likes to have the monopoly in miracles is in no way a more extraordinary phenomenon than that of the Greek history'.[158] Although Renan concedes that Christianity has become 'an element as important as liberal rationalism of the Greeks' to the European civilizations, its hold, nevertheless, is 'less assured' than many might think.[159] He also asserts that 'Greek mythology, or, in a wider sense, the mythology of the Indo-European peoples', was quite different from those of the revealed books, because they had initially 'envisaged to reflect solely the youthful and delicate sensations of the organs, without resorting to dogmas, theologies, or prescriptions of any sort'.[160]

As far as the Iranian world was concerned, Renan does not examine it within the context of its relationship with the Greek world.[161] Instead, the templates of Islam and the Semitic cultures are used. In *L'Islam et Sciences* (1861), he argues that 'those who are aware of the contemporary world affairs, see clearly the unmistakable inferiority of Muslim countries, the decadence of states governed by Islam, and the vapidity of the intellectual life, both culturally and educationally, of the various races under the tutelage of this religion'.[162] Being a Muslim in the Islamic world, according to Renan, took precedence over being a member of a nationality, with one notable exception: 'Persia here is the only exception. It managed to retain its own genius, and it did so because it was successful in safeguarding its own legacy from Islam.'[163] Moreover, as far as the Iranian world was concerned, dire consequences followed when the

> centre of the Islamic world shifted towards the region of the Tigris and Euphrates. This land was full of traces of one of the most brilliant civilisation that the Near East had ever witnessed – those of the Sasanians. The march of Islam brought to an end a civilization that under the reign of Chosroes Noushirvan was a flourishing centre for arts and industry for centuries. The terrible blow from Islam suddenly stopped this beautiful Iranian development for a hundred years.[164]

In her paper entitled 'The Critique of Orientalism', S. Freitag quotes from Renan's *Journal de Debats* (1883) and states that in Renan's eyes, 'the Arab lack of scientific advancement was [...] enhanced by the inherent hostility of the Arab race – as opposed to the Aryan one – to science. What was known as Arabic science was, according to Renan, either pure linguistics or else due to the influence of the Christians and Persians.'[165]

Hegel, Renan and Gobineau refrained from situating the Persians within an explicitly Oriental framework for very different reasons.

With comparative philology still in its infancy, no form of doublethink could have impinged on Hegel. As far as the other two were concerned, their framework was entirely predicated upon the 'Aryan race' theories, which imposed a conceptually racist requirement to downplay the differences between the Greeks and Persians. Another case which is of some significance here is that of Gordon Childe. As argued in Chapter 4, Childe's methodology had unintentionally mimicked the 'Aryan race' theories of the period, and as a consequence, it was of limited use. The following passage from *The Aryans* demonstrates this point:

> The accession to power of the Iranian Achaemenids brought in its train an aesthetic, political and religious revolution. No doubt the Persians had the benefit of the experience of their predecessors. The transformation achieved is none the less startling. Achaemenid art is characterized by a sobriety and verisimilitude unknown in Hither Asia since the Sumerian period, and yet incorporated all the technical improvements of the intervening centuries. Most striking is the lively individuality of the human figures as contrasted with the stiff and expressionless types of the Hittites, Babylonians or Assyrians. It is further very significant that the Persians should at once have proceeded to create a simple and almost alphabetic syllabary out of the clumsy and incredibly complicated cuneiform script [...] the Persian Empire was not only infinitely wider than even the greatest domains conquered by a Sargon or Sennacherib. It was organised with statesmanlike genius by the great Darius and for two hundred years brought peace to the war-scarred lands of the Near [...]. Its official religion, Zoroastrianism, was inspired by genuinely moral conceptions and was international in its appeal and monotheistic in its essence.[166]

John Linton Myres, however, is a different proposition altogether. Although he shares with the others (apart from Hegel) a deep interest in the Indo-European languages, cultures and peoples, he nonetheless chooses to pursue this interest within the contexts of anthropology and historico-scientific Hellenism[167] (see Chapters 3, 4 and 6). In *The Dawn of History* (1911), Myres writes the following words:

> The newcomers of the North marshalled the whole eastern world, from the Adriatic to the Caspian and the Persian Gulf, into final camps, Eastern and Western in name,[168] but held and directed on both sides by long-last brothers and true kinsman [...] the efficient civil-service of Darius the 'counter of pence', the men who kept the Persian empire working for nearly two centuries after it lost its intellectual head. For it was these whom the greatest of the Hellenes, Alexander – himself, too, by birthright, a 'horse-tamer' – could recognise as fit to share with his own 'companions' from Macedon the rule of the world. It was these, too, whose ideals of old parkland chivalry, Herodotus [...] defined with Hellenic insight and happy epigram – 'to ride, and to shoot, and to tell the truth'.[169]

This theme is continued in *Who Were the Greeks?* (1930). 'This precarious tenure of the Olympian gods,' as Myres commented on Greek myth,

> has its counterpart in Norse, and (above all) in Iranian belief, wherein it is only if all good things, and good men, do their utmost in support of the source and champion of all good, that the good cause can ultimately win; a conception which illuminates for us the amazing successes of Persian imperial administration under Cyrus and Darius, and makes the collision between Persians and Greeks one of the world's great tragedies.[170]

Myres, in E. Eyre's (ed.) *European Civilisation: Its Origin and Development* (1935), has a chapter entitled 'The Ethnology, Habitat, Linguistic, and Common Culture of Indo-Europeans up to the Time of the Migration'. In it, Myres writes:

The product [Persians after Persian education of riding, shooting and telling the truth] was a nation of boy scouts, happy warrior, wise and tolerant administrator. This naturally puzzled and amused the rationalized and commercialized Greeks; and Cyrus, on his part, had no use (they said) for men who 'had a place where they met daily to cheat each other'. The tragic result of this initial misunderstanding between two of the world's gifted peoples was two centuries of war, intrigue, and deadlock, until Persian grit and integrity had been sapped by alien vices, and a Greek prince, bred to 'ride and shoot and tell the truth' in Macedon, made himself King of Kings.[171]

Moreover, looking at the myths, legends and religious practices of the Persians – many of which he felt indicated that 'the earliest Iranian migration was from a colder region to the country round Bokhara and Merv' – Myres asserts that by 'comparing Aryan and Iranian peoples in the light of such legend [...] it is possible to form an estimate of their spread and its significance, which is of the highest value as a clue to events farther north and farther west'.[172] This statement is revealing because it indicates that for Myres, the European ('farther north and farther west') and Iranian cultures were not mutually exclusive phenomena.

The phrases such as 'Eastern and Western in name'; 'the collision between Persians and Greeks [being] one of the world's great tragedies'; and 'this initial misunderstanding between two of the world's gifted peoples', counterpoise nearly all that were quoted from the mainstream Hellenist historians. If these are Myres' views concerning the Greeks and Persians, then how did he analyse and relate the inner workings of the Achaemenid Empire? In his published works, there is very little concerning only the Achaemenids, but among his unpublished papers, there are some interesting historical and anthropological writings on Persia.

In a 1938 paper entitled 'Greece and Persia', Myres begins by contending that:

in 500 BC, as in 1914 AD [...] there were two sides in the quarrel; not necessarily both right, nor even right-according-to-their-lights; but based upon, and presuming, ideals and ends; a philosophy of life, however inarticulate; and qualities of courage and devotion, foresight and generosity, 'worthy', (some will say) of a better cause – 'not unworthy' (other may believe) 'of the cause that was theirs'.[173]

It might be argued at this point that since the questions that Myres gives voice to are, in the main, of an ethical variety, then they must surely require the analytical thrust of philosophers and not the forensic skills of historians. Myres, as mentioned in Chapter 6, disagrees and maintains that historians must also be philosophers, and should respond appropriately to the following question that was posed, albeit in a different context, by Ranke: *'what really happened?'*[174] It is precisely within the limiting boundaries of this question where Myres situates his ruminations on Greece and Persia.

According to Myres, 'the victories of Cyrus and his Persians' created a new situation to which 'the whole world of the Mediterranean' had to react one way or the other. He begins by discussing 'the all-inclusive character of the Persian Empire' and accounts for 'the broad ethnological foundations on which earlier empires had been constructed, and on which the Persian kings too had to build, incorporating much of the structures of their predecessors'.[175] But of course the Iranian peoples themselves had only been dwellers in the Near East for a relatively short period of time:

> The test commonly – and even now most usefully – applied is that of the Indo-European speech, intrusive in its Aryan form into Northern India between 2000 and 1500 BC, and in its Iranian into the Plateau of Iran about the same time [...]. Permanent establishment of Iranian-speaking peoples seems to have been limited along the steep frontage of Zagros mountains, so that the whole country between the Black Sea and Levant westward, and India eastward became bisected into

an eastern half predominately Indo-European and specifically Iranian, and western half predominately Semitic.[176]

Myres, unusually among Hellenists, was deeply interested in the question of Achaemenid kingship. 'If the king's business prospers,' he writes, 'there is the largest of the royal bounty. Thus "all the Persians", in Herodotus's phrase, are in a special sense the king's men, as the Macedonians were Philip's men, and Alexander's.'[177] Moreover, he describes this state of affair as the 'personal monarchy of the "people's choice"', implying that within its remits, 'there was [...] premised an intimate social cooperation; there were benefactors of the king in all ranks of society'. In other words, meritocracy reigned and there was 'no "royal seclusion"; the line of aristocratic exclusiveness was drawn elsewhere, if at all'.[178]

On the matter of the Iranian religious and philosophical outlook, Myres, as mentioned earlier, draws similarities between them and the Greeks. In these lecture notes, however, he contrasts them with those of Vedic tradition:

> Under the sterner conditions of tropical India the reasoned answer to the problem of existence is a mystical pantheism; the individual, despairing of the universe, seeks union with the universal, losing at the same time all relation with the external world. In Iran, the individual is never absolved from direct relations with the external (phenomenal) world [...]. Consequently, in Iran there is a positive moralist, with active secular social duties, a lifelong sequence of acts of individual free choice; there are no mystical or magical substitutes or disguises for definite personal responsibility. Goodness and truth are attainable by Man, by intercourse with Nature and other Men, exploiting and enhancing the world's resources, cooperating with other individual like oneself. An Indian (it would not be unfair to say) looks forward, like the Thracian in Herodotus [I, 133], to the day of his death. A Persian – as we know on the same authority – celebrates above all other days of the year, his birthday: for it was then that he was given his chance.[179]

After this slight digression, Myres resumes his analysis of the political history of the period by discussing the annexation of Lydia. 'It was not only that the master at Sardis had been replaced by a master at Susa,' but more importantly, Sardis was no longer an autonomous kingdom, 'looking after its own interests with its own experience.'[180] Moreover,

> the master of Susa needed wealth, on a vast scale, to make and to acquire conquests, of which Lydia was only the first. Empire is a snowball; problem succeeds problem till natural limits are reached; and there were no natural or political limits for Persia until all that had been held by the Four Despots had been incorporated. There was no peace otherwise. But the attainment of natural limits involved national and cultural anomalies. Conquest of Babylon raised the whole question of its Semitic culture, and the Persians were not Semites nor Semitized.[181]

A very important point of order concerning the governance of the Ionian city-states was the Persian alleged penchant for tyrannical vassals:

> The effect of this 'tyrant'-system was to create a general impression that Persians 'could not understand democracy', from the sarcasm of Cyrus to the warning of Artaphernes; and the popular element in every Greek city was consequently at cross-purposes with the Great King from the first. The King therefore looked to the non-democratic elements as affording greater security for loyalty and stability – as indeed it did – as well as for revenue. And consequently the non-democratic elements looked to the king for support, in their local quarrels with the popular parties.
>
> (Exactly the same thing happened after the Italian occupation of the Dodecanese in 1912. Some of the island communities – the last survivors of the city-state – were democratic, others were oligarchic. The Italians tried to work with both, but the 'liberal' and also irresponsible outlook of the 'democracies' involved them in frequent disputes with the High Commissioner, and within a

few years all oligarchies were supporting Italian rule, and all democracies were irredentists.)[182]

So what is to be made of Myres' treatment of the Iranian world and the Achaemenid Empire? This lengthy quote is a good place to start. It argues that it was skilful statecraft and not an innate inability to 'understand democracy' that directed the Persian king to support the non-democratic elements within the Greek city-states. Furthermore, this approach is given a fairly recent historical analogy from within Europe – which is not without significance. In other words, the actions of the Achaemenids and the reactions of the city-states are not situated within the usual 'Europe–Asia' template, but shown neutrally as political actors going about their business rationally. Myres' comparison of 1914 and 500 BC, again refraining from taking sides ('two sides in a quarrel'), also suggests that the wars between the Persians and the Greeks, as was the case between the Germans and the British, was an intra-regional affair, and not necessarily a struggle between the Europeans and Asiatics. The way in which he visualized the spatial relationships between various protagonists was a matter of great importance to him. He is quite clear: Persian advance altered the nature of the power-relationships in 'the whole world of the Mediterranean' considerably. In other words, 'Europe' as a spatial entity does not even come into play. His analysis of the nature of the Achaemenid kingship is also out of kilter with the favoured conceptualization of 'oriental despotism'. Instead, Myres describes it approvingly as the 'personal monarchy of the "people's choice"'. In addition he, wrongly or rightly, attributes philosophical moderation to Persians' religious practices vis-à-vis the Vedic Indians, as well as suggesting strong similarities between Greek and Iranian mythologies. And specifically on matters Indo-European, although he does not consider it useful for revealing the inner workings of the empire itself, nonetheless, the anthropologist in him touches on what he considers to be the cultural challenges of ruling over Semitic peoples.

Of course Myres was not immune from the forms of expression which could perhaps stray a little too near to those of the mainstream

Hellenists. For example, in 'The Geographical Aspect of Greek Colonisation', he writes that:

> already in the fifth century BC, when Herodotus was first writing continuous history of a European nation, it was to commemorate the successful struggle of a league of Greek sea-powers, not to win, but to reclaim, the Mediterranean as a Greek sea, from the combined aggressions of rivals in Tyre, Carthage, and Etruria, leagued under the patronage of the greatest land-empire which the world had known till then, and backed by the full weight of the armed forces of Persia.[183]

Two points need to be made here. First, having looked very closely at his output, this is one of the very few instances[184] that have been found where, by using the term 'European nation', Myres deviates from his usual neutral ways of expressing his thoughts. Second, in this passage, the Mediterranean is not a European, but, significantly, a Greek sea; and it is a Greek sea with accompanying geographical and demographical constraints:

> To clear up the features of the Greek cradle-land: It is not until we replace the Mediterranean region itself in its own geographical setting, as we see fully how remarkable its position is in relation to the Old World as a whole. Note how centrally the Greek lands lie, in the heart of the Eastern Mediterranean, and then see how centrally the Mediterranean lies, between the River Cultures of the Ancient East on the one side, and the Transalpine, Atlantic facing regions [...]. See, no less, how it lied encircled on nearly three sides by three of the great flatlands and potential grasslands of the planet, in North Africa, in Arabia, and in the great level between Carpathian and the highland core of Asia; beset, therefore, and for ever threatened, in its human aspect, by three great reservoirs of unspent Man; the Libyan enemies of ancient Egypt, the Semites of Arabia, and the Aryan-speaking folks of the mainland North.[185]

In other words, the geographical and demographical realities with which the Greeks had to deal were not in any way predominantly or exclusively European in character (see below).

II – Analysis

Why produce such a lengthy survey, and what is it supposed to achieve? The fact that nearly all of the works discussed are underpinned by a small corpus of classical sources and uniformly informed by aesthetic Hellenism is not without significance. The lengthiness of this survey has a dual purpose. First, its function is to act as a rhetorical device and demonstrate that there was an overwhelming historiographical consensus which was repeated – with only minor stylistic alterations – *ad nauseam*. It aims to strike the reader (the way in which Lord Curzon was struck by the 'Persepolitan platform') 'with a sense of monotony and fatigue. It is all the same, and the same again, and yet again.' Second, it strives to catalogue the very powerful intellectual forces that were arrayed against the type of approach that Myres was advocating. It also seemed necessary (after having established in earlier chapters that there was a tendency to classify cultures, languages and peoples into broad categories) to gauge the manner in which Greeks and the various Iranian peoples were classified as Indo-Europeans in relevant texts of the period, and how these classifications interacted with the following type of historiographical consensus that has been gleaned from this survey: the Achaemenid rulers were not averse to displaying 'Asiatic manners', shedding 'feminine tears', and being blissfully ensconced in well-populated seraglios. As far as the Persian Wars were concerned, the 'lord of Asia' had only one thing on his mind: the 'conquest of Europe'. This 'peril from the East' resulted in the 'supreme struggle between the Persian Empire and the West'; and as a consequence of this, the 'illimitable East' went down 'before a few thousand Europeans' with the greatest of ease. 'Greece was saved, and with Greece, the future of European civilisation.' A century and half later, Alexander felt, in a manner of speaking, the 'white man's burden' most acutely; and as a result, he set out to endow 'the East [with] an entirely new intellectual and moral outlook upon life'. In the short period that was available to him, he achieved a great deal, but ultimately there was only so much that he could do. After all, '[W]hen the Persians attempted to accept everything that was Greek; they did not grasp the reason and proportion, but were satisfied with the semblance'.

These snippets of quotes, although culled randomly from the survey, exhibit, on the one hand, a very precise and far from random geographical or spatial conception that underscored these works, and on the other, they underline the manner in which these authors dichotomized the political, social and cultural life of Greece and the Achaemenid Empire. The fact that these historical accounts take place between two very different realms (Europe v. Asia; West v. East) is the most consequential and indispensable framing device that has been available to mainstream Hellenists throughout the ages. But what has happened to the other component of this 'doublethink', namely the Indo-European similarities that are supposed to have existed between the Greeks and Persians? Doublethink, as a description of the historiographical consensus, is in need of some qualification. There was a simultaneous holding of contradictory views in a number of sources, which contended that although there were fundamental commonalities between Greeks and Persians, the Persians should nevertheless be regarded as the polar opposite of the Greeks and as 'Asiatic' as all other nationalities of the Near East, such as the Babylonians, Assyrians and Egyptians. This was paradoxical in the extreme. Moreover, these two contradictory strands of thoughts were not expressed with the same vigour. Whereas the 'otherness' and the non-European credentials of the Persians was forcefully, copiously and repeatedly stressed, the supposed Indo-European commonalities, in a manner of speaking, were relegated to the small print of these historical documents and only mentioned, if at all, tersely and in passing. In other words, the sheer power and dominance of one strand of thought was so superior that the weaker strand was barely noticed. 'Europe' ('West' and 'Occident' being its nearest substitutes), 'freedom' and, less frequently, 'democracy' appear along with their antonyms in nearly all of the works discussed from I.a to I.c. This was done for one overriding purpose: to signify a set of ideological precepts, which reflected a tendency towards teleology and presentism.[186] After all, what else is James hinting at (see above) when he writes that the Greek victory 'meant in the long run for us the preservation of a distinctive European civilization and the emancipation of the human spirit'?

But in what way is teleology or presentism a conceptual problem? According to Bernard Bailyn (a prominent critic of presentism), '[T]here is always a need to extract from the past some kind of bearing on contemporary problems, some message, commentary, or instruction to the writer's age, and to see reflected in the past familiar aspects of the present'. There is, of course, nothing wrong with this, but without 'critical control', this need 'generates an obvious kind of presentism, which at its worst becomes indoctrination by historical example'.[187] Within his area of research – the American Revolution – Bailyn is concerned that 'too much of the historical research for social and economic roots and purposes in the revolutionary movement is presentist', thus reflecting 'the assumption that the impulses to revolution in eighteenth century America must in some way have been analogous to impulses that account for modern social protests and revolutions'.[188] Gordon S. Wood argues in 'The Creative Imagination of Bernard Bailyn' that the presentist type of interpretation is 'essentially unhistorical: it violates the historian's central concern for authenticity of the past, and it breeds anachronism – what Marc Bloch called "the most unpardonable of sins" that a historian can commit'.[189] Although Wood concedes that Bailyn's 'emphasis on what the past actors actually thought and intended' can be 'a healthy antidote', nevertheless, 'to stress only the pastness [...] is to evade the historian's responsibility to connect the past with what came after. The historian needs to recover not just past meaning, not just past intentions, but also the unanticipated future consequences of those intentions.'[190] It is, in Wood's view, 'a question of degree, of getting the balance right'.[191] This might very well be true; the historian should try to 'connect the past with what came after', but how long is this 'after', and is it an 'after' or a sequence of 'afters'? For instance, should we not distinguish between historians looking at the Persian Wars in order to connect them to the events of fifth- and fourth-century Greece and Persia, and historians looking at the same wars in order to make sense of the 9/11 atrocities?[192] Bailyn has no doubt on the primary function of historians:

> [H]istorians must be, not analysts of isolated technical problems abstracted from the past, but narrators of worlds in motion – worlds as complex, unpredictable, and transient as our own. The historian must re-tell, with a new richness, the story of what some one of the worlds of the past was, how it ceased to be what it was, how it faded and blended into new configurations, how at every stage what was, was the product of what had been, and developed into what no one could have anticipated.[193]

This idea that historians should be conceptually bounded within 'one of the worlds of the past'[194] – its being, its ceasing to be, its fading and blending into 'new configurations' – has an interesting antecedence. In his 1862 paper, 'Schlosser and the Problem of Universal History', Wilhelm Dilthey develops a framework which has some core similarities with Bailyn's school of thought.[195] 'Immanent teleology', according to the editors of Dilthy's *Hermeneutics and the Study of History* (1996),

> is that property of a whole, which allows it to develop its structure and meaning out of itself and not from some externally given end or purpose. Applied to history, immanent teleology involves the rejection of a pure teleological philosophy of history that projects a purpose of history or searches for God's providential intent by which all historical epochs are to be judged.[196]

This second form of rejection is crucial, because it chimes with 'Ranke's famous phrase that each epoch stands "in immediate relation to God"'. This, in turn, allows Ranke to reject external teleology in favour of an immanent one, thereby indicating that his over-quoted phrase of 'reconstructing the past in its own term' (*wie es eigentlich gewesen*) is not insensitive to the requirements of the present.[197] And with Myres' approving nod towards Ranke in his 'Greece and Persia' paper, the importance of this implicit concurrence between the two is not without importance (see below).

The fact that historians, in their endeavours to understand the past, cannot ignore the present is beyond dispute. The manner in which they choose not to ignore it, however, continues to remain a point of debate and disagreement. Bailyn, Ranke and Dilthey qualify their interest in the present by adopting well-defined methodological frameworks. Interestingly, their respective approaches also tend to concur with one of Collingwood's more nuanced points of analysis. In discussing the past and its relation to the present (see Chapter 6), he asks whether it is correct to state that 'an act of thought by being subjective ceases to be objective, and thus, by being present, ceases to be past'. He does not believe this to be the case: 'because a person who states this has understood by subjectivity not the act of thinking, but simply consciousness as a flow of immediate state.'[198] What should we make of this? He seems to be saying that if a term or a word is posited in this 'state', then it can do no other but to take full account (as 'immediate' strongly suggests) of that word's or term's meanings, which have been acquired or accumulated throughout the ages since the coinage of that word or term. Spatial and political terms, such as 'Europe', 'freedom' and 'democracy' store a miscellany of such meanings; thus, it cannot be asserted with any authority that they denote 'past thought incapsulated in a context of present thought'.[199] This is so because the past and present meanings of these words are, as I shall argue, so fundamentally different that without prior terminological clarifications, their continuing usage in discussing the histories of ancient Greece and Persia is anachronistic and signals nothing but deeper ideological preferences on the part of the authors.

a) Spatial Terms

The following example should set the scene: In *Hellenica* (1880), E. Abbott quotes the following line from Euripides' *Helen* and footnotes its Greek original (here in brackets): 'Among the *Easterns* all save one are slaves (τά βαρβάρων γάρ δοῦλα πάντα πλήν ἑνός.).'[200] Why mistranslate 'βαρβάρων' (barbarians) as 'Easterns'? Surely the Greeks did not only consider the peoples to the east of them as barbarians. So why assign them and them alone such a description? Bearing this and the quote from Toynbee in Chapter 5 in mind, it is evident that those involved in the writing of Greek history seem to have had, at the very least, a keen ideological penchant for depicting the Iranians in an a priori-arranged fashion. Phrases such as 'Europe in Peril' signify or symbolize a certain type of mentality that goes well beyond the mere rudiments of teleological prespectivity. A closer look at the language of the discourse may tell us whether or not these vocabularies carry with them hidden or larger ideological and non-historical meanings.

It was largely believed by the philologists of the latter half of the nineteenth century that the etymological root of the word 'Europe' was 'derived from [an] Assyrian or Hebrew root, which signifies the west or the setting sun, and [that of Asia] from a corresponding root meaning the east or rising sun, and that they were used at one time to imply the west and the east'.[201] Moreover, the same piece makes the following points:

> There is ground for supposing that they may at first have been used with a specific or restricted local application, a more extended signification having eventually been given to them. After the word Asia had acquired its larger sense, it was especially used by the Greeks to designate the country around Ephesus. The idea of Asia as originally formed was necessarily infinite, and long continued to be so; and the area to which the name was finally applied, as geographical knowledge increased, was to a great extent determined by arbitrary and not very precise conceptions, rather than on the basis of natural relations and differences subsisting between it and the surrounding regions.[202]

Of course, the problem lies with the tendency that begins with some 'specific or restricted local application' of a word, and then goes on to acquire 'extended signification' in due course. 'Europe', for instance, begins life as a Semitic[203] word denoting regular movement of the sun, and ends up as a term brimful with meanings and applications: Hellenism, the Roman Empire, Christianity, the Carolingian Age, Renaissance, the discovery of the New World, the white man (and his burden!), Reformation, Enlightenment, the Industrial Revolution, mechanized warfare, etc. The list is as endless as it is arbitrarily drawn. One thing is certain, however: it has become 'a matter of honour, emotion and [European] continental pride' whether or not populations and cultures have moved across the imaginary line that divides Europe from Asia.[204] It is precisely such a 'Europe' – as witnessed in section I – that tends to delineate the thoughts of many of those examining the Persian Wars or the conquests of Alexander. But what is the right 'Europe' for the purposes of ancient history? The answer is 'none'.

In order to justify this sweeping assertion, we need to return to Myres and his long-term interest in geography. He begins his 'The Coming of the North' chapter in *The Dawn of History* by 'looking at the theatre of lands and waters, in which the drama of history'[205] is generally played out. In 'The Place of Man and his Environment in the Study of Social Sciences',[206] Myres argues that the 'province' of historians tends to overlap with those of geographers, because 'historians are preoccupied by their study of sequences in time within particular regions and environments'.[207] In *The Man of Science and the Science of Man* (1933), he develops this theme further:

> History, like geography, stands in relation to its subject matter different from any of the specific and 'systematic sciences', such as chemistry or morphology, in that its function is to correlate and interpret the coexistences and the interactions, of different kinds of facts and events, in the order of time, as geography studies and tries to interpret their regional co-distributions. History and geography, then, are in a special sense 'applied sciences', in that they are concerned with the data of many

'systematic' sciences in so far as they are relevant here and now in respect (that is) of particular periods or regions. Hence their intimate mutual relations. All history has its geographical or regional aspect; and (though this is not quite so obvious) all geography has its historical aspect.[208]

In his 1935 'Races and Cultures' paper, moreover, Myres sees 'geographical fact' to be a corrective counterweight to the potential dangers of 'historical myth'. 'Few recent events,' he writes, 'have been more significant, more unexpected, more alarming and pathetic, than the rapid, almost unquestioned propagation [...] of statements and beliefs on matters which until recently were rather abstruse topics in branches of knowledge.'[209] Since some of these statements and beliefs – many of which relate to physical anthropology, ethnology and philology – 'are antiquated or obsolete, some vigorously disputed, some unsupported by verifiable references to published scientific work',[210] then, in Myres' opinion, geographical forms of enquiry might be able to undermine the dominance of myth in 'historical teaching' and 'historical research'. This is so because the methodologies of 'historical and geographical' sciences (see Chapters 3 and 5) have deepened the perspective of the past, and widened the perspective of the present. When an enquiry is situated within these boundaries, 'we expect – and rightly – so much, if only because in these aspects in all events "earth's young significance is all to learn" – what is it for which we are looking? And why – on the word of a geographer, no less than a historian – are we looking for it in the past?'[211]

These slightly untidy ponderings on the topic of geography, its intimate relationship with history and its various applications, in my view, have equipped Myres' approach with precisely the kinds of attributes required for mounting a direct challenge to the unquestioning geographical or spatial constant that has always framed the history of the ancient world. As early as 1910, he is not only interested in the 'Greek people', but also in the 'Greek lands'. In other words, he sees the need to accommodate the anthropology and the geography of the Greeks equally and simultaneously. This is precisely why he had added a geographical component to Herodotus' quartet of anthropological characteristics in *Who Were the Greeks?* Elsewhere, he writes:

> The Greek cradle and home in fact are not, and never have been, on the mainland of Greece exclusively [...] the art, and thought, and commerce of classical Greece began, and long continued to grow, on the Asiatic shores.[212]

As a consequence of this way of thinking, he pays no attention whatsoever to the notion that Europe and Asia (or for that matter, East and West) are two separate and well-delineated entities, where human or cultural leakages can be discounted as largely inconsequential. He argues instead that the region with any practical spatial or topographical meaning for the Greeks and non-Greeks alike was not Europe and Asia respectively, but an amalgam of certain areas of what we now call the three continents of Europe, Asia and Africa. In a lecture for the BBC (broadcast May 1930) entitled 'The Bread and Olive Civilization', Myres invites the listeners to view the map of the ancient world in the following way:

> If you look at a Map of the Mediterranean Sea – still better if you will turn it upside down, so as to overlook it from the North instead of from the South – you will see, first, that what we call the Mediterranean is only part of a whole lake-region of inland seas, such as the Black Sea and the Caspian; next [that] what breaks up this lake-region into distinct basins is a great belt of rugged country lying obliquely across it, from the Pyrenees and the Atlas range, through the Alps and Carpathians, to Asia Minor, Armenia and the Persian plateau.[213]

Now if a historian were to be constrained within this cartographical representation, as opposed to the zonal division of Europe and Asia, then his ability to depict the wars, or any other aspect of the Graeco-Persian relationship, within an Orientalist context would become increasingly untenable. It can be argued that there was a historian who had managed to sidestep the ubiquitous Hellenocentrism and the Orientalism of the period, and provide a fair analysis of the Persians without needing to approach the subject geographically, anthropologically or with any considerations of Indo-European matters. It is indeed true that in general Grundy gave a fair summary of the wars in his 1901 publication. He was also sanguine with regard to Persian rule. Even if the Persians had won, it does not, in his view, 'warrant the assertion that such a victory would have brought about the substitution of an Eastern for a Western civilization in south European lands'.[214] He does, however, concede that a Persian victory 'would have immensely modified the political development of Greece in the last three quarters of the fifth century [...] and such a modification could not but have seriously affected the genius of Hellenism'.[215] Moreover, in his 1926 publication, Grundy writes that 'it is difficult to guess what instigated Darius to carry his rule into Europe'.[216] In other words, the spatial aspect together with its innate cultural components continued to play a part, *pace* Myres, in Grundy's *oeuvre*. It is also worth mentioning that Myres' cartography of the ancient world is not entirely incongruous with those available to the ancient Greeks themselves. The geographical account of Hecataeus (550–476 BC) in his *Periegesis* is instructive. Hecataeus' 'map' of the world has the Greek archipelago and the Mediterranean at its centre. This centre, moreover, is delineated with (inaccurate) bits of Africa, Asia and Europe. When this map is studied alongside Myres' spatial discussions, it becomes quite clear that Myres is doing no more than reasserting the geographical sensibilities of the Greeks.

b) Political Terms

Spatial concepts aside, there are other, more political concepts which have evolved to mean something qualitatively different or more than what they had meant originally. Uniquely in the English language, 'freedom' and 'liberty' are both used, and used synonymously. In most of the Romance languages, however, a variant on the Latin '*libertas*' is often used; and in the non-English Germanic languages, it is those with roots in the Norse '*fri*' that are generally favoured. Why should any of this be germane to this unfolding analysis? In his *Studies in Words* (1960), C. S. Lewis writes:

> Like *eleutheria* and *libertas*, *freedom* and *franchise* can of course mean the legal freedom of a community. But the ancient words are used chiefly, if not entirely, in reference to the freedom of a state. The contrast implied is sometimes between autonomy and subjection to a foreign power; sometimes between the freedom of a republic and the rule of a despot. The Medieval words nearly always refer to something different; to the guaranteed freedoms or immunities (from royal or baronial interference) of a corporate entity which cut across state, or which exists within the state, like a city or guild.[217]

Moreover, according to D. H. Fischer there is a fundamental difference between these two concepts:

> Northern European traditions centred on freedom as a form of belonging and rights of connection to a community of free people. They imply tribal membership, and the existence of inalienable rights among all free born people. The Mediterranean tradition of liberty is an idea of separation and independence. It is an idea of hierarchy, in the variable possession of privileges that might be given or taken away by a higher power.[218]

The differences that flow from this are noteworthy. 'Legal possessions', in the classical Mediterranean world, for instance, are things that 'may be given'.[219] In the North European world, at least since the Late Middle Ages, it is something that 'must be given'. This is one of the differences that implies, in Fischer's judgment, that 'the original meanings of freedom and liberty were not merely different but opposed. Liberty meant separation. Freedom implied connection [...]. A person with *eleutheria* in ancient Greece has been granted some degree of autonomy [...]. A person in northern Europe [...] was united by kinship or affection to a tribe or a family of free people.'[220] All of which suggests that the condition in 'the

Mediterranean civilizations was in some ways more limited than freedom in northern Europe'.[221] It therefore cannot be stated with any degree of confidence that when mainstream Hellenists use the term 'freedom' or 'liberty', they are genuinely cognizant (as Lewis and Fischer happen to be) of the real differences between the limited and modest concept that was accessible to the ancient Greeks, and the more substantial and sophisticated variety that has been available to the peoples of Northern Europe intermittently (including to the authors themselves) for almost a millennium. After all, when Webster writes that the 'Greek victory saved Europe for better things. It was a victory for human freedom,'[222] one may assume the author did not consciously differentiate between the 'freedom' that was available to him in the USA of 1915, and the *'eleutheros'* that was at the disposal of the non-slave Greek men of the classical period.[223] Even some modern historians claim that Greek victory has 'secured a *permanence* of freedom for Europe',[224] without paying due attention to the *sui generis* political developments that have been taking place in Northern Europe for centuries. But as far as the Persian Empire is concerned, it can be argued that it may not have trampled all that heavily on the *'eleutheros'* of their Greek and non-Greek subjects. Bozeman's inference in *Politics and Culture in International History* (1994) is persuasive:

> In apology for this lacuna [the Persian Empire's 'disregard for the individual'] in applied ethics and politics, it can be said that within his national or cultural group, which was more fully recognized by the Persians than by any other great power, the individual seems to have been free to follow his calling and engage in his speculations, and that it was only in relation to the pivot of the whole cosmopolitan structure – the imperial administration itself – that no rights were presumed to inhere in man.[225]

From the latter half of the nineteenth century to the first four decades of the twentieth, 'democracy', as a political concept, was not bandied about as often as it is now. This was so because many had viewed it with some suspicion and considered it to be no more than a *carte blanche* for the 'great unwashed' to behave horridly. Despite this, it was still a political term which embodied positive connotations, largely because it was believed to have been invented by the Athenians. Once again, however, as in the case of 'freedom', 'democracy' tends to be discussed far too abstractly, thus allowing for far too many post-Hellenic and modern characteristics to be grafted onto it. 'In Greece,' writes Rousseau in *The Social Contract* (1765), 'all that people had to do, it did for itself; it was constantly assembled in the public square. The Greeks lived in a mild climate; they had no natural greed; slaves did their work for them; their great concern was with their own liberty.'[226] The problem with this type of narrative, which celebrates the notion that the Greeks had laudably possessed a direct or participatory form of democracy, overlooks a very important point that has recently been developed by John Keane. In *The Life and Death of Democracy* (2009), Keane sets the scene in the following manner:

> Fans of 'direct' or 'participatory' democracy usually overlook a point [...] that a 'people' cannot govern itself unless it relies upon institutions that in turn have the effect of sundering 'the people'. So despite the fact that they may try to imagine themselves to be standing shoulder to shoulder, face to face, seeing eye to eye, a body that calls itself 'the people' always finds in practice that it is a fictional entity made up of different individuals and groups interacting through institutions that materially shape not only how they make decisions and what they decide as a body, but also who they are as a 'people'.[227]

This was the primary drawback of the Athenian democracy. Keane validates this inference by pointing out that not only was there a practical need to delegate many functions to particular citizens, thereby undermining the idea of direct participation, but also that this democracy had to accommodate pre-democratic institutions, such as the Areopagus ('the seat of the oldest and most august court in Athens'[228]). At various times, during the 250 years of Athenian democracy, according to the author, this body's 'considerable power cut like an axe through the assembly principle that the people always ruled'.[229] In addition, 'the modern meaning of "representation" [was] not known to the Athenians'; they had also no real understanding of 'what would later be called the separation of power[s]'.[230] Keane is unequivocal: 'Athenian democracy was not based on anything like "the rule of law", as we now call a type of government in which no power can be exercised except according to principles, procedures and constraints in law that are designed to protect citizens.'[231] To a modern democrat – to paraphrase one of Peter Winch's central points of analysis in *The Idea of a Social Science* (1958) – the Athenian democracy was, to all intents and purposes, an anachronism. In addition, as was the case with 'freedom', 'democracy' must also have evolved. B. Flyvbjerg in his study of democracy in Denmark,[232] for instance, tries to understand what impact pre-modern structures of governance have had on the manner in which the Danish form of democracy eventually configured. In order to do this, he contextualizes Danish democracy within the political history of Denmark and the Germanic world, and not within what had taken place millennia ago somewhere in the eastern Mediterranean.[233]

To what extent was democracy itself a Hellenic innovation? There is a great deal of evidence that strongly suggests that 'the art of self-government by assemblies of people who regard each other as equal was *not* an invention of the Athenians'.[234] This form of self-government had a long prehistory not only in other parts of the Greek-speaking world,[235] but more crucially in much of Mesopotamia. The various civilizations of this region were not averse to making political decisions within a recognizably 'democratic' context. 'The existence of assemblies in Phoenician cities like Byblos,' according to Keane, 'has been given greater credence during the past generation by evidence that the Phoenicians practised government by assembly much more widely than had previously been thought.'[236] Indeed, the non-Greek's propensity for creating assemblies was temporally and spatially widespread, thus compelling Keane to conclude that 'the lamp of assembly-based democracy was first lit in the East'.[237]

Perhaps it can be countered that those writing about democracy from the 1850s to 1940s were genuinely unaware that the various Semitic civilizations of the Near East possessed systems of government more akin to Athens, and quite different from the expected norm of Oriental despotism. Perhaps. But the historiographical evidence suggests otherwise. The evidence from Byblos, for example, was translated by Breasted and published in the *Ancient Record of Egypt* as early as 1906.[238] In a 1943 paper, entitled 'Primitive Democracy in Ancient Mesopotamia', T. Jacobsen induced that 'democratic forms of political organisation in Mesopotamia all points to a time before the earliest historical inscriptions',[239] i.e. that democracy is an extremely old concept that predated the Greeks. In addition, Jacobsen is unambiguous in his conclusion that the 'indicators which we have, point to a form of government in which the normal run of public affairs is handled by a council of elders, but ultimate sovereignty resided in a general assembly composing all members of community'.[240] Admittedly, by describing the Mesopotamian tradition of collective political life as a 'democracy', Jacobsen exposes his arguments to some noteworthy criticisms.[241] In *Democracy's Ancient Ancestors* (2004), D. E. Fleming asserts that he has kept the word 'democracy' in the title of his work in order 'to recall Jacobsen and to invite consideration of [the] Near Eastern evidence as a backdrop to the Greek development'.[242] Fleming asserts, however, that his analysis of the Mari archives suggests that the 'collective political forms' in Mesopotamia were not in any way 'democratic' – 'primitive' or otherwise. In other words, 'Mari preserves not the direct antecedents of Greek democracy but a cross-section of its ancestry in the larger region'.[243] Fleming qualifies this inference by the following remarks:

> From an ancient Near Eastern perspective, pre-democratic Greece seems to be cut out of the same cultural cloth as its eastern neighbours, in broad political and social terms. I emphasize the word 'broad', in that I acknowledge entirely not only the possibility of finding essential distinctions but the necessity of doing so. At the same time, however, it is not

possible to treat cultural geography as if it were divided into nation-states with absolute boundaries.²⁴⁴

Two final points regarding the idea of 'democracy'. First, the political process which has given the contemporary world what it understands as 'democracy' should be regarded as an organic whole, whose earliest history resides in an ancient world where, as Fleming avers (and not entirely at odds with Jacobsen's contention), 'Greece was not a world away from Mesopotamia'.²⁴⁵ Second, the assertion that the Mesopotamian political traditions were not 'the direct antecedents of Greek democracy but a cross-section of its ancestry in the larger region' also seems to be an adequate definer, *mutatis mutandis*, of the relationship between Greek democracy and the democracies of the present. After all, the *sui generis* and cumulative democratic innovations of the non-Greek world (Denmark, Italy, the US, etc.) suggest that not everything can or should be traced back to Athens, and to Athens alone.

III – Conclusions

It has been established that much of the paradoxical thinking of the Hellenists was posited – and continues to be posited – upon a very rigid teleological perspective. It has also been ascertained that in order to induce this teleology to function adequately, it was necessary to equip it with an appropriate vocabulary.²⁴⁶ A provoked Europe preserving itself (better still, 'herself'), her freedom and one of her glorious inventions (democracy) against the Asiatic hordes, evokes such an irresistibly dramatic and pathetic *mise-en-scène* that it makes it extremely difficult for an observer not to be intellectually stimulated or emotionally moved by it. The observer's response, furthermore, takes place within a cultural context that, by and large, considers the achievements of the ancient Greeks as the apotheosis of human endeavour – sublime, beautiful and unsurpassable (see the previous two chapters). Now, how can a fair rendition of who the ancient Iranian peoples were and what they did in human affairs be situated within this context? On both counts, Myres' thoughts are of some relevance. He recognized, as he had done with the Greeks, that the anthropological characteristics of the Iranian peoples ('*Who were the Iranians?*' as it were) were as important as their historical footprints. Since this represents his methodological and indeed philosophical points of departure, then, as a matter of logic, he effectively disqualifies himself from introducing the widely-accepted notion of spatial dichotomy of Europe and Asia (where democracy and despotism reigned, respectively), and Romantic aestheticism into his thinking. In other words, his framework ('Eastern and Western in name') can do no other – and did no other – but to regard the Persians and Greeks as 'long-lost brothers and true kinsman', fighting a regrettable regional war (and emphatically not an epochal clash of Europe against Asia), which was caused by a simple 'misunderstanding'. During the period under discussion, no one else had come close in putting into words such atypical inferences. But is Myres being given too much credit? Or can it be argued that perhaps his writings have been taken out of context, and as a consequence, the overarching case that is being made here is a gross overstatement? Before responding to these crucial questions in the next and final chapter, it is necessary at this point to bring the analysis of this chapter to a close.

What should be done with words which have acquired 'massive and misleading resonances, even though [they] had little purchase in the mind of the contemporaries?'[247] In 2008, the early modern British historian, Clifford Davis, penned an article for the *Times Literary Supplement* in which he argued that 'we are wrong to talk about "the Tudors"', because it was a term that was 'hardly used in the sixteenth century, either by the monarchs or their subjects'.[248] Whether this is a valid assertion or not is secondary to the more fundamental point that Davis is making, namely: why persist with words that *in situ* would have been regarded as meaningless? And as argued here, terms such as 'Europe', 'freedom' and 'democracy' have evolved in meanings and applications to such an extent that their continuing usage in Graeco-Iranian historiography should now be considered as anachronistic and amended accordingly. After all, unreflecting use of unsuitable terms, as Davis argues, gives a 'misleading impression of [...] reality'. He goes on: 'To use the cant term, it is "Whiggish" in implying a spurious unity, a sense of outcomes implicit in origins.'[249] The key word here is 'reality'. Nothing does away with reality more swiftly than the tendency (both past and present) to produce works that consider the Graeco–Persian Wars as being merely the first round of an ongoing '2,500-Year Struggle between East and West'.[250]

In his 1945 essay entitled, 'Politics and the English Language', George Orwell (the neologist of 'doublethink') samples a number of problematic writings and concludes that they all have two qualities in common: 'staleness of imagery' and 'lack of precision'.[251] Although one cannot accuse the authors discussed here as being seriously deficient in their manufacture of memorable imageries, their aptitude for precision, however, is open to doubt. It is not their overwhelming reliance on the classical sources that renders their works problematic; but it is the combination of uncritical engagement with these sources (Collingwood), and their reluctance to augment their methodologies with other academic disciplines which are a cause for concern (see Murray's antipathy towards anthropology in Chapter 5). The purpose of using terms such as 'democracy' or 'freedom' was never an end to itself, but a necessary means to a specific end, namely the celebration of aesthetic Hellenism through historical teleology. There are, however, many instances, as Orwell warns, where the meanings of words fall by the wayside. Two of the words that he had in mind were, coincidentally, 'democracy' and 'freedom'. They, according to Orwell, 'have each of them several meanings which cannot be reconciled with one another'.[252] If this was a serious worry in the political discourse of 1945, then surely the problem becomes even more acute when such terms are employed in describing ancient events in faraway places.

CHAPTER 8

CONCLUDING REMARKS

Throughout the writing of this book, I have been made aware by my intellectual superiors that objectivity, sensible use of evidence, sobriety in criticism, clear exposition and a sense of balance in inferring hypotheses and drawing conclusions must override all else. As I now meander towards the end of this particular intellectual journey, I am compelled to ask: how have I fared? After rereading the preceding chapters, it has come to my attention that it is possible that I might have made a number of core assertions and inferences that, on closer examination, could very well be construed as examples of clumsy overstatement, elaborate but ultimately futile use of philosophy and woolly reasoning. It is not, admittedly, improbable that having ploughed through my sources, I might have begun to regard my chosen field of study as a 'personal fiefdom'. This 'Keep Out' mentality could have led to a growing sense of intellectual superciliousness, and caught in this fervour of infallibility, I could have very easily overstated my case and reasoned maladroitly.

It is in three broad areas where an attentive reader might require further clarifications. First, the notion that the 'race–culture debate' of the 1930s had moved on from the pseudoscience of the earlier period is perhaps overdone. Moreover, the 'positive' depiction of Myres' 'Races and Cultures' paper cannot be justified, because he had considered 'race' to be something more substantial than what it is now generally accepted to be, namely a 'social construct' (Chapters 3 and 4). Second, by situating Myres' Hellenism within the well worked-out contexts of the philosophies of history and science, I might have given the impression that it has been endowed with greater intellectual weight and sophistication than it genuinely deserves. In addition, this 'inaccurate' depiction of Hellenism could go on to underpin an eccentric view of Persian history which was wildly at odds with the consensus of the day (Chapters 5, 6 and 7). Finally, the criticism concerning what this work calls 'aesthetic' Hellenism is too severe. After all, the problem does not lie with the appreciation of the undoubted beauty of ancient Greece, but more narrowly, with the defective treatment of the various historical subject-matters (Chapters 2, 5 and 6).

This monograph has demonstrated that Hellenism is not constrained by a single narrative. The mainstream or the 'aesthetic' variety engages, by and large, uncritically with the ancient sources and is presentist in its historical methodology. It also exists in a state of historiographical stupor brought about by ideas concerning the beauty and sublimity of the Greek civilization. As a consequence, it often chooses to depict the powerful empire that was gnawing at the eastern borders of Hellas in an unflattering light. Within this well-entrenched context, the 'European' attributes of the Greeks have their counterparts in the 'Asiatic' shortcomings of the Iranian and non-Iranian peoples. The alternative narrative of 'historico-scientific' Hellenism, as advocated by Myres, is much more interested in a Rankean type of historical approach, which is augmented by appropriate methodological borrowings from the disciplines of the social sciences, such as anthropology, philology, geography and archaeology. In this context, unsurprisingly, the Greek and the Iranian peoples are depicted very differently from the still popular 'East is East and West is West' formulism. In this guise, the Graeco-Iranian world is considered not only to be an integral part of the Near Eastern political space, but also to be the representative of a larger Indo-European *oecumene*. As a consequence, their martial entanglements (the Persian Wars) are rendered as a purely regional matter, and not qualitatively different from those experienced by (say) the United Kingdom and Germany in the first half of the twentieth century.

It can also be equally argued that by discussing the *inner* and *outer* aspects of two very different types of Hellenism, as well as singling out some Hellenists' tendency to use supposedly inappropriate terms or words (Chapter 7), I am over-analysing and problematizing the study of ancient Greece unnecessarily. Perhaps. But the fact that two fundamentally different types of 'aims and procedure' defined the works of Murray and Myres can no longer be doubted. Chapters 5 and 6 provided the reader with an ample amount of evidence and criticism in demonstrating that primary differences had truly existed between the anthropological and non-anthropological approach towards the study of the ancient world. Moreover, the idea of examining, on the one hand, the literature relevant to the subject matter (*outer*), and on the other, its philosophical underpinnings (*inner*) was merely an attempt to treat a much-neglected subject as comprehensively as possible. In order to acquire a better understanding of these philosophical sensibilities, it seemed necessary to search out clues directly from the texts themselves; hence, the need to look closely at certain terms and phrases. Words such as 'beauty', 'perfection', 'freedom', 'democracy', as well as concepts such as the historically- and culturally-determined geographical spaces of Europe and Asia, were precisely the necessary textual and semantic fragments of information that were required for a better understanding of each and every philosophical undercurrent that this work tried to analyse; be they 'aestheticism', 'normal science', 'Collingwoodian history', or 'teleological history'.

The pertinent question here is why, as witnessed in the preface, Chapter 1 and by numerous endnoted examples, it is the 'aesthetic' and/or the 'teleological' narrative that is still going strong, while the 'historico-scientific' has fallen out of favour. The primary foundation blocks of this latter approach, as discussed, is the assumed relationship that exists between the concept of race (defined as a biological or zoological phenomenon), and the concept of culture (language, customs, myths, manmade goods, etc.). Myres' 'Races and Cultures' paper, together with many of his other writings, particularly his 1930 anthropological treatments of the ancient Greeks, were very much defined by his thoughts concerning this alleged relationship between race and culture. With the demise of a brutal racist regime in 1945, however, the moral appetite for the notion that 'race' could be a biological or genetic phenomenon was (and still is) understandably absent.

While there was no meeting of minds in the 1930s concerning the relationship or otherwise between 'race' and 'culture', there was, however, a near-complete consensus regarding the manner in which cultures had configured in the prehistorical Europe: it was believed that they were the result of repeated diffusions from Mesopotamia and Egypt. Everyone on the RAI committee had in one way or another conceded this point. But was this not a conceptual anomaly? After all, if the characteristics of a given race (which was believed to be a 'biological' or 'zoological' phenomenon) were instrumental in the configuration of a given culture, then how can the theory that the main components of that 'culture' were imported from elsewhere be maintained? Elliot-Smith's position was the only one that was entirely logical. This was so because nothing, in his view, links race to culture, and therefore it was not peculiar for him to suggest that 'while Egypt was laying the foundation of our civilization', there was 'nothing' happening in the rest of the world (including Europe). Childe, from the early 1930s onwards, had also held a similar position to that of Elliot-Smith, but unlike the latter, Childe's work, as discussed at length in Chapter 4, was riddled with problems concerning evidence and methods of analysis.

The picture, however, becomes more complicated with those committee members (including Myres) who believed that some form of relationship between race and culture was morphologically verifiable. They can be divided into three groups. First, there were those maintaining that some minor aspects of racial character can affect cultural life to a modest degree. Haldene, Firth, Fleur and Morant, broadly speaking, belong to this group. Second, there were those (Gates and Pitt-Rivers) asserting with some confidence that race almost always affects cultural life in a substantial manner. And finally there was Myres, who argued that the relationship between race and culture is a symbiotic phenomenon, meaning that each has a functional relationship with the other. Of course, as long as there is an a priori concession that 'culture' was diffused from the Semitic East, none of these views, apart from those of Elliot-Smith's, can be held rationally. In other words, this stance can do no other but to negate the role that 'race' was supposed to have played in the configuration of European 'culture'.

With the paradigm shift brought about by the applications of radiocarbon dating and dendrochronology, the hypothesis of diffusionism is now considered by a critical mass of prehistorians and archaeologists to be largely inappropriate for explaining the cultural life of prehistoric Europe. In other words, Elliot-Smith might have been consistent in his argument, but he was also largely mistaken in his adherence to hyper-diffusionism. Does this, therefore, imply that after diffusionism was overturned in the 1950s and 1960s, the earlier discussions concerning 'race' and 'culture' were given another lease of analytical life? While diffusionism was being decommissioned as a working hypothesis, the idea that 'race' should be regarded as a biological phenomenon was also downgraded drastically. A very authoritative 1950 report by UNESCO, entitled *The Race Question*, declared that '[t]he biological fact of race and the myth of "race" should be distinguished. For all practical social purposes "race" is not so much a biological phenomenon as a social myth.'[1] Thenceforth, a powerful consensus emerged that considered 'race' to be nothing more than a morally dubious social or cultural construct. This consensus, moreover, is still going strong. E. Barkan's *The Retreat of Scientific Racism* (1992), which was discussed at length in Chapter 3, and Kenan Malik's *The Meaning of Race* (1996) and *Strange Fruit: Why Both Sides are Wrong in the Race Debate* (2008), for instance, echo the pronouncement of UNESCO, by contending that '[r]ace exists only as a statistical correlation, not as an objective fact. The distinction we make between different races is not naturally given but is socially defined.' As a consequence the author is in no doubt that 'the division of humankind into discrete groups is entirely manmade'.[2] With the widespread acceptance of this definition of 'race', serious considerations could scarcely have been given to those, such as Myres and most of the committee members, who had considered 'race' to be partly a biological ('zoological') phenomenon.

If it were to be argued that, after all that has been said and done, the concept of 'race' does indeed possess genetic or biological underpinnings as well as social and cultural ones, would it then be possible to examine the writings of Myres and others within this new context of 'race'? In recent years, with the emergence of the new academic disciplines of evolutionary biology and genetics, there have also emerged new voices making the following kind of arguments: 'The claim that there is no such a thing as race is understandable but wrong [...]. We should recognise both the genetic reality of race and the unique human ability to transcend it.' This assertion was made by the evolutionary biologist Mark Pagel in a critical review of Malik's 2008 publication. The reviewer also states that 'if we measure large numbers of genetic markers from populations around the world and then use them to form clusters, we get back groupings that bear a striking resemblance to what have conventionally been recognised as the major racial groups on the planet'. He also warns against the desire 'to swap the word race for something less politically charged', and argues that this is 'just an act of self-denial and certainly no more accurate than the dreaded "r" word'. In addition, the 'more we measure, the more genetic differences we find among populations; and no kinds of difference can be absolutely ruled out'. Consequently, Pagel argues that '[w]e may in future need a language, and maybe even a new ethics, to discuss the new genetics'.[3] Indeed, the entry for 'race' in the *Oxford Encyclopaedia of Evolution* (2002) seems to have done precisely that. By treating the subject-matter from two 'perspectives' ('Population Genetics Perspective' and 'Sociological Perspective'[4]), this publication is effectively outlining the terms of reference for this 'new ethics'.

As far as contextualizing the writings of Myres and others in this new 'double-perspective' of 'race' is concerned, the following observations can be made. Apart from Elliot-Smith at one end of the analytical divide, and Gates and Pitt-Rivers on the other end, positions held by the rest of the committee were too fuzzy and equivocal to merit further investigations. Although 'race' was a major factor in the thinking of Gates and Pitt-Rivers, nevertheless, their approach cannot be accommodated within the context provided by today's evolutionary biology, because first, the attachment of hierarchical values to 'race' – implying that the configuration of cultures and civilizations moves along deterministic lines – is completely at odds with the ethos of the modern science of genetics. Second, in their framework it is always culture that is a function of race and never race a function of culture. The modern practitioners of biology, unlike Gates and Pitt-Rivers, do not discount the importance of culture, nor do they dismiss the contention that 'race' is partially a social or cultural construct.

Myres, however, due to the manner in which he had conceptualized his framework, had largely managed to avoid these two major pitfalls. As discussed in Chapters 3 and 6, his starting point was straightforward: 'race' and 'culture' are in a simultaneous functional relationship, the result of which is a symbiotic product called 'people'. But this 'people' is not a static concept; it is a time-dependent variable: the two variables of 'race' and 'culture' tend to converge as we go back in time and vice versa. One practical application of this for (say) the positioning of Greeks and Persians within the context of ancient history is the probable convergence between these two Indo-European 'peoples' (which for Myres are a complex amalgam of 'race' and 'culture'). By arguing against evaluating 'people', moreover, Myres frames his historical analysis in such a way that it becomes illogical for him to introduce any stock-in-trade ideas from the ubiquitous schools of Orientalism or Hellenocentrism. In his scheme of things, the 'Europeans v. Asiatics' template is conspicuous by its absence. It is therefore safe to infer that Myres' thinking on 'race' can be analysed afresh within what is current in contemporary human sciences. In other words, this reappraisal of Myres is not merely an exercise in antiquarianism, but a concerted effort to recommend his thinking to a modern intelligentsia that is well versed in the sciences of genetics and evolutionary biology. Having spent a good three years in the company of his multifaceted writings, it is my sense that if he had read Pagel's contention that 'we should recognise the genetic reality of race and the uniquely human ability to transcend it', he would have nodded in agreement.

But is this not an example of overstating Myres' position, and claiming too much on his behalf? There might be something in this observation. Within the post-war intellectual climate, Myres, by that point an emeritus professor, reappraised and amended significantly some important areas of his pre-war writings, and in the process he uncharacteristically adopted an unmistakably Orientalist mindset. In a 1953 paper entitled 'Persia, Greece and Israel', he writes of 'Oriental aggression'[5] experienced by the Ionians at the hand of the Persian Empire, which, in turn, is described as an 'Oriental despotism'[6] possessing an 'Oriental culture'.[7] As my extensive analysis of Myres' works has shown, this new way of depicting the Persians is not congruent with what Myres had produced during the most productive period of his academic life (1910–38). The underlying reason for this fundamental revision is hard to pinpoint. In my judgement it could have been due to one of the following two explanations. First, writing in the early 1950s, Myres, after witnessing the tragic consequences of the 'Aryan race' theories, might have made a conscious decision to abandon his earlier interest in matters Indo-European (however carefully they were formulated) for purely moral or ethical reasons. Or second, as a result of a thorough intellectual re-examination, he had revised the foundations of his earlier drawn inferences.

The evidence in support of such a Damascene conversion, however, is thin. There is nothing in his private papers or published works c.1940s that in any way hints at a fundamental rethink. In other words, there is not a paper-trail that can demonstrate the ideological shift from his 1938 'Greece and Persia' to this late essay under discussion. In fact, a careful reading of this 1953 paper suggests that Myres had neither undertaken new lines of enquiries, nor had he come, by way of new evidence, to a conclusion that required the 're-orientalizing' of the Persians. What this essay was trying to achieve was to understand the underlying reasons for Jews' better relationship with the Persian Empire than the one enjoyed by the Greek city-states. This question seems to be somewhat contrived.

The recreation of the Jewish realm was an act of Achaemenid patronage, whereas the state structures of the Greeks existed prior to and independent of any substantial Persian input. Consequently therefore, Jews and Greeks could not have reacted similarly to the demands of the empire. In addition, the fact that he takes a number of key sentences[8] from his earlier works, and alters their syntactical structures sufficiently enough in order for them to chime with the sensibilities of the post-war and post-1948 readership of the *Palestine Exploration Quarterly* does not suggest that Myres was making a serious attempt to produce an original piece of research. When he mentions the 'misunderstanding' between the Persian nation of 'boy scouts' and the 'rationalized and commercialized Greeks', he no longer situates the protagonists within the framework of the 'Ethnology, Habitat, Linguistic, and Common Culture of Indo-Europeans'. Moreover, when he discusses a Greek prince, who was brought up like Persian nobles 'to ride and to shoot, and to tell the truth', Myres does not dwell (as he had done in 1911) on what Alexander and these 'clear eyed' nobles had in common, namely that favourite euphemism for Indo-European descent: the commonality of 'horse-taming'. In addition, in his 1938 paper, Myres argues that there were 'benefactors of the king in all ranks of society', and that the 'no "royal seclusion" policy defined the social relationship within the Achaemenid power structure [a power structure, moreover, founded on the 'personal monarchy of the "people's choice"']'. He also contends that 'the line of aristocratic exclusiveness was drawn elsewhere, if at all'. In the 1953 paper, in contrast, he contradicts these points by asserting that the 'social structure' of Persia was 'archaic'.[9]

The reason why Myres had produced such a paper, in my view, was largely to do with the necessity of coming to terms with this new and UNESCO-sponsored definition of 'race'. In turn, this made it more difficult for him to situate Indo-Europeanism in a predominately anthropological context, which, in his thinking, would invariably have touched upon the concept of 'race'.[10] In other words, it was a moral and a practical and not an intellectual response to an entirely new *modus vivandi*. Indeed, a year earlier, commenting on two UNESCO publications on the question of 'race', Myres was equivocal:

> The reason why there was so little race prejudice among the ancient Greeks was not because their culture 'arose in a human environment in which miscegenation appears to have been rampant', but because the limits of race mixture in Greek lands were so narrow, that the question did not arise. The significant differences – as between Greeks and Persians or Scythians [i.e., Indo-Iranians] – were cultural, not racial at all. Can U.N.E.S.C.O. pamphlets produce a single instance of a Greek who married a Negro?[11]

Of course, some of the groundwork for this new outlook on 'race' was prepared before the war. '[T]he impetus for the shift in ideologies of race,' as Barkan argues, 'came from the inclusion of outsiders (women, Jews, and leftists) who infused greater egalitarianism into scientific discourse.'[12] One of the main consequences of such a move was an implicit jettisoning of the core philosophies that had underwritten Myres' form of Hellenism. As a result, the relevant intellectual arena was surrendered to mainstream Hellenism. With no alterative available to this 'aesthetic-cum-teleological' variety, many aspects of Graeco-Persian history reverted back to a more polished version of the earlier Orientalism and Hellenocentrism. In this contemporary manifestation, the tone of the discourse, admittedly, has become more nuanced; and the inferences drawn, less gung-ho and triumphalist. The ideological sensibilities, however, that frame the current discourse have continued to rely heavily on a number of thematic topoi, which, broadly speaking, suggest that the freedom-loving European Greeks were in the fight of their lives against the despot-worshipping, prostrate-junkie hordes of Asiatic Persians.[13]

Come what may, the pre-war intellectual legacy of Sir John Linton Myres should now be recognized as a vital part of modern British intellectual history and classical scholarship. How and whether his methods and ideas pertaining to science, history, anthropology, geography, race, culture, people, Greeks and Persians might influence the evolution of the academic discipline of ancient history can only be ascertained in the years – perhaps decades – to come. Meanwhile, the following epitaph from one of his obituary-writers should suffice:

> It is unlikely that his mastery of so many branches of study will often be rivalled; for he was a specialist in all, a classical scholar, a prehistoric archaeologist, an ethnologist, geographer, and geologist, and was at home also in the literature of other sciences. His quick wide-ranging mind could fertilize one of these disciplines from another; but all were related to one end, the study of man and his setting on the earth.[14]

Now that this intellectual journey is drawing near its conclusion, there are two loose ends in need of tidying up. First, in Chapter 1, I stated that the locus of the Indo-European debate from 1850s to 1930s 'was constructed *mostly* within the contours of the highly dubious foundation of "Aryanism"'. This italicized 'mostly' is hugely significant. It is within the limiting conditionality of what remains from this 'mostly' (i.e., the works of Myres) that the evidence for this discourse has been, in a manner of speaking, mined. Without it, this work would have lacked a moral centre, and without a moral centre, I would have refrained from writing it. The second point is the question that I posed at the beginning of this chapter: 'How have I fared?' This, of course, is not a question for me but for the reader. What I want the reader to bear in mind when considering it is the contention that in demonstrating that there perhaps exists an alternative and arguably a better way of doing Persian/Iranian ancient history, this work has acted as a methodological point of departure for future investigations.

POSTSCRIPT

I concluded the final chapter of this book by asserting that there might exist a better way of doing Persian/Iranian history. What do I mean by this? One of the most important academic areas which might have some relevance for ancient history and/or Iranian studies is the modern and multifaceted discipline of Indo-European studies. Of course, as witnessed in this work, Indo-European studies have often been perceived as a morally questionable framework of historical analysis. But this academic field has progressed so fundamentally in the recent decades that the continuing adherence (which I had frequently encountered during my research) to its supposed moral bankruptcy should now be reconsidered with an open mind. In order to aid this process, I propose this brief bibliographical essay.

The doyen of the modern Indo-European studies has undoubtedly been the American archaeologist J. P. Mallory. Since the publication of his seminal *In Search of the Indo-Europeans: Language, Archaeology and Myth* (1989), he has also co-written (with W. H. Mair) *The Tarim Mummies: Ancient China and the Mystery of the Earliest Peoples from the West* (2001). This influential work brought to public attention the discovery of well-preserved Tocharian mummies in north-western China in the 1990s. By doing so, it has brought into play the sub-discipline of biological anthropology in a decisive fashion. This approach has recently been augmented by the publication of G. Cochran's and H. Harpending's *The 10,000 Year Explosion: How*

Civilization Accelerated Human Evolution (2009). This work argues that because dairying produces five times as many calories as raising cattle for slaughter, the 'carrying capacity' of the Indo-Europeans allowed them to 'raise and feed more warriors' to such an extent that it handed them a comparative advantage in warfare and conquest (p. 181). Furthermore, in 2006, Mallory along with D. Q. Adams published a very comprehensive Indo-European handbook, entitled *The Oxford Introduction to Proto-Indo-European and Proto-Indo-European World*.

Indeed between the early 1990s and 2006, a large number of authors, from varied academic backgrounds (including classics, anthropology and ancient history) contributed to the debate in a substantial way. N. Ascherson's *Black Sea: The Birthplace of Civilisation and Barbarism* (1995); C. Watkins' *How to Kill a Dragon: Aspects of Indo-European Poetics* (1995); B. Sergent's *Homosexualité et Initiation chez les Peuples Indo-Européens* (1996); A. Sherratt's 'The Archaeology of Indo-European: An Alternative View', in *Economy and Society in Prehistoric Europe* (1997) and J. V. Day's *Indo-European Origins: The Anthropological Evidence* (2001) are good examples of this trend. Moreover, the interdisciplinary nature of the subject is very much on view in *Indo-European Perspectives: Studies in Honour of Anna Morpurgo Davis* (2004). The fact that 43 contributors (all of whom were drawn from the leading universities of Europe and North America) can come together and discuss matters Indo-European shows a subject in a reasonably good health.

In 2007, the *annus mirabilis* of publications concerning this field, three groundbreaking works were produced. First, Martin West, a distinguished Hellenist, published a magisterial book, entitled *Indo-European Poetry and Myth*. By linking two of the most important cultural building-blocks in this way, he situates the Greeks and Persians, *inter alia*, in a context that is the converse of the 'East v. West' template. The fact that a bona fide Hellenist does this is also significant. Second, D. W. Anthony's *The Horse, the Wheel and Language: How Bronze-Age Riders from the Eurasian Steppes Shaped the Modern World* is a tour de force of archaeological analysis at its most cutting-edge. By bringing not only the recent discoveries into view, but the newly-available reservoir of Russian materials (archaeological finds, decades of research and publication and the post-Soviet ease with which one can investigate the most important sites), Anthony has been able to produce an original, and possibly a paradigm-shifting, work. Third, and as a consequence of the opening up of the Russian sources, E. E. Kuz'mina's magnificently erudite *The Origin of the Indo-Iranians* is without a doubt one of the most important and primary sources for a better understanding of the Iranian world and civilization at its inception. Its bibliography alone is a cornucopia of knowledge: it lists almost 3,000 sources, three-quarters of which are only available in Russian. (It would be useful for some enterprising publishers to step in and produce some of these works in English.) Finally, in March 2010, the highly respected French academic journal, *Dossiers d'Archéologie*, dedicated an entire issue to 'Les Indo-Européens'. Many of the 11 lengthy essays, produced by eminent international scholars, dealt with a wide range of current Indo-European areas of interest.

Some aspects of contemporary Indo-European studies, undoubtedly, may still be contaminated by the racism of the past (for a counterblast, refer to S. Arvidsson's *Aryan Idols* [2000]). As Anthony points out, however, the academic world has moved on, and it has moved on decisively:

> For Indo-European archaeology, the errors of the past cannot be repeated as easily today. When the nineteenth-century fantasy of the Aryans began there were no material remains, no archaeological findings, to constrain the imagination [...]. Archaeology really played no role. The scattered archaeological discoveries of the first half of the twentieth century could still be forced into this previously imaginary mould. But that is not so easy today. A convincing narrative about the speakers of Proto-Indo-European must today be pegged to vast array of archaeological facts, and it must remain un-contradicted by the facts that stand outside the chosen narrative path.[1]

GLOSSARY

Arnold, Mathew (1822–88): English-born cultural critic and HM Inspector of schools, educated at Rugby, Winchester and Balliol, where he was involved in the 'Oxford Movement'. While he was a fellow at Oriel, he produced a number of essays regarding the classics, including the essay entitled 'Culture and Anarchy'.

Boas, Franz (1858–1942): German-born American anthropologist, widely known as the 'father of American anthropology', studied physics and geography at the Universities of Heidelberg and Kiel, respectively. One of his first major publications was *The Mind of the Primitive Man* (1911).

Breasted, Henry (1865–1935): American archaeologist, Egyptologist and historian, studied at Yale University and became the first American to be awarded a doctorate in Egyptology from the University of Berlin. The University of Chicago became his academic home, where he was instrumental in establishing its world-renowned Oriental Institute. *Ancient Times* (1916) and *Ancient Record of Egypt* (1906) in five volumes are two of his major publications.

Childe, Gordon (1892–1957): Australian-born prehistorian and classicist. After studying classics at the University of Sydney, Childe attended Queen's College, Oxford, where he took a BLitt in 1916 under the supervision of Myres and Sir Arthur Evans. At Oxford, he had also become involved in Marxism. After a brief spell in Australia in the early 1920s, he returned to England and became in 1927 the first holder of the Abercromby Chair of Prehistoric Archaeology at the University of Edinburgh. In 1946, six years after becoming a fellow of the British Academy, Childe became a professor of archaeology at the Institute of Archaeology, and eventually its director. He was widely regarded, according to Peter Gathercole in the *Oxford Dictionary of National Biographies* (2005), 'as the most distinguished European prehistorian of his time, with a bibliography of over 600 items' (p. 438). His staunch political beliefs sat rather uneasily not only with his appreciation of the 'Aryans', but also with his seemingly patrician affection for lunching and staying regularly at the Athenaeum. The anonymous person who was given the task of sorting out his papers at the University of London Special Collection left the following intriguing remarks with his collected papers: 'Only of some interest to a biographer [...] they also show the dichotomy – a theoretical liking for the working class and a dislike of the cultural implications of its domination – that was so marked a feature of this author' (Box 13, folio 5). In 1957 he returned to Australia, and in the October of that year, he committed suicide.

Collingwood, Robin George (1889–1943): English-born historian, philosopher and a fellow of the British Academy, who studied at Rugby and University College, Oxford. After attaining a first in Classics Mods followed by Greats, he became a fellow of Pembroke in 1912, where he remained for most of his academic career. His interests were wide-ranging; apart from the philosophy of history he was also interested in Roman history (publishing *Roman Britain and the English Settlements* in 1936), metaphysics and the philosophy of art.

Coulanges, Numa Denis Fustel de (1830–89): Paris-born historian and anthropologist, he studied at the École Normale Supérieure, where he excelled in the ancient languages. Later at the Sorbonne, he concentrated on the history of ancient France, producing a book on its political institutions in 1875. He also published the well-known book entitled *La cité antique* (1864).

GLOSSARY

Elliot-Smith, Sir Grafton (1871–1937): Australian-born anatomist and anthropologist and the holder of the Chair of Anatomy at University College London from 1919 until 1936. His theories of cultural diffusionism resulted in a number of publications, such as *Migration of Early Culture* (1915), *Elephants and Ethnologists* (1924) and *The Diffusion of Culture* (1933).

Fleure, Herbert John (1877–1969): Guernsey-born geographer and anthropologist, who studied zoology and geology at the Universities of Aberystwyth and Zurich, where he also taught. In 1930 he became a professor of geography at Manchester. In the 1930s he attacked the Nazis' 'Nordic myth' of racial purity. Two of his main publications were *Human Geography in Western Europe* (1918) and *A Natural History of Man in Britain* (1951).

Gates, Reginald Ruggles (1882–1962): Canadian-born McGill- and Chicago-educated botanist and geneticist, who became a professor of botany at King's College London in 1921, and Fellow of the Royal Society in 1931. After the war he undertook research at Harvard until his retirement in 1957. *Heredity in Man* (1929) and *Human Genetics* (1946) are two of his noteworthy publications.

Gobineau, Joseph Arthur de (1816–82): A Paris-born aristocrat, who had intermittently attended Collège de France in the 1840s. He was also a man of letters and a diplomat (serving for four years in Tehran *c*.1850s). He expounded his influential socio-historical and racial theories in *Essai sur l'inégalité des races humaines* (1855). In 1846 he married a 'Creole' from Martinique, and in 1869 he published *Histoire des Perses*.

Haldane, John Burdon Sanderson (1892–1964): Oxford-born, and Eton- and Oxford-educated (mathematics, classics and philosophy), Haldane taught at both Oxford and Cambridge and became a Fellow of the Royal Society in 1932. He held a number of posts, including that of professor of genetics at University College London. He published copiously, including *Daedalus, or, Science and the Future* (1923) and *The Inequality of Man* (1932).

Herzfeld, Ernst Emil (1879–1948): German-born archaeologist and Iranist who studied at the Universities of Munich and Berlin and worked extensively in Persia in the inter-war period. Among his publications are *Archaeological History of Iran* (1935) and *The Persian Empire* (1968).

Inge, William Ralph (1860–1954): English-born classicist, who studied at Eton and Kings' College, Cambridge, and spent most of his academic career at Eton and Hertford College, Oxford. His main interest was Greek religious practices and their relationship to the theological teaching of the Church of England (*The Platonic Traditions in English Religious Thought* was published in 1926).

Jones, Sir William (1746–94): London-born Orientalist, radical Whig and judge, who studied at University College, Oxford. After acquiring Persian and Arabic, and translating the *1001 Nights*, he travelled extensively in Persia and India, where he was one of the very first European philologists to adduce linguistic links between a number of languages (the Indo-European family of languages). He published a number of books, including *Grammar of the Persian Language* (1771).

Kossinna, Gustav (1858–1931): German-born prehistorian and professor of archaeology at the University of Berlin. He situated the cradle of the 'Aryans' in modern Germany and displayed extreme nationalism and 'Aryanism' sensibilities. Gordon Childe was heavily influenced by him at the beginning of his career.

Livingstone, Sir Richard Winn (1880–1960): Liverpool-born classicist who studied at Winchester and New College, Oxford. His first publication, *Greek Genius and its Meaning to Us* (1912), was very close to ideas which were being entertained by Gilbert Murray and others.

GLOSSARY 253

Mahaffy, John Penland (1839–1919): Swiss-born Irish classicist, who studied and taught at Trinity College, Dublin, where he also tutored Oscar Wilde. *Alexander's Empire* (1887) and *A Survey of Greek Civilization* (1897) were two of his main publications.

Meyer, Eduard (1855–1930): German-born ancient historian, polymath and polyglot. He held professorial positions at the Universities of Halle and Berlin. One of his main contributions to the history of the Near East came with the publication of *Geschichte des Altertums* (1902). He also wrote the entry for 'Persia' in the now famous 1911 edition of *Encyclopaedia Britannica*.

Morant, Geoffrey Miles (1899–1964): London-born anthropologist and statistician, educated and taught at University College London. By the late 1920s, Morant was regarded as the leading authority in the biometric school of physical anthropology. Between 1926 and 1930, he published a number of essays in the *Annals of Eugenics*. His most noteworthy publication was *The Races of Central Europe* (1939).

Müller, Max (1823–1900): German philologist, studied at Leipzig and Paris (Sanskrit), moved to Oxford, where he spent most of his life in academia, and was a professor of comparative theology at All Souls (1868–75). In 1861, he published his *Lectures on the Science of Language*.

Murray, George Gilbert Aimé (1866–1957): Australian-born and Oxford-educated (Classics), Murray began his academic career at Glasgow (until 1899) and continued it at Oxford (regius professor of Greek from 1908 onwards). He was interested in every aspect of Hellenism, in particular its literary canon. He translated a number of important works, concentrating mainly on the Greek dramatists. Via the Cambridge Ritualists, Murray immersed himself in the religious practices of the Greeks. This spiritual life was further supplemented, according to Thomson in *Proceedings of the British Academy* (1957), by being an able telepathist (often, apparently, he would get in touch with the ancients). As a scholar, however, his legacy is questionable. According to *The Dictionary of British Classicists* (2004), he 'disliked the loneliness of those private labours that produce great scholarship' (p. 690). Moreover, the same publication assesses Murray in the following forthright manner: 'It now takes a considerable effort in moral imagination to engage with his claim that "if Europe can preserve the standards that we call classic or Christian or Hellenic, there will be at least one great centre round which the higher, gentler, nobler influences of the world can gather and stand fast"' (p. 692). See the bibliography for some of his numerous publications.

Myres, Sir John Linton (1869–1954): Myres was born in Preston, Lancashire to a Church of England clergyman. After attending the local grammar school, he won a scholarship to Winchester in 1882. Another scholarship in 1888 took Myres to New College, Oxford, where he obtained a first in Classical Moderations and *Literae Humaniores*. A fellowship at Christ Church was followed by a lectureship in classical archaeology; and in 1907, he was appointed the Gladstone Professor of Greek at the University of Liverpool. But in 1910 he came back to Oxford and remained there until his death: he was appointed the Wykeham Professor of Ancient History at New College Oxford. He retired in 1939, aged 70. Almost at the midpoint of his tenure, he was elected to the British Academy (1923). Myres was also heavily involved in the discipline of anthropology: he served as the honorary secretary (1901–3) and then as the president (1928–31) of the RAI, and edited its journal, *Man*, for some years. Myres' deep interest in science, according to *The Dictionary of British Classicists* (2004), began when he was still at Winchester. He attended his first meeting of the British Association for the Advancement of Science in 1890, becoming the secretary of its anthropological section in 1893. He was also one of the very few scholars who gave the Sather Lectures at Berkley on two different occasions – 1914 and 1927 (1916's *Influence of Anthropology on the Course of Political Science* and 1930's *Who Were the Greeks?* were the resultant publications). A number of honorary positions followed, such as the presidency of the Hellenic Society (1935–8), and the chairmanship of the British School at Athens (1934–47).

While his obituary in the *Proceedings of the British Academy* (T. J. Dunbabin, vol. 41 (1955), pp. 348–65) and his entry in the *Oxford Dictionary of National Biographies* (J. Boardman [2005], pp. 87–9.) touch upon his interest in science and anthropology, they do not do what this book has striven to do; namely to demonstrate, via close analysis of his published and unpublished works, that his writing on Greece and relevant subjects was largely predicated on the understanding and the utility of a number of scientific disciplines, such as geography, comparative philology, prehistory archaeology and, of course, anthropology.

Pater, Walter Horatio (1839–94): London-born, Oxford-educated art historian and essayist. He was hugely influenced by Jowett (and therefore by Hegel), and took a fellowship at Brasenose in 1864, where he taught modern German philosophy. His book *The Renaissance* (1873) has proven to be very influential, even to this day.

Pitt-Rivers, George Henry Lane-Fox (1890–1966): London-born, Eton- and Oxford-educated, Pitt-Rivers served with the Royal Dragoons in the First World War. Although not a professional academic, he published a number of books, including *The Clash of Culture and the Contact of Races* (1927). Throughout his life, Pitt-Rivers displayed extreme right-wing views: he was an internee during the war, and one of the sponsors of A. K. Chesterton's National Front.

Ranke, Leopold van (1795–1886): German historian and historiographer, who studied classics and Lutheran theology at the University of Leipzig. He taught mostly in the University of Berlin. His empirical approach was truly a revolution in methodology. He wrote on a variety of historical subjects, one of his best works being the *History of the Latin and Teutonic Nations from 1494–1514*.

Rawlinson, George (1812–1901): English-born ancient historian, who studied a Trinity College, Oxford, where he became Camden Professor of Ancient History (1861–89). The series of books on 'Oriental' monarchies remain his most important publications.

Renan, Ernst (1823–92): Breton-French philosopher, who studied in a number of Catholic seminaries across France, and taught intermittently at the Sorbonne. He wrote on a wide variety of subjects, touching on the questions of ethnicity, race, religion and the attributes of civilizations: *De l'origine de Langage* (1862), *L'Islam et Sciences* (1883), *Qu'est-ce qu'une nation?* (1882), to name but three.

Thomson, James Alexander Kerr (1879–1957): English classicist, who taught at King's College London for a large part of his career. Intellectually he was very close to Gilbert Murray's school of thought. Among his publications were *The Greek Tradition: Essays in the Reconstruction of Ancient Thoughts* (1915) and *Greeks and Barbarians* (1922).

Toynbee, Arnold Joseph (1889–1975): English historian, a fellow at Balliol and later a Professor of Modern Greek and Byzantine History at King's College London, and Gilbert Murray's son-in-law. He published extensively and his best work (if seldom read these days) is the Spengler-inspired *A Study of History* in 12 volumes.

Winckelmann, Johann Joachim (1717–68): German art historian, Hellenist and aesthete. After studying theology at Halle University, he toured Italy extensively. But his love was always Greece (where he never visited). His influence among the Romantics was substantial. His 1764 publication, entitled *The History of Ancient Art among the Greeks*, became one of the bibles of Romanticism.

NOTES

Preface

1. N. Davis, *Europe: A History* (1997), p. 103.
2. *Aeschylus' Persians* (Edith Hall's 1996 translation): 'Two beautifully dressed women seemed to appear to me, one decked out in Persian robes, the other in Dorian clothing. In statue they were conspicuously larger than people are today, and were faultlessly lovely; they were sisters of one race. One of them lived in her fatherland, Greece, which she obtained by lot, the other in the lands of the barbarians,' p. 61.
3. S. Goldhill, 'Review', *The Classical Review* (2001), pp. 9–10.
4. S. Goldhill, 'Letter', November 2001.
5. J. Podlecki, *Aeschylus' Persians* (1971), p. 42.
6. P. Briant, 'Alexandre le Grand, "héros civilisateur"', *Le Monde*, 6 January 2005.
7. Peter Green, 'Letter', *Times Literary Supplement* (hereafter *TLS*), February 2005: '[A]s several commentators noted', Stone's Darius did 'bear a certain resemblance' to Osama bin Laden.
8. A. Murray, 'Review', *TLS*, 23 June 2006, p. 12. The book that was under review, J. Folda's *Crusader Art in the Holly Land* (2006), comes with a CD-ROM, which reproduces an image of a turbaned and sallow-complexioned Xerxes from *Histoire d'Outremer*.
9. M. Wood, 'At the Movies', *London Review of Books* (hereafter *LRB*), 26 April 2007, p. 19.
10. Reader: what is your visceral reaction when you read the deliberately offensive 'Scotch' instead of the more appropriate 'Scot'?
11. There appears to be a continuing tendency to render the threatening 'other' as different as possible. The famous darkened mugshot of O. J. Simpson on the cover of *Time Magazine* is a good example of this. A more recent example is the manipulation (darkening) of Jean Charles de Menezes' image. According to *The Times* (October 17, 2007), 'a picture designed to show the similarity between [...] de Menezes and a convicted terrorist [of Ethiopian background] was manipulated by the Metropolitan Police to make it look more convincing'.
12. P. Cartledge, *The Greeks: A Portrait of Self and Others* (1993), p. 60.

13. P. Cartledge, 'Historiography and Ancient Greek Self-Definition', in M. Bentley (ed.), *Companion to Historiography* (1997), p. 26.
14. Both definitions are taken from *The Shorter Oxford Dictionary* (2002).
15. P. Cartledge, *Thermopylae* (2007), p. xii.
16. H. Sancisi-Weerdenburg, J.W. Drijvers (eds.), *Achaemenid History V: The Roots of the European Tradition* (1995), pp. xi–xii. They write: 'One only needs to compare the publication numbers of this novel [Gore Vidal's *Creation*] with the best-seller in the scholarly field, Olmstead's *History of the Persian Empire*, to realize that the former has contributed much more to general ideas about Achaemenid period than the latter [p. xi.].'
17. R. Kipling, *The Ballad of East and West* (1892).
18. A. Pagden, *Worlds at War: The 2,500-Year Struggle between East and West* (2008).

Chapter 1   Introduction

1. J. Herder, *Reflections on the Philosophy of History of Mankind* (1968), p. 131.
2. G. Rawlinson, *The Five Great Monarchies of the Ancient Eastern World* (1862), p. 316.
3. G. W. Cox, *The Greeks and the Persians* (1887), p. 204.
4. Taken from T. Garton Ash, '1989!' *New York Review of Books* (hereafter, *NYRB*) 5 November 2009, p. 4.
5. T. Holland, *Persian Fire: The First World Empire and the Battle for the West* (2006), p. xxi.
6. J. B. Bury, *A History of Greece* (1909), pp. 185–6.
7. B. Bull, 'Alexander, the First Neo-Con', *FT Magazine*, 22 January 2005. Note that the phrase 'a vast oriental culture' suggests the existence of a homogenized and monolithic cultural construct. He also writes: 'Alexander wanted to bring what Greeks saw as the light of Hellenic civilisation to new lands. "We must bring change to the east", says Alexander in Stone's film. "We will build an empire not of land and gold, but of the mind."' At the other end of the ideological spectrum, there are those who regard Alexander as a brutal destroyer. A. B. Bosworth, for instance, regards Hernán Cortés, the *conquistador* of Mexico, as a latter-day Alexander (*Alexander and the East* [1996], pp. 35–41). Also see A. B. Bosworth and E. J. Baynham, *Alexander the Great in Fact and Fiction* (2001).
8. P. Green, *The Years of Salamis* (1970), p. xxiii.
9. This is a peculiar assertion. As Lloyd Llewellyn-Jones has argued in *Aphrodite's Tortoise: The Veiled Women of Ancient Greece* (2007), 'veiling was so routine a practice [in Greece] that it seldom receives a mention in the ancient sources' (p. 1). Moreover, 'Greek veiling and the philosophy behind it operated within the general milieu of the ancient Near East' (p. 6).

10. V. Davis-Hanson in Cowley (ed.), *What if?* (1999), p. 34.
11. R. Lane Fox, *The Classical World: An Epic History from Homer to Hadrian* (2005), pp. 106–7. In a review of this work, even Tom Holland takes Lane Fox to task: '[His] lack of interest in non-classical cultures is evident in almost everything he writes about them. The word "barbarian" itself is employed with total lack of irony' ('Review', *The Guardian*, 17 December 2005).
12. J. A. Gobineau, *The World of the Persians* (1971), p. 131.
13. E. Renan, *De l'origine de Langage* (1862), *passim*.
14. E. Renan, *L'Islam et Sciences* (1883), p. 378. 'La Perse seule fait ici exception; elle a su garder son génie propre; car la Perse a su prendre dans l'islam une place à part.'
15. J. W. Jackson, 'Iran and Turan', *Anthropological Review* (1868), pp. 121–37 (126).
16. J. L. Myres, *The Dawn of History* (1911), p. 217.
17. H. Breasted, *Ancient Times* (1916), pp. 239–40.
18. G. Childe, *The Aryans: A Study of Indo-European Origins* (1926), p. 4.
19. S. Jones and M. Keynes (eds.), *Twelve Galton Lectures: A Centenary Selection with Commentary* (2007), p. vii.
20. Ibid., p. xi
21. Ibid.
22. Revealingly, two of Galton's publications were entitled *Hereditary Genius* (1869) and *Natural Inheritance* (1889). M. Keynes (2007) writes: 'from his [Galton's] perception of a national decline, he felt "the augmentation of favoured stock" by deliberate breeding ought to be encouraged' (p. 5).
23. The change in name had a great deal, according to Hauser, to do with the 'ideological closeness between Iran and [Nazi] Germany' of the period. For more see Hauser, 'German Research on the Ancient Near East', in W. G. Schwanitz (ed.), *Germany and the Middle East 1871–1945* (2004), pp. 166–7. This 'closeness' was bolstered significantly in 1936 when the German economic minister, Hjalmar Schacht, visited Iran and, according to Bernard Lewis in *The Multiple Identities of the Middle East* (1998), 'assured the Iranians that since they were "pure Aryans", the anti-Semitic Nuremberg race laws did not apply to them' (p. 45).
24. J. Wiesehöfer, *Ancient Persia* (2001).
25. Some of the Indo-Iranian dwellers in and around the Iranian plateau were the Persians, Medians, Parthians, Drangians, Sogdians, Chorasmians, Bactrians and Arians.
26. Some of the Indo-Iranian dwellers outside the plateau were the Scythians, Alans, Cappadocians and Sarmatians.
27. It should, however, be stressed that the reasons usually given for 'othering' the Persians have nothing to do with the fact that many important aspects of the Achaemenid Persians (culture and ethnicity) were non-Indo-Iranian. I have yet to locate a document which asserts that the Persians are 'orientalized' because they happen to be partly Elamite or Babylonian.

28. Indeed, it is not implausible to think of the Greeks as also being a 'Eurasian people'. This is so because first, Greeks did not differentiate between a well-delineated 'Europe' and a clear-cut 'Asia' (see Chapter 7); and second, many Greeks dwelled in lands – only described much later as 'Asia' – for centuries.

Chapter 2 Setting the Scene: Anthropology, Linguistics and Romantic Hellenism in Victorian Britain

1. T. K. Penniman, *A Hundred Years of Anthropology* (1952), p. 7. The following are the author's periodizations: before 1835, the 'Formulary Period'; 1835–59, the 'Convergent Period'; 1859–1900, the 'Constructive Period'; and 1900–35, the 'Critical Period'.
2. Ibid., p. 53.
3. Penniman, *A Hundred*, p. 73.
4. L. Poliakov, *The Aryan Myth* (1971), p. 189.
5. Ibid.
6. Ibid.
7. A. H. Sayce, *Introduction to the Science of Language* (1880), vol. 1, p. 61.
8. Ibid., p. 63.
9. Ibid., p. 70.
10. Ibid., p. 73.
11. Ibid., p. 63.
12. Ibid., p. 66.
13. Ibid., p. 68.
14. Ibid., p. 75.
15. Penniman, *A Hundred*, p. 151.
16. M. Müller, *Lectures on the Science of Language* (1861), p. 1.
17. Ibid., pp. 3–20.
18. Ibid., p. 22.
19. Ibid., pp. 23–24.
20. Ibid., p. 199.
21. Oglilvie in *The Imperial English Dictionary* (1882), *passim*.
22. Poliakov, *Aryan*, p. 209.
23. Taken from Poliakov, *Aryan*, p. 213.
24. C. Chauvin, *Renan* (2000), p. 94. 'Renan tient à opposer la race sémitique, don't Israël est le Rameau le plus élevé et le plus pur, à la race indo-européenne. Pour lui, les carctères des peoples sont en relation avec leurs langues: le sémite a une langue à structure géométrique qui ne peut manier les abstractions, à la différence des langues aryennes: aux races qui les parlent peuvent être attributes tous les grand mouvements politiques, sociaux et intellectuals de l'historie du monde' (my translation).

25. Ibid. 'Aussi "l'oeuvre juive aura sa fin (...), l'oeuvre grecque (c'est-à-dire la science) se continuera san fin"' (my translation).
26. E. Renan, *De l'origine de Langage* (1862). Taken from M. Rowlands, 'Childe and the Archaeology of Freedom', in D. Harris (ed.), *The Archaeology of Vere Gordon Childe* (1994), p. 44.
27. Chauvin, *Renan*, p. 94. 'Renan, peut-être influencé par Gobineau, défendra toujours cette inégalité.'
28. The English translation of this work, published in 1915, was dedicated to HM George V.
29. J. A. Gobineau, *Essay Concerning the Inequalities of Races* (1915), p. 33.
30. Poliakov, *Aryan*, p. 233.
31. Ibid.
32. For an excellent overview of the nineteenth-century debate, refer to P. Mandler's '"Race" and "Nation" in mid-Victorian Thought', in S. Collini, R. Whatmore, S Young (eds.), *History, Religion, and Culture: British Intellectual History 1750–1950* (2000), pp. 198–223.
33. Gobineau was followed, most notably, by Gustave Le Bon's (1841–1931) 'evolutionist racialism and social Darwinism' and Georges Vacher de Lapouge's (1854–1936) 'theories of race and eugenics'. For a critical analysis of all three, refer to P-A. Taguieff's *La Couleur et le Sang: Doctrines Racistes à la Française* (1998).
34. Poliakov, *Aryan*, p. 231.
35. Ibid.
36. Ibid.
37. J. W. Jackson, 'Iran and Turan', *Anthropological Review* (1868), pp. 121–37.
38. Ibid., p. 122.
39. Ibid., p. 130.
40. J. W. Jackson, 'The Aryans and the Semites', *Anthropological Review* (1869), pp. 333–65 (295).
41. Ibid., p. 334.
42. F. M. Turner, *The Greek Heritage in Victorian Britain* (1980), p. 8.
43. A phrase borrowed from Oliver Elton.
44. J. W. Johnson, *The Formation of English Neo-Classical Thought* (1967), p. 30. Also see Johnson's 'What was Neo-Classicism?', *The Journal of British Studies* (1971), pp. 49–70.
45. M. L. Clarke, *Greek Studies in England 1700–1830* (1945), p. 9.
46. In his *Ancient Greek Literature* (2004), Tim Whitmarsh, according to Mary Lefkowitz, is aware of the problems involved in interpreting classical texts, namely the desire to give 'priority to the concerns of our own society': 'He points out how in the past interpreters of the texts have in effect recast the Greeks in their own image, making them into ideal nineteenth-century Englishmen and Germans' (*TLS*, June 3 2005, p. 10).
47. Turner, *Greek Heritage*, p. 5.
48. Ibid., pp. 189–90.

49. J. Priestley, *An Essay on the First Principles of Government* (1768), p. 132. Taken from Turner, *Greek Heritage*, p. 191.
50. Ibid., p. 195.
51. W. Mitford, *History of Greece* (1784–1810), vol. 1, p. 335; vol. 5, p. 9, emphasis in the original. All taken from Turner, *Greek Heritage*, p. 198.
52. Ibid., pp. 204–9.
53. Ibid., p. 215.
54. G. Grote, *History of Greece* (1846–1856), vol. 4, p. 81.
55. Ibid., vol. 3, p. 146.
56. Turner, *Greek Heritage*, p. 215. Turner's analysis of this subject area remains unsurpassed – hence my (over)reliance upon it. For other perspectives refer to R. Jenkyns, *The Victorian and Ancient Greece* (1980); P. Cartledge, 'Ancient Greeks and Modern Britons', *History Today* (April 1994); K. Demetriou, 'In Defence of the British Constitution: Theoretical Implication of the Debate over Athenian Democracy in Britain, 1770–1850', *History of Political Thought*, XVII (1996); and C. A. Ataç, 'Imperial Lessons from Athens and Sparta: Eighteenth-Century British Histories of Ancient Greece', *History of Political Thought*, XXVII (2006).
57. S. L. Marchand's *German Orientalism in the Age of Empire: Religion, Race and Scholarship* (2009) is a detailed and up-to-date treatment of subjects discussed in this chapter. Many of its discussions (particularly those on pp. 123–41) can profitably be read in conjunction with the analysis here.
58. E. M. Butler, *The Tyranny of Greece over Germany* (1958), p. 6.
59. Ibid., p. xi.
60. D. T. De Laura, *Hebrew and Hellene in Victorian England* (1969), pp. 167–8.
61. J. J. Winckelmann, *The History of Ancient Art* (2006), vol.1, pp. 286–9; vol. 2, p. 241.
62. Winckelmann quoted in H. Trevelyan's *The Popular Background to Goethe's Hellenism* (1934), pp. 80–1.
63. Turner, *Greek Heritage*, p. 41.
64. Butler, *Tyranny*, p. vii.
65. W. Pater, *The Renaissance* (1873), p. 137.
66. Cited in Butler, *Tyranny*, p. 46.
67. Laocoön was a Trojan priest who warned his fellow citizens against accepting the gift of a wooden horse, to no avail ('A deadly fraud is this'). He was subsequently murdered by serpents sent across the sea by his Greek enemies.
68. Winckelmann cited in Butler, *Tyranny*, p. 46.
69. Taken from H. Trevelyan, *Popular*, p. 83.
70. Winckelmann quoted in Butler, *Tyranny*, p. 48.
71. Winckelmann, *History*, pp. 133–4.
72. Butler, *Tyranny*, p. 46.
73. Ibid., p. 62.
74. John Dryden's translation.
75. Butler, *Tyranny*, p. 62.

76. H. Trevelyan, *Goethe and the Greeks* (1941), p. 77.
77. Some commentators have asserted that Goethe was influenced by Herder. See Trevelyan, *Goethe*, p. 73: 'Doubtless Herder had convinced him [...] that this ["the Greek closeness to nature"] was the fundamental quality in the Greek genius.'
78. Ibid., p. 70.
79. S. Atkins, *Goethe: Collected Works* (1984), vol. 2, p. 237.
80. Ibid., p. 240.
81. Goethe cited in Butler, *Tyranny*, p. 144.
82. Ibid.
83. For an up-to-date analysis consult L. Maguire's *Helen of Troy: From Homer to Hollywood* (2009), pp. 154–9.
84. Goethe cited in Pater, *Renaissance*, p. 119.
85. Turner, *Greek Heritage*, p. 18.
86. P. A. Dale, *The Victorian and the Idea of History* (1977), p. 130.
87. M. Arnold, *On the Classical Tradition* (1869), p. 24.
88. Arnold cited in Turner, *Greek Heritage*, p. 29.
89. M. Arnold, *Culture and Anarchy* (1994), p. 164.
90. Ibid., p. 165.
91. Ibid.
92. Ibid.
93. Ibid., p. 170.
94. Ibid., p. 169.
95. Ibid., p. 172.
96. Ibid.
97. Ibid., p. 174.
98. Ibid., p. 172.
99. Ibid., p. 175.
100. See Turner, *Greek Heritage*, p. 22 and p. 69.
101. De Laura, *Hebrew*, pp. 172–3.
102. Ibid., p. 177.
103. Pater, *Renaissance*, p. 116.
104. Ibid., pp. 122–3.
105. Ibid., pp. 127–8.
106. Ibid., p. 137.
107. W. Pater, *Greek Studies* (1895), p. 141.
108. Ibid., p. 197.
109. Ibid., p. 191.
110. Ibid., p. 199.
111. De Laura, *Hebrew*, p. 177.
112. Pater cited in Turner, *Greek Heritage*, p. 73.
113. Ibid., pp. 73–4.
114. Hegel's *Philosophy of Art* cited in Pater, *Renaissance*, p. 114.

115. Benjamin Jowett's analysis of Plato, for instance, was very much influenced by Hegelianism (see Turner, p. 417). In a 1884 letter to Lord Arthur Russell, Jowett writes: 'It is more than forty years since I began to read his [Hegel's] writings, and I think that in those days my mind received a greater stimulus from him than from any one [...] I still retain a great reverence for my old teacher and master.' Taken from E. Abbott and L. Campell (eds.), *Life and Letters of Benjamin Jowett* (1897), vol. 2, p. 249.
116. Pater, *Greek Studies*, p. 220.
117. F. Hegel, *The Philosophy of Fine Art* (1916), vol. 3, p. 208.
118. Ibid., p. 210.
119. Ibid., vol. 2, p. 169.
120. D. Forbes in F. Hegel's *Lectures on the Philosophy of World History* (1975), p. xviii. Hegel's examples here are Herodotus and Thucydides.
121. Ibid., pp. 23–4.
122. Ibid., p. 47.
123. Ibid., p. 51.
124. There will be a critical analysis of this aspect of Hegel's thought in Chapter 7.
125. S. Houlgate, *An Introduction to Hegel: Freedom, Truth and History* (2005), p. 17.
126. Ibid.
127. F. Hegel, *Philosophy of World History* (1975), p. 223.
128. Ibid., p. 239.
129. H. Butterfield, *Man on his Past: The Study of the History of Historical Scholarship* (1955), p. 41.
130. Ibid., p. 43.
131. All the quotes from Ranke are taken from T. H. Von Laue, *Leopold Ranke: The Formative Years* (1950), p. 122.
132. Arnold, 'Our Liberal Practitioners', *Anarchy*, p. 208.
133. Ibid., 'Hebraism and Hellenism', p. 173.
134. G. L. Hersey, 'Aryanism in Victorian England', *Yale Review* (1976), vol. 66, pp. 104–13 (108).
135. Ibid., pp. 110–11. Leighton is echoing ideologies of Renan and Richard Wagner.
136. B. Disraeli, *Lothair* (1870), quoted in Hersey (1976), p. 107. It should, however, be remembered that Disraeli was not a believer in the equality of man. According to him, Jews 'are a living and most striking evidence of the falsity of that pernicious doctrine of modern times, the natural equality of man'. See Wheatcroft's review of A. Kirsch, *Benjamin Disraeli* (2008); 'Review', *NYRB*, 4 December 2008, p. 30.
137. F. de Coulanges, *The Antique City* (1975), p. 11.
138. Ibid., p. 15.
139. A. Momigliano, 'Forward', in De Coulanges, *The Antique City* (1975), p. x.
140. Ibid., p. xxii.
141. Ibid.

142. C. Schultze, "'People Like Us" in the Face of History: Cormon's *Les Vainqueurs de Salamine*', in E. Bridges, E. Hall, and P. J. Rhodes (eds.), *Cultural Responses to the Persian Wars* (2007), p. 368.
143. F. Nietzsche, *The Birth of Tragedy* (1997), p. 109. Here Nietzsche is reacting to the Rankean historical scholarship of 'as it really was' (*wie es gewesen ist*).
144. This was also Pater's position.
145. In *Thus Spoke Zarathustra*, Nietzsche uses a 'historical' Persian as his 'Aryan' vehicle.
146. Ibid., p. 57.
147. Ibid.
148. MSS. Murray, 172, folio 27. Murray's letter to J. A. K. Thompson, 21 December 1921.
149. J. L. Myres, *Who were the Greeks?* (1930), p. xi.
150. Because during the period of our interest, 'Helleno-Aryanism' played almost no role in the study of ancient Greece in this country, I concluded that it need not be analysed any further.

Chapter 3 The 'Race–Culture' Debate: 1900s–1930s

1. The reason why the 'Aryan race' theories are in the foreground here is largely due to the framing requirements of this narrative. In no way am I suggesting that these theories had *dominated* the racial discourse of the period.
2. The full guide to the teaching of anthropology at the University of London can be found in A. C. Haddon's *History of Anthropology* (1910), pp. 4–5.
3. T. K. Penniman, *A Hundred Years of Anthropology* (1952), pp. 210–219.
4. A. Sherratt, *Economy and Society in Prehistoric Europe* (1997), footnote 26, p. 65.
5. MSS. Myres 8. Letters written by Childe in 1922 (folio 3) and 1925 (folio 31) to his B. Litt. Supervisor J. L. Myres.
6. Royal Anthropological Institute (hereafter RAI) 58/2/3/2.
7. Ibid.
8. RAI. 58/2/4/4.
9. RAI. 58/2/4/6.
10. RAI. 58/2/4/18.
11. Ibid.
12. Ibid.
13. MSS. Myres 119 (*Geography and History – General*), folio 58.
14. J. B. Bury, S. A. Cook, F. E. Adcock (eds.), *The Cambridge Ancient History* (1924), p. 3.
15. T. Ballantyne, *Orientalism and Race: Aryanism in the British Empire* (2002), pp. 50–1.
16. See Haddon, *History*, pp. 4–5.

17. J. Whatmough, 'Review', *Classical Philology* (1928), pp. 130–5.
18. G. V. Childe, *The Aryans: A Study of Indo-European Origins* (1926), p. xi.
19. Ibid., p. xii.
20. Ibid., p. 11.
21. G. Childe, 'Races, Peoples and Cultures in Prehistoric Europe', *Man*, XVIII (October 1933), p. 200.
22. Ibid., p. 199.
23. G. Childe, *The Danube in Prehistory* (1929), p. v–vi.
24. Childe's Papers (UCL), Box 13, 8/2/1.
25. Of course, this report, the composition of the committee and those taking part have already been covered extensively by a number of academics. The primary reason for these potted summaries is due to the need to provide the non-(anthropology) specialist reader with some appropriate historical and analytical backgrounds. Those interested in more in-depth analyses should refer to the following publications: E. Barkan, *The Retreat of Scientific Racism* (1992); D. Stone, *Breeding Superman: Nietzche, Race and Eugernics in Edwardian and Interwar Britain* (2002); C. Hutton, *Race and the Third Reich: Linguistics, Racial Anthropology and Genetics in the Dialect of Volk* (2005); P. Mazumdar, *Eugenics, Human Genetics and Human Failings: the Eugenics Society, its Sources and its Critics in Britain* (1992); D. Kevles, *In the Name of Eugenics: Genetics and the Uses of Human Heredity* (2001); G. W. Stocking, *Race, Culture, and Evolution: Essays in the History of Anthropology* (1968).
26. RAI. 114/12/2 (*Race and Culture*), p. 2.
27. Ibid., p. 3.
28. Ibid., pp. 3–4.
29. Ibid., pp. 5–6.
30. The following extracts are the edited-out sections of his contributions to this published paper. They were found among Myres' papers. MSS. Myres 121 (*Anthropology: Culture and Race*), folios 201–4.
31. Evidently, peoples of Iranian descent were not part of Elliot-Smith's thinking!
32. MSS. Myres 121, folios 201–4.
33. G. Elliot-Smith, *Diffusion of Culture* (1933), pp. 208–39.
34. RAI (*Race and Culture*), pp. 6–8.
35. Ibid., pp. 18–19.
36. R. Firth, *Human Types* (1938), p. 21.
37. Ibid., p. 16.
38. RAI (*Race and Culture*), pp. 20–21.
39. Ibid., p. 24.
40. G. Morant, *The Races of Central Europe* (1939), *passim*.
41. RAI (*Race and Culture*), pp. 8–11.
42. Morant, *Races*, p. 6.
43. R. Gates, *Heredity in Man* (1929), p. 1.
44. RAI (*Race and Culture*), pp. 11–15.
45. Ibid., pp. 15–18.

46. Taken from E. E. Evans Pritchard et al. (eds.), *Essays Presented to C. G. Seligman* (1934), p. 247.
47. RAI (*Race and Culture*), p. 18.
48. According to the RAI's senior archivist, Sarah Walpole, the archives indicate that this interim report was not followed by more substantial ones later on, thus, hinting at a hurried abandonment of the project.
49. RAI (*Council Minutes A 10:4*).
50. Between them, the files MSS.119–22 have more than 500 folios of archival material concerning race, culture and language.
51. J. L. Myres, *Herodotus and Anthropology* (1908), p. 125.
52. Ibid., p. 136.
53. MSS. Myres 121, folio 4.
54. J. L. Myres, *Greek Lands and the Greek People* (1910), p. 13.
55. J. L. Myres, *Science and the Humanities: The Use and Abuse of Information* (1933), p. 23.
56. MSS. Myres 121, folio 4.
57. Ibid., folio 5.
58. Ibid.
59. Ibid., folio 7.
60. Ibid., folio 6.
61. Ibid., folio 8.
62. Ibid.
63. Ibid., folio 10.
64. Ibid., folio 11.
65. Ibid., folio 12.
66. Ibid., folio 15.
67. Ibid., folios 16–17.
68. Ibid.
69. Ibid.
70. Ibid., folios 18–19.
71. Ibid. Interestingly, the phrase 'Manners makyth Man' is the motto of the institution where Myres had spent most of his academic life: New College, Oxford.
72. Ibid., folio 24.
73. Ibid., folio 30.
74. Ibid., folios 31–2.
75. Ibid., folio 33. 'But the question "*what are mammals for*" only has its full significance, when we return to our classification of human races, and the corresponding question "*what is man for*". And this we are compelled to do, if only to equip ourselves to criticise answers implied (and sometimes outspoken) in [the] attempt to classify the races of man in an order of importance or *value*.'
76. Ibid.
77. Ibid., folio 30. Discussing languages in general, Myres writes: '...let [sic] assume it to be Indo-European – some how excelling them all? The question

has only to be put in this comparative way, to show how silly it is to ask such question [sic] at all.' The question in this context is: 'Is it possible to classify, and can we classify, in a scale of some sort of goodness?'

78. In *Economy and Society*, Sherratt contends that Myres' interest in ethnology 'was based on a belief in the unity of language, culture and race, balanced by sensitivity to geography' (p. 58).' Although this statement is not incorrect, it does not take into account the symbiotic and functional relationships which delineate this 'unity'.
79. *Report*, p. 1.
80. Childe writes that 'the Aryans must have been gifted with exceptional mental endowment'. *Aryans*, p. 4.
81. G. Childe, *What Happened in History?* (1942), p. 150. But to be fair, Childe prefixes this assertion by the following words: 'As used by Nazis and Anti-Semites generally.'
82. MSS. Myres 88 (*Papers Concerning the* Dawn of History), letter to Brooks, dated 30 October 1911, folios 58–9.
83. In *The Aryans*, Childe opines that 'the Indo-European languages and their assumed parent-speech have been throughout exceptionally delicate and flexible instruments of thought' (p. 4).
84. Barkan, *Retreat*, p. 288.
85. Ibid., p. 289.
86. Ibid., p. 295.
87. Ibid., p. 287.
88. Ibid., p. 289.
89. Ibid., p. 35.
90. Ibid., pp. 35–6.
91. Ibid., p. 81. Boas writes in the 1938 edition of *The Mind of the Primitive Man*: 'The term race, as applied to human types, is vague. It can have a biological significance only when a race represents a uniform, closely interbred group, in which all family lines are alike – as in pure breeds of domesticated animals. These conditions are never realised in human types and impossible in large populations' (p. 254).
92. The 1904 study at the Louisiana Purchase Exposition is highly representative of this pseudoscientific trend (see Stocking, *Essays*, pp. 217, 347).
93. I am not implying that Barkan's labelling is inaccurate; I am merely suggesting that everyday racism was so very rife in the Europe of the period that even the 'anti-racist' members of the committee may not have been entirely immune from it. Moreover, since the indisputable racist tendencies of Gates and Pitt-Rivers were kept at bay within the context of the report by their fairly measured contributions, it therefore seems to me to be an unnecessary act to dwell upon them inordinately. But to be fair, Barkan's intellectual canvass, unlike mine, transcends the report.

Chapter 4 The 'Diffusionism v. Evolutionism' Theoretical Debate, Gordon Childe and the Prehistory of Europe

1. Taken from R. Slobodin, *W. H. R. Rivers* (1978), p. 148.
2. C. Renfrew, *Before Civilization: The Radiocarbon Revolution and the Prehistoric Europe* (1973), p. 35.
3. Ibid., p. 38.
4. For detailed analysis see C. Renfrew, *Problems in European Prehistory* (1979).
5. Ibid., p. 17.
6. Renfrew, *Before Civilization*, p. 124. 'The old controversy between the diffusionists and the evolutionists has become irrelevant, and is not worth pursuing further. As we shall see, new approaches can offer a far more satisfactory solution.'
7. Malinowski in G. Elliot-Smith (ed.), *Culture: A Symposium* (1928), *passim*.
8. C. Wissler, *Man and Culture* (1923), p. 105.
9. The two papers by White are 'Diffusionism versus Evolutionism: An Anti-Evolutionist Fallacy', *American Anthropologist*, 47 (1945), pp. 339–56; and 'History, Evolutionism, and Functionalism: Three Types of Interpretations of Culture', *Southwestern Journal of Archaeology*, 1 (1945), pp. 2214–8. Indeed, in a review over 20 years later, John Rowe conceded that the 'Doctrine of diffusionism is a hardy weed', which had led Radcliffe-Brown to move towards the creation of 'Social Anthropology' as a direct response, p. 334. J. H. Rowe, 'Diffusionism and Archaeology', *American Antiquity*, 31 (1966), pp. 334–7.
10. White, 'Diffusionism versus Evolutionism', p. 354.
11. MSS. Myres 8, folio 11.
12. Ibid., folio 13.
13. G. Childe, *The Dawn of European Civilization* (1925), p. xiii.
14. Ibid., p. xiii–xiv.
15. *The Shorter Oxford English Dictionary* (2003).
16. Childe, *Dawn* (1939), p. xvii.
17. Childe, *Dawn* (1925), p. 24.
18. Ibid., pp. 23–4.
19. Ibid., p. 22.
20. Ibid., pp. 27–8.
21. Ibid., p. 29.
22. Ibid., p. 33.
23. Ibid., p. 34.
24. For how these improvements were made, refer to *Dawn* (1925), pp. 33–5.
25. Ibid., p. 36.
26. Childe, *Dawn* (1939), p. 27.
27. Childe, *Dawn* (1925), p. 148.
28. Ibid., pp. 150–1.
29. Ibid., p. 151.

30. Childe, *Dawn* (1939), pp. 149, 151, 153.
31. Ibid., p. 175.
32. Childe, *Dawn* (1925), p. 216.
33. Ibid., p. 302.
34. Ibid., p. 301.
35. Ibid., p. 302.
36. Childe, *Dawn* (1939), p. 334.
37. Ibid., pp. 334–5.
38. G. Childe, 'Retrospect', *Antiquity*, XXXII (1958), p. 69.
39. G. Childe, *The Aryans: A Study of Indo-European Origins* (1926), p. 5.
40. Ibid., p. 4.
41. Ibid., pp. 209–10.
42. Ibid., p. 211.
43. With Childe touching so explicitly here on the 'positive' physical attributes of the Nordic peoples, Renfrew's categorical assertion that 'Childe was not a racist' becomes highly debatable. Renfrew in Harris (ed.), p. 131.
44. Childe, *Aryans* (1926), p. 212.
45. Ibid., p. xvii.
46. Childe, *Dawn* (1939), p. xvii: 'Indeed, *revolutionary discoveries* [my emphasis] published even during 1938, warns us that the picture here presented is still in high degree provisional.'
47. In the 1939 edition, the sections on Crete and the steppes have 101 footnotes in total. Nearly all of them are from newer sources (those published between 1925 and 1938) but almost none of them are explicit examples of the much-heralded 'revolutionary' finds. Meanwhile, the real building-blocks (the illustrated archaeological finds) remained almost entirely unchanged.
48. In the chapter on Crete, the same and the same number of illustrations (nine in total) are provided. In sections on the Steppes, out of six illustrations from the 1925 edition, five of them are reproduced in the 1939 edition.
49. G. Clark, 'Prehistory since Childe', *Bulletin of the Institute of Archaeology*, 13 (1976), p. 4. Clark also writes that '[O]ne has only to glance through the pages of *The Dawn* to see how vestigial is the evidence used to define the dimensions of time and space, by comparison with that needed to reconstruct living systems' (p. 10).
50. These notebooks can be viewed at UCL's Special Collection.
51. Trigger, 'Childe's Relevance to the 1990s', p. 27.
52. MSS. Myres 124, folio 24.
53. MSS. Myres 88, folios 58–9.
54. MSS. Myres 8, folios 53–5.
55. UCL, Box 13, Misc. 1/3–4. This extract was dropped from the published work.
56. Childe, 'Retrospect', p. 74.
57. C. F. C. Hawkes, *The Prehistoric Foundation of Europe* (1940), p. 381.
58. Ibid., p. 383.
59. Childe, *Dawn*, p. xv.

60. G. Daniel, *The Idea of Prehistory* (1962), p. 39.
61. B. Trigger, 'If Childe were Alive Today', *Bulletin of the Institute of Archaeology* (1982), p. 3.
62. M. Rowland in Harris, D., *Archaeology*, p. 43.
63. Renfrew, *Before Civilization*, p. 39.
64. P. A. Boghossian, *Fear of Knowledge: Against Relativism and Constructivism* (2007), p. 129.
65. Ibid., p. 130.
66. In his 'Preface to the Sixth Edition' of *The Dawn* (1957), Childe indeed makes such a 'balanced' revision: '[T]he new technique of radio-carbon dating [...] offer at least the hope of an independent time-scale against which archaeological events in several regions can be compared chronologically. These advances allow and demand drastic revision and rearrangement of my text. At the same time the fresh data [...] have induced a less dogmatically "Orientalist" attitude I adopted in 1925. [...] Radio-carbon dating has indeed vindicated the Orient's priority over Europe in farming and metallurgy. But the speed and originality of Europe's adaptation of Oriental traditions can now be better appreciated; it should be clear why [...] a distinctively European culture had dawned by the Bronze Age!' (p. xiii). Childe got his editions of *The Dawn* muddled-up. It was the 1939 *Dawn* that took a 'dogmatically "Orientalist" attitude'. The 1925 edition, as discussed, was much closer in inference to the notion that the Orient had a 'priority over Europe', but the 'speed and originality of Europe's adaptation' resulted in the dawning of 'a distinctively European culture [...] by the Bronze Age'. In 1957, Childe, circuitously, went back to his 1925 stance without, deliberately or otherwise, acknowledging his return journey. It is ironic that Childe had managed, in 1925, to draw conclusions, almost intuitively it seems, which were broadly verified, years later, by radiocarbon dating.
67. For substantially more on 'presentism', refer to Chapter 7.
68. Trigger, 'If Childe were Alive Today', p. 18.
69. G. Clark, 'Prehistory since Childe', p. 4.
70. It should be noted that the thesis had dealt solely with Greece, whereas only about a fifth of the book does so.
71. There are those who disagree. Trigger, in 'Childe's relevance to the 1990s', writes: 'Childe gradually abandoned the search for an Indo-European homeland as something that could never be determined for certain on the basis of archaeological evidence' (p. 12). And Renfrew in 'Childe and the Study of Cultural process' in Harris (ed.): '[Childe] had, I feel, despaired of finding a clear archaeological solution to the problem of Indo-European' (p. 129).
72. I. Berlin, 'The Hedgehog and the Fox', in *Russian Thinkers* (1947), pp. 22–82.
73. Childe, 'Retrospect', p. 69. Interestingly, Childe was not 'guided' in his reading by Myres, his supervisor at Oxford.

Chapter 5   Hellenisms Reassessed (1890s–1940s): Part I

1. MSS. Murray, 172, folio 27.
2. R. W. Livingstone, *The Greek Genius and its Meaning to Us* (1915), p. 24.
3. Ibid., pp. 27–8.
4. Ibid., p. 29.
5. Ibid., p. 30.
6. Ibid., pp. 33–4.
7. Ibid., pp. 38–9.
8. For an excellent analysis of these individuals and their milieu refer to R. Overy, *The Morbid Age: Britain between the Wars* (2009).
9. A. Toynbee, 'History' in R. W. Livingstone (ed.), *The Legacy of Greece* (1921), p. 289.
10. Ibid., p. 297.
11. Ibid., p. 299. It has to be borne in mind that Toynbee and many of his like-minded colleagues were greatly influenced by Oswald Spengler's cyclical historical writing, and in particular *The Decline of the West* (1918). The essence of the historical vision of this work, according to J. Farrenkopf in *The Prophet of Decline* (2001), 'is that world history forms a magnificent cosmic spectacle. A grand harmony of perpetual struggle, of becoming and degradation' (p. 15). It is also interesting to note that Spengler was himself influenced by a work on the history of the ancient world, namely O. Seeck's 1897 publication entitled *Geschichte des Untergangs der Antike Welt* (*Decline of Antiquity*). For more on Spengler's effect on Toynbee see Farrenkopf: *Prophet, passim*.
12. Ibid., p. 300.
13. Ibid.
14. Ibid., p. 301.
15. Ibid.
16. MSS. Murray 172, folio 1.
17. J. A. K. Thomson, *Greeks and Barbarians* (1921), p. 148.
18. Ibid., p. 153.
19. Ibid., p. 158.
20. Ibid.
21. Ibid., p. 156.
22. Ibid., p. 157.
23. Ibid., p. 176.
24. Ibid., p. 188.
25. Ibid., p. 186.
26. Ibid., p. 203.
27. Ibid., p. 158. Thomson, for instance, contrasts 'the extreme Romantic temper' of the Celts with that of the 'Hellenic temper' by comparing W. B. Yeats' *The Shadowy Waters* with the *Odyssey*. This would have surprised and dismayed Yeats. Along with a number of Irish intellectuals of his age, such as James

Joyce and J. M. Synge, Yeats believed that Irish culture had very close affinities with that of the Greeks. See J. Curtis (ed.), *Sophocles' Oedipus at Colonus: Manuscript Materials by W. B. Yeats* (2010).
28. A. Toynbee, *Greek Historical Thought; From Homer to the Age of Heraclius* (1924), p. xxiv.
29. Thomson, *Greeks*, p. 181.
30. It has been argued that this work shares a number of Indo-European tropes with a Persian epic. See C. Monettee, 'Indo-European Elements in Celtic and Indo-Iranian Epic Tradition: the Trial of Champions in the *Táin Bó Cúailnge* and the *Shahnameh*', *The Journal of Indo-European Studies* 32 (2004), pp. 61–78.
31. MSS. Murray, 172, folio 19. Murray (23 August 1921): 'It is so exceedingly well written; and I get to feel more and more that you cannot expound classical literature unless you write well. You have first to see the subtleties and then make other people see them; and that needs literary power.'
32. G. Murray, *A History of Greek Literature* (1935), pp. xiv–xv.
33. MSS. Murray 476, folios 191–4.
34. Towards the end of his life, Murray had not only supported the Suez adventure, he had also 'disparaged the new members of the United Nations as "nearly all of them uncivilized, Asiatic, Arabic or South American nations with a violent anti-west prejudice or anti-civilization majority"'. See M. Ceadel, 'Gilbert Murray and International Politics', in C. Stray (ed.), *Gilbert Murray Reassessed* (2007), p. 237. Richard Seaford, however, in a 2009 article entitled 'World without Limits', gives a very sanitized profile of Gilbert Murray, entirely bereft of the kind of sentiments expressed in the above quote. Seaford writes: '[H]e was the last prominent proponent of the idea that Hellenism has implications for every sphere of life, including politics. And this I cannot help admiring' (*TLS*, June 2009, p. 15).
35. G. Murray, *Rise of the Greek Epic* (1907), p. v.
36. Ibid., p. 26. Murray writes: 'The combination of [. . .] the appreciation of good things and the power to refuse them, is characteristic of the spirit of progress. I think most scholars will admit that it is also eminently characteristic of Greek civilization.'
37. G. Murray, *Greek Studies* (1946); see also the 1941 paper entitled 'Hellenism' in the same publication, pp. 1–2.
38. G. Murray, 'The Value of Greece to the Future of the World' in R. W. Livingstone (ed.) *Legacy of Greece* (1921), p. 9.
39. G. Murray, 'Humane Letters and Civilization', (1937) published in *Greek Studies* (1946), p. 216.
40. Taken from W. Bruneau, 'Gilbert Murray, Bertrand Russell, and the Theory and Practise of Politics', in Stray, *Gilbert Murray*, p. 213. For an interesting review of this publication see Oswyn Murray's piece in the *TLS*, 21 and 28 December 2007, p. 31.
41. Murray, *Rise*, p. 2.
42. Murray, *Legacy*, pp. 22–3.

43. G. Murray, 'Greece and England' in *Greek Studies* (1946), p. 193.
44. Ibid., p. 194.
45. This scholar was probably Wilamowitz-Moellendorff. In a letter (2 May 1896), Murray suggests that 'Wilamowitz thinks that Aristotle's principal work in his life was to preach "little-Englandism"'. Taken from MSS. Murray 476, folio 106.
46. Murray, *Greek Studies*, p. 195. Of course, as it will be discussed in the next section, it was not only the German scholars who had found this form of scholarship *unwissenschaftlich* (unscientific).
47. Taken from Stray, *Gilbert Murray Reassesed*, p. 2.
48. J. S. Mill, *Discussions and Dissertations* (1859), vol. II, p. 283. Taken from an 1846 essay in the *Edinburgh Review* entitled, 'Early Grecian History and Legend'. Mill continues this analysis by presenting the reader with the following counter-factual: 'If the issue of that day had been different, the Britons and the Saxons might still have been wandering in the woods.'
49. J. L. Myres, 'Herodotus and Anthropology' in J. L. Myres (ed.), *Anthropology and Classics* (1908), p. 122.
50. Ibid., p. 125.
51. J. L. Myres, *Greek Lands and the Greek People* (1910), pp. 10–11.
52. Ibid., p. 13.
53. J. L. Myres, 'The Value of Ancient History' (1910), in *Geographical History in Greek Lands* (1953), p. 38.
54. Ibid., p. 39.
55. Ibid., p. 46.
56. Ibid., p. 47.
57. Ibid., p. 49.
58. J. L. Myres, *The Dawn of History* (1911), p. 8.
59. Ibid., p. 11.
60. Ibid.
61. Ibid.
62. Ibid., p. 209.
63. Ibid., p. 211.
64. Ibid., p. 216.
65. J. L. Myres, *Influence of Anthropology on the Course of Political Science* (1916), p. 74.
66. Ibid., pp. 74–5.
67. J. L. Myres, *The Political Ideas of the Greeks* (1927), p. 4.
68. Ibid., p. 8.
69. Ibid., p. 29.
70. Ibid., pp. 15–23.
71. Ibid., p. 58.
72. Ibid., p. 79.
73. Ibid., p. 84.
74. Ibid., p. 100.

75. Ibid., p. 208.
76. Myres draws the attention of the reader to some philological similarities between these specifically Greek 'notions' and their Indo-European correspondences. For instance, he compares *demos* with the 'Iranian *dam*' (p. 38); *arkhé* with the Sanskrit verb *arhami* (p. 84); and *Dikê* with Latin *dica* (p. 100).
77. MSS. Murray, 172, folio 27. Murray's letter to J. A. K. Thompson, 21 December 1921.
78. Myres (1927), p. 1.
79. J. L. Myres, *Who Were the Greeks?* (1930), p. xi.
80. Ibid., p. xvi.
81. Ibid., p. xvii.
82. Ibid., 'Contents', p. ix.
83. Ibid., p. 90.
84. Ibid., p. 533.
85. Most reviews of this work were extremely positive. A. T. Olmstead (*The Classical Journal* [1931], p. 214–16): 'The whole long argument is a unity and must be read as such to be understood, much less criticised [...]. Myres has enabled us to answer, with more assurance than ever before, the question, Who were the Greeks?' An anonymous reviewer (*Journal of Hellenic Studies* 51 [1931], pp. 291–2): 'The vast quantity of information conveyed will instruct, excite or mystify but never weary the reader. The conclusions reached may be convincing, controversial or unacceptable, but they are always suggestive.' A. J. B. Wace (*The Classical Review* [1931], p. 128): 'Professor Myres in this stimulating book subjects the Greek claim to unity to a very searching analysis and decides that they were never really one, but always in process of becoming one.'
86. Myres, *Who*, p. xxix.
87. Ibid., pp. xxix–xxx.
88. Myres, unsure in how to proceed with this type of investigation, asked for some clarification on the question of 'Colouring of statues as evidence for complexion' from one of his expert proofreaders. S/he replies: 'This is a subject full of horrid pitfalls. What, for instance will you do with the Korai, who mostly had red eyes and brown indigo hair? Personally I think the Greeks didn't care tuppence whether their statues imitated natural colours or not...Don't forget, however, a monument where there is full naturalism and careful distinction – the Alexander sarcophagus. There all the faces have brown eyes, except two who have blue.' MSS. Myres 90, folio 50.
89. Myres, *Who*, p. 74.
90. Ibid. p. 80.
91. Indeed he argues that physical types can be altered in the most unpredictable way. The blondness of inhabitants of a village (Heraklio) near Athens is due to the nineteenth-century introduction of Germans from Bavaria by King Otho. Ibid., p. 42.

92. Ibid., pp. 101–7.
93. Ibid., pp. 107–13.
94. Ibid., p. 149.
95. Ibid., p. xxx.
96. Ibid., p. 166.
97. Ibid., p. 168.
98. Ibid., p. xxx.
99. Ibid., p. xxxii.
100. 'Illustrate (a book) by later insertion of material, esp. prints cut from other works (Granger's *Biographical History of England* had blank pages to allow for this).' *Shorter Oxford English Dictionary* (2002).
101. J. L. Myres, *The Man of Science and the Science of Man* (1933), p. 15.
102. In his 1933 pamphlet (*The Man of Science and the Science of Man*), Myres writes on science in business, in leisure and in education with some authority. He also argues for a 'need for popular exposition of scientific outlook'. 'Science in propaganda' – which was in the 1930s emerging from both Germany and the Soviet Union – was also discussed in order to forewarn against the normalization of the idea that 'might is right'. See pp. 5–20.
103. Myres, *Influence of Anthropology*, pp. 58–61.
104. Ibid., p. 55.
105. It has to be borne in mind that during the period under discussion, it was an accepted fact that there were a number of peoples, residing both in Asia and Europe, who should be labelled '(Indo-)Iranian'. 'Iranians' for M. Rostovtzeff, writing in 1922, for instance, were the Scythians, Sarmatians, and Alans (present-day Ossetians are the descendents of the Alans) as well as the various Iranian peoples of the Iranian plateau and north-western India; *Iranians and Greeks in South Russia* (1969). It is also worth remembering that, etymologically, 'Danube' – a word with strong European cultural connotations – is 'an Iranian name'. See the entry for the 'Indo-European Languages' in H. Bussmann's *Routledge Dictionary of Language and Linguistics* (1998).
106. J. L. Myres, 'The Ethnology, Habitat, Linguistic, and Common Culture of Indo-Europeans up to the Time of the Migration' in E. Eyre's *European Civilization* (1935), p. 211.
107. Myres, *Dawn*, p. 8.
108. This pencil-written manuscript is not dated. My reason for opting for 1935 is as follows: Myres writes that 'within the last few months, Professor Collingwood [...] has formulated afresh the philosophical basis of history' (MSS. Myres 116, folio 87). Collingwood's inaugural essay, 'The Historical Imagination', from which a number of passages is quoted, was published in 1935.
109. MSS. Myres 116, folio 74.
110. Ibid.
111. Ibid., folio 75.

112. Ibid.
113. Ibid., folio. 76.
114. Ibid.
115. Ibid., folio 80.
116. Ibid., folio 82.
117. Ibid., folio 83.
118. Ibid.
119. Ibid.
120. Ibid., folio 84.
121. Ibid.
122. Ibid., folio 85.
123. Ibid.
124. Ibid.
125. Ibid., folio 87.
126. Ibid.
127. Ibid. For the backgrounds to these episodes, see Herodotus I.5.
128. Ibid., folio 92.
129. Ibid.
130. Ibid., folio 92.
131. Ibid., folios 93–4.
132. Ibid., folio 94.
133. Ibid., folio 95.
134. Ibid., folio 97.
135. Ibid., folio 137.
136. T. Kuhn, *The Structure of the Scientific Revolution* (1962), pp. 2–3.
137. See, for instance, A. Momigliano, 'Time in Ancient Historiography', in *Essays in Ancient and Modern History* (1975), pp. 179–204; P. Corfield, *Time and the Shape of History* (2007); and K. Clarke, *Making Time for the Past: Local History and the Polis* (2008).
138. MSS. Myres 116, folio 92.
139. Ibid., folio 137.
140. J. A. K. Thomson's 'The Present and Future of Classical Scholarship' in J. A. K. Thomson's and A. Toynbee's (eds.) *Essays in Honour of Gilbert Murray* (1936), p. 279.
141. Ibid.
142. Ibid., p. 291.
143. Murray, *Rise*, p. 42.
144. Murray (1897), pp. xiv–xv.
145. Thomson, *Greeks*, p. 205.
146. Ibid., p. 10.
147. Murray, *Rise*, p. 47. Although the same point could have been made with regard to the Persian Wars, Murray, as far as I know, never made it. In fact, Murray's Herodotus 'saw the world [...] as an age-long conflict between West and East, Greece and Asia, the principles of freedom and intelligence and the

principles of riches and force. The climax of the conflict has been reached in the invasion of Greece by the Persians under Xerxes, and his almost miraculous repulse.' Who the 'Semites' and 'Aryans' are in this scheme of 'East v West' is not at all clear. MSS. Murray 436, folio 26.
148. Murray, 'Beginning of Grammar' in *Greek Studies*, p. 171.
149. Bearing this and many of Murray's other comments in mind, it is rather puzzling to read a paper by Mark Griffith, entitled 'Gilbert Murray on Greek Literature' (in Stray, *Gilbert Murray Reassessed*), which states that Murray 'did not buy deeply into the racist notion of a superior "spirit" or "character" shared by all Greeks or all Indo-Europeans' (p. 59). The fact that he did not buy into the 'superior "spirit"' of the Indo-Europeans cannot be doubted (accommodating the Persians would have been problematic); but not buying into the 'superior "spirit"' of the Greeks, as shown in section I, is debatable. Even Griffith cannot but undermine his own statement by arguing a few pages earlier that Murray was above all a 'spreader of the word and especially of the *spirit* [emphasis in the original] of the ancient Greeks to a larger public' (p. 55). Why spread it, if it is of inferior quality?
150. Myres, *Who*, p. xxxiv.
151. W. H. Dray, *History as Re-enactment: R. G. Collingwood's Idea of History* (1995).

Chapter 6 Hellenisms Reassessed (1890s–1940s): Part II

1. The aim of this section is to discuss only those specific areas of Collingwood's philosophy which are directly relevant to a better understanding of Myres' Hellenism. Moreover, when dealing with Collingwood, it is necessary to be aware of the manner in which he studied his topics. As W. H. Dray and W. J. van der Dussen have argued in their introductory notes to Collingwood's *The Principles of History* (1999), since Collingwood 'did not mind "thinking on paper", his ideas sometimes appear to change significantly over time, and in some cases over a very short time' p. xv. By concentrating mainly on 'The Historical Imagination' (1935), I think it is possible to sidestep this problem.
2. MSS. Myres 116, folio 87.
3. R. G. Collingwood, 'The Historical Imagination' (1935), in *The Idea of History* (1946), p. 233.
4. Ibid., p. 247.
5. Ibid., p. 233.
6. Ibid.
7. Ibid., pp. 234–5.
8. Ibid., p. 235.
9. Ibid., p. 236.
10. Ibid.

11. Ibid., p. 237.
12. Ibid.
13. Ibid.
14. Collingwood, *The Idea of History*, p. 8.
15. R. G. Collingwood, *An Autobiography* (1939), p. 109.
16. Collingwood, 'The Historical Imagination', p. 242.
17. Ibid.
18. Ibid., p 243.
19. See M. H. Nielsen, 'Re-enactment and Reconstruction in Collingwood's Philosophy of History', *History & Theory*, 20 (1981), pp. 1–31 (30–1) for a highly technical treatment of this subject.
20. Collingwood, 'History as Re-enactment of Past Experiences', in *The Idea of History*, p. 284.
21. Ibid., p. 288.
22. Collingwood, 'Human Nature and Human History', in *The Idea of History*, p. 157.
23. Collingwood, *Autobiography*, p. 112.
24. Collingwood, 'The Historical Imagination', p. 247.
25. Collingwood, 'The Limits of Historical Knowledge' (1928), in *Essays in the Philosophy of History* (1985), p. 99.
26. Collingwood, 'Philosophy of History' (1930), in *Essays*, p. 138.
27. R. G. Collingwood, 'History as the Understanding of the Present (1934), in *The Principles of History* (1999), p. 140.
28. Ibid., p. 141.
29. It is this tendency which, as I shall argue in Chapter 7, has given rise to the 'presentism' that is in vogue today. On the question of Collingwood's attitude towards 'presentism', see W. H. Dray, *History as Re-enactment: R.G. Collingwood's Idea of History* (1995), pp. 267–8 & ff. p. 297.
30. R. G. Collingwood, 'History as Re-enactment of Past Experience', pp. 290–1. A real difficulty with this analysis, according to P. Winch, is the fact that 'Collingwood pays insufficient attention to the manner in which a way of thinking [present] and the historical situation to which it belongs [past] form one indivisible whole'. See P. Winch, *The Idea of a Social Science and its Relation to Philosophy* (1958), pp. 132–3.
31. Collingwood, *Autobiography*, p. 114.
32. Collingwood, 'Nature and Aim of Philosophy of History' (1924), in *Essays*, p. 35.
33. Ibid.
34. Ibid.
35. Ibid., p. 36.
36. Ibid., p. 43.
37. Ibid.
38. Collingwood, 'The Philosophy of History' (1930), in *Essays*, pp. 136–9.
39. Collingwood, 'Can a Historian be Impartial?' (1936), in *The Principles of History* (1999), p. 211: 'The fact that Rostovtseff hates the Communists who

have ruined himself and his friends is the fact which enriched us all with a new interpretation of third-century history.'
40. Ibid., pp. 217–8. For a concise discussion on 'value judgment in history' see W. H. Dray, 'Philosophy and Historiography' in *Routledge Companion to Historiography* (1997), pp. 770–4.
41. Collingwood (1924), p. 44.
42. J. L. Myres, *Herodotus: The Father of History* (1953), p. 1.
43. J. L. Myres, *Who Were the Greeks* (1930), p. xi.
44. J. L. Myres, 'The Value of Ancient History' (1910), in *Geographical History in Greek Lands* (1953), p. 49.
45. Collingwood, *The Idea of History*, p. 20.
46. Ibid., pp. 24–5.
47. MSS. Myres 116, folio 97.
48. As was the case with the previous section, I am only discussing those areas of the philosophy of science which are relevant to the way in which Myres pursues his academic goals.
49. C. B. Joynt and N. Rescher, 'The Problem of Uniqueness in History', *History & Theory* 1 (1961), p. 154: 'The generalizations provided by anthropology, sociology, psychology, etc., are used by the historian in the interests of his mission of facilitating our understanding of the past.'
50. For detailed analysis refer to 'The Problem of Inductive Logic', in R. Carnap, *Logical Foundation of Probability* (1950), pp. 161–2.
51. B. Farrington, *The Philosophy of Francis Bacon* (1964), p. 89.
52. W. S. Jevons, *The Principle of Science* (1958), pp. 510–11.
53. W. H. Newton-Smith, *A Companion to the Philosophy of Science* (2000), p. 88.
54. T. S. Kuhn, *The Structure of Scientific Revolutions*, (1962), p. 3.
55. Ibid., p. 5.
56. Ibid.
57. Ibid., p. 10.
58. J. Losee, *A Historical Introduction to the Philosophy of Science* (2001), p. 198.
59. Kuhn, *Structure*, p. 36.
60. Ibid., p. 52.
61. Ibid.
62. Ibid, p. 52.
63. Ibid., p. iii.
64. Myres, *Who*, p. 62.
65. J. Watkins, 'Against "Normal Science"' in I. Lakatos & A. Musgrave (eds.), *Criticism and the Growth of Knowledge* (1970), p. 31.
66. Ibid, p. 1.
67. Ibid., K. Popper, 'Normal Science and its Dangers', p. 52.
68. Ibid., p. 53.
69. Ibid., p. 55.
70. Ibid., p. 57.
71. Ibid., Popper quoted in T. S. Kuhn, 'Reflections on my Critics', p. 242.

72. Ibid.
73. Ibid., L. P. Williams, 'Normal Science, Scientific Revolution, and the History of Science', p. 49.
74. Ibid., p. 249.
75. Ibid., p. 252.
76. Ibid., p. 253.
77. See for instance A. Sesonske, 'Truth in Art', *Journal of Philosophy*, LIII (1956), pp. 345–6.
78. For the historical background concerning the relationship between truth and aestheticism refer to P. Lamarque and S. H. Olsen, 'Truth', in M. Kelly (ed.), *The Encyclopaedia of Aesthetics* (1998), pp. 406–15.
79. For more context on this refer to J. Stolnitz, *Aesthetic and the Philosophy of Art Criticism* (1960), pp. 1–5; N. Pappas, 'Beauty: Classical Concepts', in M. Kelly (ed.) *Encyclopaedia of Aesthetics* (1998), pp. 244–247; H. Dickermann, 'Theories of Beauty' in *Dictionary of History of Ideas* (1973), pp. 196–8.
80. Aristotle, *Poetics* (1917), VIII. 3, p. 35. In *Speculum Mentis* (1924), Collingwood discusses not the universality of truth, but that of history: 'History is the knowledge of the infinite world of facts. It is therefore itself an infinite whole of thought: history is essentially a universal history, a whole in which the knowledge of every fact is included' (p. 231).
81. Sesonke regards *embedded* and *embodied* truths to be different from each other. The first refers to truth being conveyed by the use of metaphor; the second truth 'conveyed by the work as a whole'. See 'Truth in Art', pp. 350–1.
82. S. Carritt, *What is Beauty?* (1932), p. 19.
83. Ibid., p. 26.
84. Ibid., p. 24.
85. Ibid., p. 32.
86. J. Hospers, *Meaning and Truth in Art* (1946), p. 145.
87. The chances of success or failure, according to the author, entirely depend on the chosen branch of art; 'abstract' arts, such as painting and music, have less chance of success than the more 'human-based' ones, such as literature. See Hospers, *Meaning*, pp. 174–96.
88. In 'Is There Artistic Truth?' *Journal of Philosophy*, XLVI (1949), pp. 285–91, K. B. Price argues that it cannot be shown that all artistic truths can be rendered as being 'true-*to* human nature; they can equally be true-*about* something including the larger humanity' (p. 287).
89. Hospers, *Meaning*, p. 173.
90. J. Hospers (ed.), *Introductory Readings in Aesthetics* (1969), p. 9.
91. Ibid., p. 227.
92. H. Dieckmann, 'Theories of Beauty', in P. P. Wiener (ed.) *Dictionary of History of Ideas* (1973), p. 200.
93. Hospers, *Introductory*, p. 11.
94. Ibid., p. 276.

95. This new subjective way of looking at things of aesthetic quality began sometime in the late seventeenth century. Beauty was no longer, according to Dieckmann (1973), 'self-subsistent, an essence, an objective nature, or a relation' (p. 201), or, as David Hume had put it: 'Beauty is no quality in things: it exists merely in the mind which contemplates them; and each mind perceives a different beauty' (ibid).
96. Hospers, *Introductory*, p. 294.
97. Ibid., p. 295.
98. Although the more recent literature concerning this topic has not altered the terms of the debate substantially, it has, nonetheless, resulted in a number of focal and methodological changes. When the perennial question – is beauty subjective or objective? – is asked, it is asked within the context of another question: 'Are there principles of beauty?' See J. A McMahon, 'Beauty', in B. Gaunt and D. M. Lopes (eds.) *Routledge Companion to Aesthetics* (2005), pp. 307–19.
99. G. Murray, 'Humane Letters and Civilization' (1937), published in *Greek Studies* (1946), p. 216.
100. Taken from A. Savile's interpretation of Adorno's *Ästhetische Theorie* in his 'Beauty and Truth: the Apotheosis of an Idea', in R. Shusterman (ed.), *Analytic Aesthetics* (1989), p. 128.
101. A. Toynbee, *Greek Historical Thought: From Homer to the Age of Heraclius* (1924), p. xii. For more on Ranke refer to Chapters 2 and 7.
102. Murray, *Greek Studies*, p. 216.
103. Dieckmann, *Dictionary*, p. 202. It is interesting to note how often these words cropped up in the last chapter's analysis of aesthetic Hellenism.
104. G. Murray, 'The Value of Greece to the Future of the World', in R. W. Livingstone (ed.), *Legacy of Greece* (1921), p. 14.
105. Ibid.
106. Ibid., p 15.
107. Note that it is 'spiritual' and not 'legal' rights which Murray chooses to mention.
108. Ibid.
109. R. Ackerman, 'The Cambridge Group: Origin and Composition', in W. M. Calder III (ed.), *The Cambridge Ritualists Reconsidered* (1991), p. 4.
110. Ibid.
111. My viva examiner and the chairperson of the Gilbert Murray Trust, Edith Hall, described my labelling of Murray as an 'aesthetic Hellenist' as a case of 'Aunt Sally' in action. Perhaps, but bearing in mind that Murray practised telepathy, and was often in touch with the ancient Greeks, he brings to mind not so much Aunt Sally, but Madame Arcati (the dotty medium from Noel Coward's *Blithe Spirit*).
112. J. Levinson, *The Oxford Handbook of Aesthetics* (2005), p. 4.
113. Ibid., p. 6.
114. Ibid.

115. Joynt and Rescher, 'Problem of Uniqueness', p. 154.
116. Ibid., p. 156.
117. MSS. Myres, 121, folio 5.
118. MSS. Myres, 121, folio 7.
119. Ibid., folio 24.
120. Ibid., folio 33. Myres contends that languages and races cannot be 'easily or cogently arranged in any hierarchy from primitive to advanced'.
121. Myres, as discussed in Chapter 3, has followed the example of Herodotus' description of ethnicity (comprising 'the community of blood and language, temple and ritual [and] common customs') very closely. It should be noted that here the concept of race (community of blood) is embedded in the broader concept of *ethnos*. See *The Histories*, viii, p. 144.
122. In *The Two Cultures: A Second Look* (1964), Snow writes: 'The non-Scientists have a rooted impression that the scientists are shallowly optimistic, unaware of man's condition. On the other hand, the scientists believe that the literary intellectuals are totally lacking in foresight, peculiarly concerned with their brother men, in a deep sense anti-intellectual, anxious to restrict both art and thought to the existential movement' (p. 5).
123. This brings Nietzsche's *The Birth of Tragedy* to mind. See Chapter 2.

Chapter 7 Hellenisms and the Historiography of Ancient Persia

1. This section mainly covers the period between 1890s and 1930s (some select texts from earlier period are also discussed). The material selected here aims to be a representative sample rather than an exhaustive list of relevant publications.
2. *Oxford English Dictionary*.
3. J. Herder, *Reflections on the Philosophy of History of Mankind* (1968), p. 129. But because of the date, 'race' may signify only the similarities in the behaviour of the Persian and German aristocrats.
4. Ibid.
5. Ibid., p. 131.
6. Ibid.
7. Ibid., p. 165.
8. Ibid., p. 207.
9. G. W. Cox, *The Greeks and the Persians* (1887), p. 1.
10. Ibid., p. 2.
11. Ibid., p. 5.
12. Ibid., p. 7.
13. Ibid., pp. 11–12.

14. Ibid.
15. Ibid., p. 74.
16. Ibid., p. 75.
17. Ibid., p. 204.
18. G. N. Curzon, *Persia and the Persian Question* (1892), p. 4.
19. Ibid., p. 5.
20. Ibid., p. 10.
21. Ibid., p. 195.
22. Ibid.
23. J. B. Bury, *A History of Greece* (1909), pp. 229–30.
24. Ibid., p. 55. This is further echoed by C. D. Edmond. In *Greek History for Schools* (1914), he writes: 'the spirit that urged on the vast majority of the king's army was that of slavery and the lash; the Greeks were animated by patriotism, however narrow, and their love of liberty' (p. 138).
25. J. Boardman et al. (eds.), *The Cambridge Ancient History*, Volume IV, p. v.
26. Ibid., p. vii. Why, then, call the volume 'The Persian Empire and the Greeks'? After all, the table of contents suggests that Persia or the Persians were not at the top of the editorial agenda: 16 chapters in total: 2 on Persia, 3 on the Wars, 1 each on Carthage, Sicily, the Etruscans and Lydia; and 7 chapters on the Greece.
27. Ibid., p. 1.
28. M. G. W. Laistner, *A Survey of Ancient History* (1929), pp. 190–1.
29. Ibid.
30. R. W. Rogers, *The History of Ancient Persia* (1929), p. 165.
31. Ibid., p. 167.
32. E. Herzfeld, *Archaeological History of Iran* (1935), pp. 51–2.
33. Ibid., p. 75.
34. Ibid.
35. J. M. Todd in *The Ancient World* (1938), p. 30. Much of the discourse concerning the wars has changed very little in the past 150 years. In *Worlds at War: The 2,500-Year Struggle Between East and West* (2008), A. Pagden opines: 'The battles of Thermopylae, Marathon, and Salamis had [...] secured a permanence of freedom for Europe. Had Xerxes succeeded [...] had Greek democracy been snuffed out [...] that incredible burst of creative energy which took place during the fifth and fourth centuries BCE and which laid the foundation for all later Western civilization, would never have happened' (p. 30).
36. J. Mahaffy, *Alexander's Empire* (1887), p. 2.
37. Ibid., p. 42.
38. Bury, *History*, pp. 185–6.
39. Ibid., p. 749.
40. H. Webster, *A History of the Ancient World* (1915), p. 277.
41. Ibid., p. 278.
42. J. Bury, *The Hellenistic Age* (1923), p. 4.

43. U. Wilcken, *Alexander the Great* (1932), p. 80.
44. Ibid., p. 246.
45. Ibid., p. 284.
46. Ibid., pp. 314–5.
47. I am aware that 'these Oriental peoples'are not all of Indo-Iranian descent.
48. G. Rawlinson, *The Five Great Monarchies of the Ancient Eastern World* (1862), p. 316. Rawlinson clearly did not think this analysis through: if the Persians had had unusually thin skulls and, according to the author, bigger than usual brain size, then their brains must have been bigger than those of the Greeks (why else would Herodotus bother mentioning the unusual thinness of their skulls?). If this was so then the Persians must also have had superior 'intellectual power' compared to the Greeks. Although Rawlinson would not have admitted to such an unlikely scenario, his analysis nonetheless recommends it.
49. Ibid., p. 317.
50. G. Rawlinson, *Parthia* (1893), p 32. The 'anti-Turkic' views on offer from the 1880s to 1920s – Rawlinson; J. W. Jackson, 'Iran and Turan', *Anthropological Review*, 21/22, 1868; Bury, *History*, etc. – seem to suggest that the European intelligentsia was preoccupied by the collapse of the Ottoman Empire and its messy aftermath.
51. Ibid., pp. 32–3.
52. J. Mahaffy, *A Survey of Greek Civilization* (1897), p. 109.
53. Ibid., p. 110.
54. Ibid., pp. 110–11.
55. Ibid., p. 121.
56. Ibid., p. 122.
57. I referred to the French edition of this work: Meyer, *Histoire de l'antiquité*, Vol. 1 (1912). See the section entitled 'Race, famille linguistique, group ethnique', pp. 79–87.
58. A. Momigliano, 'Introduction to a Discussion of Eduard Meyer', in *Studies in Historiography* (1966), p. 214.
59. E. Meyer, 'Persia' in *Encyclopaedia Britannica* (1911), p. 211. In *The Classical Foundations of Modern Historiography* (1990, p. 6), Momigliano contends that Meyer's article is 'still fresh'. The use of the word 'vizier' in the main body of the text, and the more appropriate *'chiliarch'* relegated to the parentheses, along with the inevitability of 'degeneration in oriental states' suggest not freshness, but a propensity to orientalize the Persians according to norms of the day. Besides, as Pierre Briant has argued (June 2009 lecture), the finding of the Persepolis and other tablets has revolutionized Achaemenid studies beyond recognition, thus casting doubt on the freshness of any document from 1911.
60. Webster, *Ancient World*, pp. 16–18.
61. Ibid., p. 150.
62. Ibid.

63. Ibid.
64. Ibid., pp. 166–7.
65. D. G. Hogarth, *The Ancient East* (1914), p. 13.
66. Ibid., p. 16.
67. Ibid., pp. 165–6.
68. Ibid., p. 168.
69. Ibid., p. 170.
70. Ibid., pp. 177–8.
71. Ibid., p. 186.
72. Ibid., p. 188.
73. Ibid., p. 193.
74. Ibid., p. 217.
75. H. Breasted, *Ancient Times* (1916), pp. 239–40.
76. Ibid., p. 177.
77. Ibid., p. 279.
78. Ibid., p. 382.
79. P. Sykes, *History of Persia* (1915), vol. I, pp. 154–5.
80. Ibid., p. 104.
81. Ibid., p. 225.
82. Ibid., pp. 300–3.
83. Ibid.
84. H. R. James, *Our Hellenic Heritage* (1921), p. 255.
85. Ibid., p. 277.
86. Ibid., p. 384.
87. Ibid., p. 386.
88. Ibid., p. 387.
89. Ibid., p. 389.
90. Ibid.
91. Ibid., p. 393.
92. G. W. Botsford, *Hellenic History* (1922), p. 26.
93. Ibid., p. 160.
94. Ibid.
95. Ibid., p. 169.
96. Ibid., pp. 173–4.
97. Ibid., pp. 190–1.
98. C. W. C. Oman, *A History of Greece* (1924), p. 19.
99. Ibid., p. 124.
100. Ibid., pp. 125–6.
101. Ibid., p. 188.
102. Ibid., p. 543.
103. A. Blunt, *The Ancient World and its Legacy to Us* (1932), p. 43.
104. Ibid., p. 44.
105. Ibid., p. 46.

106. Ibid., p. 47. In *Persia* (1888), R. G. W. Benjamin (the US's first ambassador to Persia), writes with reference to the outcome of the Persian Wars that 'it had been ordained that Europe should never belong to the races of Asia' (p. 121).
107. Ibid., p. 68
108. M. Rostovtzeff, *A History of the Ancient World* (1928), p. 333.
109. F. Howell, *Our Aryan Ancestors: The World's Historical People* (1935), p. 69.
110. Ibid., p. 90.
111. Ibid., p. 340.
112. Ibid., p. 354.
113. Ibid., pp. 53–4.
114. Ibid., p. 359.
115. Ibid., p. 371.
116. Ibid., p. 372.
117. D. M. Robinson, *History of Greece* (1936), p. 389.
118. Ibid., p. 393.
119. Ibid., p. 400.
120. Ibid., p. 409.
121. Ibid., pp. 411–12.
122. G. B. Grundy, *The Great Persian War and its Preliminaries* (1901), p. vii.
123. Ibid., p. 577.
124. Ibid., p. 579.
125. Ibid., pp. 2–3.
126. Ibid., p. 16.
127. Ibid., pp. 32–5.
128. G. B. Grundy, *A History of the Greek and Roman World* (1926), p. 121.
129. Ibid., pp. 124–5.
130. A. Jardé's *The Formation of the Greek People* (1970), p. xiii. Berr takes this from H. Ouvré's *Les Formes littéraires de la pensée grecque* (1900), p. 2.
131. This is the same series of books (Ogden) in which Childe's *Ancient East* (1925) and *The Aryans* (1926) had appeared.
132. Jardé, *Formation*, p. xiv.
133. Ibid., p. 71.
134. Ibid., p. 73.
135. Ibid., pp. 266–7.
136. Ibid., p. 269.
137. C. Huart, *Ancient Persia and Iranian Civilisation* (1928), p. xv.
138. Ibid., p. 60.
139. Ibid., p. 217.
140. H. G. Wells, *A Short History of the World* (1929), p. 64.
141. Ibid., p. 68.
142. T. R. Glover, *The Ancient World* (1935), p. 88.
143. Ibid., p. 91.
144. Ibid., p. 97.
145. Ibid., pp. 109–10.

146. Ibid., p. 112.
147. Ibid.
148. Ibid., p. 211.
149. F. Hegel, *Lectures in the Philosophy of History* (1884), p. 180.
150. F. Hegel, *Lectures in the Philosophy of World History* (1975), pp. 200–1.
151. K. Löwith, *From Hegel to Nietzsche* (1941), p. 32.
152. S. Houlgate, *Introduction to Hegel: Freedom, Truth and History* (2005), p. 18.
153. These types of Hegelian complexities have also been lost on those nonspecialist discussants of this aspect of Hegel's analysis. T. Holland in *Persian Fire* (2006), p. xii; and P. Cartledge in *Thermopylae* (2006), p. xvii, for instance, furnish the reader with the following quote concerning the Persian Wars from Hegel's *Philosophy of History* without situating it within its proper Hegelian context: 'the interest of the whole world's history hung trembling in the balance.' Surely we can say exactly the same thing about the Napoleonic Wars, the Great War, World War II and the Cuban Missile Crisis.
154. J. A. Gobineau, *Essay Concerning the Inequalities of Races* (1915), p. 171.
155. This is an abridged publication in English of Gobineau's *Histoire de Perse* (1869).
156. J. A. Gobineau, *The World of the Persians* (1971), p. 131.
157. E. Renan, *Oeuvres Complètes de Ernest Renan* (1961), vol. 10, p. 203: 'Vous avez fait là un livre des plus remarquables, plein de vigueur et d'originalité d'esprit'.
158. E. Renan, *Histoire de Peuple d'Israël* (1889), 'L'histoire juive, qui voudrait avoir le monopole du miracle n'est pas un fait plus extraordinaire que l'histoire grecque.' Taken from H. Peyre, *Sagesse de Renan* (1968), p. 168.
159. Renan, *Histoire*. 'Le christianisme, en un mot, devient dans l'histoire un élément aussi capital que le rationalisme liberal des Grecs, quoique à certains égards moins assuré de l'éternité.' Ibid., p. 170.
160. E. Renan, *Ètude's d'Histoire religieuse* (1862). 'La mythologie grecque, ou, dans un sens plus general, la mythologie des peoples indo-européens, envisagée dans son premier essor, n'est que le reflet des sensations d'organes jeunes et délicats, sans rien de dogmatique, rien de théologique, rien d'arrêté.' Ibid., pp. 170–1.
161. Renan, *Histoire*. 'Cette culture fut loin de produire un abaissement militaire, puisqu'à l'heure même où la Grèce créait le cadre absolu de la civilisation, que tout le monde devait accepter après elle, elle résistait victorieusement à tout l'effort de l'empire achemecide et lui infligeait des defaites repetees.' Ibid, p. 177. And when Renan mentions the Persian Wars, he does so in a publication concerning Jewish history.
162. 'Toute persone un peu instruite des choses de notre temps voit clairement l'infériorité actuelle des pays musulmans, la décadence des Etats gouvernés par l'islam, la nullité intellectuelle des races qui tiennent uniquement de cette religion leur culture et leur éducation.' E. Renan, *L'Islam et Sciences* (1883), pp. 376–7.

163. Ibid., p. 378. 'La Perse seule fait ici exception; elle a su garder son génie propre; car la Perse a su prendre dans l'islam une place à part.'
164. Ibid., p. 381. 'Le centre de l'Islam se trouve transporté dans la region du Tigre et de l'Euphrates. Or ce pays était plein encore des traces d'une des plus brillantes civilisation que l'Orient ait connues, celle des Perses Sassanides, qui a été portée a son comble sous le règne de Chosroe Noushirvan. L'art et l'industrie florissaient en ces pays depuis des siècles. Le terrible coup de vent de l'Islam arrêta net, pendant une centaine d'années, tout ce beau développement iranien.' (All translations are mine.)
165. S. Freitag, 'The Critique of Orientalism', in *Companion to Historiography* (1996), p. 624.
166. G. Childe, *The Aryans* (1926), pp. 208–9. Also see his comments on the 'Aryan Darius' in Chapter 4.
167. The reader should be reminded that Myres at no point asserted that the Indo-European family of languages are 'superior' to all others.
168. As mentioned in Chapter 5, Myres believed that Herodotus had also set aside 'the East is East and West is West' theory when dealing with the Persians and the Greeks.
169. J. L. Myres, *The Dawn of History* (1911), p. 217.
170. J. L. Myres, *Who Were the Greeks?* (1930), p. 168.
171. J. L. Myres, 'The Ethnology, Habitat, Linguistic, and Common Culture of Indo-Europeans up to the Time of the Migration', in E. Eyre's (ed.) *European Civilisation: Its Origin and Development* (1935), p. 203.
172. Ibid., p. 204.
173. MSS. Myres 115 ('Greece and Persia from Cyrus to Alexander'), folio 2. The reason why I think this essay was written in 1938 is because it reads 'in 500 BC, as in 1914 AD and 1938...'
174. Ibid., folio 3.
175. Ibid., folio 20.
176. Ibid., folio 26.
177. Ibid., folio 36.
178. Ibid. 'Mardonios {a satrap} is an early example of Darius new "civil service".'
179. Ibid., folio 42. Myres adds: 'For him as for Stevenson's Happy Child: "The world is so full of a number of things, I am sure we should all be as happy as kings."' Myres takes this from R. L. Stevenson's *A Child Garden of Verses* (1885). Note: this contrast between Iranian and Indian religions is also made in Myres (1933), p. 38; and Myres (1935), p. 202.
180. Ibid., folio 67.
181. Ibid.
182. Ibid., folio 69.
183. MSS. Myres 117, folio 34.
184. The only other example that I have managed to locate is the following: 'Though in a sense the soul of Persia died with Darius, the dead hand of his

Empire maintained its paralysing constraint over the Greek world for nearly two hundred years' (MSS. Myres115, folio 13).
185. MSS. Myres 117, folio 44.
186. In *Hobbes and Republican Liberty* (2008), Quentin Skinner, taking his cue from Wittgenstein (*Philosophical Investigations* [1958], p. 146.), makes a very interesting suggestion which might be of some relevance when thinking about these select words under discussion: 'To interpret and understand [Hobbes'] texts, I suggest, we need to recognise the force of the maxim that words are also deeds [p. xv.].'
187. Bailyn quoted in G. S. Wood's 'The Creative Imagination of Bernard Bailyn', in J. A. Heretta et al. (eds.), *The Transformation of Early American History: Society, Authority and Identity* (1991), p. 38.
188. Ibid.
189. Ibid.
190. Ibid., p. 41.
191. Ibid., p. 42.
192. The example of connecting the Persian Wars with 9/11 is not given here for the purpose of shocking the reader. This connection was actually made in the preface of P. Cartledge's *Thermopylae: The Battle that Changed the World* (2006): 'The events of "9/11" in New York City and now "7/7" in London have given this project a renewed urgency and importance within the wider framework of East-West cultural encounter' (p. xv). In his 6 December 2007 review of this book in *The New York Review of Books* (*NYRB*) J. Griffin is not unsympathetic towards this teleological approach: 'Perhaps the claim of a link with September 11 may look a little insecure, but something like it was worth saying; and it falls into place, when we consider these events as part of that long series of return matches, in which East and West have in turn invaded and conquered each other. That has regularly meant some rewriting of history' (p. 64).
193. B. Bailyn, 'The Challenge of Modern Historiography', *The American Historical Review*, 87 (1982), pp. 1–24 (24).
194. In other words, refraining from conflating the Persian Wars with 9/11.
195. W. Dilthey, *Hermeneutics and the Study of History* (1999), R. A. Makkreel and F. Rod (eds.), pp. 309–13.
196. Ibid., pp. 21–2.
197. Ibid., p. 22.
198. R. G. Collingwood, 'History as Re-enactment of Past Experience', in *The Idea of History* (1946), pp. 290–1.
199. R. G. Collingwood, *An Autobiography* (1939), p. 114.
200. E. Abbott, *Hellenica* (1880), p. 7 (Euripides, 276 [added emphasis]).
201. In a similar way, the Latin roots of 'Occident' and 'Orient' describe western and eastern portions of the sky, respectively.
202. *Encyclopaedia Britannica*, (1911), p. 734.

203. The notion that 'Europe' has Semitic philological roots has come under some criticism of late. M. L. West, for instance, believes that 'Europe' has Greek roots and states that 'phonologically, the match between Europa's name and any form of the Semitic word is very poor'. See *The East Face of Helicon: West Asiatic Elements in Greek Poetry and Myth* (1997).
204. A. Sherratt, *Economy and Society in Prehistoric Europe* (1997), p. 12. He also writes: '"Europe" appeared as an ideological entity only with the spread of Christianity, and has only the faintest geographical justification as a physical unit' (ibid.).
205. Myres, *Dawn*, p. 189.
206. J. L. Myres, 'The Place of Man and his Environment in the Study of Social Sciences', *Man* 23, pp. 162–8.
207. Ibid., p. 164.
208. J. L. Myres, *Man of Science and the Science of Man* (1933), p. 25.
209. MSS. Myres 121 ('Anthropology'), folio 6.
210. Ibid.
211. Ibid., folio 7.
212. MSS. Myres 117 ('The Geographical Study of Greece and Roman Culture'), folio 5.
213. MSS. Myres 77, unnumbered folio.
214. Grundy, *The Great*, p. 4.
215. Ibid.
216. Grundy, *A History*, p. 121.
217. C. S. Lewis, *Studies in Words* (1960), pp. 124–5.
218. D. H. Fischer, *Liberty and Freedom: A Visual History of America's Founding Ideas* (2005), p. 10.
219. Ibid.
220. Ibid., p. 5. The limitedness of this freedom, however, continues to go unregistered by many of the present-day Hellenists. Christian Meier's *A Culture of Freedom: Ancient Greece and the Origins of Europe* (2011) is a teleological case in point.
221. Ibid., p. 7. Hannah Arendt, however, equates *eleutheros* with *freedom* and differentiates it from *liberty*. For more details on this see her *On Revolution* (1965) and 'What is Freedom?' in *Between Past and Present* (1961). For a well-argued critique of her approach refer to H. F. Pitkin, 'Are Freedom and Liberty Twins?' *Political Theory* 16 (1988), pp. 523–52.
222. Webster, *Ancient World*, pp. 166–7.
223. The modern discourse has changed very little. In *The Greek World 479–323 BC* (2002), Simon Hornblower borrows Isaiah Berlin's *Two Concepts of Liberty* ('non-interference with my own activity' and 'being one's own master') and argues that 'Greeks valued the second kind, which included freedom to oppress and dominate, at least as much as the first' (p. 69). As the discussions in the main body of this text have illustrated, adopting modern frameworks concerning freedom/liberty can be problematic. D. H. Fischer observes that Berlin's idea is very much of its time and place: 'His thinking was embedded

in a German cultural context, which routinely distinguishes between *Freiheit von* and *Freiheit zu*. It also was part of a Jewish tradition of freedom that developed in response to many centuries of persecution in Christian Europe' (*Liberty and Freedom: A Visual History of America's Founding* Ideas [2005], endnote 6, p. 740).
224. Pagden, *Worlds at War*, p. 30. Emphasis added.
225. Bozeman, *Politics and Culture in International History* (1994), pp. 54–5. See also Momigliano's 'Persian Empire and Greek Freedom' (1979), pp. 139–51.
226. J. J. Rousseau, *The Social Contract* (1993), Book 3, Chapter 15, p. 267.
227. J. Keane, *The Life and Death of Democracy* (2009), p. 42.
228. Ibid.
229. Ibid., pp. 42–3.
230. Ibid., p. 44.
231. Ibid., p. 46.
232. See Flyvbjerg's *Rationality and Power: Democracy in Practice* (1998). Similar works concerning Italy have been undertaken by R. Putnam in his *Making Democracy Work: Civic Tradition in Modern Italy* (1993). Putnam traces the roots of the civic community back to medieval Italy: 'Although medieval Italy was closer to ancient Rome than to present, nevertheless, social pattern plainly traceable from early Medieval Italy to today turn out to be decisive in explaining why some communities are better able than others to manage collective life and sustain effective institutions' (p. 121).
233. As far as Flyvbjerg is concerned, 'democracy' is a modern creation (*Rationality*, p. 90), which is 'young and fragile when compared to traditions of class and privilege' (p. 231).
234. Keane, *The Life*, p. 90.
235. Ibid., pp. 92–101. According to Keane, 'democracy' has an etymological root going back to Linear B.
236. Ibid., p. 107. For a detailed look at Byblos see pp. 104–6.
237. Ibid., p. 113.
238. Similar examples were also published in R. H. Pfeiffer, *State Letters of Assyria* (1935).
239. T. Jacobsen, 'Primitive Democracy in Ancient Mesopotamia', *Journal of Near Eastern Studies*, 2 (1943), pp. 158–72 (167).
240. Ibid., p. 172.
241. Of course, the quality or otherwise of the arguments are very much beside the point. Jacobsen is being analysed here in order to demonstrate that ideas concerning the non-Athenian forms of 'democracy' were discussed during the first half of the twentieth century.
242. D. A. Fleming, *Democracy's Ancient Ancestors: Mari and Early Collective Governance* (2004), p. 235.
243. Ibid. Mari is a northern region of modern-day Iraq, where a number of texts have been excavated since the 1930s.

244. Ibid., p. 239. Fleming's view concerning 'cultural geography' is not that different from that held by Myres (see above).
245. Ibid., p. 240.
246. An alternative way of looking at the role of words or terms is a structuralist approach. In 'Myth Today' (*Mythologies*, 1957), Barthes goes back to the semiology of Saussure and makes an explicit link between *language* and *myth* and states that 'myth is not defined by the object of its message, but by the way in which it utters this message' (p. 109). Putting it simply, Barthes endows his structure of myth with three components: 1) the 'signifier'; 2) the 'signified'; and 3) the 'signification'. For example the phrase, 'The Persian Wars – Greece Saves Europe' (taken from Du Pontet's *Ancient World* [1912], p. 225), can be analysed in the following way: the signifier is a combination of lexical (Europe vis-à-vis Persia), typographical (big fonts titling a chapter) and rhetorical (Greece *saves*…) devices. Since it is Greece that is solely and dynamically instrumental in this text, then, the signified can be called 'Hellenicity'. The association of these two terms, or the signification, would be the assertion that there was a 'Europe', which was recognized by the ancients as a quantifiable and describable whole that the non-European Persians wanted to destroy and/ or enslave, but their plans were thwarted by a Greece determined to save this entity of 'Europe' for presumably better things. See Barthes' *Mythologies* (1957) and *Image, Music, Text* (1977). I, however, abandoned this approach, because, first, I lack the right expertise for its proper application and second, the more straightforward analysis of the way in which these terms have evolved seemed to have been adequate for the purposes of this discourse.
247. Quoted from a letter to *TLS* by Clifford Davis, 3 July 2009, p. 6.
248. C. Davis, 'A Rose by Another Name', *TLS*, 13 June 2008, p. 14.
249. Ibid., p. 15.
250. This phrase is taken from the title of Pagden, *Worlds at War*, in which he also produces an excellent example of presentism in the following remark: 'One morning, over breakfast, my wife, the classical scholar Giulia Sissa, was looking at a picture in the *New York Times* of a group of Iranians prostrate in prayer. "How ironic!" She remarked. "It was just this habit of prostration which most horrified the Greeks about the ancient Persians."' (p. xxi).
251. G. Orwell, 'Politics and the English Language', in *Essays* (2002), p. 956.
252. Ibid., p. 959.

Chapter 8   Concluding Remarks

1. UNESCO, *The Race Question* (1950), p 8. This document can be found online: http://unesdoc.unesco.org/images/0012/001282/128291eo.pdf.
2. K. Malik, *The Meaning of Race* (1996), pp. 4–5.

3. M. Pagel, *Prospect*, June 2008, p. 72. He also writes: 'Humans still speak about 7,000 distinct languages. You don't get that by hanging out with each other' (p. 73). In an email (17–18 September 2009) to the author, I sought clarification. The following are two relevant extracts from his reply: 'My position is that there are not fixed boundaries defining races, but merely that there are background – what are known as neutral – genetic differences among populations of people and these coincide in many instances with groups we have traditionally defined as different races.' 'The point I was trying to make in my essay was that we could imagine finding differences among groups of people and that it is possible these differences would correspond to old classifications of race. But that says nothing about one group being better or worse.' See also Pagel's *Wired for Culture: The Natural History of Human Co-operation* (2012).
4. M. Pagel (ed.), *Oxford Encyclopaedia of Evolution* (2002), pp. 979–84. The essays are by H. Harpending ('Population Genetic Perspective') and D. Jones ('Sociological Perspective').
5. J. L. Myres, 'Persia, Greece, and Israel', *Palestine Exploration Quarterly*, vol. 83 (1953), p. 8.
6. Ibid., p. 14.
7. Ibid., p. 19.
8. The following two examples should illustrate this point. Myres ('The Ethnology, Habitat...' [1953]), p. 203: 'The product was a nation of boy scouts, happy warriors, wise and tolerant administrators. This naturally puzzled and amused the rationalized and commercialized Greeks.' Myres ('Persia, Greece, Israel' [1953]), pp. 10–11: 'The result was a nation of boy-scouts, of happy warriors, of grave, polite, considerate, honest, and efficient gentlemen. To the sophisticated Greeks, much of this was foolishness and pedantry.' Also, Myres (1935), ibid.: 'The tragic result of this initial misunderstanding between two of the world's gifted peoples was two centuries of war, intrigue, and deadlock, until Persian grit and integrity had been sapped by alien vices.' Myres (1953), p. 19: 'The sequel was two hundred years of frustration and political anxiety for Persia [...] and that nightmare ended only when the vitality of Persia itself has been sapped by contact with less desirable subjects and advisors.' It should be noted that the phrase 'Alien vices' is replaced by a more neutral phrase in 1953.
9. Myres, 'Persia, Greece', p. 18.
10. Incidentally, the word 'Indo-European' does not appear in this paper.
11. J. L. Myres, 'Review', *Man* 52 (1952), p. 73.
12. E Barkan, *The Retreat of Scientific Racism* (1992), p. i. I am puzzled by this idea that a science community can ever be in need of social engineering. I do not see how the cause of science is furthered (or not furthered, for that matter) by the infusion of individuals, whose identities are primarily defined by their gender, religion, or voting habits. This seems to be a little too close for comfort to the postmodern concepts of relativism and constructivism. See P. A. Boghossian, *Fear of Knowledge* (2007), and the relevant discussions in Chapter 4.

13. *Plus ça change*! With this type of classical history-writing going from strength to strength (if the present trend of academic postings, publications and the reception of these publications are anything to go by), then it would not be too fantastic to paraphrase the words of a former British prime minister – in whose 'presence' Gilbert Murray felt or imagined to feel 'a certain Hellenic atmosphere' (see C. Stray, *Gilbert Murray Reassessed* [2007], p. 221) – and argue that the current batch of aesthetic Hellenists 'have never had it so good'.
14. T. J. Dunbabin, 'Sir John Linton Myres', *Proceedings of The British Academy* 41 (1955), p. 365.

Postscript

1. D. W. Anthony, *The Horse, the Wheel and Language: How Bronze-Age Riders from the Eurasian Steppes Shaped the Modern World* (2007), p. 465.

BIBLIOGRAPHY

Unpublished Primary Sources

G. Childe's Papers, Special Collection, UCL, London.
G. Murray's Papers, Bodleian Library, Oxford.
J. L. Myres' Papers, Bodleian Library, Oxford.
The Archives of the Royal Anthropological Institute, London.

Published Primary Sources

Abbott, E., *Hellenica* (London, 1880).
────── and Campell, L. (eds.), *Life and Letters of Benjamin Jowett* (London, 1897).
Anonymous, 'Review of *Who Were the Greeks?* by J.L. Myres', *The Journal of Hellenic Studies*, 51 (1931), pp. 291–2.
Arnold, M., *Culture and Anarchy* (Yale, CT, 1994).
Atkins, S. (ed.), *Goethe: Collected Works* (Princeton, NJ, 1984).
Bender, H.H., *The Home of the Indo-Europeans* (Princeton, NJ, 1922).
Benjamin, S.G.W., *Persia* (New York, NY, 1888).
Blunt, A., *The Ancient World and its Legacy to Us* (London, 1932).
Boas, F., *The Mind of the Primitive Man* (New York, NY, 1938).
Borovka, G., *Scythian Art* (London, 1928).
Botsford, G.W., *Hellenic History* (New York, NY, 1922).
Breasted, H., *Ancient Times* (Boston, MA, 1916).
────── *Origins of Civilisations* (Scientific Monthly, 1920).
Breasted, J.H., *Ancient Record of Egypt* (Chicago, IL, 1906).
Bury, J.B., *A History of Greece* (London, 1909).
────── *The Hellenistic Age* (Cambridge, 1923).
Bury, J.B., Cook, S.A., Adcock, F.E. (eds.), *The Cambridge Ancient History* (Cambridge, 1924).

BIBLIOGRAPHY

Childe, G., *The Dawn of European Civilization* (London, 1925, 1939, 1957).
———— *The Aryans: A Study of Indo-European Origins* (London, 1926).
———— 'Traces of the Aryans on the Middle Danube', *Man*, 26 (1926), pp. 153–4.
———— *The Most Ancient East* (London, 1928).
———— *The Danube in Prehistory* (Oxford, 1929).
———— 'Races, Peoples and Cultures in Prehistoric Europe', *Man*, xviii (1933), pp.193–203.
———— *New Light on the Most Ancient East* (London, 1934, 1952).
———— 'Review of *European Civilization*, by E. Eyre', *Man*, 35 (1935), pp. 91–2.
———— *What Happened in History?* (London, 1942).
———— 'The Future of Archaeology', *Man*, 44 (1944), pp. 18–19.
———— 'Archaeology and Anthropology', *Southwestern Journal of Anthropology*, vol. 2, no. 3. (Autumn 1946), pp. 243–51.
———— 'Retrospect', *Antiquity*, xxxii (1958), pp. 69–75.
Collingwood, R. G., *Speculum Mentis* (Oxford, 1924).
———— *An Autobiography* (Oxford, 1939).
———— *The Idea of History* (Oxford, 1946).
———— *Essays in the Philosophy of History* (Oxford, 1985).
———— *The Principles of History*, edited by Dray, W. H., and van der Dussen, W. J. (Oxford, 1999).
Cox, G.W., *The Greeks and the Persians* (London, 1887).
Curzon, G. N., *Persia and the Persian Question* (London, 1892).
De Coulanges, F., *The Antique City* (London, 1975).
Dilthey, W., *Hermeneutics and the Study of History*, Makkreel R. A. and Rod, F. (eds), (Princeton, NJ, 1999).
Disraeli, B., *Lothair* (London, 1870).
Duchesne-Guillemin, *The Western Response to Zoroaster* (Westport, CN, 1958).
Dunbabin, T.J., 'Myres's Obituary', *Proceedings of the British Academy*, 41 (1955), pp. 48–65.
Du Pontet, C, *Ancient World* (London, 1912).
Edmond, C.D., *Greek History for Schools* (Cambridge, 1914).
Edmonds, J.M., *An Introduction to Comparative Philology for Classical Students* (Oxford, 1906).
Elliot-Smith, G., *Culture: A Symposium* (London, 1928).
———— *Diffusion of Culture* (London, 1933).
Evans-Pritchard, E. (ed.), *Essays Presented to C G Seligman* (London, 1934).
Eyre, E. (ed.), *European Civilisation: Its Origin and Development* (Oxford, 1935).
Fergusson., J., *Rude StoneMonuments in All Countries* (London, 1872).
Firth, R., *Human Types* (London, 1938).
Frankfort, H., *The Intellectual Adventure of Ancient Man* (Chicago, IL, 1946).
Galton, F., *Hereditary Genius* (London, 1869).
———— *Natural Inheritance* (London, 1889).
Gates, R., *Heredity in Man* (London, 1929).
Glover, T.R., *The Ancient World* (London, 1935).
Gobineau, J.A., *Histoire de Perse* (Paris,1869).
———— *Essay Concerning the Inequalities of Human Races* (London, 1915).
———— *The World of the Persians* (Geneva, 1971).
Gordon, G.S. (ed.), *English Literature and the Classics* (Oxford, 1912).

Grote, G., *History of Greece* (London, 1846–1856).
Grundy, G.B., *The Great Persian War and its Preliminaries* (London, 1901).
────── *A History of the Greek and Roman World* (London, 1926).
Haddon, A.C., *History of Anthropology* (London, 1910).
Harrison, J., *Themis: A Study of the Social Origins of Greek Religion* (Cambridge, 1927).
Hawkes, C.F.C., *The Prehistoric Foundation of Europe* (London, 1940).
Hegel, F., *Lectures on the Philosophy of History* (London,1884).
────── *The Philosophy of Fine Art* (London, 1916).
────── *Lectures on the Philosophy of World History* (Cambridge, 1975).
Herder, J., *Reflections on the Philosophy of History of Mankind* (Chicago, IL, 1968).
Herodotus, *The Histories* (London, 1996).
Herzfeld, E., *Archaeological History of Iran* (Cambridge, 1935).
────── *The Persian Empire: Studies in Geography and Ethnography of the Ancient Near East* (Wiesbaden, 1968).
Hogarth, D.G., *Ionia and the East* (London, 1909).
────── *The Ancient East* (London, 1914).
Howell, F., *Our Aryan Ancestors: The World's Historical People* (New York, NY, 1935).
Huart, C., *Ancient Persia and Iranian Civilisation* (London, 1928).
Jackson, J.W., 'Iran and Turan', *Anthropological Review*, 21/22 (1868), pp. 121–37 and 286–301.
────── 'The Aryans and Semites', *Anthropological Review*, 27 (1869), pp. 333–65.
Jacobsen, T., 'Primitive Democracy in Ancient Mesopotamia', *Journal of Near Eastern Studies*, 2 (1943), pp. 158–72.
James, H. R., *Our Hellenic Heritage* (London, 1921).
Jardé, A., *The Formation of the Greek People* (New York, NY, 1970).
Laistner, M.G.W., *A Survey of Ancient History to the Death of Constantine* (Boston, MA, 1929).
Lane-Fox, A., *The Evolution of Culture* (Oxford, 1906).
Levy-Bruhl, H., *La Mentalité Primitive* (Paris, 1922).
Livingstone, R.W., *The Greek Genius and its Meaning to Us* (Oxford, 1915).
────── (ed.), *The Legacy of Greece* (Oxford, 1921).
Mahaffy, J.P., *Social Life in Greece from Homer to Menander* (London, 1877).
────── *Alexander's Empire* (London, 1887).
────── *A Survey of Greek Civilization* (London, 1897).
Meyer, E., 'Persia', *Encyclopaedia Britannica* (Cambridge, 1911), pp. 202–24.
────── *Histoire de l'antiquité* (Paris, 1912).
Mill, J.S., *Discussions and Dissertations* (London, 1859).
Mitford, W., *History of Greece* (London, 1784–1810).
Montelius, O., *Der Orient und Europa* (Stockholm, 1899).
Morant, G., *The Races of Central Europe* (London, 1939).
Morgan, L H., *Ancient Society* (London, 1877).
Müller, M., *Lectures on the Science of Language* (London, 1861).
Murray, G., *The Rise of Greek Epic* (Oxford, 1907).
────── 'The Value of Greece to the Future of the World' in R.W. Livingstone (ed.), *Legacy of Greece* (Oxford, 1921).
────── *A History of Greek Literature* (London, 1935).
────── *Greek Studies* (Oxford, 1946).

―――― *Five Stages of Greek Religion* (Oxford, 1955).
Myres, J.L., 'Alpine Races in Europe', *The Geographical Journal*, 28 (1906), pp. 537–53.
―――― 'Herodotus and Anthropology', in Myres, J.L., *Anthropology and Classics* (Oxford, 1908).
―――― *Greek Lands and the Greek People* (Oxford, 1910).
―――― *The Dawn of History* (London, 1911).
―――― *Influence of Anthropology on the Course of Political Science* (Berkeley, CA, 1916).
―――― *The Political Ideas of the Greeks* (London, 1927).
―――― *Who Were the Greeks?* (Berkeley, CA, 1930).
―――― *The Man of Science and the Science of Man* (Liverpool, 1933).
―――― *Science and the Humanities: The Uses and Abuses of Information* (Oxford, 1933).
―――― 'The Ethnology, Habitat, Linguistic, and Common Culture of Indo-Europeans up to the time of the Migration', in Eyre, E., (ed.), *European Civilisation: Its Origin and Development* (Oxford, 1935a), pp. 179–244.
―――― 'Review of What Happened in History, by G. Childe', *Man*, 44 (1944), pp. 27–8.
―――― *Herodotus: The Father of History* (Oxford, 1953).
―――― 'Persia, Greece and Israel', *Palestine Exploration Quarterly*, 83 (1953), pp. 8–22.
―――― 'The Value of Ancient History' (1910), in Myres's *Geographical History in Greek Lands* (Oxford, 1953).
―――― 'The Place of Man and his Environment in the Study of Social Sciences', *Man*, 23, pp. 162–8.
Nietzsche, F., *Thus Spoke Zarathustra* (London, 1961).
―――― *The Birth of Tragedy* (London, 1997).
Ogilvie, J. (ed.), *The Imperial Dictionary of the English Language* (London, 1882).
Olmstead, A.T., 'Review of *Who Were the Greeks?* by J.L. Myres', *The Classical Journal*, 27 (1931), pp. 214–16.
Oman, C.W.C., *A History of Greece* (London, 1924).
Ouvré, H., *Les Formes littéraires de la pensée grecque* (Paris, 1900).
Pater, W., *The Renaissance* (London, 1873).
―――― *Greek Studies* (London, 1895).
Peyre, H., *Sagesse de Renan* (Paris, 1968).
Pfeiffer, R.H., *State Letters of Assyria* (Millwood, NY, 1935).
Pitt-Rivers, G., H., 'Anthropological Approach to Ethnogenics' in Evans Pritchard, E.E., et al. (eds.), *Essays Presented to C.G. Seligman* (London, 1934).
Poliakov, L., *The Aryan Myth* (Sussex, 1971).
Priestley, J., *An Essay on the First Principles of Government* (London, 1768).
Rawlinson, G., *The Five Great Monarchies of the Ancient Eastern World* (London, 1862).
―――― *A Manual of Ancient History* (Oxford, 1869).
―――― *Parthia* (London, 1893).
Renan, E., *De l'origine de Langage* (Paris, 1862).
―――― *Qu'est-ce qu'une nation?* (Paris, 1882).
―――― *L'Islam et Sciences* (Paris, 1883).
―――― *Oeuvres Complètes d'Ernest Renan* (Paris, 1961).
Robinson, D.M., *History of Greece* (London, 1936).
Rogers, R.W., *The History of Ancient Persia* (London, 1929).

Rose, H.J., 'Review of Who Were the Greeks? by J.L. Myres', *Man*, 30 (1930), pp. 159–60.
Rostovtzeff, M., *A History of the Ancient World* (Oxford, 1928).
—— *Iranians and Greeks in South Russia* (New York, NY, 1969).
Sayce, A.H., *Introduction to the Science of Language* (London, 1880).
Schrumpf, G.A., *A First Aryan Reader* (London, 1890).
Spengler, O., *The Decline of the West* (London, 1918).
Sykes, P., *History of Persia* (London, 1915).
Thomson, J.A.K., *Greeks and Barbarians* (London, 1921).
—— 'The Present and Future of Classical Scholarship' in J.A.K. Thomson's and A. Toynbee's (eds.), *Essays in Honour of Gilbert Murray* (London, 1936).
—— and Toynbee, A. (eds.), *Essays in Honour of Gilbert Murray* (London, 1936).
Todd, J.M., *The Ancient World* (London, 1938).
Toynbee, A.J., 'History' in R.W. Livingstone (ed.), *The Legacy of Greece* (Oxford, 1921).
—— *Greek Historical Thought: From Homer to the Age of Heraclius* (London, 1924).
—— *A Study in History* (Oxford, 1954).
—— *Greeks and their Heritages* (Oxford, 1981).
Trevelyan, H., *The Popular Background to Goethe's Hellenism* (London, 1934).
—— *Goethe and the Greeks* (Cambridge, 1941).
Tylor, E.B., *Anthropology: An Introduction to the Study of Man and Civilization* (London, 1881).
Wace, A.J.B., 'Review of *Who Were the Greeks?* by J.L. Myres', *The Classical Review*, 45 (1931), pp. 128–30.
Wagner, R., *Das Judenthum in der Musik* (Leipzig, 1869).
Webster, H., *A History of the Ancient World* (London, 1915).
Wells, H.G., *A Short History of the World* (London, 1929).
Whatmough, J., 'Review of *The Aryans*', in *Classical Philology*, 4 (1928), pp. 130–5.
Wilcken, U., *Alexander the Great* (London, 1932).
Winckelmann, J.J., *The History of Ancient Art* (Los Angles, CA, 2006).
Wissler, C., *Man and Culture* (London, 1923).
Worsaae, J.J., *The Prehistory of the North* (London, 1886).

Secondary Sources

Ackerman, R., 'The Cambridge Group: Origin and Composition', in W.M. Calder III (ed.), *The Cambridge Ritualists Reconsidered* (Illinois, IL, 1991).
Adams, W.Y., 'Invasion, Diffusion, Evolution?' *Antiquity*, xlii (1968), pp. 194–216.
Arendt, H., *Between Past and Present* (New York, NY, 1961).
—— *On Revolution* (London, 1965).
Aristotle, *Poetics* (New York, NY, 1917).
Arvidsson, S., *Aryan Idols* (Chicago, IL, 2000).
Ataç, C.A., 'Imperial Lessons from Athens and Sparta: Eighteenth-Century British Histories of Ancient Greece', *History of Political Thought*, xxvii (2006), pp. 642–60.
Bailyn, B., 'The Challenge of Modern Historiography', *The American Historical Review*, 87 (1982), pp. 1–24.

Baldick, J., *Homer and the Indo-Europeans* (London, 1994).
Ballantyne, T., *Orientalism and Race: Aryanism in the British Empire* (Basingstoke, 2002).
Barkan, E., *The Retreat of Scientific Racism* (Cambridge, 1992).
────── 'Review of *Defender of the Race: Jewish Doctors and Race Science in fin-de-siecle Europe*, by J.M. Efron', *American Historical Review*, 101 (1996), pp. 838–9.
Barth, F., *Models of Social Organisations* (London, 1966).
Barthes, R., *Mythologies* (Paris, 1957).
────── *Image, Music, Text* (London, 1977).
Beard, M., *The Invention of Jane Harrison* (Harvard, MS, 2000).
Beardsley, M.C., 'Beauty since the Mid-Nineteenth Century', in P.P. Weiner (ed.) *Dictionary of the History of Ideas* (New York, NY, 1973).
Bentley, M. (ed.), *Companion to Historiography* (London, 1997).
Berlin, I., *Russian Thinkers* (London, 1947).
Bernal, M., *Black Athena* (London, 1991).
Bews, J.W., *Human Ecology* (Oxford, 1935).
Binford, L.R., 'Archaeology as Anthropology', *American Antiquity*, 28 (1962), pp. 217–25.
────── 'Some Comments on Historical versus Processual Archaeology', *Southwestern Journal of Anthropology*, 24 (1968), pp. 267–75.
Bloch, M., *The Historian's Craft* (Manchester, 1953).
Boardman, J., *Persia and the West* (London, 2000).
Boardman, J., 'Myres, J. L.', in *Oxford Dictionary of National Biographies* (Oxford, 2005).
Boardman, J., Brown, M., Powell, T. (eds.), *The European Community in Later Prehistory* (London, 1971).
Boardman, J., Edwards, I. E. S., Hammond, N. G. L., Sollberger, E., (eds.), *Cambridge Ancient History*, Vol. IV (Cambridge, 1988).
Boghossian, P.A., *Fear of Knowledge: Against Relativism and Constructivism* (Oxford, 2007).
Bosworth, A.B., *Alexander and the East* (Oxford, 1996).
────── and Baynham, E.J., *Alexander the Great in Fact and Fiction* (Oxford, 2001).
Bosworth, C.E., 'The Hon. George Nathaniel Curzon's Travels in Russian Central Asia and Persia', *Iran*, vol 19 (1981), pp. 127–36.
Boyle, J.A., *Persia: History and Heritage* (London, 1978).
Bozeman, A.B., *Politics and Culture in International History* (London, 1994).
Bradly, R., 'Review of *In Search of the Indo-Europeans*, by J.P. Mallory', *Nature*, 338 (1989), pp. 675–676.
Braudel, F., *The Mediterranean World in the Age of Philip II* (New York, NY, 1949).
────── *On History* (Chicago, IL, 1980).
Briant, P., *From Cyrus to Alexander: A History of the Persian Empire* (Wionna Lake, IN, 2002).
Bridges, E., Hall, E., and Rhodes, P.J. (eds.), *Cultural Responses to the Persian Wars* (Oxford, 2007).
Brosius, M., 'Alexander and the Persians', in J. Roisman (ed.), *Brill's Companion to Alexander the Great* (Leiden, 2003), pp. 169–93.
Brough, J., 'The Tripartite Identity of Indo-Europeans: An Explanation in Method', *Bulletin of SOAS*, 22 (1959), pp. 69–85.

Bunton, M., 'Sykes P.M.', in *Oxford Dictionary of National Biographies* (Oxford, 2005).
Burkert, W., *Babylon, Memphis, Persepolis: Eastern Context of Greek Culture* (Harvard, MA, 2004).
Burn, A.R., *Persia and the Greeks: The Defence of the West* (London, 1984).
Bussmann, H., *Routledge Dictionary of Language and Linguistics* (London, 1998).
Butler, E.M., *The Tyranny of Greece over Germany* (Boston, 1958).
Butterfield, H., *Man on his Past: The Study of the History of Historical Scholarship* (Cambridge, 1955).
Calder III, W.M., and Kopff, E.C., 'The Student-Teacher Topos in Biographical Fiction: Gilbert Murray and Ulrich von Wilamowitz-Moellendorff', *Classical Philology*, vol 43 (1977), pp. 53–4.
────── (ed.), *The Cambridge Ritualists Reconsidered* (Illinois, IL, 1991).
Carnap, R., *Logical Foundation of Probability* (London, 1950).
Carritt, E.F., *What is Beauty?* (London, 1932).
Cartledge, P., *The Greeks: A Portrait of Self and Others* (Oxford, 1993).
────── 'Ancient Greeks and Modern Britons', *History Today*, April (1994), pp. 27–31.
────── 'Historiography and Ancient Greek Self-Definition', in M. Bentley (ed.), *Routledge Companion to Historiography* (London, 1997).
────── *Thermopylae: The Battle that Changed the World* (London, 2007).
Cavalli-Sforza, L.L., *The History and the Geography of Human Genes* (Princeton, NJ, 1994).
Ceadel, M., 'Gilbert Murray and International Politics', in C. Stray (ed.), *Gilbert Murray Reassessed* (Oxford, 2007).
Chauvin, C., *Renan* (Paris, 2000).
Clark, G., 'The Invasion Hypothesis in British Archaeology', *Antiquity*, xl (1966), pp. 172–200.
────── 'Prehistory since Childe', *Bulletin of the Institute of Archaeology*, 13 (1976), p. 1–21.
Clarke, K., *Making Time for the Past: Local History and the Polis* (Oxford, 2008).
Clarke, M.L., *Greek Studies in England 1700–1830* (Cambridge, 1945).
Cochran G., and Harpending, H., *The 10,000 Year Explosion: How Civilization Accelerated Human Evolution* (New York, NY, 2009).
Collini, S., *Victorian Thinkers* (Oxford, 1993).
────── (ed.), *History, Religion, and Culture: British Intellectual History 1750–1950* (Cambridge, 2000).
────── *Absent Minds: Intellectuals in Britain* (Oxford, 2006).
Corfield, P., *Time and the Shape of History* (Yale, CT, 2007).
Curtis, J., (ed.), *Sophocles' Oedipus at Colonus: Manuscript Materials by W.B. Yeats* (Cornell, NY, 2010).
Dale, P.A., *The Victorian and the Idea of History* (Cambridge, MA, 1977).
Daniel, G., *The Idea of Prehistory* (London, 1962).
────── 'Elliot-Smith, Egypt and Diffusionism', in Lord Zuckerman (ed.), *The Concept of Human Evolution* (London, 1973).
────── *150 Years of Archaeology* (London, 1975).
────── 'From Worsaae to Childe: The Models of Prehistory', *Bulletin of the Institute of Archaeology*, vol 13 (1979) pp. 140–53.

Davidson, J., *Greeks and the Greek Love: A Radical Reappraisal of Homosexuality in Ancient Greece* (London, 2007).
Davis, N., *Europe: A History* (Oxford, 1997).
Davis-Hanson, V., *The Western Way of War: Infantry Battle in Classical Greece* (Oxford, 1989).
——— 'No Glory That Was Greece', in R. Cowley (ed.), *What If* (London, 2001).
De Laura, D.T., *Hebrew and Hellene in Victorian England* (Austin, TX, 1969).
Demetriou, K., 'In Defence of the British Constitution: Theoretical Implications of the Debate over Athenian Democracy in Britain, 1770–1850', *History of Political Thought*, xvii (1996), pp. 280–97.
Derrida, J., *Of Grammatology* (Baltimore, MD, 1976).
Detienne, M., *Greeks and Us* (Cambridge, 2007).
Dickermann, H., 'Theories of Beauty' in P.P. Wiener (ed.) *Dictionary of History of Ideas* (New York, NY, 1973), pp. 196–8.
Dray, W.H., 'Collingwood on Reflective Thought', *Journal of Philosophy*, 57 (1960), pp. 157–63.
——— *History as Re-enactment: R.G. Collingwood's Idea of History* (Oxford, 1995).
——— 'Philosophy and Historiography' in *Routledge Companion to Historiography*, M. Bentley (ed.), (London, 1997), pp. 770–4.
Dunbabin, T.J., 'Sir John Linton Myres', *Proceedings of The British Academy*, 41, (1955), pp. 353–365.
Evison, M.P., 'Genetics, Ethics and Archaeology', *Antiquity*, 70 (1996), pp. 512–14.
Farrenkopf, *The Prophet of Decline* (Baton Rouge, 2001).
Farrington, B., *The Philosophy of Francis Bacon* (Liverpool, 1964).
Fischer, D.H., *Liberty and Freedom: A Visual History of America's Founding Ideas* (Oxford, 2005).
Fleming, D.A., *Democracy's Ancient Ancestors: Mari and Early Collective Governance* (Cambridge, 2004).
Flyvbjerg, B., *Rationality and Power: Democracy in Practice* (Chicago, IL, 1998).
Folda, J., *Crusader Art in the Holy Land: From the Third Crusade to the Fall of Acre, 1187–1291* (New York, NY, 2006).
Fotiadis, M., 'Factual claims in Late Nineteenth Century European Prehistory and the Descent of a Modern Discipline's Ideology', *Journal of Social Archaeology*, 6 (2006), pp. 5–27.
Franklin, M.J., 'Jones, W.', in *Oxford Dictionary of National Biographies* (Oxford, 2005).
Freitag, S., 'The Critique of Orientalism', in *Routledge Companion to Historiography*, M. Bentley (ed.), (London, 1997).
Frye, R., *Greater Iran* (2005).
Ganim, J.M., *Medievalism and Orientalism* (New York, NY, 2005).
Gathercole, P., 'Gordon Childe: Man or Myth', *Antiquity*, lvi (1982), pp. 195–9.
——— 'Childe, G.', in *Oxford Dictionary of National Biographies* (Oxford, 2005).
Gaunt, B., and Lopes, D.M. (eds.), *Routledge Companion to Aesthetics* (London, 2005).
Georges, P., *Barbarian Asia and the Greek Experience* (London, 1994).
Gilmour, D, 'Curzon, G. N.', in *Oxford Dictionary of National Biographies* (Oxford, 2005).
Gilson, J.C., 'Morant, G. M.', in *Oxford Dictionary of National Biographies* (Oxford, 2005).

Gnoli, *The Idea of Iran* (Roma, 1989).
Goldhill, S., 'Review', *The Classical Review*, vol 5 (2001), pp. 9–10.
Goldstein, L.J., 'Collingwood's Theory of Historical Knowing', *History & Theory*, 9 (1970), pp. 3–36.
Green, P., *The Years of Salamis* (London, 1970).
Green, S., *Prehistorian: A Biography of Gordon V. Childe* (Bradford-on-Avon, 1981).
Griffith, M., 'Gilbert Murray on Greek Literature' in C. Stray (ed.), *Gilbert Murray Reassessed* (Oxford, 2007).
Gruffudd, P., 'Fleure, H. J.', in *Oxford Dictionary of National Biographies* (Oxford, 2005).
Gunter, A.C., Hauser, S.R. (eds.), *Ernst Herzfeld and the Development of Near Eastern Studies 1900–1950* (Leiden, 2005).
Halbwach, M., *La Memoire Collective* (Paris, 1997).
Hall, E., *Inventing the Barbarian* (Oxford, 1989).
——— *Aeschylus' 'Persians'* (Warminster, 1996).
Hall, E., Macintosh, F., Wrigley A. (eds.), *Dionysus since 69: Greek Tragedy at the Dawn of the Third Millennium* (Oxford, 2004).
Hall, J., *Ethnic Identity in Greek Antiquity* (Cambridge, 1997).
Haller, J., *Outcast from Evolution: Scientific Attitudes of Racial Inferiority* (Carbondale, 1971).
Harpending, H., 'Population Genetic Perspective', in M. Pagel (ed.), *Oxford Encyclopaedia of Evolution* (Oxford, 2002).
Harris, D.R. (ed.), *The Archaeology of Vere Gordon Childe* (London, 1994).
Haugen, E., 'Language and Ethnicity' in Jazayery, M.A., et al. (eds.), *Language and Culture* (The Hague, 1978), pp. 235–44.
Hauser, S.R., *German Studies in the Ancient Near East* (Princeton, NJ, 1998).
Herrenschmidt, C., Vernant, J-P., (eds.), *Ancestors of the West: Writing, Reasoning, and Religion in Mesopotamia, Elam, and Greece* (Chicago, IL, 2000).
Hersey, G.L., 'Aryanism in Victorian England', *Yale Review* (1976), 66, pp. 104–13.
Herzfeld, M., *Anthropology through the Looking-Glass* (Cambridge, 1987).
Hobsbawm, E., *On History* (London, 1975).
Holland, T., *Persian Fire: The First World Empire and the Battle for the West* (London, 2006).
Hornblower, S., *Greek Historiography* (Oxford, 1994).
——— *The Greek World 479–323 BC* (London, 2002).
Hospers, J., *Meaning and Truth in Art* (North Carolina, NC, 1946).
——— (ed.), *Introductory Readings in Aesthetics* (New York, NY, 1969).
Houlgate, S., *An Introduction to Hegel: Freedom, Truth and History* (Malden, MA, 2005).
Humphreys, S.C., *Anthropology and the Greeks* (London, 1978).
Hutton, C., *Race and the Third Reich: Linguistics, Racial Anthropology and Genetics in the Dialect of Volk* (Cambridge, 2005).
Ingold, T., 'The Trouble with "Evolutionary Biology"', *Anthropology Today*, 23, No. 2 (2007), pp. 13–18.
Irwin, R., *For Lust of Knowing: The Orientalists and Their Enemies* (London, 2006).
Isaac, B., *The Invention of Racism in Classical Antiquity* (Princeton, NJ, 2004).
Jenkyns, R., *The Victorian and Ancient Greece* (London, 1980).
Jevons, W.S., *The Principle of Science* (London, 1958).

Johnson, J.W., *The Formation of English Neo-Classical Thought* (Princeton, NJ, 1967).
——— 'What was Neo-Classicism?', *The Journal of British Studies*, vol 10 (1971), pp. 49–70.
Jones, C.P., '*Ethnos* and *Genos* in Herodotus', *Classical Quarterly*, 46 (1996), pp. 315–20.
Jones, D., 'Sociological Perspective' in M. Pagel (ed.), *Oxford Encyclopaedia of Evolution* (Oxford, 2002).
Jones, S., and Keynes, M., (eds.), *Twelve Galton Lectures: A Centenary Selection with Commentary* (London, 2007).
Joynt, C.B., and Rescher, N., 'The Problem of Uniqueness in History', *History & Theory*, 1 (1961), pp. 150–62.
Keane, J., *The Life and Death of Democracy* (London, 2009).
Kevles, D., *In the Name of Eugenics: Genetics and the Uses of Human Heredity* (2001).
Kipling, R., *The Ballad of East and West* (London, 1892).
Koerner, E.F.K., 'Ideology in 19th and 20th Century Study of Language: A Neglected Aspect of Linguistic Historiography', *Indogermanische Forschungen*, 105 (2000), pp. 1–26.
Körner, A., *Politics of Culture in Liberal Italy: From Unification to Fascism* (London, 2009).
Kuhn, T.S., *The Structure of the Scientific Revolutions* (London, 1962).
——— 'Reflections on my Critics' in I. Lakatos and A. Musgrave (eds.), *Criticism and the Growth of Knowledge* (Cambridge, 1970).
Kuhrt, A., *The Ancient Near East: c.3000–330 BC* (London, 1995).
Lakatos, I., and Musgrave, A. (eds.), *Criticism and the Growth of Knowledge* (Cambridge, 1970).
Lamarque P., and Olsen, S.H., 'Truth', in M. Kelly (ed.), *The Blackwell Guide to Aesthetics* (Oxford, 2004), pp. 406–15.
Lamberg-Karlovsky, C.C., 'Archaeology and Language: The Indo-Iranians', *Current Archaeology*, 41 (2002), pp. 63–88.
Lane Fox, R., *The Classical World: An Epic History from Homer to Hadrian* (London, 2005).
Lawrence, A.W., 'The Acropolis and Persepolis', *Journal of Hellenic Studies*, LXXI (1951), pp. 111–19.
Le Goff, Nora P. (ed.), *Constructing the Past: Essays in Historical Methodology* (Cambridge, 1974).
Lehmann, W.P. (ed.), *A Reader in Nineteenth Century Historical Indo-European Linguistics* (Bloomington, IN, 1967).
Lembke, J. and Herrington, C.J., *Aeschylus' Persians* (London, 1980).
Levinson, J., *The Oxford Handbook of Aesthetics* (Oxford, 2005).
Lewis, B., *The Middle East: A Brief History of the Last 2,000 Years* (New York, NY, 1995).
——— *The Multiple Identities of the Middle East* (London, 1998).
Lewis, C.S., *Studies in Words* (Cambridge, 1960).
Littleton, C.S., *The New Comparative Mythology: An Anthropological Assessment of the Theories of Georges Dumezil* (Berkeley, CA, 1966).
Llewellyn-Jones, L., *Aphrodite's Tortoise: The Veiled Women of Ancient Greece* (Swansea, 2007).
Losee, J., *A Historical Introduction to the Philosophy of Science* (Oxford, 2001).

Löwith, K., *From Hegel to Nietzsche* (London, 1941).
Magee, B., *Wagner and Philosophy* (London, 2000).
Maguire, L., *Helen of Troy: From Homer to Hollywood* (Chichester, 2009).
Malik, K., *The Meaning of Race* (London, 1996).
——— *Strange Fruit: Why Both Sides are Wrong in the Race Debate* (London, 2008).
Malkin, I. (ed.), *Ancient Perceptions of Greek Ethnicity* (Harvard, MA, 2001).
Mandler, P., '"Race" and "Nation" in mid-Victorian Thought' in S. Collini, R. Whatmore, and S Young (eds), *History, Religion, and Culture: British Intellectual History 1750–1950* (Cambridge, 2000).
Marchand, S.L., *German Orientalism in the Age of Empire: Religion, Race, and Scholarship* (Cambridge, 2009).
Mazumdar, P., *Eugenics, Human Genetics and Human Failings: The Eugenics Society, its Sources and its Critics in Britain* (London, 1992).
McMahon, J.A., 'Beauty', in B. Gaunt and D.M. Lopes (eds.) *Routledge Companion to Aesthetics* (London, 2005).
McNairn, B., *Method and Theory of Childe* (Edinburgh, 1980).
Meier, C., *A Culture of Freedom: Ancient Greece and the Origins of Europe* (Oxford, 2011).
Miller, M.C., *Athens and Persia in the Fifth Century BC: A Study in Cultural Receptivity* (Cambridge, 1997).
Mitchell, L.G., 'Greeks, Barbarians and Aeschylus' *Suppliant*', *Greece & Rome*, 53 (2006), pp. 205–33.
Momigliano, A., *Studies in Historiography* (London, 1966).
——— 'Georges Dumézil and the Trifunctional Approach to Roman Civilization', *History & Theory*, 23 (1984), pp. 312–30.
——— *The Classical Foundations of Modern Historiography* (Berkeley, CA, 1990).
Monettee, C., 'Indo-European Elements in Celtic and Indo-Iranian Epic Tradition: the Trial of Champions in the *Táin Bó Cúailnge* and the *Shahnameh*', *The Journal of Indo-European Studies*, 32 (2004), pp. 61–78.
Murray, G., *Aeschylus' Persae* (London, 1939).
Neer, R., *The Emergence of the Classical Style in Greek Sculpture* (Chicago, IL, 2011).
Newton-Smith, W.H., *A Companion to the to Philosophy of Science* (Oxford, 2000).
Nielsen, M.H., 'Re-enactment and Reconstruction in Collingwood's Philosophy of History', *History & Theory*, 20 (1981), pp. 1–31.
Nylander, C., 'Darius III – 'The Coward King Point and Counterpoint' in J. Roisman (ed.), *Brill's Companion to Alexander the Great* (Leiden, 2003), pp. 143–59.
Olender, M., *The Language of Paradise: Race, Religion and Philology* (Cambridge MA, 1992).
Orwell, G., *Essays* (London, 2002).
Overy, R., *The Morbid Age: Britain Between the Wars* (London, 2009).
Pagden, A., *Worlds at War: The 2,500-Year Struggle between East and West* (London, 2007).
Pagel, M. (ed.), *Oxford Encyclopaedia of Evolution* (Oxford, 2002).
——— *Wired for Culture: The Natural History of Human Co-operation* (London, 2012).
Pappas, N., 'Beauty: Classical Concepts', in M. Kelly (ed.) *Encyclopaedia of Aesthetics* (New York, NY, 1998), pp. 244–7.
Penniman, T.K., *A Hundred Years of Anthropology* (London, 1952).

Pitkin, H.F., 'Are Freedom and Liberty Twins?' *Political Theory*, 16 (1988), pp. 523–52.
Pitt-Rivers, G.H., *The Clash of Cultures and the Contact of Races* (Oxford, 1927).
Podlecki, J., *Aeschylus' Persians* (London, 1971).
Popper, K., *Poverty of Historicism* (London, 1961).
——— 'Normal Science and its Dangers' in I. Lakatos and A. Musgrave (eds.), *Criticism and the Growth of Knowledge* (Cambridge, 1970).
Potter, R., *Aeschylus' Persae* (London, 1886).
Price, K.B., 'Is There Artistic Truth?' *Journal of Philosophy*, XLVI (1949), pp. 285–91.
Putnam, R., *Making Democracy Work: Civic Tradition in Modern Italy* (Princeton, 1993).
Quirke, V.M., 'Haldane, J.B. S.', in *Oxford Dictionary of National Biographies* (Oxford, 2005).
Renfrew, C., 'New Configurations in Old World Archaeology', *World Archaeology*, 2 (1970), pp. 199–211.
——— *Before Civilization: The Radiocarbon Revolution and the Prehistoric Europe* (London, 1973).
——— *Problems in European Prehistory* (Edinburgh, 1979).
——— *Archaeology and Language* (London, 1987).
——— 'Childe and the Study of Cultural Process' in Harris (ed.), *The Archaeology of Vere Gordon Childe* (London, 1994).
——— 'The Identity of Europe in Prehistoric Archaeology', *Journal of European Archaeology*, 2 (1994), pp. 153–73.
Renton, D., 'Pitt-Rivers, G.H.L. F.', in *Oxford Dictionary of National Biographies* (Oxford, 2005).
Richards, G., 'Elliot-Smith, G.', in *Oxford Dictionary of National Biographies* (Oxford, 2005).
Root, M.C., 'The Parthenon Frieze and the Apadana Reliefs at Persepolis: Reassessing Programmatic Relationship', *American Journal of Archaeology*, 89 (1985), pp. 103–20.
Rousseau, J.J., *The Social Contract* (London, 1993).
Rowe, J.H., 'Diffusionism and Archaeology', *American Antiquity*, 31 (1966), pp. 334–37.
Rowlands, M., 'Childe and the Archaeology of Freedom' in D. Harris (ed.), *The Archaeology of Vere Gordon Childe* (1994).
Rushton, A.R., 'Gates, R. R.', in *Oxford Dictionary of National Biographies* (Oxford, 2005).
Said, E.W., *Orientalism* (London, 1977).
Sancisi-Weerdenburg, H. and J.W. Drijvers (eds.), *Achaemenid History V: The Roots of the European Tradition* (Leiden, 1995).
——— 'Alexander and Persepolis' in J. Roisman (ed.), *Brill's Companion to Alexander the Great* (Leiden, 2003), pp. 177–88.
Sangren, P.S., 'Anthropology of Anthropology? Further Reflection on Reflexivity', *Anthropology Today*, 23, no. 4 (2007), pp. 13–16.
Scheffler, T., '"Fertile Crescent", "Orient", "Middle East": The Changing Mental Maps of Southwest Asia', *European Review of History*, 10 (2003), pp. 253–73.

Schultze, C., '"People Like Us" in the Face of History: Cormon's *Les Vainqueurs de Salamine*', in E. Bridges, E. Hall, and P.J. Rhodes (eds.), *Cultural Responses to the Persian Wars* (Oxford, 2007)

Schwanitz, W.G. (ed.), *Germany and the Middle East 1871–1945* (Princeton, NJ, 2004).

Sesonske, A., 'Truth in Art', *Journal of Philosophy*, liii (1956), pp. 345–6.

Sherratt, A., 'Review of *In Search of the Indo-Europeans*, by J.P. Mallory', *Journal of Field Archaeology*, 17 (1990), pp. 89–93.

―――― *Economy and Society in Prehistoric Europe* (London, 1997).

Shusterman, R. (ed.), *Analytic Aesthetics* (Oxford, 1989).

Sinor, D. (ed.), *Orientalism and History* (Cambridge, 1954).

Skinner, Q., *Hobbes and Republican Liberty* (Cambridge, 2008).

Slobodin, R., *W. H.R. Rivers* (Sutton, 1978).

Snow, C.P., *The Two Cultures and the Scientific Revolution* (Cambridge, 1959).

―――― *The Two Cultures: A Second Look* (Cambridge, 1964).

Stepan, N., *The Idea of Race in Science: Great Britain 1800–1960* (Hamden, MA, 1982).

Stephens, S.A. and Vasunia, P. (eds.), *Classics and National Cultures* (Oxford, 2011).

Steward, J.H., *Theory of Culture Change The Methodology of Multi-linear Evolution* (Urbana, IL, 1955).

Stocking, G.W., *Race, Culture, and Evolution: Essays in the History of Anthropology* (Chicago, IL, 1968).

―――― *After Tylor: British Social Anthropology 1888–1951* (Wisconsin, WI, 1995).

Stolnitz, J., *Aesthetic and the Philosophy of Art Criticism* (Boston, MA, 1960).

Stone, D., *Breeding Superman: Nietzsche, Race and Eugenics in Edwardian and Interwar Britain* (Liverpool, 2002).

Stray, C., 'Murray, G. A.', *Oxford Dictionary of National Biographies* (Oxford, 2005).

―――― (ed.), *Gilbert Murray Reassessed* (Oxford, 2007).

Sykes, P., 'A Fifth Journey in Persia', *The Geographical Journal*, 28 (1896), pp. 425–50.

Taguieff, P.A., *La Couleur et le Sang: Doctrines Racistes à la Française* (Paris, 1998).

Tashjean, J.E., 'Indo-European Studies and the Sciences of Man', *History of Political Thought*, ii (1981), pp. 447–67.

Todd, R.B. (ed.), *The Dictionary of British Classicists* (Bristol, 2004).

Tombs, I., and Tombs, R., *That Sweet Enemy: The French and the British from the Sun King to the Present* (London, 2006).

Trigger, B.G., 'Aims in Prehistoric Archaeology', *Antiquity*, xliv (1970), pp. 26–38.

―――― 'If Childe Were Alive Today', *Bulletin of the Institute of Archaeology*, (1982), pp. 1–20.

―――― 'Childe's Relevance to the 1990s' in D.R. Harris (ed.), *The Archaeology of Vere Gordon Childe* (London, 1994).

Turner, F.M., *The Greek Heritage in Victorian Britain* (Yale, CT, 1980).

UNESCO, *The Race Question* (New York, 1950).

Vallacott, P., *Aeschylus' The Persians* (London, NY, 1961).

―――― *Aeschylus' The Suppliants* (London, 1961).

Venturi, F., 'Oriental Despotism', *Rivista Storica Italiana*, lxxii (1960), pp. 117–26.
Voegelin, E., *History of Political Ideas: Hellenism, Rome, and Early Christianity* (Columbia, MO, 1997).
Von Laue, T.H., *Leopold Ranke: The Formative Years* (Princeton, NJ, 1950).
Watkins, J., 'Against "Normal Science"' in I. Lakatos and A. Musgrave (eds.), *Criticism and the Growth of Knowledge* (Cambridge, 1970).
West, M.L., *The East Face of Helicon: West Asiatic Elements in Greek Poetry and Myth* (Oxford, 1997).
White, L.A., 'Diffusionism versus Evolutionism: An Anti-Evolutionist Fallacy', *American Anthropologist*, 47 (1945), pp. 339–56.
——— 'History, Evolutionism, and Functionalism: Three Types of Interpretations of Culture', *Southwestern Journal of Archaeology*, 1 (1945), pp. 221–48.
——— 'Review of *Theory of Culture Change*, by J.H. Steward', *American Anthropologist*, 59 (1957), pp. 540–2.
Whitmarsh, T., *Ancient Greek Literature* (Cambridge, 2004).
Wiesehöfer, J., *Ancient Persia* (London, 2001).
Williams, L.P., 'Normal Science, Scientific Revolution, and the History of Science' in I. Lakatos and A. Musgrave (eds.), *Criticism and the Growth of Knowledge* (Cambridge, 1970).
Winch, P., *The Idea of a Social Science and its Relation to Philosophy* (London, 1958).
Winnington-Ingram, R.P., *Studies in Aeschylus* (Cambridge, 1987).
Wittfogel, K.A., *Oriental Despotism* (Yale, CT, 1957).
Wood, G.S., 'The Creative Imagination of Bernard Bailyn', in Henretta J.A., Kammen, M. and Katz, S.N. (eds.). *The Transformation of Early American History: Society, Authority, and Ideology* (New York, NY, 1991).
Wright, D., 'Curzon, G. N.', in E. Yar-Shater (ed.) *Encyclopaedia Iranica* (London, 1991).
Zangwill, N., 'Beauty', in D.E. Cooper (ed.) *Oxford Companion to Aesthetics* (Oxford, 1992).

Miscellaneous Secondary Sources

Briant, P., 'Alexandre le Grand, "héros civilisateur"', *Le Monde*, 6 January 2005.
——— 'Lecture', UCL, June 2009.
Bull, B., 'Alexander, the First Neo-Con', *FT Magazine*, 22 January 2005.
Collini, S., 'Historian of the Future', *TLS*, March 2008.
Cousin, M., 'Film Review', *Prospect*, May 2007.
Davis, C., 'A Rose by another Name', *TLS*, 13 June 2008.
——— 'Letter', *TLS*, 3 July 2009.
Goldhill, S., 'Private Letter to the author', November 2001.
Green, P., 'Letter', *TLS*, February 2005.
Griffin, J., 'Review', *NYRB*, 6 December, 2007.
Holland, T., 'Review', *The Guardian*, 17 December 2005.
http://unesdoc.unesco.org/images/0012/001282/128291eo.pdf
Janko, R., 'Born of Rhubarb', *TLS*, 22 February 2008.
Lefkowitz, M., 'Review', *TLS*, 3 June 2005.
Murray, A., 'Review', *TLS*, 23 June 2006.

Pagel, M., 'Review', *Prospect*, June 2008.
―――― 'email to the author', 7 September 2009.
Seaford, R., 'Worlds without Limits', *TLS*, June 2009.
Wheatcroft, G., 'Review', *NYRB*, 4 December, 2008.
Wood, M., 'At the Movies', *LRB*, 26 April 2007.

INDEX

Abbott, E., 221-2
Achaemenid, xiii, 4, 5, 9, 47, 176, 178, 180-1, 205, 207, 209, 259, 287
Ackerman, R., 169, 170
Adorno, T., 167
Aeschylus, xiii, 282
Aesthetics, (philosophy of), 163-171, 232
Aesthetics of wonder (*thauma*), 12, 171
Alexander the Great, xiv, 2, 13, 176, 179, 187-188, 243
Anthony, D. W., 247-8
Anthropology, 5, 8, 12, 64, 68-9, 76, 112, 116-119, 130, 168, 224, 236
History of, 15-23, 49-53
Arabs, 204, 208
Archaeology, 8, 51, 54, 66, 85, 99, 103, 123, 127-8, 161, 236, 248
Arendt, H., 291
Arnold, M., 10, 32-34, 41-2, 249
Arnold, T., 22, 32
Aryan, 23, 41, 74, 91-93, 97, 143-4, 189, 212
Aryanism, 5, 4, 49, 245
'Aryan Race', 48, 51, 53, 63, 144, 265
Ashurbanipal, 5, 29
Asia, xv, 10, 218, 222
Assyria (Assyrians), 9, 42, 82, 184, 207, 209

Athens, 2, 25, 26, 33, 181, 183, 191, 204, 229, 232

Bacon, F., 138
Bailyn, B., 219-20
Balfour, H., 50
Ballantyne, T., 52
Barkan, C., 75-6, 268, 294
Barthes, R., 293
British Broadcasting Cooperation (BBC), 225
Beauty (philosophy of). *See* Aesthetics
Bender, H, 92
Benjamin, R. G. W., 287
Berlin, I., 103
Blunt, A., 197-8
Boas, F., 76-7, 249, 268
Boghossian, P., 101
Bopp, F., 17
Botsford, G. W., 195-7
Bozeman, H., 228
Breasted, H., 4-5, 192-4, 249
Briant, P., xiv, 287
Bronze Age, 80, 83-5, 89, 91, 93, 98, 99, 106, 120
Bury, J. B., 2, 184
Butler, E., 29
Butterfield, H., 40

Cambridge Ritualism, 169
Carnap, R., 45
Carritt, E. F., 164
Cartledge, P., xvi–xvii, 288, 290
Chauvin, C., 21
Childe, G., 5, 11–12, 53–4, 74–5, 50, 75–6, 79–83, 209, 238–9, 249–50, 268, 270, 271
China, 147, 207
Christianity, 34–6, 41–2, 207
Clark, G., 102
Collingwood, R. G., 12, 134, 135, 139, 148–55, 221, 250, 279
Comparative Philology. *See* Linguistics
Constructivism, 101
Coulanges, Fustel de., 43, 250
Cox, G. W., 1–2, 181–3
Culture, 11, 48–78
Curzon, G. N., 183
Cyrus the Great, 2, 191, 199

Daniel, G., 100
Darius I, 5, 92
Darius III, xiv
Davis, C., 233–4
Davis-Hanson, V., 3
De Laura, D., 35
Democracy, 229–32
Diffusionism. *See* Childe
Dilthey, W., 220
Disraeli, B., 42, 264
Doublethink, 180–1, 217–18
Dray, W., 146
Ducasse, C. J., 166

Egypt (Egyptians), 2, 4, 30, 37, 42, 57, 84, 88, 92, 124, 144, 204, 218
eleutheria (liberty), 227–8
Elliot Smith, G., 51, 56–7, 77, 80–1, 238–9, 251
Europe, 86, 218, 222–3, 233
Evans, A., 83–106
Evolutionism. *See* Childe

Falaize, E. N., 50–1
Fergusson, J., 80
Firth, R., 58
Fischer, D. H., 227–8
Fleming, D. E., 231–2
Fleure, H., 57–6, 252
Flyvbjerg, B., 292
Freedom, 226–8
Fri, 226
Freitag, S., 208

Galileo, 160
Galton. F., 259
Gates, R., 60–1, 241, 252
Gatterer, J., 40
Germany, 31–2, 170
Romantics, German, 10
Geist (Spirit), 28
Gibbon, E., xv
Glover, T. R., 204–5
Gobineau, A., 3, 22, 206–7, 208, 252
Goethe, J., 28, 31–2
Goldhill, S., xiii
Goldsmith, O., 26
Greece (Greeks), xv, 3, 21, 23, 30, 26–41, 112, 119, 124, 127, 142, 165, 168–9, 176, 183, 184–191, 221, 225, 231
Green, P., xiv, 3, 257
Grimm, J., 17
Grote, G., 7, 27
Grundy, G. B., 200–2

Haldane, J., 59–60, 252–3
Hall, E., xiii, 257, 282
Harrison, J., 107
Hawkes, C. F. C., 98
Hebraism. *See* Judaism
Hecataeus, 226
Hegel, F., 28, 37–40, 205–6, 288
Hellenism, 10, 33, 34, 168, 176
Mainstream (Romantic), 106–116
Historico-scientific, 116–137
Helleno-Aryanism, 41–5

INDEX

Herder, xv, 1, 28, 181
Herodotus, 65, 116–17, 138, 172, 200, 282
Hersey, G. L., 42
Herzfeld, E., 186, 252
History (philosophy of). *See* Collingwood
Hogarth, D. G., 191–92
Holland, T., 2, 259, 288
Hornblower, S., 291–2
Hospers, J., 164–5
Houlgate, S., 206
Howell, F., 198–9
Humboldt, W. von, 17
Humphreys, S. C., 43

Iliad, 111
India, 207
Indo-European, xv, 3–4, 6, 13, 16–17, 43, 78, 90, 92, 97–8, 129, 144–5, 189, 212–13, 217, 236, 246–7
Indo-Iranian, xviii, 10, 129, 143, 188, 244, 259
Inge, W., 131–2, 252
Iran (Iranians), 8–9, 23, 98–9, 212, 213
Islam, 205, 208

Jackson, J. W., 22
Jacobsen, T., 231
James, H. R., 195
Japhetic, 16
Jardé, A., 202–3
Jessop, T. E., 165–6
Jevons, W., 158
Jews. *See* Judaism
Johnson, J. W., 24
Jones, W., 16–17, 252
Jowett, B., 264
Judaism, 22, 33–4, 42, 57, 76, 121, 204, 242, 244, 264

Keane, A. H., 19, 229–30
Keats, J., 110

Kossinna, G., 77, 80–1, 103, 252
Kuhn, T., 12–13, 138, 145, 159–60
Kuhrt, A., xiii
Kuz'mina, E. E., 248

Laistner, M., 185
Lane Fox, R., xiv, 3, 259
Laocoön and his Sons, 39, 262
Leibniz, W., 16
Leighton, F., 42
Lessing, G., 28, 31
Levinson, J., 171
Lewis, C. S., 227
Libertas, 225
Linguistics, 15–23
Livingstone, R., 107–8, 252
Losee, J., 160–1
Löwith, K., 206

Macauley, T. B., 27
Macedonia, 2, 204
Mahaffy, J., 187, 189, 253
Malik, K., 240
Malinowski, B., 82
Mallory, J. P., 246
Mesopotamia, 83, 87, 90, 144, 230, 231, 232, 238
Meyer, E., 189–90, 253, 285
Mill, J. S., 115, 158
Minoan Civilization, 86–7
Mitford, W., 26–7
Momigliano, A., 43, 285
Montelius, O., 80
Morant, G., 58–9, 253
Morgan, D. N., 165
Müller, M., 19–21, 253
Murray, G., 12, 107, 112–16, 141–2, 144–5, 166–7, 168–70, 176, 253–4, 274, 276–7, 285, 295
Myres, J. L., 11, 51–2, 73–4, 76–7, 83, 96, 145, 148, 155–7, 161, 172–6, 223–6, 232–3, 236–245, 254–5, 267–8, 275–6, 294

On Hellenism, 116–41
On Persian (Achaemenid) Empire, 209–17
On race and culture, 64–72

Nebuchadnezzar, 5, 92
Neer, R., 171
National Socialism (Nazism), 47, 101
Nietzsche, F., 28, 44–5, 265
Normal Science, 160–3

Ogden, C. K., 91
Old Testament, 189
Oman, C., 197
Orientalism. *See* Said and Hall
Orwell, G., 234
Ouvré, H., 202

Pagden, A. 284, 293
Pagel, M., 240–1, 294
Parthia, 189
Pater, W., 10, 35–6, 255
Penniman, P. K., 15–17
Perry, W., 80
Persepolis, 133, 189, 285
Persian Wars, 3, 9, 13, 176, 179, 181, 185, 191, 197, 204, 217, 219, 234
Persians. See Aeschylus
Petrie, F., 83
Pitt, W. (The Elder), 241
Pitt-Rivers, G., 61–2, 74, 77, 241, 255
Podlecki, A., xiii
Poliakov, L., 20
Popper, K., 145, 162–3
Pott, F., 18
Presentism, 13, 102, 219–20
Priestley, J., 26
Principle of Zoning, 95

Race, xvi, 5, 19, 11, 48–78, 240
Radiocarbon Dating, 81
Ranke, L. van, 40–1, 212, 220–1, 25
Rassentheorie, 52, 78
Rawlinson, G., 1, 188–9, 255, 285

Renan, E., 3–4, 21–2, 207–8, 256
Renfrew, C., 81, 270
Robinson, D. M., 199–200
Rogers, R. W., 185–6
Rostovtzeff, M., 276, 287
Rousseau, J. J., 229
Rowlands, M., 100
Royal Anthropological Institute (RIA), 11, 48–51, 55
Russia, 90–1, 96

Said, E., xiii
Sasanians, 131, 207, 201, 208
Sassetti, F., 16
Sayce, A. H., 18–19
Scandinavia, 91, 96, 144
Schiller, F., 28
Science, (philosophy of), 159–63
Schlegel brothers, A & F, 17
Schleicher, A., 18
Schliemann, H., 106
Schlozer, L. von, 16
Schultze, C., 43
Scythians, 145, 244, 284
Semites, 23, 41, 43, 216
Semitic, 3, 4, 16, 18, 20, 118, 121, 143, 184, 192, 194, 197, 201, 208, 213–14, 223, 231
Sergent, B., 247
Skinner, Q., 290
Snow, C. P., 177, 282
Spengler, O., 292
Steinthal, H., 18
Sumerians, 194
Sykes, S., 194–5
Stanyan, T., 26

Táin Bó Cúailnge, 111
Thomson, J. A. K., 108, 109–11, 141, 143–4, 256
Todd, J. M., 184, 284
Toynbee, A., 108–9, 222, 256, 272
Tocqueville, A. de, 22
Trevelyan, H., 31

Trigger, B., 96, 100, 102, 271
Turan, 4, 23
Turner, F. M., 28–9, 36, 262

UNESCO, 239, 244
University College London (UCL), 6

Virgil, 31

Wace, A. J. B., 120, 275
Walker, E. M., 184
Watkins, C., 247
Watkins, J., 162
Webster, H., 187–8, 190–1
Weitz, M., 165

Wells, H. G., 203
West, M., 247, 291
Whatmough, J., 53
White, L., 82–3
Wilamowitz-Moellendorff, U. von, 103
Wilcken, U., 188
William, Archbishop of Tyre, xiv
Winch, P., 230
Winckelmann, J., 28–31, 256
Wissler, C., 82
Wood, G. S., 219–20

Xerxes, 181, 191, 197

Zoroastrianism, 92, 209